Python Scripting in Blender

Extend the power of Blender using Python to create objects, animations, and effective add-ons

Paolo Acampora

BIRMINGHAM—MUMBAI

Python Scripting in Blender

Copyright © 2023 Packt Publishing

All rights reserved. No part of this book may be reproduced, stored in a retrieval system, or transmitted in any form or by any means, without the prior written permission of the publisher, except in the case of brief quotations embedded in critical articles or reviews.

Every effort has been made in the preparation of this book to ensure the accuracy of the information presented. However, the information contained in this book is sold without warranty, either express or implied. Neither the author, nor Packt Publishing or its dealers and distributors, will be held liable for any damages caused or alleged to have been caused directly or indirectly by this book.

Packt Publishing has endeavored to provide trademark information about all of the companies and products mentioned in this book by the appropriate use of capitals. However, Packt Publishing cannot guarantee the accuracy of this information.

Group Product Manager: Rohit Rajkumar

Publishing Product Manager: Kaustubh Manglurkar

Senior Editor: Keagan Carneiro

Senior Content Development Editor: Debolina Acharyya

Technical Editor: Simran Ali

Copy Editor: Safis Editing

Project Coordinator: Sonam Pandey

Proofreader: Safis Editing

Indexer: Sejal Dsilva

Production Designer: Vijay Kamble

Marketing Coordinators: Nivedita Pandey, Namita Velgekar, and Anamika Singh

First published: June 2023

Production reference: 1120523

Published by Packt Publishing Ltd.
Livery Place
35 Livery Street
Birmingham
B3 2PB, UK.

ISBN 978-1-80323-422-9

www.packtpub.com

*To my daughters, Noè and Dedè, for all the games we play together, which are
the best part of the whole thing.*

– Paolo Acampora

Contributors

About the author

Paolo Acampora is a software developer at Binary Alchemy and a veteran technical director for animation, visual effects, and prototyping. He is a long-time Blender user and advocates for the widespread adoption of open source software and code literacy.

He works with studios to kickstart their computer graphics pipelines and shares his tools with the Blender community.

I want to thank my life companion, Dona, for her support and for tolerating my snoring. My parents and the whole bunch of rascals who make my family such a fun lot. My friends, who still invite me to parties, and everyone else I met along the way: a little piece of each one of us lies hidden in these pages.

About the reviewer

Dr. Edward Tate is an engineer who has used Blender for more than 15 years for both technical illustration and communication. He has extensively used Python for scientific work. He holds a **bachelor of science in mechanical engineering (BSME)** and a **bachelor of science in electrical engineering (BSEE)** from Kettering University, a **master of science in electrical engineering** (MSEE) from Stanford, and a **doctor of philosophy (Ph.D.)** from the University of Michigan. He is the author of more than 40 patents. He has worked on electric vehicles, scientific software, aerospace, and wireless power transfer.

Table of Contents

Preface   xv

Part 1: Introduction to Python

1

Python's Integration with Blender   3

Technical requirements	4	External editor – Visual Studio Code	17
Installing Blender	4	Loading our scripts folder	18
Installing Blender on Windows	4	Keeping Blender's text blocks in sync	19
Installing multiple versions on macOS	6	Version control and backup	19
The Scripting workspace – first steps with Python	8	Initializing the repository	19
		Making changes	20
The Python console	8	Summary	21
The Info Log	12	Questions	22
The Text Editor	14		

2

Python Entities and API   23

Technical requirements	23	Accessing Blender data	33
Useful features of Python	24	Creating new objects	37
Options for developers	24	Removing elements	40
Python console's utilities	26	Understanding the user context	40
Accessing Blender modules	30	Summary	46
The bpy module	30	Questions	46
API documentation	32		

3
Creating Your Add-Ons 47

Technical requirements	47	Refreshing the add-on list	57
Installing our add-ons in Blender	48	Running from the Search Toolbar	57
Add-on requirements	49	**Improving our code**	**59**
Installation	50	Saving our edits automatically	59
Uninstall	51	Ignoring bytecode files (.pyc)	59
The scripts path	51	Fixing the operator logic	62
Creating our first add-on –		Reloading scripts	64
object collector	**53**	Avoiding re-assignment errors	64
Operators	54	Our final operator	65
Writing a basic operator	54	Extending menus	66
Loading operators in our add-on	56	**Summary**	**67**
Running our add-on	**57**	**Questions**	**68**

4
Exploring Object Transformations 69

Technical requirements	69	Creating rest offsets with	
Moving objects in space	70	the parent inverse matrix	83
Transforming objects	70	**Writing the Elevator add-on**	**84**
Transforming objects indirectly	**76**	Setting the environment	84
Using Object Constraints	77	Writing the first draft	85
Using object hierarchies	79	Using input properties	87
Understanding the transform matrix	**80**	Setting the height in the world matrix	89
Accessing matrices	81	Avoiding duplicate transformations	90
Storing object matrices	82	Adding the constraints switch	91
Copying matrices	82	Avoiding duplicate constraints	92
Restoring transformations using		**Summary**	**93**
the world matrix	83	**Questions**	**94**

5

Designing Graphical Interfaces 95

Technical requirements	95	Checking whether an object is active	118
Areas, regions, and panels	96	Drawing layouts in red or gray	118
Creating a simple panel	97	**Displaying buttons**	**120**
Setting the environment	97	Using the operator method	120
Drafting our panel add-on	97	Setting the operator's text and visibility	121
Setting display attributes	99	Overriding an operator's settings	123
Adding a panel to the Object Properties area	102	Setting operator properties	124
Using layouts in our panels	**109**	Adding buttons for our functions	125
Arranging in columns and rows	109	Displaying the operator properties	127
Adding frames with box layouts	110	**Using different regions**	**129**
Using composite layouts	111	**Summary**	**130**
Providing color feedback	**117**	**Questions**	**131**
Checking whether an object has been selected	118		

Part 2: Interactive Tools and Animation

6

Structuring Our Code and Add-Ons 135

Technical requirements	135	**Adding a user interface**	**145**
Folders, packages, and add-ons	136	Writing the UI module	145
Creating a package folder and the init file	136	Importing the UI	146
Writing the init file	137	Completing the Objects panel	147
Guidelines for separating modules	138	**Reloading cached modules**	**148**
Writing the structured panel	139	Reloading via importlib	148
Packing external images	**140**	Implementing a refresh module	148
Writing an icon library	141	Reloading the package modules	149
Loading pictures from a folder	141	Using Developer Extras as a condition	150
Unregistering icons	143	**Using add-on preferences**	**151**
Getting the collection	143	Creating preferences	151
Using relative imports	144	Populating the preferences	153

Using add-on preferences in code	154	Creating a .zip file using 7-Zip	159
Adding operators	**155**	Creating a .zip file using Windows File Manager	160
Writing the operators module	156	Creating a .zip file on Mac using Finder	161
Registering operator classes	157	Creating a .zip file using Gnome	161
Refreshing operators on reload	157	Installing .zip add-ons	161
Adding operator buttons	158	**Summary**	**162**
Packaging and installing add-ons	**159**	**Questions**	**162**
Cleaning up bytecode	159		

7

The Animation System — 163

Technical requirements	**163**	Animation curves and the Graph Editor	179
Understanding the animation system	**163**	**Accessing animation data in Python**	**181**
Timeline and Current Frame	164	Adding keyframes in Python	181
Duration and Frame Rate	165	Retrieving keyframes in Python	182
Current frame and preview range	166	**Writing the Vert Runner add-on**	**185**
Animation keyframes	167	Setting the environment	185
Writing the Action to Range add-on	**168**	Writing the Vert Runner information	186
Setting the environment	168	Writing the Vert Runner operator	186
Writing the Action to Range information	168	Writing the operator methods	187
Writing the Action to Range operator	169	Writing the menu and register functions	188
Writing the operator methods	169	Creating cyclic animations	189
Writing the menu function	171	Adding rotations	190
Finishing the add-on	172	Using Vert Runner	195
Enabling and running	174	**Summary**	**195**
Fixing context for other operators	177	**Questions**	**196**
Editing keyframes	**179**		

8

Animation Modifiers — 197

Technical requirements	**197**	Adding F-Curve Modifiers in the Graph Editor	198
Using F-Curve Modifiers	**198**	Adding F-Curve Modifiers in Python	200

Writing the Shaker add-on	**201**	Finding the class names of context menus	206
Setting up the environment	201	Registering the Shaker add-on	207
Writing the Shaker add-on info	201	Using the Shaker add-on	208
Writing the Add Object Shake operator class	202	**Summary**	**208**
Writing the operator methods	203	**Questions**	**209**
Adding menu items	206		

9

Animation Drivers 211

Technical requirements	**211**	Implementing the pendulum equation	220
Creating drivers	**212**	Controlling the amplitude	226
Creating quick drivers via the right-click menu	212	**Writing the pendulum add-on**	**228**
Setting up a wheel with the Drivers Editor	214	Setting the environment	229
Creating driver expressions in properties	216	Writing the information	229
Driving a cyclic motion	**216**	Writing the Operator class	230
Changing the rotation pivot via constraints	217	Writing the menu and registering the class	233
Controlling the period of the sin function	219	**Summary**	**234**
		Questions	**234**

10

Advanced and Modal Operators 237

Technical requirements	**237**	**Adding modal behavior**	**245**
Understanding the operator flow	**237**	Adding the operator to the modal handlers	246
Steps of execution	238	Writing the modal method	247
Writing the "PunchClock" add-on	**240**	**Styling the operator panel**	**250**
Creating the add-on script	240	Writing the draw method	250
Using invoke to initialize properties	243	**Summary**	**252**
Ensuring default invoke in pop-up menus	244	**Questions**	**252**

Part 3: Delivering Output

11

Object Modifiers — 255

Technical requirements	255	Adding object subdivisions	269
Understanding object modifiers	255	Changing lattice resolution	269
Adding modifiers	256	**Using armature deformers**	**271**
Subdividing an object	257	Adding armature objects to the scene	271
Changing the object's shape using Cast	259	Adding armature bones	272
Adding modifiers in Python	**259**	Binding objects to armatures	274
Finding collection-type items	259	**Scripting a lattice armature**	**275**
Using modifiers.new	260	Adding an armature condition	275
Deformation objects	**262**	Adding an armature to the scene	275
Using the Lattice modifier	262	Creating edit bones	276
Writing the Latte Express add-on	**263**	Assigning vertices to bones	278
Setting the environment	264	Creating the Armature modifier	279
Writing the Latte Express information	264	**Adding custom bone shapes**	**279**
Writing the Latte Express operator	264	Creating mesh objects in Python	279
Finding the center of a model	265	Finalizing the setup	281
Adding a Create Lattice menu item	267	**Summary**	**283**
Using the Latte Express add-on	268	**Questions**	**283**
Improving Latte Express options	**268**		

12

Rendering and Shaders — 285

Technical requirements	285	Understanding the Node Tree	289
Render and materials	286	**Writing the Textament add-on**	**291**
Setting the Render Engine	286	Using texture images	291
The Shading workspace	286	Setting up the environment	292
Understanding object materials	287	Writing an import operator	292
Setting Material Properties	287	Connecting nodes	298
The Shader Editor	**289**	Adding a header button	299

Using Load Textures	300	Mixing the Base Color	306
Improving Load Textures	**302**	**Summary**	**308**
Arranging shader nodes	303	**Questions**	**309**

Appendix 311

Part 1: An Introduction to Python	**311**	Chapter 6, Structuring Our Code and Add-Ons	316
Chapter 1, Python's Integration with Blender	311	Chapter 7, The Animation System	317
Chapter 2, Python Entities and API	312	Chapter 8, Animation Modifiers	318
Chapter 3, Creating Your Add-Ons	314	Chapter 9, Animation Drivers	318
Chapter 4, Exploring Object Transformations	315	Chapter 10, Advanced and Modal Operators	319
Chapter 5, Designing Graphical Interfaces	316	**Part 3: Delivering Output**	**320**
Part 2: Interactive Tools and Animation	**316**	Chapter 11, Object Modifiers	320
		Chapter 12, Rendering and Shaders	321

Index 323

Other Books You May Enjoy 336

Preface

Blender is a free, open source application for 3D modeling and animation. It has evolved over the years and, since version 3.0, is on par with state-of-the-art software in many aspects.

It provides a Python **Application Programming Interface** (**API**) for automating tasks, adding functionalities, and integrating Blender in large productions.

Python is a free, open source programming language for quick yet powerful scripting. Its syntax, akin to simplified English, automatic memory management, and ease of integration, makes it the standard in software APIs and 3D pipelines.

This book goes through the steps of the 3D process, starting with the creation and manipulation of objects, then animation and deformation follow, with rendering as the closing chapter. Though this order is a linear path, every chapter can stand on its own, with the exception perhaps of *Chapter 6*, and *Chapter 8*, which rely on examples introduced in their immediate predecessor.

Who this book is for

This book is for users of Blender who want to expand their skills and learn to script, technical directors who want to automate laborious tasks, and professionals and hobbyists who want to learn more about the Python architecture of Blender.

What this book covers

Chapter 1, *Python's Integration with Blender*, teaches you how to run Python instructions in Blender, and use external editors and version control.

Chapter 2, *Python Entities and APIs*, teaches you how to set up options for developers, and how to use Blender modules and access the current context and objects.

Chapter 3, *Creating Your Add-Ons*, teaches you how to write Blender add-ons using Python, how towrite operators, and how to add entries to Blender menus.

Chapter 4, *Exploring Object Transformations*, teaches you how location, rotation, and scale are handled in Python, how to use object constraints and transform matrices, and how to use input properties in operators.

Chapter 5, *Designing Graphical Interfaces*, provides information on how the Blender user interface works, how to create and arrange your own panels, and how to load custom icons and display buttons for custom functions.

Chapter 6, *Structuring Our Code and Add-Ons*, teaches you how to write and distribute modular addons, how to display add-on preferences, and how to update changes in your modules.

Chapter 7, *The Animation System*, teaches you how to access and create animation data, how to script procedural motions, and how to extrapolate rotations.

Chapter 8, *Animation Modifiers*, instructs you on how to add non-destructive modifiers to animations, and how to use them for animated procedural effects.

Chapter 9, *Animation Drivers*, teaches you how to set up inputs for animation channels, how to drive animations with Python expressions, and how to convert the oscillation formula to animated objects.

Chapter 10, *Advanced and Modal Operators*, teaches you how to customize the operator execution flow and how to respond to input events in your operators.

Chapter 11, *Object Modifiers*, provides information on how object modifiers, armatures, and lattices work, and how to set up animation controls of deformed objects.

Chapter 12, *Rendering and Shaders*, teaches you how color and material information is applied to objects and how that process can be automated.

To get the most out of this book

The examples in this book were written and tested using Blender version 3.3. Version 3.3 is a long-term support release and can be found on most application platforms, besides being available for free at `Blender.org`.

Using a programmer text editor is advised. Microsoft Visual Studio Code 1.70, a lightweight free editor available on most operating systems, is used in this book, but any other editor can be used.

More instructions on how to install the software are provided in *Chapter 1*.

The scripts contained in the book were written with forward compatibility in mind. The code available online will be updated to accommodate changes in future releases.

It is assumed that you have some experience with Blender and at least a basic understanding of how Python works, but special effort was put into keeping those requirements low and providing explanations for every concept used in this book.

Preface xvii

Software/hardware covered in the book	Operating system requirements
Blender 3.3	Windows, macOS, or Linux
Visual Studio Code 1.70 or later	

If you are using the digital version of this book, we advise you to type the code yourself or access the code from the book's GitHub repository (a link is available in the next section). Doing so will help you avoid any potential errors related to the copying and pasting of code.

Download the example code files

You can download the example code files for this book from GitHub at https://github.com/PacktPublishing/Python-Scripting-in-Blender. If there's an update to the code, it will be updated in the GitHub repository.

We also have other code bundles from our rich catalog of books and videos available at https://github.com/PacktPublishing/. Check them out!

Download the color images

We also provide a PDF file that has color images of the screenshots and diagrams used in this book. You can download it here: https://packt.link/G1mMt.

Conventions used

There are a number of text conventions used throughout this book.

`Code in text`: Indicates code words in text, database table names, folder names, filenames, file extensions, pathnames, dummy URLs, user input, and Twitter handles. Here is an example: "The `fcurve.modifiers.new(type)` method creates a new modifier according to the type provided in the argument. It returns the new modifier."

A block of code is set as follows:

```
bl_info = {
    "name": "Object Shaker",
    "author": "Packt Man",
    "version": (1, 0),
    "blender": (3, 00, 0),
    "description": "Add Shaky motion to active object",
    "location": "Object Right Click -> Add Object Shake",
    "category": "Learning",
}
```

When we wish to draw your attention to a particular part of a code block, the relevant lines or items are set in bold:

```
sin((frame / fps) * 2 * pi / (2 * pi * sqrt(length/9.8)))
```

Any command-line input or output is written as follows:

```
['ASSETBROWSER_MT_context_menu',
...
['VIEW3D_MT_edit_metaball_context_menu', 'VIEW3D_MT_gpencil_edit_context_menu', 'VIEW3D_MT_object_context_menu', 'VIEW3D_MT_particle_context_menu',
...
```

Some of the code is meant to be used as input for the interactive Python Console. In that case, the user input is preceded by the >>> prompt, unlike the console output:

```
>>> print("Hello")
Hello
```

Bold: Indicates a new term, an important word, or words that you see onscreen. For instance, words in menus or dialog boxes appear in **bold**. Here is an example: "Before we delve into how f-modifiers are scripted, we will have a look at how to create them in **Graph Editor**."

> **Tips or important notes**
> Appear like this.

Get in touch

Feedback from our readers is always welcome.

General feedback: If you have questions about any aspect of this book, email us at `customercare@packtpub.com` and mention the book title in the subject of your message.

Errata: Although we have taken every care to ensure the accuracy of our content, mistakes do happen. If you have found a mistake in this book, we would be grateful if you would report this to us. Please visit `www.packtpub.com/support/errata` and fill in the form.

Piracy: If you come across any illegal copies of our works in any form on the internet, we would be grateful if you would provide us with the location address or website name. Please contact us at `copyright@packt.com` with a link to the material.

If you are interested in becoming an author: If there is a topic that you have expertise in and you are interested in either writing or contributing to a book, please visit `authors.packtpub.com`.

Share Your Thoughts

Once you've read, we'd love to hear your thoughts! Scan the QR code below to go straight to the Amazon review page for this book and share your feedback.

`https://packt.link/r/1803234229`

Your review is important to us and the tech community and will help us make sure we're delivering excellent quality content.

Download a free PDF copy of this book

Thanks for purchasing this book!

Do you like to read on the go but are unable to carry your print books everywhere?

Is your eBook purchase not compatible with the device of your choice?

Don't worry, now with every Packt book you get a DRM-free PDF version of that book at no cost.

Read anywhere, any place, on any device. Search, copy, and paste code from your favorite technical books directly into your application.

The perks don't stop there, you can get exclusive access to discounts, newsletters, and great free content in your inbox daily

Follow these simple steps to get the benefits:

1. Scan the QR code or visit the link below

```
https://packt.link/free-ebook/9781803234229
```

2. Submit your proof of purchase
3. That's it! We'll send your free PDF and other benefits to your email directly

Part 1: Introduction to Python

In this part, we will familiarize you with Blender's Python interface. This part will illustrate the fundamentals of scripting and provide an overall understanding of how to code tools for Blender.

This section comprises the following chapters:

- *Chapter 1, Python's Integration with Blender*
- *Chapter 2, Python Entities and APIs*
- *Chapter 3, Creating Your Add-Ons*
- *Chapter 4, Exploring Object Transformations*
- *Chapter 5, Designing Graphical Interfaces*

1
Python's Integration with Blender

Blender accepts code instructions in the same way as it interacts: via a graphical user interface.. That allows artists and studios to implement their own features and automation.

Python, a highly extensible programming language with low barriers to entry, is widely used in computer graphics.

Though Blender's core is written in C and C++, menus and graphic elements use Python. That allows custom and factory functionalities to share the same look and feel.

In this chapter, we'll learn how to run Python commands in Blender and where to look for their outcome. We will also see where a history of past instructions is found and how to use that to our advantage. Lastly, we will introduce a code editor and a version control system and see how they help make our work easier.

By the end of this chapter, you will understand how a programmer works and why it is not so different from using software in the first place.

In this chapter, we will cover the following main topics:

- The scripting workspace
- Python execution
- Version control

Technical requirements

Besides Blender 3.3+ or in this case, Blender 3.3 (https://www.blender.org/download/lts/3-3), you will require the following free tools:

- Visual Studio Code, available at https://code.visualstudio.com/Download. Version 1.66 is used in this book, and is available at https://code.visualstudio.com/updates/v1_66
- Git (optional), found at https://git-scm.com/downloads

You are encouraged to write your own code; the examples for this chapter can be found at the following URL: https://github.com/PacktPublishing/Python-Scripting-in-Blender/tree/main/ch1.

Since it is a free, open source software, there are plenty of ways to install Blender. We are going to look at the most common install solutions.

Installing Blender

The procedure for installing Blender varies with the operating system. Like most applications, installers for *Microsoft Windows* and *Apple macOS* are provided. Also, portable versions, such as archives that can be uncompressed and executed everywhere in the system, are available for *Linux* and Windows.

The version of Blender used in this book, 3.3, might differ from other versions already installed on the system. In that case, we can install different versions of Blender on the same machine.

Installing Blender on Windows

There are more ways to install a program on Microsoft Windows: Windows Installer, *Microsoft Store*, and *using a portable archive*. While most application publishers choose one of those options, all of them are available for Blender.

Installing multiple versions via Windows Installer

The most common way to install Blender on Windows is to download **Windows Installer** from Blender's download page. Executing the downloaded .msi file installs Blender. Before Blender 3.4, only one of the multiple installed versions was available in the **Start** menu.

If that is the case for you, the other versions can be accessed by navigating to the Program Files folder, usually C:\Program Files\Blender Foundation, using Windows Explorer.

We can execute blender.exe directly from the Blender 3.3 folder or use right-click > **New** > **Shortcut** in Windows Explorer and create a shortcut to it:

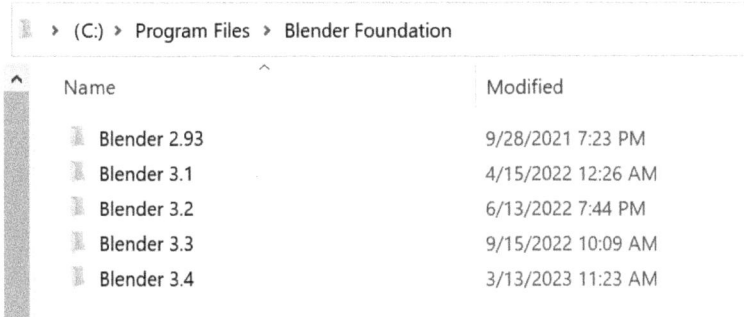

Figure 1.1: Multiple versions of Blender in Program Files

Alternatively, since version 3.3 is a *Long-term Support* version, it is also available in the Microsoft Store.

Installing Blender from the Microsoft Store

The download page of Blender 3.3 provides a link to the Microsoft Store installer. Alternatively, we can start **Microsoft Store** from the **Start** menu and look up `blender` in the top bar. Once we get to the **Blender** page, we make sure that it's published by **Blender Foundation** and click the **Get** button:

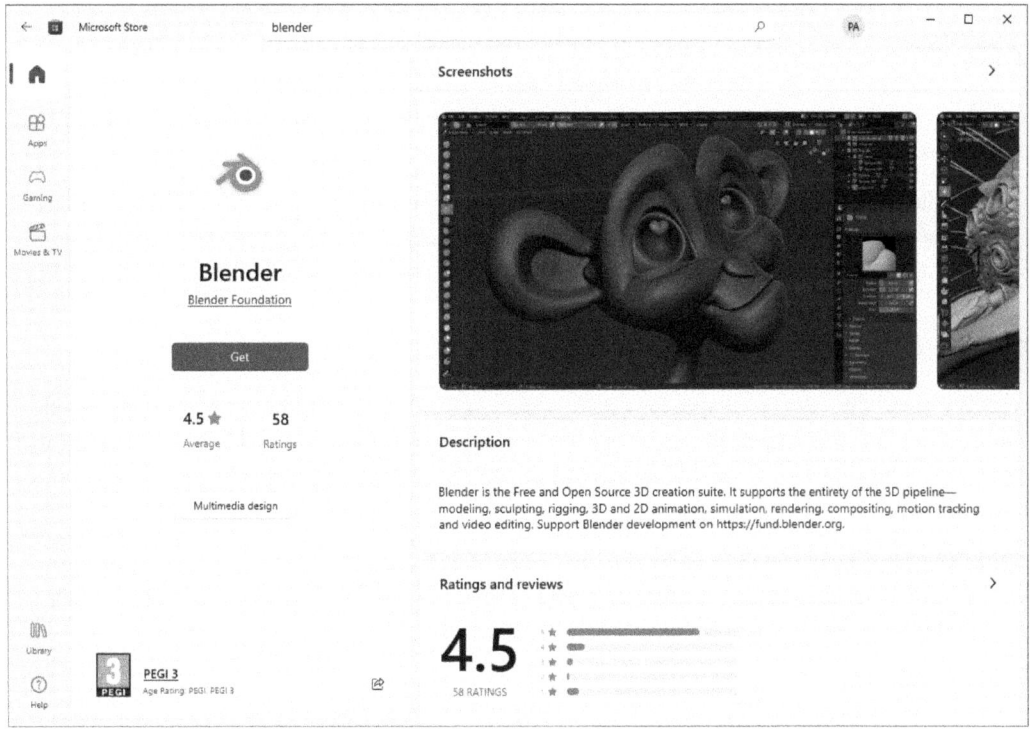

Figure 1.2: Installing Blender from the Microsoft Store

That will add a Blender 3.3 entry in the **Start** menu:

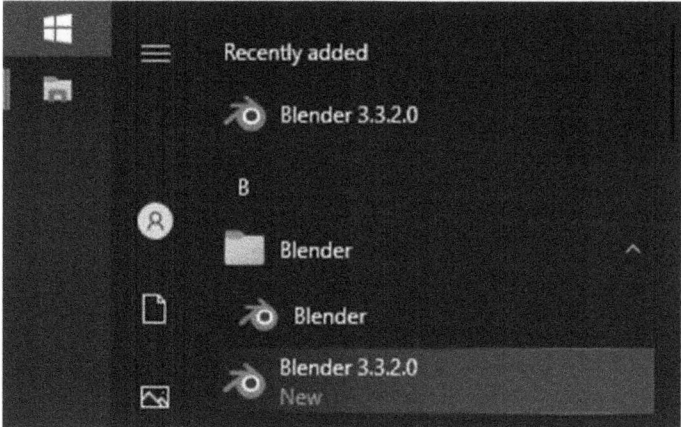

Figure 1.3: Multiple versions in the Start menu

Microsoft Store gives the advantage of always adding a shortcut for the installed version. If, for some reason, Microsoft Store is not an option, we can download a portable archive.

Downloading a portable archive

To avoid any application packaging, we can download a Windows portable `.zip` file, or a Linux `.tar.xz` archive.

Portable versions can be used from any location of the system, even removable drives. We only need to extract the archive in a directory of choice via right-clicking -> **Extract** in the file manager and then executing the `blender.exe` or `blender` executable in the unpacked folder.

Installing multiple versions on macOS

We can download the `.dmg` packages for *Apple Intel* or *Apple Silicon* computers. Once downloaded, double-clicking the file will open the installer window. If another version of Blender is already present in the system, a prompt dialog will ask whether we want to keep both or replace the installed version with the new one.

Selecting **Keep Both** will install the new version as **Blender 2**. The digit depends on the installation order and doesn't reflect the actual version of Blender. We can rename it `Blender 3.3` using right-click -> **Rename** on the **Application** entry in the file manager:

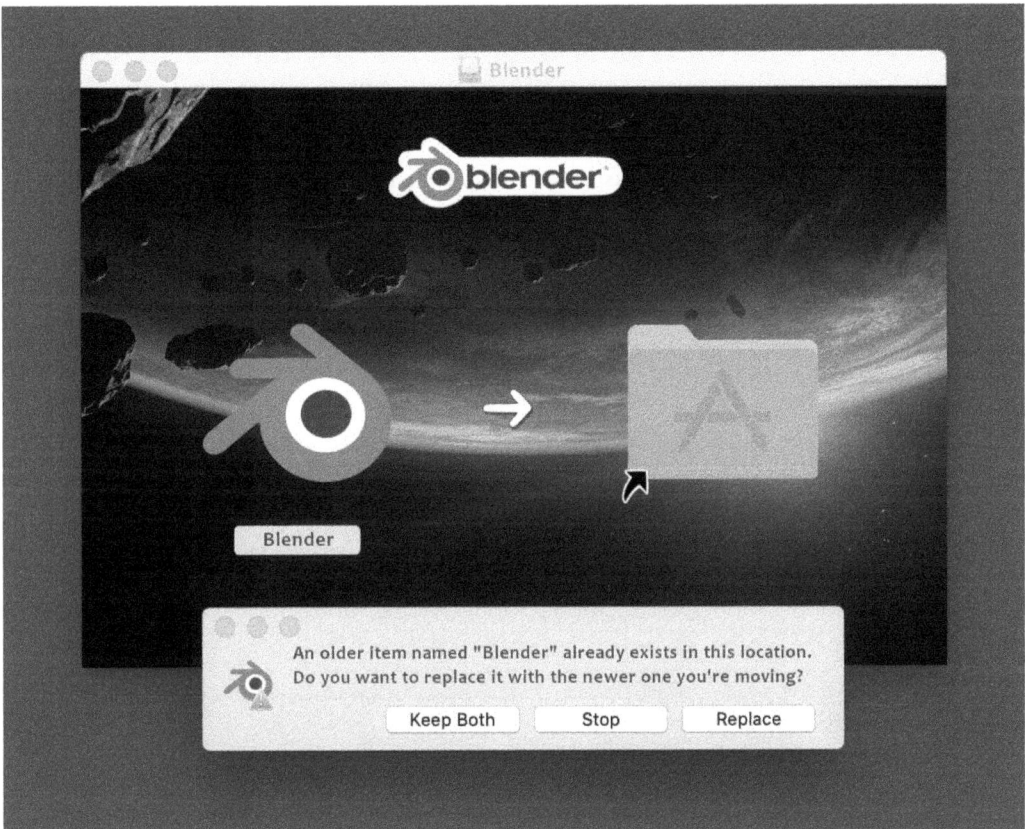

Figure 1.4: Installing an additional version of Blender on macOS

There are many other ways to install Blender: a link to stores such as *Steam* (Windows, macOS, or Linux) or *Snapcraft* (Linux only) is provided on the download page, not to mention the package manager of Linux distribution (*apt* on *Ubuntu*, *yum* on *CentOS*, and so on). It is worth mentioning that it is possible to build Blender from the source code, but that's an advanced topic beyond the scope of this book.

While this book sticks to version 3.3, the examples should work on future releases of the 3.x series with minor corrections at worst.

A future major release, such as Blender 4 or 5, is almost guaranteed to break compatibility with past scripts. Still, the knowledge from this book about best practices and thought patterns will stand the test of time.

Now that we have installed Blender on our system, we can dive into its scripting capabilities.

The Scripting workspace – first steps with Python

A sequence of Python instructions is often referred to as a **script**. Likewise, the activity of producing Python code is usually called **Scripting**.

Blender's interface consists of different **workspaces**. Each of them is a tab meant for a different activity. At the time of writing, the **Scripting** tab is the last on the right side of the screen. Clicking on it switches to the interface designed for Python users.

The most significant elements are the **Python console**, the **Info Log**, and the **Text Editor**:

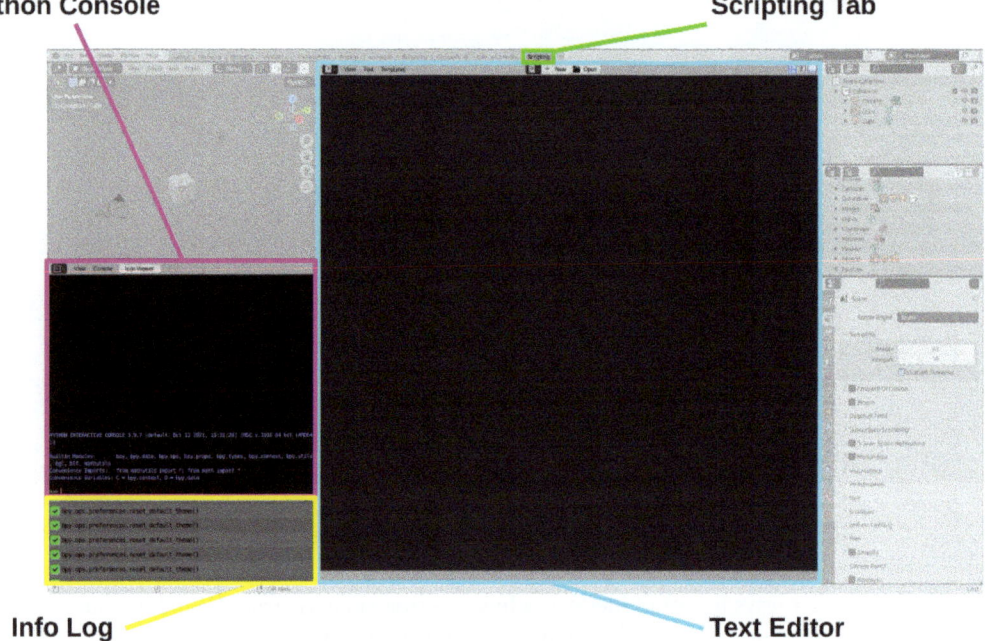

Figure 1.5: Blender scripting interface

We will start our journey in Python by typing commands in the Python console.

The Python console

The console is an interactive terminal with a header that displays the current version of Python (3.10.2, at the time of writing) and a >>> prompt sign to advertise that it's waiting for interactive text. All we need to do is hover the cursor on it and type an instruction:

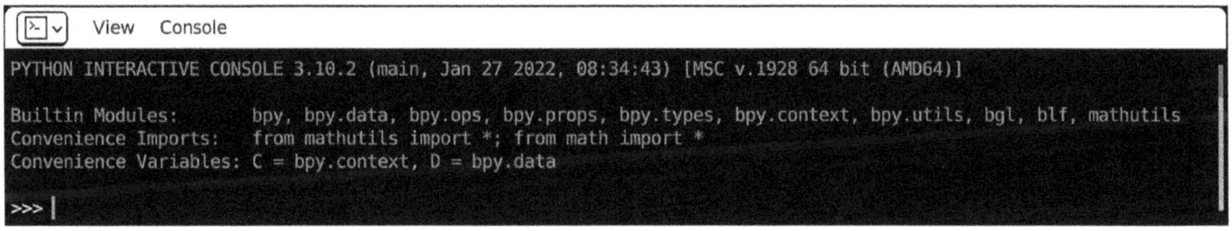

Figure 1.6: The Python console

"Hello World!" from the console

The practice called *Hello World!* is a way to familiarize yourself with a new programming language. It's about displaying the titular phrase using a command.

We will use the `print` function for that. Example code for the interactive console starts with the `>>>` prompt symbol. We don't need to type that as well in the console: it is already there. We click on the console area and type `print("Hello World")`:

```
>>> print("Hello World")
```

Then press *Enter*. The console output is displayed in a different color and doesn't start with the prompt:

Figure 1.7: Displaying our output on the console

We can use the Python console to query information about the Python version.

Checking the Python release

The current version of Python can be displayed anytime using the `sys` module. We need to import this module and look for its `version` attribute. That takes the following two lines:

```
>>> import sys
>>> sys.version
```

The console prints out verbose information about the version in use:

```
'3.10.2 (main, Jan 27 2022, 08:34:43) ...'
```

The three digits of the version number stand for *major*, *minor*, and *micro* versions. A different major release number implies heavy changes in the language syntax: *Python 3.0* is very different from any Python 2.x releases. A minor release introduces new features but doesn't break compatibility with older code. A micro release doesn't bring changes to the language; it consists of bug fixes and other forms of maintenance.

The changes brought with each new Python version are available as *Release Notes* on the download page of the **Python Software Foundation**:

https://www.python.org/downloads/

If our script relies on a feature introduced with a minor release, we can check the version numbers individually using `version_info`, as seen here:

```
import sys
if sys.version_info.minor < 6:
    print("Warning: This script requires Python 3.6.x")
```

Compared with other software, Blender follows the Python release cycle very tightly. This is done mostly to take advantage of the latest improvements in terms of performance and bug fixes.

Checking the Blender release

The current Blender release can be checked in the graphical user interface or in Python scripts.

Checking the Blender release in the interface

Starting from version 3.0, the most immediate place to check for the version number of Blender is in the lower-right corner of the window. In version 3.3, the version number is followed by the current time and frame set for the scene:

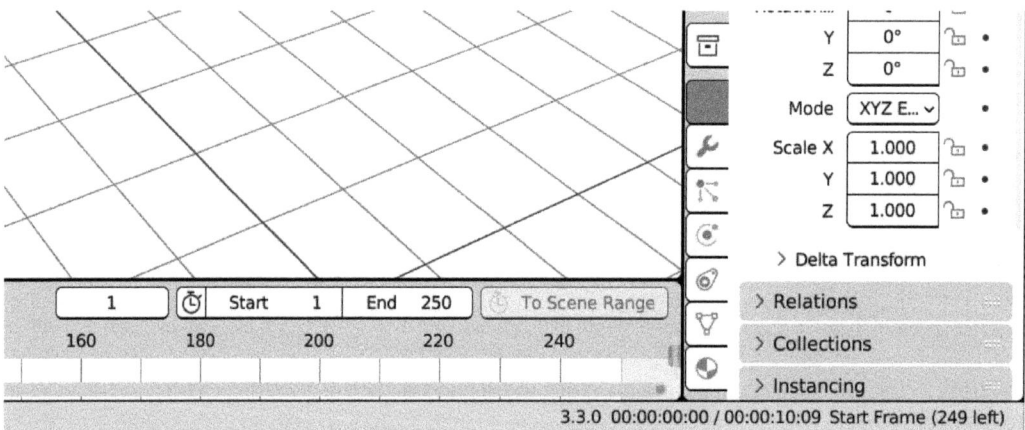

Figure 1.8: Blender version number in the status bar

Another way to display the version number is by clicking the Blender icon in the top-right corner of the menu bar and then selecting **About Blender** from the menu.

We can also get Blender's version number via Python scripts.

Checking the Blender release in Python scripts

If our scripts rely on features from a specific version, they must be able to determine on which release of Blender it is running. That information is contained in the bpy.app module. We can display the current version by typing these lines in the console:

```
>>> import bpy
>>> bpy.app.version
```

In *Blender 3.3.2*, the console returns the following:

```
(3, 3, 2)
```

Unlike sys.version_info, bpy.app.version doesn't contain names, just numbers. Nevertheless, we can store them in variables using the Python syntax:

```
>>> major, minor, micro = bpy.app.version
```

Then, we can use print to display the single version numbers:

```
>>> print("Major version:", major)
Major version: 3
>>> print("Minor version:", minor)
Minor version: 3
>>> print("Micro version:", micro)
Micro version: 2
```

A new major release of Blender brings drastic changes to the interface and workflow, while a minor release introduces new tools for animation or for generating images.

To display the information, we have used the print function. Since functions are the first step toward structured programming, we will have a better look at how they work and how we can change the "Hello World!" message to something else.

Invoking functions

When we use a *function*, we say that we *call* or *invoke* that function. To do that, we type its name, followed by parentheses. Between parentheses, there is the function's *argument*, such as the input on which it operates:

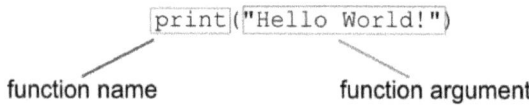

function name   function argument

Figure 1.9: Function and argument in a Python script

When invoked, the `print` function reads the argument and displays it on a new line.

The `"Hello World!"` argument is a *string literal*: it can be any sequence of characters enclosed between quotation marks (`" "`).

We can feed any other message to `print`; the output will vary accordingly:

```
>>> print("We are learning Python here")
We are learning Python here
```

Figure 1.10: Printing text in the Blender Python console

Now that we have gained confidence, we will look at some Blender commands.

The Info Log

The user activity is displayed as Python commands in the log area, at the bottom left of the **Scripting** workspace. We can open Blender and perform the following operations:

1. Delete the default cube in the Viewport via right-click -> **Delete**.
2. From the Viewport top bar, click **Add** -> **Mesh** -> **Cylinder**.
3. From the Viewport top bar, click **Add** -> **Mesh** -> **UV Sphere**. We will find these three lines in the Info Log area:

```
bpy.ops.object.delete(use_global=False)
bpy.ops.mesh.primitive_cylinder_add(radius=1, depth=2, enter_editmode=False, align='WORLD', location=(0, 0, 0), scale=(1, 1, 1))
bpy.ops.mesh.primitive_uv_sphere_add(radius=1, enter_editmode=False, align='WORLD', location=(0, 0, 0), scale=(1, 1, 1))
```

Figure 1.11: History of actions in the Info Log area

The entries of the Info Log are the Python commands triggered by our recent activity. We can copy those lines and use them in our scripts.

Using the lines from the log

Clicking or dragging with the left mouse button selects the log lines. We can copy them to the clipboard via right-click -> **Copy**:

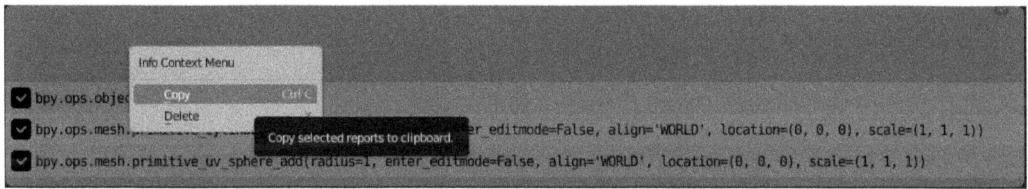

Figure 1.12: Copying Python commands from the Info Log

We can go back to the startup scene and paste them into the console:

1. Restart Blender or click **File** -> **New** -> **General**.
2. Go to the **Scripting** workspace.
3. In the Python console, right-click -> **Paste**, and press *Enter*.

Executing those lines will delete the initial cube, then add two objects: the same steps run manually earlier. We will see how we can change their content and affect the outcome.

Changing parameters

Let's not focus too much on the code for now: it will be clearer in the next chapter. Anyway, we might recognize a pattern from the "Hello World!" example:

```
function(arguments between parentheses)
```

And at least one argument is self-explanatory in its purpose:

```
bpy.[...]_uv_sphere_add(..., ..., location=(0, 0, 0), ...)
```

location=(x, y, z) represents the 3D coordinates where a new object is added. We can change the last line and create our sphere just above the cylinder.

Let's revert to the startup scene once more and paste our lines again, but before we press *Enter*, this time, we change the last zero to 2:

```
bpy.ops.mesh.primitive_uv_sphere_add(radius=1, enter_editmode=False,
align='WORLD', location=(0, 0, 2), scale=(1, 1, 1))
```

We have just run our first script. It deletes the selected objects and stacks two new shapes on top of each other:

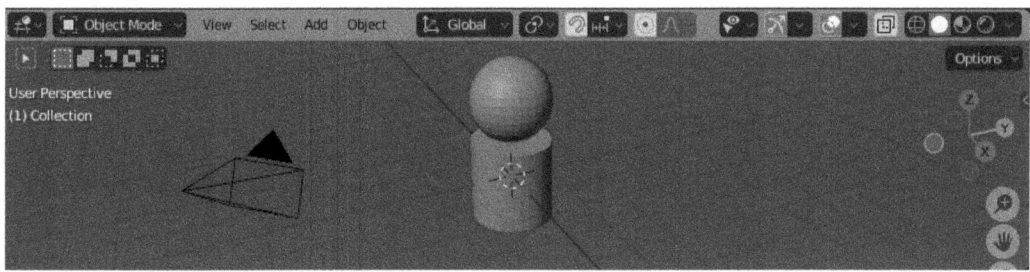

Figure 1.13: Cylinder and Sphere primitives, created via Python

The Python console can execute code with immediacy but is not very practical for more than a few lines. We will now see how to run Python scripts as documents.

The Text Editor

This is the largest element in the **Scripting** workspace. It can be used for writing text and scripts.

To add a new script, we click the + **New** button in the top bar and create a new text:

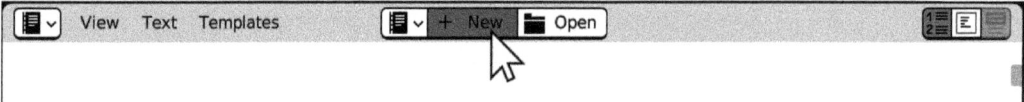

Figure 1.14: Creating a new text object in the Text Editor

Let's type some words, for instance, a more verbose version of *"Hello World!"*. Like many programmer editors, Blender displays the line numbers on the left:

Figure 1.15: Writing scripts in the Text Editor

Also, the words have different colors according to their Python meaning: white for the function, yellow for the string, and red for the parenthesis. This feature is called **syntax highlighting** and gives useful visual feedback: the color of the words depends on their role in the programming language.

Running text documents

If the current text is a Python script, we can execute it from the Text Editor:

1. Click on **Run Script** from the **Text** menu in the Text Editor menu bar.

2. Look for the execution outcome info in the Info Log:

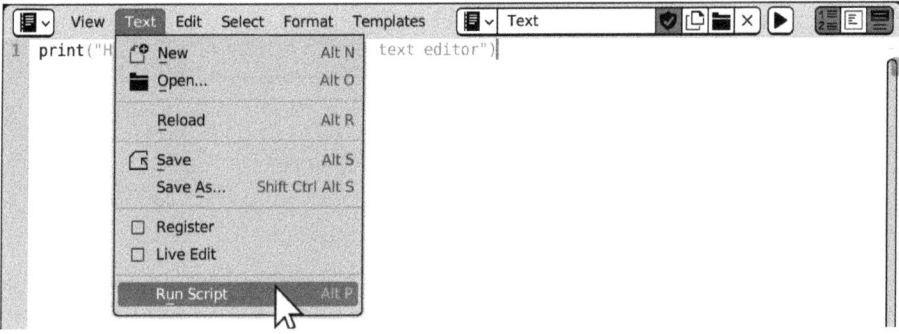

Figure 1.16: Executing scripts in the Text Editor

The Info Log confirms that something has happened:

✓ bpy.ops.text.run_script()

Figure 1.17: The script execution mentioned in the Info Log

But we might be disappointed, as the printout text is apparently nowhere to be found!

The reason is that the output of the Text Editor goes straight to the **System Console**, the *operating system's* command line.

On Windows, we can display it using **Window** ->**Toggle System Console** from Blender's top bar. To read system messages on a Unix-based system (Linux or macOS), we must start Blender from a command line in the first place.

Once brought up, **System Console** displays the output printed by the Text Editor:

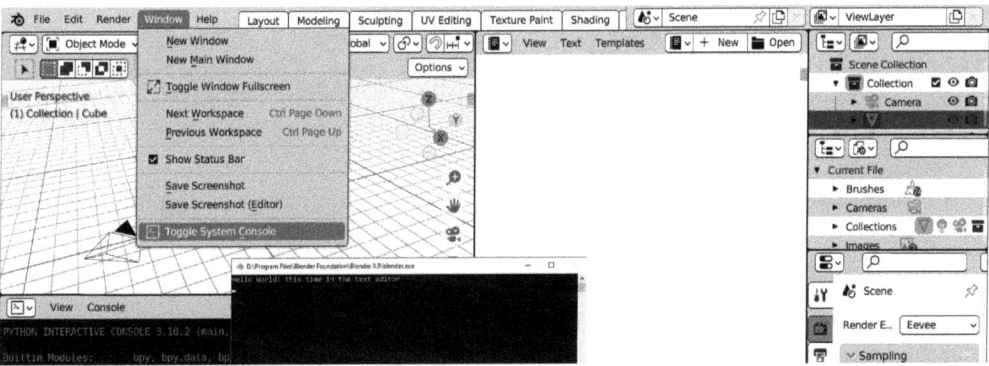

Figure 1.18: Displaying the System Console on Windows

The default name for our text block is Text. It can be renamed by clicking on it. We'll better add the .py suffix as an extension to make it clear that it's a Python script:

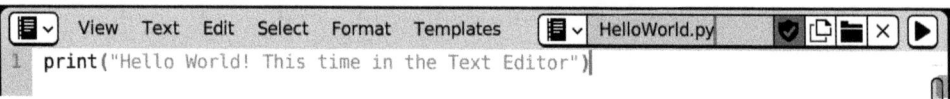

Figure 1.19: Renaming text blocks in Blender

Copying the Python console as script

Remember the lines we entered in the Python console earlier? If we haven't closed Blender or loaded a new scene, we can copy them to the *clipboard* at once.

1. From the **Console** menu in the Python console top bar, select **Copy as Script**.
2. Create another text block using **Text** > **New** from the Text Editor menu.
3. Give the text a new name, such as OurFirstScript.py.
4. Paste the lines from the clipboard via right-click -> **Paste** in the text area.

Looking at the Text Editor, it turns out that the full version of the script is a little bit longer than our three lines:

Figure 1.20: The Python console input copied to the Text Editor

The first five rows set up the console environment. They are executed behind the scenes when Blender starts.

Lines starting with a hash (#) are *comments*: they are ignored by Python and contain reminders or explanations meant for human readers.

Our own instructions are respectively at lines **13**, **17**, and **21**. This script can be executed via **Text** -> **Run Script** as we did before or via the *Alt + P* keys combination.

Exporting text files

The notepad icon lets us switch between different text blocks via a drop-down list:

Figure 1.21: Switching between text blocks in Blender

Selecting **Text | Save As...** from the editor menu bar saves the current text to disk. A new window lets us select a folder and confirm the filename:

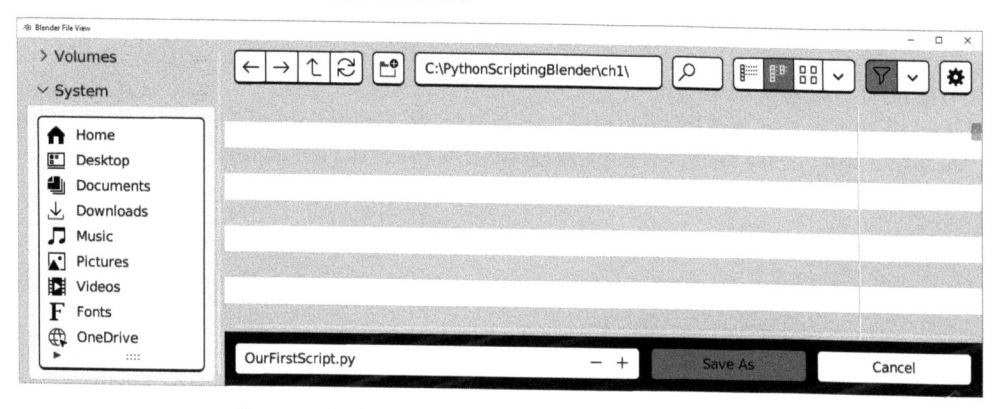

Figure 1.22: Saving the content of the Text Editor to file

Blender's Text Editor is great for quick tests, but a programmer text editor is usually preferred for more serious tasks. We are going to use *Visual Studio Code* in the next section.

External editor – Visual Studio Code

Visual Studio Code (**VS Code**), is a fast, multiplatform, free editor from Microsoft, available for Windows, macOS, and Linux. Using an external editor makes our code independent from a session of Blender. Also, a programmer text editor offers many utilities besides syntax highlighting.

VS Code 1.66 is used in this book. It is a fast, lightweight editor available for most platforms, but there are plenty of alternatives – most notably, the following:

- **Notepad++**: This is a fast but powerful editor for Windows, available at `https://notepad-plus-plus.org`.
- **PyCharm**: This is a Python **integrated development environment** (**IDE**) by **JetBrains**. A free community version can be found at `https://www.jetbrains.com/pycharm`.

- **LightTable:** This is an interesting open source editor, available at http://lighttable.com.
- **Sublime**: This is a commercial text editor, found at https://www.sublimetext.com.

Most Linux distributions come with at least one decent, ready-to-use, text editor. We encourage you to experiment and find the text editor of your choice.

In this section, we will set up VS Code for Python scripting.

> **Pick the right studio!**
>
> *VS Code* and *Visual Studio* have a similar name but are two different products from Microsoft. While VS Code is a programmer text editor, Visual Studio is a full development environment for advanced languages such as C++. While C++ projects may require a specific version of the building environment, it is safe to use any version of VS Code as long as Python is a supported language.

Loading our scripts folder

We can load the folder that contains our script files using the **Open Folder...** entry from the **File** menu. The editor will display the folder content on the first tab of the left column: the **Explorer** tab. Clicking on a .py file opens the script for editing.

Additional Python support can be installed by clicking **Install** on the bottom-right notification:

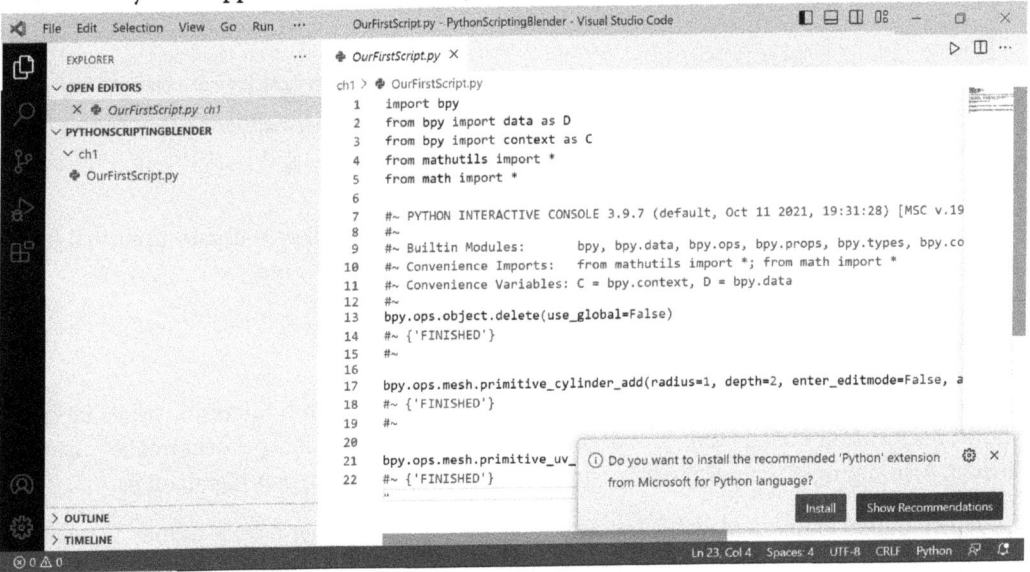

Figure 1.23: Our Python script in VS Code

Keeping Blender's text blocks in sync

When a text file open in Blender is changed by another application, a red question mark appears to the left of the filename:

```
import bpy
from bpy import data as D
from bpy import context as C
from mathutils import *
from math import *
```

Figure 1.24: Blender detects changes in a saved script

Clicking the question mark displays the viable actions:

- **Reload from disk**: This loads and displays the up-to-date file
- **Make text internal (separate copy)**: The displayed text is now part of the Blender session, no longer tied to any text file on disk
- **Ignore**: Changes are ignored; Blender will still display the old text and keep reporting that it's out of sync with the text saved on disk

To have additional help, we can add versioning to our files. That allows us to make changes without worrying about breaking things or losing our work.

Version control and backup

Version control helps to keep track of file changes, save snapshots of the code, and roll back to older versions if necessary. **Git** is the most used versioning system at present; it is free and integrated into most editors. In this section, we will use version control in combination with VS Code.

Initializing the repository

Once Git is installed, it can be used from VS Code, by activating the **Source Control** tab using the *branch* icon on the left column bar. The **Initialize Repository** button adds versioning to our folder:

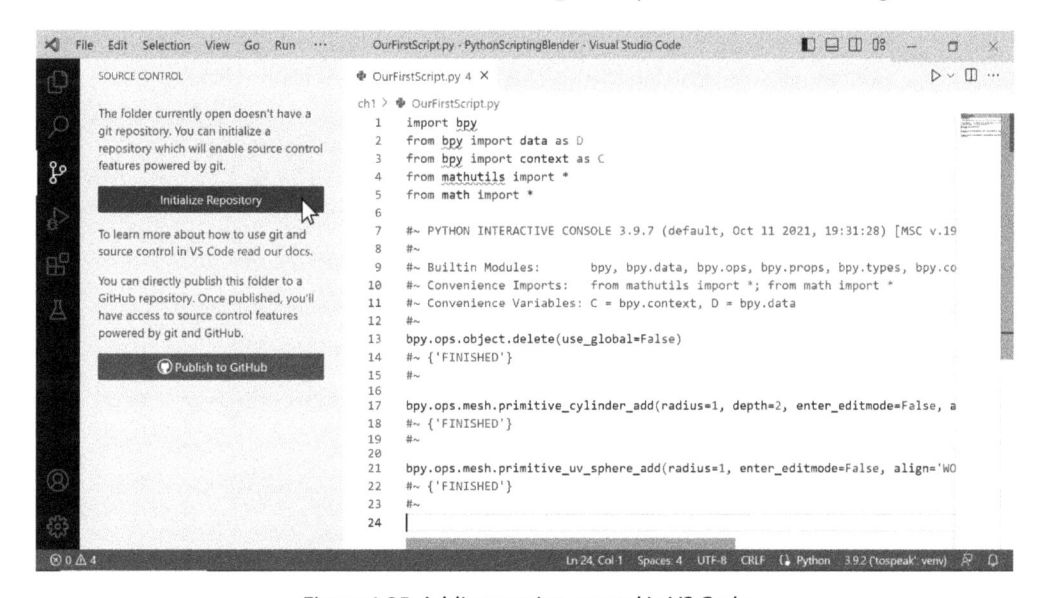

Figure 1.25: Adding version control in VS Code

The icon will change and warn us about the presence of files. We click the + icon next to the filename to add them to versioning. In Git terminology, we are going to **Stage** the current changes:

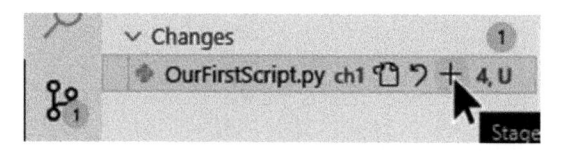

Figure 1.26: Staging changes in VS Code

The editor shows the before/after conditions of our files. We can add a message in the text field on the top left and click the *tick* icon. This will **Commit** our changes to the project history:

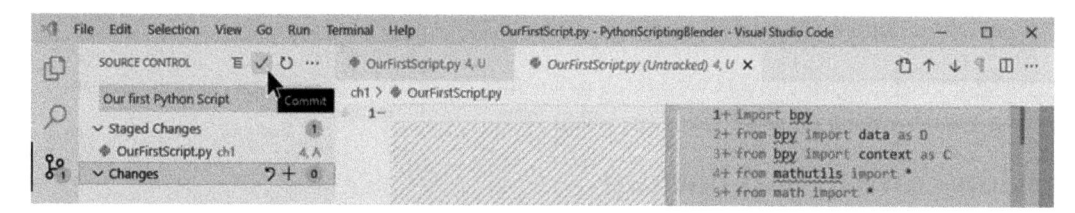

Figure 1.27: Commit changes in VS Code

Making changes

Let's say we don't want our script to delete the current objects. To do that, we delete line number **13**:

```
bpy.ops.object.delete(use_global=False)
```

When the file is saved, version control detects this change. We can stage that by clicking the + icon, as before. If we select `OurFirstScript.py` in the left column, VS Code highlights the current changes. We add a message for this new commit and click the **tick** button again:

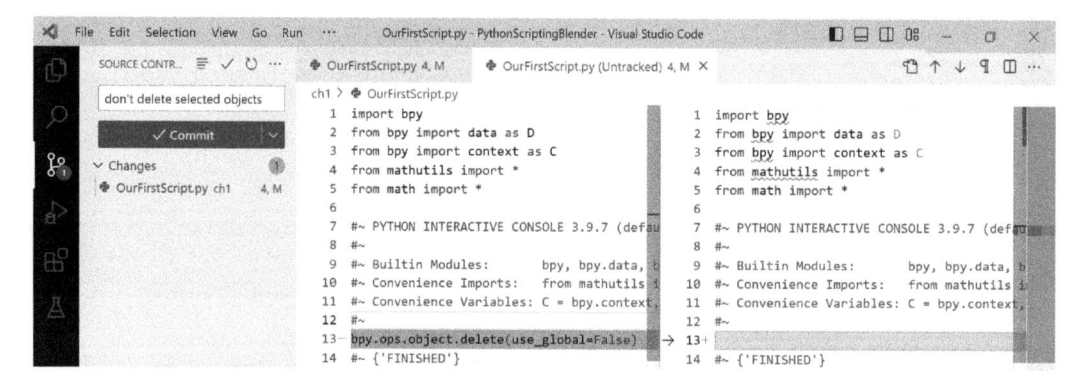

Figure 1.28: Displaying changes in VS Code

If we go back to the **Explorer** tab and select our script, we will see that a section called **Timeline** can be expanded: it contains a list of our commit messages. Selecting a commit displays the related changes, allowing us to restore old lines of code. Every change that is not committed can be easily undone using the *Revert* function.

Reverting uncommitted changes

Let's add some incorrect text at line 7 and save. If, for any reason, we cannot undo that, we can right-click our file in the **Version Control** tab and select **Discard Changes**:

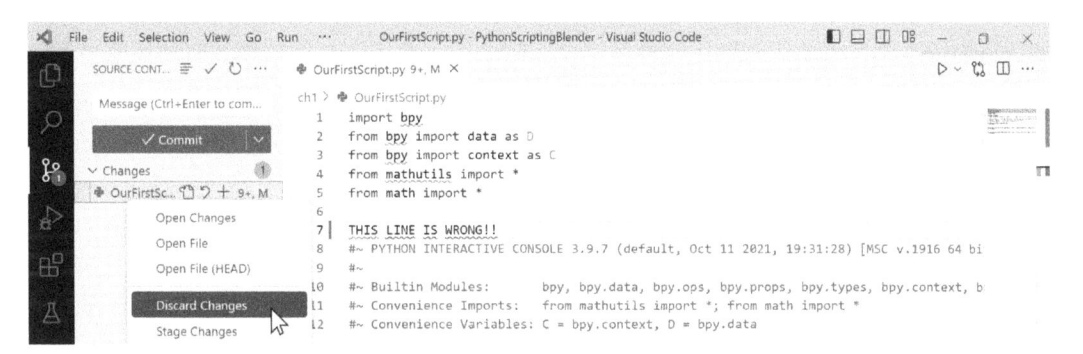

Figure 1.29: Discarding uncommitted changes in VS Code

The importance of version control can be underestimated at first but becomes vital in more complex projects. It's a wide topic that goes beyond the scope of this book, but it's important to grasp at least the basics of it.

Summary

In this chapter, we gained confidence with *scripting* and introduced the fundamental tools for Python programming. You learned how to look for Python commands in the Blender log and execute them in different contexts, and how to set up a coding environment. We also learned how to keep track of our code and edits.

In *Chapter 2*, we will refine our knowledge of Python. We will meet the most common entities and learn how to use the programming logic to write more useful scripts.

Questions

1. How do we display the sections of Blender that accept Python input?
2. How can we read the output and printout from Python execution?
3. Does Blender use Python to carry on the user actions?
4. How can we look at Blender's Python activity log?
5. How do we write scripts in Blender? Can we edit them in other applications?
6. How and in which tab can we initialize version control in VS Code?
7. How can we access a script's timeline in VS Code?

2
Python Entities and API

Blender expands Python by making the **modules** of its **Application Programming Interface (API)** available inside the app.

These modules provide **wrappers** that translate Blender's internal data into Python objects. Comprehensive documentation and an API reference are available online and can be reached from inside the application. Plus, there are some extra features to help programmers in their journey.

Much like the syntax highlight that we have met in *Chapter 1*, some features for developers are common-place in the programming world. Others, such as property tooltips and variables display, are specific to Blender.

In this chapter, we are going to look at some **snippets**, that is, chunks of code, that will help you become confident with the architecture of Blender's API.

Generally, the API is designed to be very friendly to programmers that are already experienced with Python, only deviating a few times from the standards.

By the end of this chapter, you will be able to inspect Blender objects from the Python console and change their properties, use and expand Blender collections, and check the current state of the user interaction.

In this chapter, we are going to become familiar with the following topics:

- Features of Python
- Blender modules and their structure
- Data and Context Access

Technical requirements

Only Blender is needed to follow along with this chapter.

Useful features of Python

We already met the *Python* elements of the **Scripting** workspace in *Chapter 1*. Now we are going to look at some useful features that can help us get the most out of them. When it comes to programming, automation can speed up the search for attributes and terms. That can happen both in the console, through conventional methods such as **autocompletion**, or in the interface, via shortcuts that display the Python address of a graphic element. Some of these features are already available when Blender starts, while others are left for the users to enable.

Options for developers

Developer features are disabled by default. They can be enabled in the **Preferences** dialog from the **Edit** menu in the top bar of Blender. We need to select the **Interface** tab on the left and look at the first panel: **Display**. Programmers usually enable the **Developer Extras** and **Python Tooltips** options.

Developer Extras

Developer Extras adds a right-click menu entry that can display the Python source code of the UI in the *Text Editor*. It also shows the geometry index of mesh components when the user switches to **Edit Mode**. Among other things, it allows the **search bar** to execute operators that cannot be accessed via the UI.

Python tooltips

Hovering the mouse cursor over an attribute displays a tooltip with a small description. If Python tooltips are enabled, information about how to invoke that attribute in scripts is displayed as well.

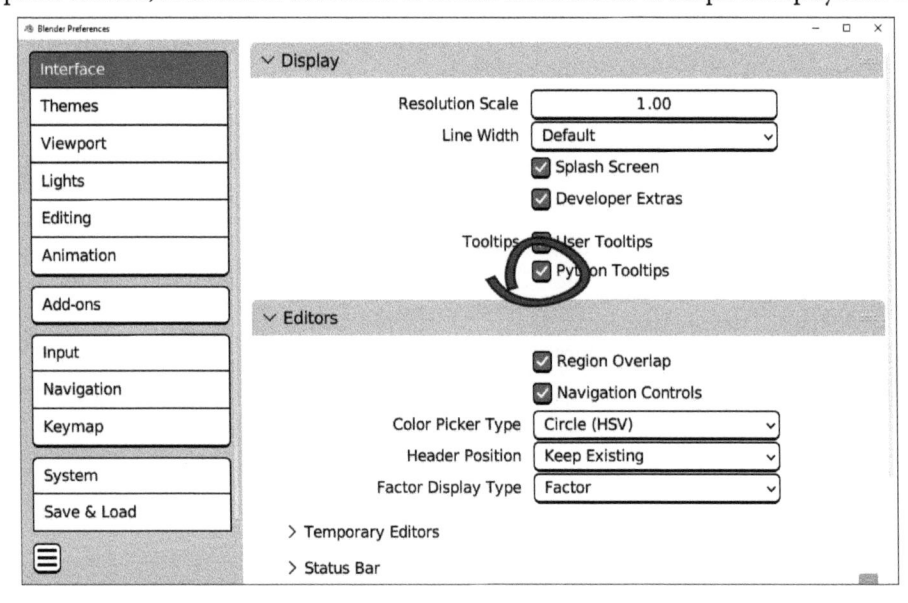

Figure 2.1: Blender's display preferences

For instance, in the 3D Viewport, we can press the *N* key to display the **transform channels** on the right-hand side of the screen. Leaving the mouse pointer over a coordinate, such as **Location: X**, for a while will show two additional lines in the description:

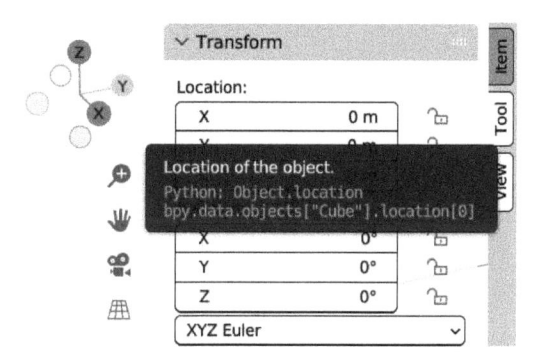

Figure 2.2: Python tooltip of an object location

The Python tooltip consists of two lines:

```
Python: Object.location
bpy.data.objects['Cube'].location[0]
```

The first line provides the Python name of the attribute; in this case, `location` is the **data path** of an `Object` position in space.

The second line is more specific: the location of this object (`'Cube'`) can be reached by typing that line in the console. This is usually referred to as the **full data path** of the property or, on some occasions, the **RNA** path. The latter term comes from a playful analogy to genetics: if Blender's internal code makes its *DNA*, its *Python* access can be seen as the *RNA* of the application.

An object's location is a simple case, other attributes can be more complex. Anyway, we can copy data paths to the clipboard following the steps in the next subsection.

Copying the data path

Right-clicking on a property opens a *context* menu. Some entries, such as **Insert Keyframes** and **Reset to Default Value**, are useful for animation. In this section, we will focus on the programming entries, **Copy Data Path** and **Copy Full Data Path**:

1. Select an object in the 3D Viewport.
2. If no transform properties are displayed on the right, press *N* to summon the **Transform** sidebar.
3. From the **Item** tab, right-click on the first location channel (**X**), then click **Copy Full Data Path**.

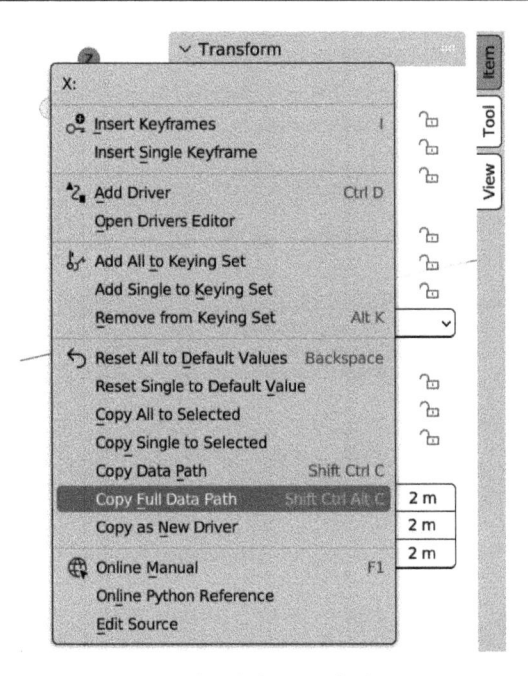

Figure 2.3: Right-click menu for location X

4. Go to the Python console, press *Ctrl* + *V* to paste, and then press *Enter*.

The console will display the location value for the *X* coordinate:

```
>>> bpy.data.objects['Cube'].location[0]
0.0
```

The full data path allows to access an attribute and, unless it is a read-only property, change its value. We can see how the copied line ends with an index, which is due to location being a three-dimensional attribute – each index refers to an axis of the space:

```
bpy.data.objects['Cube'].location[0]    # X axis
bpy.data.objects['Cube'].location[1]    # Y axis
bpy.data.objects['Cube'].location[2]    # Z axis
```

Data paths can be convoluted sometimes, but in the next section, we are going to look at some console tools that help a lot when looking for the right attribute.

Python console's utilities

The *Python console* offers some helpful utilities. Some of them, such as text completion and history, are common among programmers' tools. Others, such as the 3D representation of variables, are typical of Blender. This section provides an overview of how the Python console is used in day-to-day programming.

Autocompletion

Pressing the *Tab* button while typing in the console suggests a few possible ways to complete the line. On top of that, if the current statement is associated with internal documentation (**docstring**), that will be displayed along with the suggestion. For instance, let's try these steps to autocomplete a call to `print()`:

1. In Blender, select **Scripting Workspace** in the tabs at the top of the screen, as we learned in the *The Scripting Workspace* section, in *First steps with Python*, in *Chapter 1*.
2. In the Python console, type only `prin`, then press *Tab*.

The console fills in the missing letters and displays `print(`, with an open bracket, and its documentation. Then, it lets the programmer finish the line.

```
PYTHON INTERACTIVE CONSOLE 3.10.2 (main, Jan 27 2022, 08:34:43) [MSC v.1928 64 bit (AMD64)]

Builtin Modules:       bpy, bpy.data, bpy.ops, bpy.props, bpy.types, bpy.context, bpy.utils, bgl, blf, mathutils
Convenience Imports:   from mathutils import *; from math import *
Convenience Variables: C = bpy.context, D = bpy.data

>>> print(
print(value, ..., sep=' ', end='\n', file=sys.stdout, flush=False)
Prints the values to a stream, or to sys.stdout by default.
Optional keyword arguments:
file:  a file-like object (stream); defaults to the current sys.stdout.
sep:   string inserted between values, default a space.
end:   string appended after the last value, default a newline.
flush: whether to forcibly flush the stream.
>>> print(
```

Figure 2.4: Autocompletion in the Python console

History

Previous commands executed in Blender's Python console can be retrieved using the up/down arrow keys. This can be tested with any code. Here is an example to run in the Python console:

1. Type `print('Line One')`, then press *Enter*.
2. Press the ↑ key. The current text will change to the following:

    ```
    >>> print("Line One")
    ```

3. Delete the last letters and change the line to `print('Line Two')`, then press *Enter*.
4. Press ↑ twice to display `>>> print('Line One')` again.
5. Alternate between pressing ↓ and ↑ to switch between the two commands.

Multiline input

Snippets consisting of two or more lines can be pasted to the console and executed by pressing *Enter* twice.

Since blank lines mark the end of a snippet, they can make valid code fail when present inside indented blocks. Let's look at a simple example: a condition containing two `print` statements separated by a line:

```
if True:
    print('Line One')

    print('Line Two')
```

This code works in the *Text Editor* but fails in the *Python console*. Here is the output:

```
>>> if True:
...         print('Line One')
...
Line One

>>>         print('Line Two')
  File "<blender_console>", line 1
    print("Line Two")
IndentationError: unexpected indent
```

After the first two lines are executed, the indentation of the second `print()` is considered wrong.

Blank lines should be replaced with comments (#) in every snippet meant for the console. The following code will work:

```
if True:
    print('Line One')
    #
    print('Line Two')
```

Displaying 3D variables in the 3D Viewport

Variables that represent a 3D point or transformation can be displayed in the three-dimensional space. This is made possible by the **Math Vis (Console)** add-on. **Add-ons** are Python extensions that can be enabled at need. We are going to write our own add-ons in this book. For now, we will see how to enable an add-on that ships with Blender.

Enabling the Math Vis (Console) add-on

Add-ons can be enabled in the preferences:

1. From the top-bar menu, select **Edit | Preferences**.
2. Choose the **Add-ons** tab in the left column.

3. Type `Math Vis` in the search filter marked with the magnifier icon.
4. Click the checkbox to the left of the add-on name.

Creating 3D variables

Blender provides additional Python types for 3D entities. For instance, coordinates can be stored using a `Vector` type. We can store a vector in a variable by typing:

```
my_vector = Vector([1.0, 2.0, 3.0])
```

Since we have enabled the *Math Vis (Console)* add-on, a pink dot followed by the variable name will appear in the 3D Viewport.

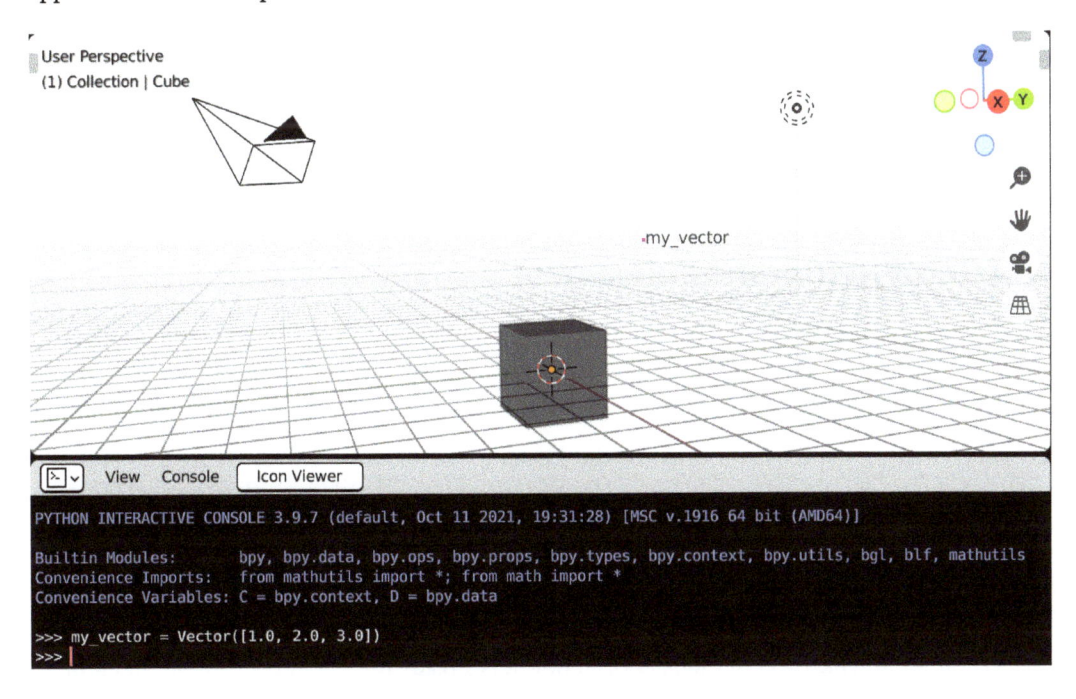

Figure 2.5: Vector coordinates [1.0, 2.0, 3.0], as displayed in the 3D Viewport

Variables are visualized only when the console is visible, as long as they exist. The drawing stops once they are deleted with the following:

```
del my_vector
```

The `del` statement is a standard Python command. We should keep in mind that it deletes Python variables, not Blender objects.

If we want to delete objects in Blender, we can use Blender's `delete()` command:

```
bpy.ops.object.delete()
```

`ops` in the preceding command stands for **operators**. We will learn more about operators in *Chapter 3*. For now, we will keep in mind that they refer to the operation performed by Blender when responding to user inputs. In the case of `bpy.ops.object.delete()`, this means pressing the *X* key or selecting the **Delete** action from the **Object** menu.

Types with a geometrical meaning, such as `Vector`, `Matrix`, and `Euler`, are mathematical constructs and belong to the `mathutils` module. This module is imported into the *console* automatically. There is no need to import it again in the console. If we were to use it in a script, we would have to import it from the module:

```
from mathutils import Vector
my_vector = Vector([1.0, 2.0, 3.0])
```

We are going to explore `mathutils` in the next chapters, when dealing with 3D objects and elements. In the next section, we'll get familiar with how Blender objects translate into Python.

Accessing Blender modules

Blender's additional modules are available throughout the application and can be used via the standard `import` statement. They are available in the Python console, the Text Editor, and generally in the scripts that are installed in the Blender system and user paths.

Some modules are very specific; for instance, the `freestyle` module handles the settings of the freestyle stylized rendering and cannot be used for any other purpose. Others, such as `mathutils`, come into play whenever numbers are concerned.

Finally, the `bpy` module and its submodules play a bigger role in Blender scripts, as they grant access to objects and data.

In this section, we will have a closer look at `bpy`, how it is already present in the console, and how we can use it in our scripts. We will also learn where to find more information about the API and its elements.

The bpy module

In *Chapter 1*, we copied the lines from the console using **Console->Copy** from the Python console editor and pasted them into a text block. In doing so, we found a few extra lines at the beginning:

```
import bpy
from bpy import data as D
from bpy import context as C
```

The first line imports bpy, the main module of the programming interface. Lines two and three import data and context and assign them, respectively, the D and C letters as convenience shortcuts. This is pointed out in the initial screen:

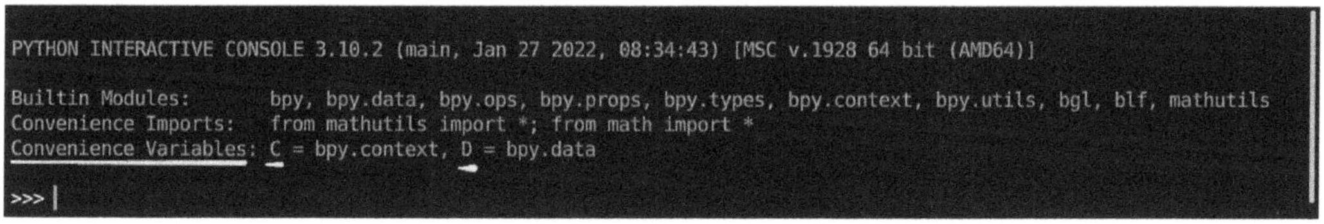

Figure 2.6: Python console's convenience variables

data represents the storage of Blender objects and context is the current state of the user interaction, such as the selection or the current mode (**Object**, **Edit**, **Pose**, etc.).

Because of their nature, context and data are always present in Blender scripts. The autocompletion gives a glimpse of the other modules. If we type bpy. and press *Tab*, we'll get a list of them.

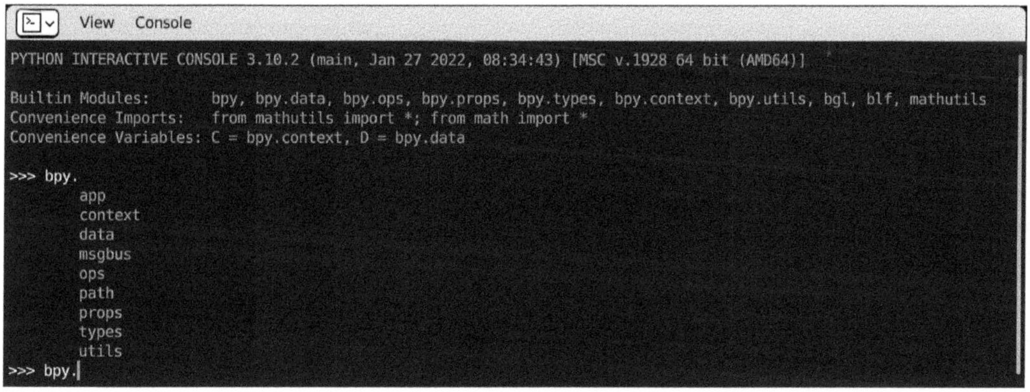

Figure 2.7: bpy's submodules

Each attribute of bpy covers a specific aspect of Blender. For instance, bpy.app contains the properties of the software (executable and version) and bpy.ops contains the operators, that is, functions that can be invoked in the interface.

bpy and the other Blender modules contain a multitude of classes, methods, and utilities. These entities are documented in the *Python API Reference*, which is available online and can be downloaded if needed.

API documentation

The reference website can be reached via **Help | Python API Reference** from the top menu bar.

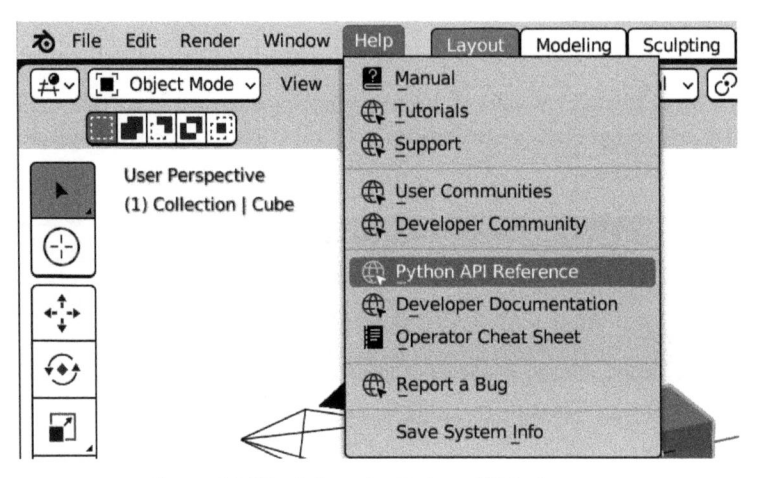

Figure 2.8: The link to the Python API Reference

The *Python Help* for the current version will open in the web browser. The documentation is generated from the docstrings using software called **Sphinx**, and adds examples and hyperlinks to the information displayed by the `help()` function.

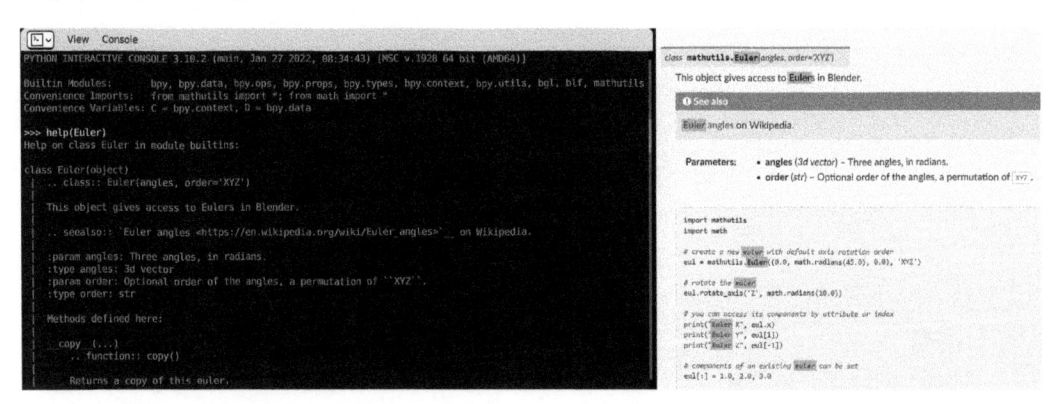

Figure 2.9: Comparison between the help() function and online help for the Euler class

The online help has the advantage of a search bar and doesn't take space from our Blender session. It contains an index of the available modules and their content.

An API reference is very useful to navigate the various modules and the attributes of bpy.

Accessing Blender data   33

In this chapter, we'll focus on `bpy.data` and `bpy.context`, leaving the specific functionalities of the other modules to the next chapters.

Accessing Blender data

All the entities created in the current session are available as part of `bpy.data`. They are grouped in categories that follow the **object types** available in Blender, so we have `bpy.data.armatures`, `bpy.data.curves`, and so on. Each category is a `bpy_collection`, a Blender type that contains more elements. Their content can be accessed with indices, like in a Python `list`, or with keywords, like in dictionaries.

Objects access

We can use Python to access the objects of a scene. For example, we can query the content of Blender's default scene, which contains a **Cube**, a **Camera** and a **Light**:

1. Open or restart Blender and select **Scripting Workspace** in the workspace tabs at the top of the screen.

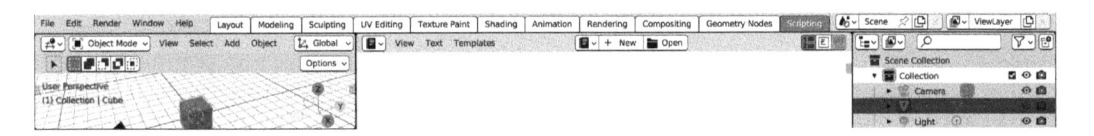

Figure 2.10: The workspace tabs

2. Type `len(bpy.data.objects)` and press *Enter*:

   ```
   >>> len(bpy.data.objects)
   3
   ```

3. In the Python console, type `bpy.data.objects`, then press *Tab*.

Figure 2.11: Blender's default objects

It might be confusing at first, since objects of different types all belong to bpy.data.objects, rather than to bpy.data.cameras, bpy.data.meshes, and bpy.data.lights.

In fact, everything that can be placed and displayed in the 3D Viewport is of the bpy.data.objects type. An **object** is a generic container in which any kind of data, or **datablock**, can be stored. The *object/datablock* system is a tenet of Blender. We are going to get a better grasp of it in the next chapters. For now, we will focus on object-level access.

List-like access

Like Python lists, individual elements of bpy_collection can be accessed by appending an index number surrounded by brackets, as in the following example:

```
>>> bpy.data.objects[0]
bpy.data.objects['Camera']
>>> bpy.data.objects[1]
bpy.data.objects['Cube']
>>> bpy.data.objects[2]
bpy.data.objects['Light']
```

If we know the name of an object we are looking for, we can get it through string keywords rather than indices.

Dict-like access

Besides using their ordinal index, we can access the elements of bpy.data.objects using their names as keywords, as we do with Python dictionaries:

```
>>> bpy.data.objects['Camera']
bpy.data.objects['Camera']
>>> bpy.data.objects['Cube']
bpy.data.objects['Cube']
>>> bpy.data.objects['Light']
bpy.data.objects['Light']
```

Iterating through collections

To execute an expression on all the objects of an aggregate type, we need to *iterate* through the collection. **Iteration** describes the action of scrolling through the elements. By iterating using loop statements, we can carry the same operation on many objects.

List-like looping

The typical `for element in list` loop works with `bpy_collection`. The following snippets print out a list of the existing objects:

```
import bpy
for ob in bpy.data.objects:
    print(ob.name, ob.type)
```

Alternatively, we use the following if we need their collection index as well:

```
import bpy
for i, ob in enumerate(bpy.data.objects):
    print(i, ob.name, ob.type)
```

Looking at the output, we can see that the elements of `bpy.data.objects` are ordered alphabetically:

```
0 Camera CAMERA
1 Cube MESH
2 Light LIGHT
```

That implies that renaming the objects changes the order in which they are listed. It can be an issue if we rename an element while we are still iterating through its collection.

For instance, this snippet adds the letter `'z'` in front of the name of the first object (**Camera**). That changes its position in the *Outliner* from first to last displayed object:

```
import bpy
bpy.data.objects[0].name ='z' + bpy.data.objects[0].name
```

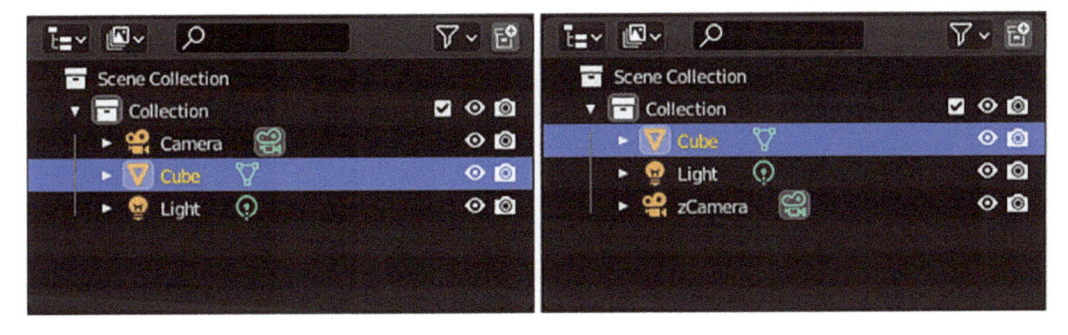

Figure 2.12: Before and after renaming – the order of the objects has changed

We will experience a reordering issue if we execute the same operation inside a loop:

```
import bpy
for ob in bpy.data.objects:
    ob.name ='z' + ob.name
```

It would be reasonable to end up with **zCamera**, **zCube**, and **zLight**. Instead, we end up with very long names where the 'z' is repeated for a long span.

Figure 2.13: Renaming added way too many "z"s

This is a bug in which neither our code nor the application does anything inherently wrong.

To understand why that happens, we need to break it down into individual steps. Blender renames the first, second, and third objects, then it should stop. But since they were renamed, **zCamera** and **zCube** come after **Light**. The query for the next object happens before `"Light"` is renamed and put last, so after that, Blender proceeds to rename `"zCamera"` to `"zzCamera"`, and the process keeps going.

That lasts until the names become too long to be renamed.

Bugs like this can cause software halts and be very hard to find. Whenever our script renames the content of a collection, we must make sure that reordering is not going to be an issue. We are going to look at some possible workarounds.

Avoiding reordering via list conversion

The first and easiest way to avoid re-iteration is to convert `bpy_collection` into a Python list. Press *Ctrl + Z* to undo the renaming.

Now we will use a slightly different line that converts the collection into a pure Python list, via the `list()` method:

```
import bpy
for ob in list(bpy.data.objects):
    ob.name = 'z' + ob.name
```

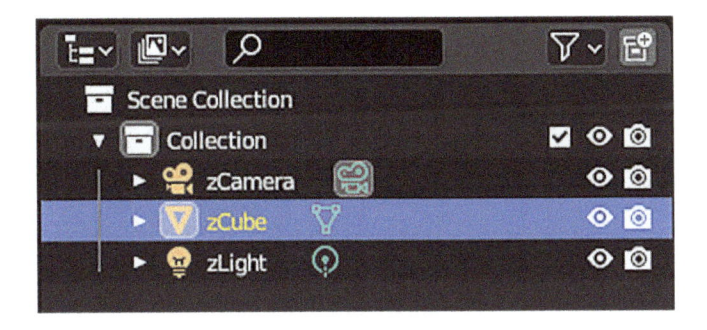

Figure 2.14: The objects have been renamed properly

In the next subsection, we'll see that dictionary methods are also supported. They are, among other things, immune to reordering.

Dict-like looping

Like in Python dictionaries, the `keys()` method returns all the names present in a collection:

```
for name in bpy.data.objects.keys():
    print(name)
```

Alternatively, we can obtain a list of the objects using the `values()` method:

```
for ob in bpy.data.objects.values():
    print(ob.name, ob.type)
```

Lastly, we can iterate both using `items()`:

```
for name, ob in bpy.data.objects.items():
    print(name, ob.type)
```

Creating new objects

Blender classes purposely lack a **constructor**. The only way to create new objects via Python is with the `new()` method of their `bpy_collection`. For instance, 3D objects are created using `bpy.data.objects.new()`.

The new() method

Adding an object to the scene takes one step with the Blender interface. Doing it in Python requires some extra work: the `new()` command stores a new object in the memory, but then we need to add it to our scene explicitly.

Typing bpy.data.objects.new and pressing *Tab* in the Python console displays its documentation:

```
>>> bpy.data.objects.new(
new()
BlendDataObjects.new(name, object_data)
Add a new object to the main database
```

The new function requires two parameters: the name that we want to give to our object and the *datablock* that it's going to contain. If we don't have any *datablocks* yet, we can create an **empty**, an object that has a position in space but no geometry or render data. To do that, we supply the None type to the argument object_data:

```
import bpy
my_empty = bpy.data.objects.new('My Empty', None)
print('New Empty created:', my_empty)
```

The print() line will confirm that the object has been created. It doesn't show up in the 3D Viewport, but we can check that **My Empty** is part of bpy.data.objects.

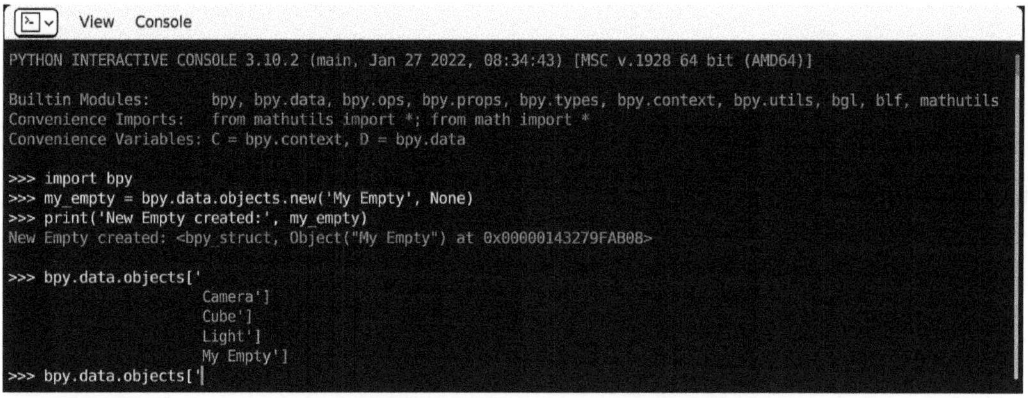

Figure 2.15: The new Empty shows up in the Python collection

This object is not part of a 3D scene yet. In order to be part of a scene, objects must belong to a **collection**.

Object collections

The term *collection* carries some ambiguity, as we have referred to `bpy_collection` as part of data access. **Scene collections** and the `bpy_collection` types, such as `bpy.data.objects`, are two distinct concepts:

- **Scene collections** are groups of objects displayed as folders in the **Outliner**. They are used to organize 3D objects in the scene.
- **bpy_collection** is a Python type. It lists objects and datablocks. Objects might exist in `bpy_collection` without being part of any scene.

All the scene collections can be accessed in Python using `bpy.data.collections`.

We are one step away from adding our object to the scene: we need to add `my_empty` to a scene collection, using the collection method `link`.

Linking to the scene

There is only one collection in the default scene, so if we type `bpy.data.collections` and press *Tab*, we get it from the autocompletion:

```
>>> bpy.data.collections['Collection']
```

The default collection is named **Collection**. Its objects can be accessed via the `Collection.objects` attribute. The Python line for linking `my_empty` is:

```
bpy.data.collections['Collection'].objects.link(my_empty)
```

My Empty is now part of the scene and shows up in the outliner.

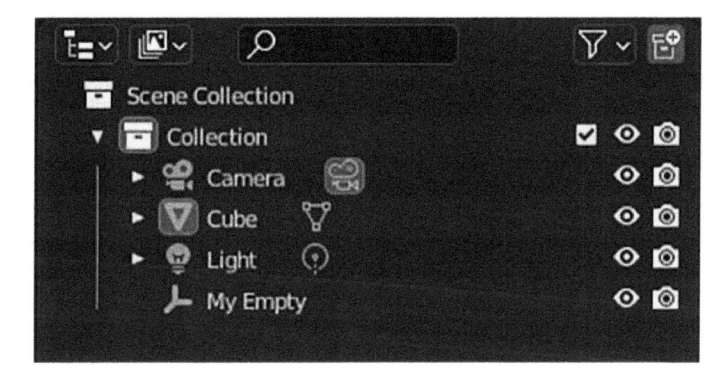

Figure 2.16: Our Empty sitting along with the other objects

Removing elements

Just like we can create new elements with `new()`, we can use the method `remove()` from `bpy.data.objects` to remove them. This line removes `my_empty` from blender:

```
bpy.data.objects.remove(my_empty)
```

Collections that link existing objects via `link()`, such as `Collection.objects`, have an `unlink()` method for removal:

```
collection = bpy.data.collections['Collection']
collection.objects.unlink(bpy.data.objects['Cube'])
```

In that case, **Cube** is not anymore in the scene, but is still in `bpy.data.objects`.

In this section, we have accessed the Blender objects via Python using `bpy.data`.

How would we fetch the current scene if there is more than just one, or the current object and active selection?

We will see how states of user interaction can be tracked in the `bpy.context` module.

Understanding the user context

The current state of interaction, the current scene, and the selection are available via `bpy.context`. Since it depends on the user actions, `bpy.context` is read-only; that is, it cannot be changed directly. Anyway, we can affect the state of the current activity via *Python*. Rather than changing the attributes of `bpy.context`, we must look for the selection and activity properties of Blender's objects, layers, and scenes.

Active scene

A `.blend` file, or an unsaved session for that matter, can contain more than one **scene**. That differs from the standard in 3D packages, where a saved file is equivalent to one scene. If more scenes are available, they can be selected from the list menu at the top right of Blender's header.

Each scene can contain any of the objects from `bpy.data.objects`, and one object can belong to more than one scene. Changes made to an object in one scene retained in the others.

We have seen how to create new objects using `bpy.data.objects.new()`. We can create new scenes in the same way, using `bpy.data.scenes.new()`:

```
import bpy
new_scene = bpy.data.scenes.new('My Scene')
print('New scene created:', new_scene.name)
```

The new scene will then be available in the top-right widget.

Figure 2.17: Blender scene menu

The currently displayed scene is contained in bpy.context.window.

If we want to create a new scene and make it active, we can assign it to the window.scene property:

```
import bpy
new_scene = bpy.data.scenes.new('Another Scene')
bpy.context.window.scene = new_scene
```

After executing this snippet, the 3D Viewport will switch to a new, empty scene. The current scene itself is part of bpy.context and can be retrieved via Python using bpy.context.scene:

```
print('The current scene is', bpy.context.scene.name)
```

View Layers

View Layers are used to render the objects of a scene separately and put them back together using **compositing**. This is done either to speed up the rendering process, for instance, rendering the background only once, or for artistic necessities. In the UI, View Layers are created in the same way as scenes, using the widget on the top bar.

When creating them in Python, we must keep in mind that they always belong to their scene rather than to bpy.data. Despite that, if we want to set the active layer, we still have to use an attribute of bpy.context.window:

```
import bpy
new_layer = bpy.context.scene.view_layers.new('My Layer')
print('New layer created:', new_layer.name)
```

```
bpy.context.window.view_layer = new_layer
print('Current layer:', bpy.context.view_layer.name)
```

The active layer must belong to the active scene. A statement that tries to assign a layer from a different scene to the current window will be ignored. Take the following example:

```
import bpy
new_layer = bpy.context.scene.view_layers.new('Another Layer')
print('New layer created:', new_layer.name)
new_scene = bpy.data.scenes.new('Another Scene')
bpy.context.window.scene = new_scene
# NOTE: the following line will not work
bpy.context.window.view_layer = new_layer
print('Current layer:', bpy.context.view_layer.name)
```

Layers can store rendering and pass properties, but also their visibility, activity, and selection status. In the next section, we'll see how a layer stores the **active object**.

Active object

When the user selects an object, that becomes the **active object** of the current layer. Its properties are displayed in the interface, and it will be the main target of the user actions.

When Blender opens, a cube is the active object by default. We can see that from the **Text Info** in the top-left corner.

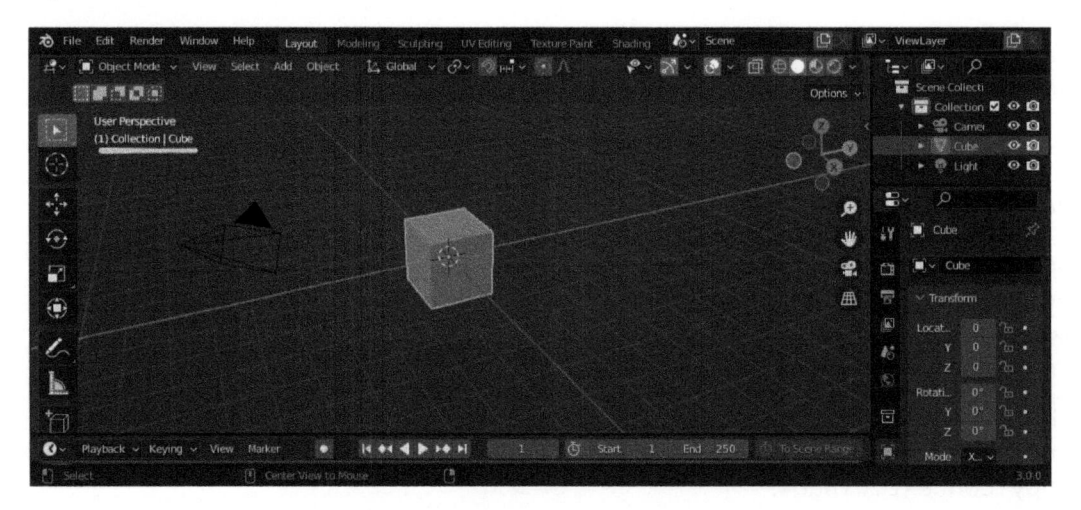

Figure 2.18: Blender's default active object

The active object can be retrieved in multiple places in the API, the most immediate being `bpy.context.object`:

```
bpy.context.object            # read only
bpy.context.active_object     # read only, same as above
bpy.context.view_layer.objects.active   # can be set
```

All three attributes point to the same object, but since `bpy.context` is read-only, only the `view_layer` attribute can be changed programmatically. If more layers are present, switching between layers can change the active object. Or we can change it using Python by following the next steps.

Changing the active object

The active object is a property of the active View Layer. With that in mind, we can just set the `view_layer.active` attribute to a different object. For instance, here is how to pick the camera instead:

1. Open Blender or revert to the default scene via **File**->**New**->**General**.
2. Go to the Scripting Workspace.
3. Type the following lines in the Python console and press *Enter*:

```
import bpy
view_layer = bpy.context.view_layer
view_layer.objects.active = bpy.data.objects['Camera']
```

We can see that the active object has changed from the 3D Viewport, the properties, and the status information.

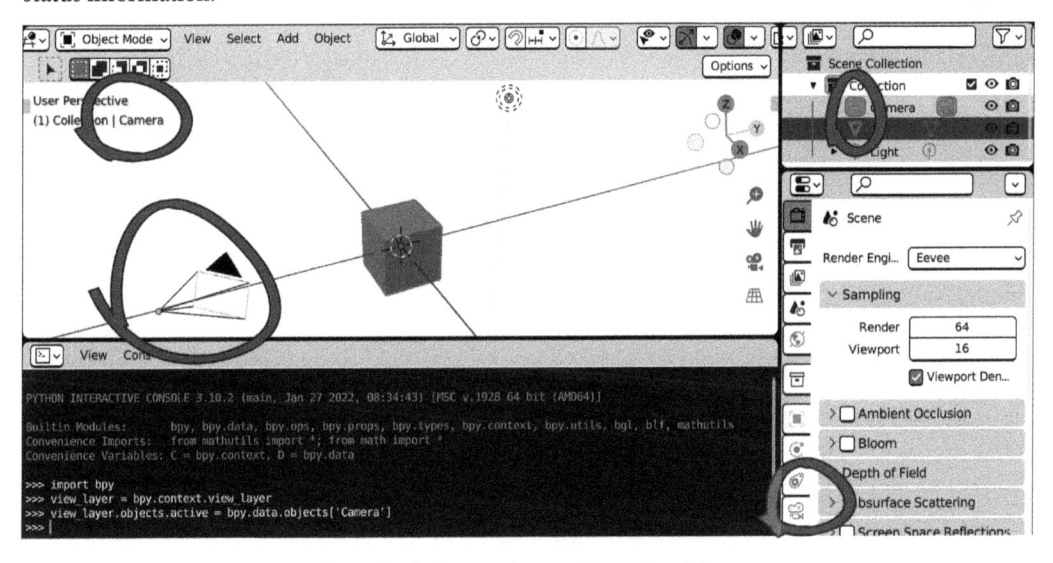

Figure 2.19: Camera is now the active object

We can also see that the cube is still selected, and that the camera, despite being the active object, isn't. That's because the active and selected statuses are two distinct concepts. We are going to see, in the next section, how they differ, and how we can query and change the current selection.

> **Keep your focus**
>
> The Blender focus policy can be confusing at first. The area under the mouse cursor takes the keyboard inputs.
>
> That's less of a problem for artists since their tasks usually involve keeping the cursor in the area in which they are operating. But it's different for programmers; we might think of typing lines of code for the console only to find out that we are triggering shortcuts in the 3D Viewport, or the other way around.

Selected objects

Let's select all the objects in the scene by pressing the *A* key in the 3D Viewport (**Select | All** from the menu bar). Then, in the console, we type the following:

```
>>> bpy.context.selected_objects
[bpy.data.objects['Cube'], bpy.data.objects['Light'], bpy.data.
objects['Camera']]
```

`selected_objects` is a Python list. Unlike `bpy.data.objects`, it sorts the objects by their creation time and not alphabetically. Objects are *never* sorted by their selection time; Blender doesn't keep that information at all. Should our tool require selecting objects in a specific sequence, we would have to store the order somewhere else.

Selecting an object usually makes it the active object of the current layer. We can print out which object is active using comparisons against `bpy.context.object`:

```
import bpy
for ob in bpy.context.selected_objects:
    if ob is bpy.context.object:
        print(ob.name, 'is active, skipping')
        continue
    print(ob.name, 'is selected')
```

Running this snippet with all default objects selected will produce this output:

```
Cube is active, skipping
Light is selected
Camera is selected
```

This pattern is useful whenever we want to propagate a property from the active object to the selection. We have already seen that we should not assume that the active object is always selected. Inverting the selection unselects the active object, but it will remain active. Or there might be no active object at all; it can be deleted or set to None via the following line:

```
bpy.context.view_layer.objects.active = None
```

A way to check whether the active object belongs to the selection is with the `in` operator:

```
is_sel = bpy.context.object in bpy.context.selected_objects
```

Even better, we can use the `select_get()` and `select_set()` object properties:

```
is_sel = bpy.context.object.select_get()
```

Like the active object, the selection status of an object is stored per View Layer. In the next section, we'll learn how to affect the current selection and where it is stored.

Changing selected objects

The selection status of an object is queried and set using `object.select_get()` and `object.select_set()` as, respectively, the **getter** and **setter** of the property. These functions accept a View Layer as an optional argument, allowing us to set selections for a specific layer. To get a glimpse of how the `select_set` function works, we can start to type it in the Python console, stopping at the parenthesis:

```
>>> bpy.context.object.select_set(
```

Pressing the *Tab* key will display a description of the function and its arguments:

```
select_set()
Object.select_set(state, view_layer=None)
Select or deselect the object. The selection state is per view layer
```

If no View Layer is given, the selection of the current layer is used. For instance, this snippet will deselect all the objects in the current layer:

```
import bpy
for ob in bpy.context.selected_objects:
    ob.select_set(False)
```

We can create layers dynamically and assign them a different selection. Here is a snippet that creates a View Layer where mesh objects are selected, and another where cameras are:

```
import bpy
m_layer = bpy.context.scene.view_layers.new('Sel_Mesh')
c_layer = bpy.context.scene.view_layers.new('Sel_Cam')

for ob in bpy.data.objects:
```

```
        ob.select_set(ob.type == 'MESH', view_layer=m_layer)
        ob.select_set(ob.type == 'CAMERA', view_layer=c_layer)
```

Selecting is the most immediate way for the user to pick objects from the scene. For this reason, `bpy.context` holds a pivotal role and is usually available in scripts, or even passed as a Python object.

Summary

In this chapter, we saw how Python can access the content of Blender via `bpy.data` and introduced space entities such as vectors. We also saw how to interact with the user activity through `bpy.context`, and how read-only attributes of context are changed by affecting the status of objects and layers.

In *Chapter 3*, we will see how to insert our routines in our own add-ons and make them ready to install and use in Blender.

Questions

1. Which helper utilities are typical of Blender?
2. How can we store and display space coordinates?
3. Which attribute of bpy gives access to all Blender entities?
4. Do Python classes of Blender objects have a constructor?
5. How do we create new Blender objects?
6. What does it mean that an object is active?
7. Is the active object a property of the Blender scene?
8. Can we affect the selection using `bpy.context`?
9. Can we affect the selection using `bpy.context.view_layer`?

3
Creating Your Add-Ons

Add-ons are extensions that expand the capabilities of Blender and can be enabled in the preferences. Some of them, such as Math Vis, encountered in *Chapter 2*, are official features distributed as optional functionalities. Others are third-party expansions that can be installed by a user.

At their core, add-ons are Python modules that contain information used by Blender to install, enable, and remove them like in a plugin system.

In this chapter, you will learn how to write and install an add-on in Blender, and how to enable add-ons while they are still in the making. We will also implement a new command that groups objects into collections and make it part of the object context menu.

This chapter will cover the following topics:

- Scripting Blender extensions
- Running and updating our add-on
- Fixing errors and improving our code

Technical requirements

We will use Blender and **Visual Studio Code** (**VS Code**). The examples created in this chapter can be found at `https://github.com/PacktPublishing/Python-Scripting-in-Blender/tree/main/ch3`.

Installing our add-ons in Blender

We can write a very simple add-on using VS Code. This add-on doesn't really do anything; it just shows up in the extensions list.

First, we must create a folder for the code of this chapter. We can use the file manager or the navigation sidebar that comes with most IDEs. In this example, we will use VS Code, which we met in the *External editors* section of *Chapter 1*:

1. Open your **PythonScriptingBlender** project in VS Code.
2. Create a new folder by clicking the **New Folder** icon.

Figure 3.1: Creating a folder in Visual Studio Code

3. Name the new folder `ch3`.

Now, we can create a Python file for our add-on:

1. Make sure the `ch3` folder is selected in the **VS Code** explorer, and then create a new file by clicking the **New File** icon.

Figure 3.2: Creating a file in VS Code

2. Name the new file `the_simplest_add_on.py`.
3. Open the file via a double click.

We are ready to write our add-on; let's look at what is required.

Add-on requirements

To be considered an add-on, our code must contain three things:

- **Script meta info** – that is, information about the add-on
- A `register()` function to enable the add-on
- An `unregister()` function to disable the add-on

Script meta info

The information displayed in the preferences tab comes from the `bl_info` variable, a dictionary located at the top of the `.py` file. The dictionary must contain the name of the author, a short description of the add-on, and the version of Blender for which it is written. Here is the info for our simple add-on:

```
bl_info = {
    "name": "The Simplest Add-on",
    "author": "John Doe",
    "version": (1, 0),
    "blender": (3, 00, 0),
    "description": "A very simple add-on",
    "warning": "This is just for Learning",
    "category": "Learning",
}
```

> **Start with a blank!**
>
> It is better to leave a blank line at the start and the end of our code – `.py` files that do not start with a blank line might fail to register as add-ons and cause a `missing bl_info` error.

Registration

The `register()` function is executed when an add-on is enabled. There is not much going on for now – only a `pass` statement, as our function doesn't do anything:

```
def register():
    # this function is called when the add-on is enabled
    pass
```

The `unregister()` function is invoked when the add-on is disabled. Much like `register()`, it doesn't do anything yet, but it is required as an add-on:

```
def unregister():
    # this function is called when the add-on is disabled
    pass
```

Installation

Now, it's time to install our add-on in Blender:

1. Open the preferences window via **Edit | Preferences** from the top menu.
2. Select the **Add-ons** tab in the left column.
3. Click the **Install** button at the top right of the add-ons preferences.
4. In the file browser, navigate to `PythonScriptingBlender\ch3` and select `the_simplest_add_on.py`.
5. Click the **Install Add-on** button at the bottom

Our add-on has been copied and installed in Blender; the filter entry on the top left is filled so that only the new add-on is displayed. We can click the add-on checkbox to enable it. Expanding the disclosure triangle displays more information from `bl_info`.

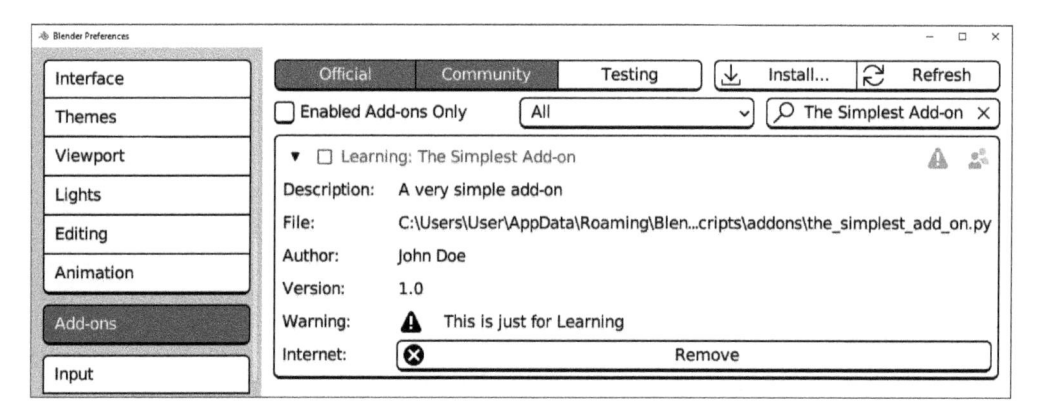

Figure 3.3: A very simple add-on as listed in Blender

The `warning` entry from our dictionary is displayed with a triangle icon. That line is to warn the users of potentially unstable code.

Now that our add-on has served its purpose, it's time to remove it.

Uninstall

Clicking the big **Remove** button in the add-on preferences will display a confirmation dialog that asks whether it is fine to delete the add-on. This operation cannot be undone, but in this case, it is fine to go along and remove **The Simplest Add-on**:

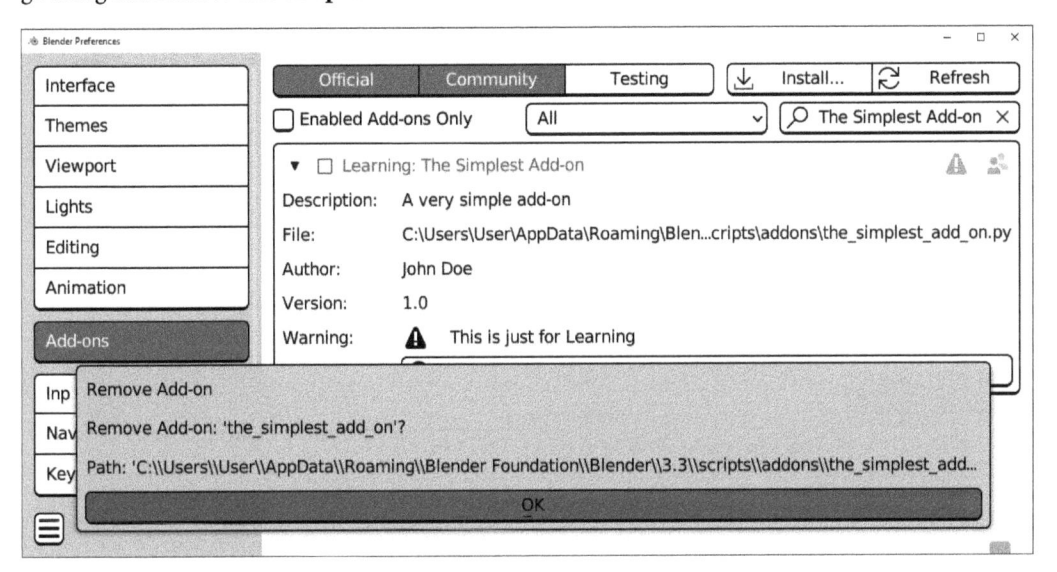

Figure 3.4: Add-on removal in Blender

The path displayed in the **Remove** dialog informs that the add-on was installed inside Blender user preferences. That's not always the case, as we will see how to point the scripts path to our working directory in the next paragraph.

The scripts path

Reinstalling an add-on at every change during development would end up being impractical. Programmers usually set up a **system path** for Python scripts and work on their add-ons from there.

System paths can be found in **Blender Preferences**, by choosing the **File Paths** tab in the left column.

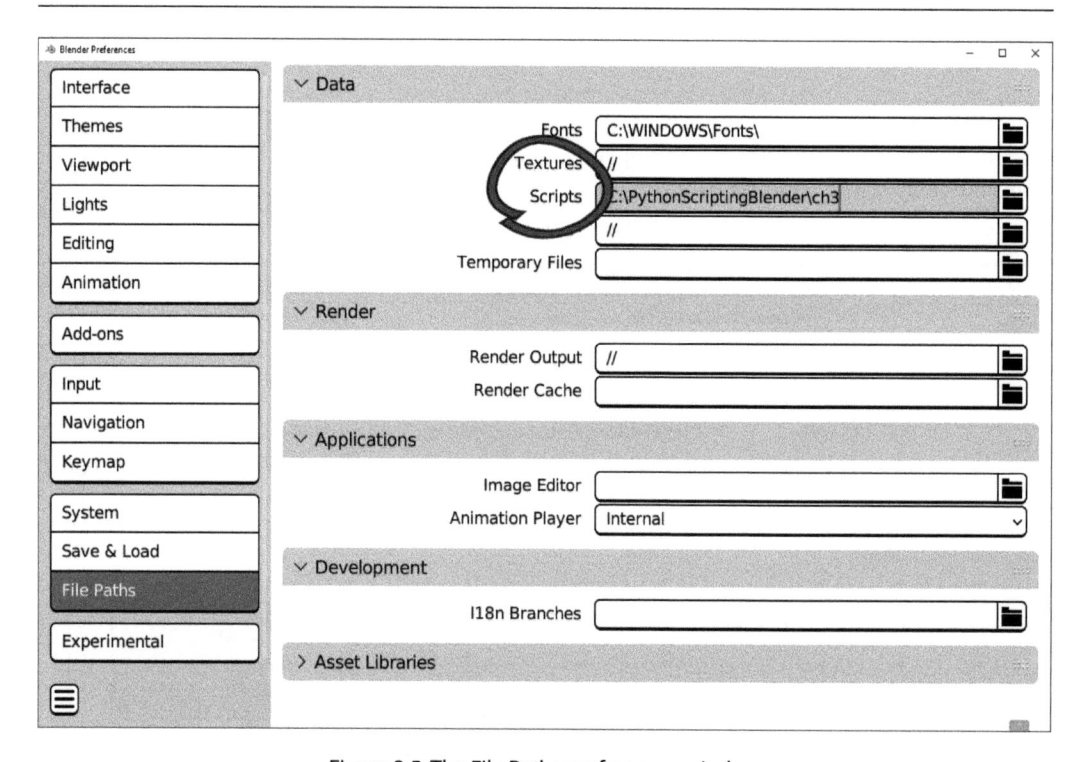

Figure 3.5: The File Paths preferences window

We can set this path to the directory that we will use for scripting, such as the `PythonScriptingBlender/ch3` folder that hosts the code of this chapter.

The addons folder

Now that blender will look in our scripting folder, we can create a directory for our add-ons. We can do that from VS Code:

1. Select `PythonScriptingBlender/ch3` in VS Code.
2. Create a new folder by clicking the **New Folder** icon.
3. Name the new folder `addons`.

It is important that `addons` is the exact name of this folder; otherwise, Blender will not look for extensions. We need to restart Blender for the **File Paths** settings to take effect, but once we do, Blender will be able to load the add-ons on which we are working, with no installation needed.

Now, we can work on a new add-on that adds functionality to Blender. In the next section, we will write an add-on that groups the objects of a scene into collections.

Creating our first add-on – object collector

We are going to write an add-on that groups the objects of a scene in collections that reflect their type – one collection for all the meshes, one for all the lights, one for the curves, and so on.

Since we have set up `PythonScriptingBlender/ch3` as the directory for our add-ons, we will proceed in VS Code:

1. Select `PythonScriptingBlender/ch3/addons` in VS Code.
2. Create a new file by clicking the **New File** icon.
3. Name the new file `object_collector.py`.
4. Open the file via a double click.

This Python script's name starts with `object`, since it affects object data. It is a *soft convention*, as this filename scheme is suggested but not enforced.

At this stage, the add-on is very similar to the previous one – we haven't added any code yet. Note how, besides the obvious difference in names and descriptions, we haven't put a `warning` entry – we intend to make a non-experimental add-on:

object_collector.py

```python
bl_info = {
    "name": "Collector",
    "author": "John Doe",
    "version": (1, 0),
    "blender": (3, 00, 0),
    "description": "Create collections for object types",
    "category": "Object",
}

def register():
    # this function is called when the add-on is enabled
    pass

def unregister():
    # this function is called when the add-on is disabled
    pass
```

> **Remove carefully!**
> It is better to not remove add-ons loaded from the script path using the **Remove** button – we risk erasing our working (and perhaps only) copy!

Blender will show up this add-on in the preferences panel. In order to add functionalities, our add-on must contain an **operator**. Operators are the entities that carry on the execution of code; we will now learn how to write them.

Operators

The `Operator` class allows calling functions from the graphic interface. They are, essentially, commands that can be run in Blender.

Therefore, we subclass the `bpy.types.Operator` class to make our code available to users.

Operator requirements

A class deriving `bpy.types.Operators` must implement these members:

- A static string named `bl_idname` that contains a unique name by which the operator goes internally
- A static string named `bl_label` that contains the displayed name of the operator
- A `poll()` class method that verifies that the conditions for executing the operator are met and return either `True` or `False`
- An `execute()` method that runs when the operator is executed, returning a set of possible running states
- Optionally, a docstring that Blender will display as additional information

We are going to fill in this information so that our add-on will contain an operator that can be executed.

Writing a basic operator

Let's start to create our operator class. Following the Blender guidelines, the name starts with OBJECT_OT. Soon after the (optional) docstring comes `bl_idname` and `bl_label`, the two attributes that Blender uses respectively as an identifier and description of the operator:

```
class OBJECT_OT_collector_types(bpy.types.Operator):
    """Create collections based on objects types"""
    bl_idname = "object.pckt_type_collector"
    bl_label = "Create Type Collections"
    @classmethod
    def poll(cls, context):
```

```
        return False
    def execute(self, context):
        # our code goes here
        return {'FINISHED'}
```

The `poll()` and `execute()` methods, at this stage, neither allow nor perform any action. We are going to implement them in the following pages, using what we have learned in *Chapter 2*, when dealing with Blender data.

Implementing the poll() method

`poll()` verifies that the conditions for running the operator are met. That restricts the possibility of error and makes the intended use of the operator more evident. This method is marked with a `@classmethod` decorator that allows us to validate the conditions before the operator is run.

Since our operator collects objects in the scene, we should not be able to use it if the scene is empty:

```
    @classmethod
    def poll(cls, context):
        return len(context.scene.objects) > 0
```

Implementing the execute() method

After an operator is invoked, Blender runs its `execute()` method. This `execute()` function contains our operations. Breaking them down into single steps will help to code them in Python.

Planning our execution

We must know what to expect when we execute our operator. For instance, running it on the default scene, we would end up with three new collections – **Mesh** for the **Cube** object, **Camera** for the **Camera** object, and **Light** for the **Light** object.

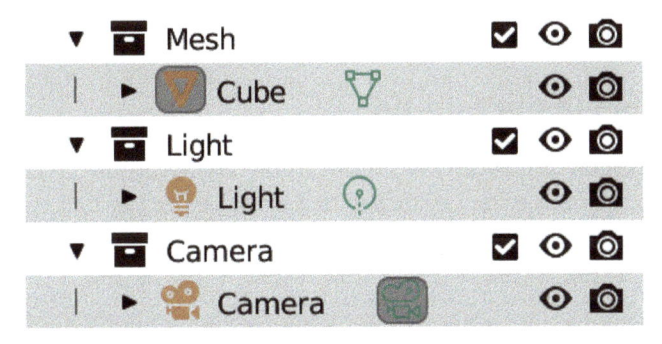

Figure 3.6: The expected result after running Collector

There is more than one way to reach this result, but to accomplish it by hand, we will need to create the **Mesh**, **Light**, and **Camera** collections and bring each object under each one of them.

Now, we will translate these actions into Python.

Writing the execution code

We have seen in *Chapter 2* how new collections can be created and linked to `scene.collection.children`:

```python
def execute(self, context):
    mesh_cl = bpy.data.collections.new("Mesh")
    light_cl = bpy.data.collections.new("Light")
    cam_cl = bpy.data.collections.new("Camera")
    context.scene.collection.children.link(mesh_cl)
    context.scene.collection.children.link(light_cl)
    context.scene.collection.children.link(cam_cl)
```

Then, we can process the objects using a `for` loop:

```python
for ob in context.scene.objects:
    if ob.type == 'MESH':
        mesh_cl.objects.link(ob)
    elif ob.type == 'LIGHT':
        light_cl.objects.link(ob)
    elif ob.type == 'CAMERA':
        cam_cl.objects.link(ob)
```

Finally, we always return an operation state when we exit the function:

```python
return {'FINISHED'}
```

This operator is still in progress and needs refining, but we can already use it. To do that, we must inform Blender of its existence using the `register_class()` function from `bpy.utils`.

Loading operators in our add-on

Our add-on adds an operator to Blender when enabled and removes it when it is disabled. This is done via the `bpy.utils.register_class()` and `bpy.utils.unregister_class()` functions that we call, respectively, inside the add-on's `register()` and `unregister()` functions:

```python
def register():
    bpy.utils.register_class(OBJECT_OT_collector_types)

def unregister():
    bpy.utils.unregister_class(OBJECT_OT_collector_types)
```

Enabling the **Collector** add-on will add **Create Type Collections** to Blender and allow you to call it from the user interface.

Running our add-on

Even if we have yet to add any graphic element, our add-on is ready for its first launch. We can use two tricks in order to run add-ons that are not yet listed, which is quite common in development.

Refreshing the add-on list

Since we have added a new script folder and just changed its content, we need to either restart Blender or refresh the add-on information. To do that, we can click the **Refresh** button at the top right in the **Add-ons** preferences window.

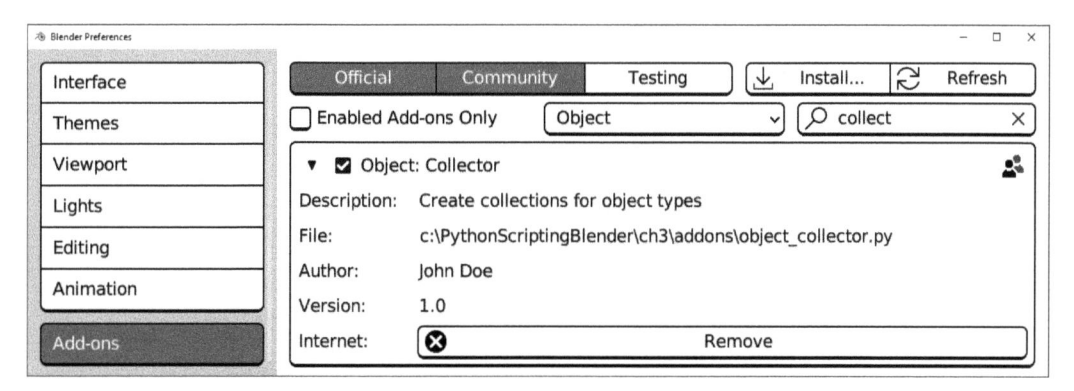

Figure 3.7: The Collector add-on, loaded from the project folder

If we start typing the name of our add-on in the filter bar, the entries in the list will narrow down until **Collector** becomes easy to find and enable. Now, it's time to execute our operator via the **Blender Source Bar**.

Running from the Search Toolbar

Operators that are not part of any graphic element are for internal usage – that is, callable by other operators but not by the user.

To make every operator searchable, make sure that **Developers Extra** is enabled in the **Preferences | Interface** tab, as we did in *Chapter 2*. If this option is active, here is how we can call our operator:

1. Press the *F3* button.
2. Start typing `create type`, and the operator will show up in the search box.

58   Creating Your Add-Ons

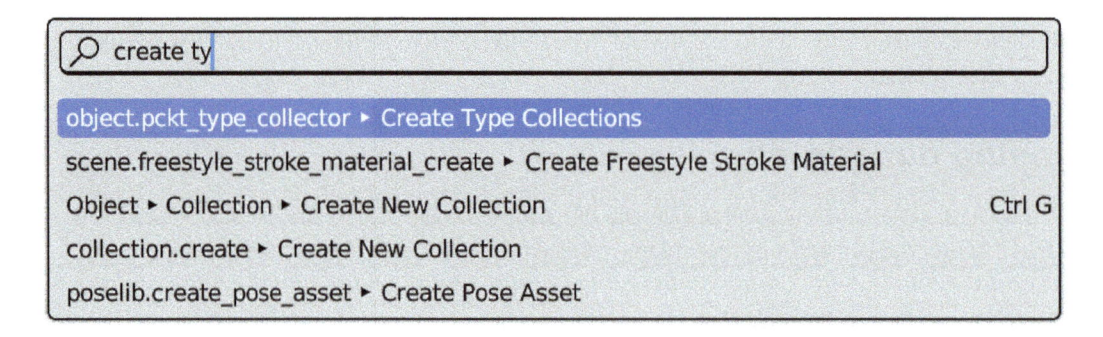

Figure 3.8: The Create Type Collections operator, showing up in the search bar

3. Click on the operator to execute it.

   We can see in the outliner that our operator succeeded.

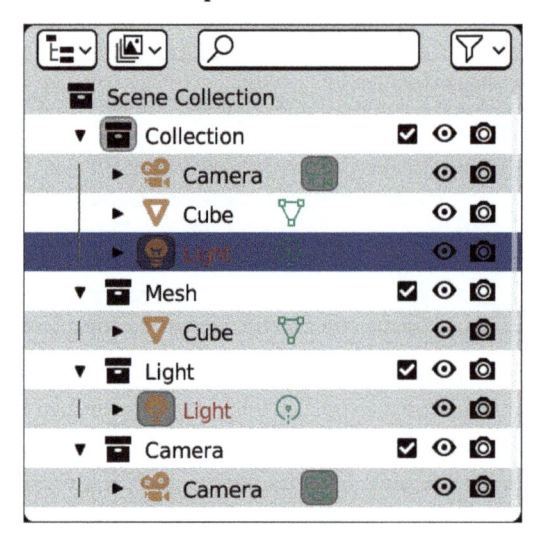

figure 3.9: Each object is grouped under its type collection

Our add-on is at an early stage; it has a few bugs and limitations that we are going to fix. For instance, the **Mesh**, **Light**, and **Camera** collections are created without checking whether they already exist, which will create duplicates. Also, we are only handling these three categories, skipping **Curves**, **Armatures**, and all the other object types entirely.

Nevertheless, if we are using version control for our folder, as seen in *Chapter 1*, we can commit our new files. We are going to improve our add-on in the next section.

Improving our code

Fixing bugs or starting with a row prototype that will be completed at a later stage is common practice in development. In this section, we will complete our add-on to its finished form, reload it in Blender, and deal with the versioning of the scripts path.

Saving our edits automatically

The **Auto Save** option will make VS Code save every file change to disk automatically. To activate this option, follow these steps:

1. Open the **File** menu in the **Visual Studio Code** menu bar.
2. Click on **Auto Save** to enable this entry.

There are developers that prefer to save manually to have more control of their files. Which solution is better depends on personal tastes and workflows. Generally, if version control is used, the advantage of **Auto Save** outweighs the danger of unwanted changes.

In some cases, we want to turn off version control on specific files. For instance, there are files that Python generates when it executes code; we have no interest in tracking them. In the following paragraph, we are going to see how to ignore specific files.

Ignoring bytecode files (.pyc)

If we execute code from our development folder, the **SOURCE CONTROL** tab in VS Code will display a `.pyc` file, along with our `.py` files.

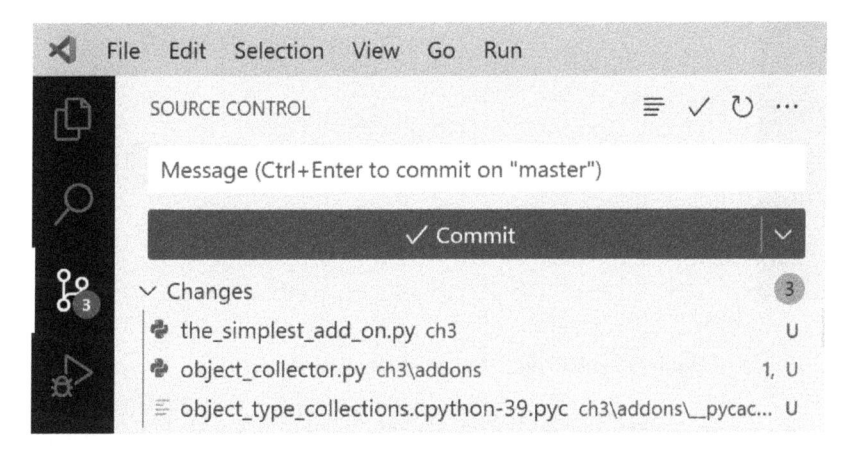

Figure 3.10: A temporary .pyc file can be seen alongside our scripts

When a `.py` file is executed, Python translates it to an internal format and saves it as `.pyc`. We don't need to concern ourselves with `.pyc` files, and usually, we don't need to keep track of them.

Creating a .gitignore file

A text file named `.gitignore`, containing the names of files and directories that we don't want to track, will have an immediate effect when placed in a version control-managed folder. We can create it manually or follow these steps inside VS Code:

1. In the **SOURCE CONTROL** tab, right-click on the `.pyc` file listed under **Changes**.
2. From the context menu, select **Add to .gitignore**.

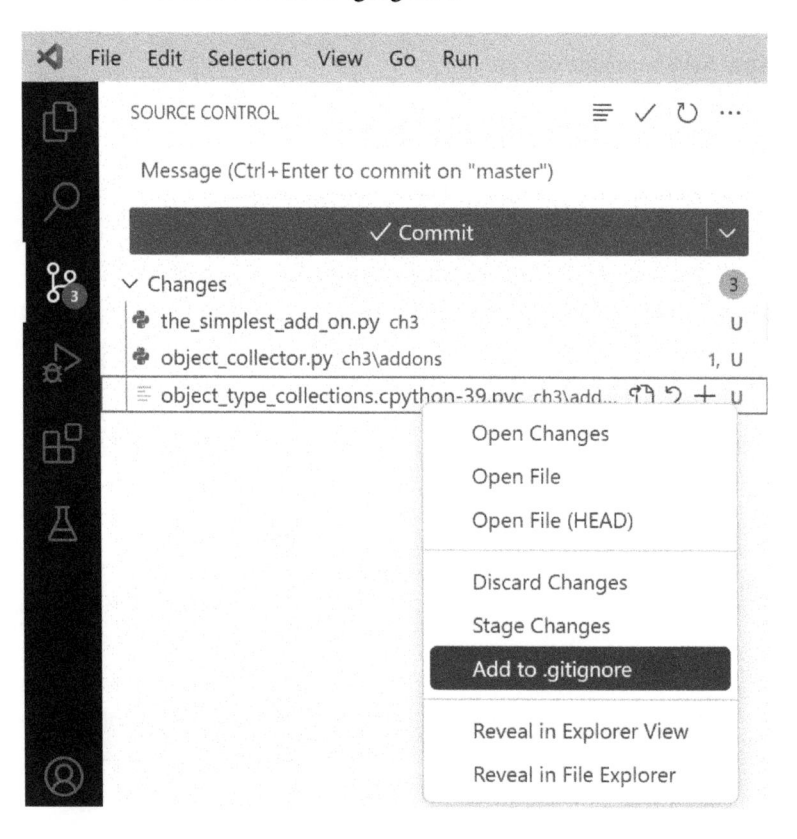

Figure 3.11: Adding to the git ignore list in VS Code

3. Once the `.gitignore` file is created, the `.pyc` file stops showing up in the changes.
4. If we open the `.gitignore` file, we will see that it contains the full path of the `.pyc` file:

```
ch3/addons/__pycache__/object_collector.cpython-39.pyc
```

5. We don't need to ignore that specific file; we can blacklist all the directories called __pycache__. To do that, we take the following code:

   ```
   ch3/addons/__pycache__/object_collector.cpython-39.pyc
   ```

   And change it to this, then save:

   ```
   __pycache__
   ```

Source control applies to the `.gitignore` file itself; we have to stage and commit this file, along with the other changes made in this chapter.

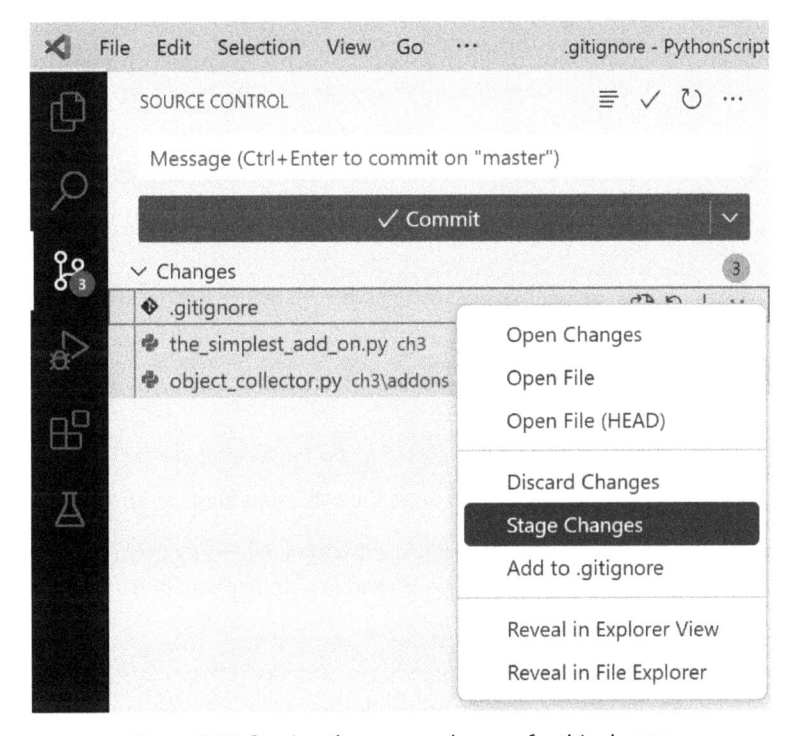

Figure 3.12: Staging the current changes for this chapter

Once we have committed our changes, we can go back to working on our script, fixing its flows, and expanding its capabilities. We will see how simplifying the logic of a script improves readability, behavior, and functionality at the same time.

Fixing the operator logic

The most evident flow in our operator is that it tries to recreate existing collections. Running it twice in a row creates the **Mesh.001** and **Light.001** collections, and so on.

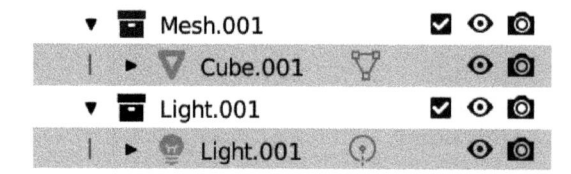

Figure 3.13: Unwanted collections are created

Avoiding duplicate collections

We should create the mesh collection only if it doesn't exist already. Note the following:

```
mesh_cl = bpy.data.collections.new("Mesh")
```

Instead of that, we should create a new one, only if looking it up causes a `KeyError` error:

```
try:
    mesh_cl = bpy.data.collections.new['Mesh']
except KeyError:
    mesh_cl = bpy.data.collections.new("Mesh")
```

To be more generic, we can write a function that takes the collection name as an argument.

The function presented in the following code block starts with a very descriptive docstring that can help to give a better idea of what a function should do and how to implement it:

```
def get_collection(name):
    '''Returns the collection named after the given
    argument. If it doesn't exist, a new collection
    is created and linked to the scene'''
    try:
        return bpy.data.collections[name]
    except KeyError:
        cl = bpy.data.collections.new(name)
        bpy.context.scene.collection.children.link(cl)
        return cl
```

Querying object types

We could create unique collections using the preceding function – for instance, `get_collection("Mesh")` – but we don't need to mention the object type explicitly; the `Object.type` parameter returns the type as a string:

```
>>> bpy.data.objects['Cube'].type
'MESH'
```

Strings can also be formatted nicely via their `.title()` method:

```
>>> bpy.data.objects['Cube'].type.title()
'Mesh'
```

Here is our operator execution block after the rewrite:

```python
@staticmethod
def get_collection(name):
    '''Returns the collection named after the given
    argument. If it doesn't exist, a new collection
    is created and linked to the scene'''
    try:
        return bpy.data.collections[name]
    except KeyError:
        cl = bpy.data.collections.new(name)
        bpy.context.scene.collection.children.link(cl)
        return cl

def execute(self, context):
    for ob in context.scene.objects:
        cl = self.get_collection(ob.type.title())
        cl.objects.link(ob)

    return {'FINISHED'}
```

This version is more elegant and supports objects of any type. There is still a bug that we will fix shortly. Before we come to that, we need to reload the script to use this new version.

Reloading scripts

Blender and Python store used scripts in memory; therefore, changes made to the code will not have an immediate effect. There is a Blender command that reloads the scripts, which we can look up in the search bar:

1. Press the *F3* key to go to the search bar.
2. Start typing `reload scr` in the search field.
3. Click the operator, **script.reload ▸ Reload Scripts**.

Figure 3.14: Invoking the Reload Scripts operator

This command reloads all the scripts and spares us from having to restart Blender every time. Our add-ons now use the latest `.py` files on disk, and we can verify that our collections are created only once.

Avoiding re-assignment errors

While executing **Create Type Collections** twice doesn't create duplicates anymore, when it tries to assign objects to collections they already belong to, it causes a `RuntimeError` error. We'll see this error pop up if we run our operator a second time:

```
    cl.objects.link(ob)
RuntimeError: Object 'Cube' already in collection 'Mesh'
```

We need to enclose object linking in a `try`/`catch` statement to avoid that:

```
            cl.objects.link(ob)
```

This should be replaced with the following:

```
            try:
                cl.objects.link(ob)
            except RuntimeError:
                continue
```

This way, no action is taken for objects that were already collected and the operator moves on to the rest of the scene.

> **Don't try too hard!**
> We should always make sure that the actions contained inside a `try` block are minimal – these statements should not be used lightly. There is no obvious rule, but if we are trying more than two lines in a block, we should probably rethink our code so that it is less error-prone.

Our final operator

We can add more objects to the scene by invoking the **Add** menu from the viewport or using the *Shift + A* shortcut. We can add objects of different types, such as **Text**, **Speaker**, **Empty** | **Plain Axes**, and even a few new meshes such as **Cylinder** and **Sphere**, and run **Create Type Collections** again. We can see that each object is assigned to a collection named after its type.

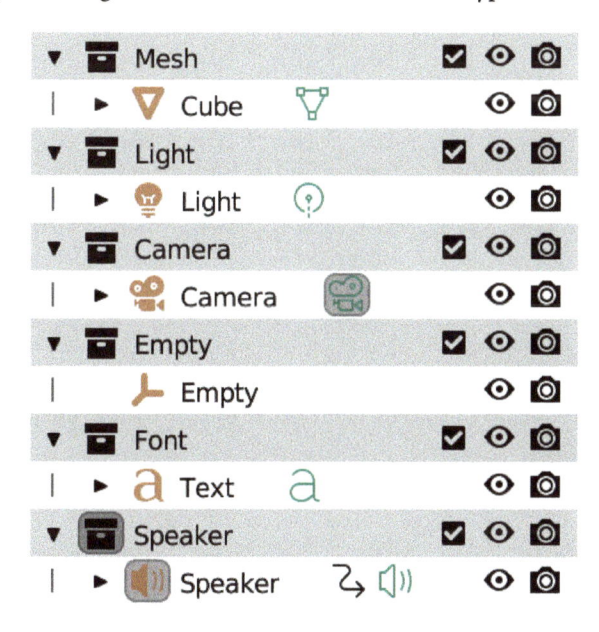

Figure 3.15: Every object type gets its own collection

The nice thing is we didn't have to account manually for all the object types – once a procedural workflow is in place, it will work with objects of all types, even those that will be added in future releases of Blender.

Our operator is complete; what is missing is an easy way to invoke it. We will finish the chapter by learning how to display an operator inside a menu of the interface.

Extending menus

Menus present many advantages – they are everywhere in the application, they cover a specific aspect of the 3D workflow, and new items can be added easily. We are going to handle the addition and removal of new menu entries in our add-on – our operator will be displayed only when our add-on is enabled.

Draw functions

Blender menus accept new items in the form of functions. These functions describe how a menu should draw a new entry; they must accept the `self` and `context` arguments passed by their menu and have the following form:

```
def draw_menu_item(self, context):
    row = self.layout.row()
```

We will gain a better grasp of UI elements in *Chapter 5*. For now, we will only add our operator to a menu row. This is how our function will look:

```
def draw_collector_item(self, context):
    row = self.layout.row()
    row.operator(OBJECT_OT_collector_types.bl_idname)
```

We can now append this function to a Blender menu and let it display our operator.

Adding menu entries

Blender menus are stored in the `bpy.types` namespace. By convention, the name of a menu type follows the following scheme:

```
bpy.types.[AREA]_MT_[NAME]
```

For instance, menus in the 3D view start with `bpy.types.VIEW3D_MT_`. Typing that in the Python console and pressing *Tab* will show the menus available in the viewport as a suggestion:

```
>>> bpy.types.VIEW3D_MT_
                    add(
                    angle_control(
                    armature_add(
                    ...
```

Since **Create Type Collections** operates on objects, we might want to look into the `bpy.types.VIEW3D_MT_object` menus:

```
>>> bpy.types.VIEW3D_MT_object
                            (
                            _animation(
                            _apply(
```

```
                    _asset(
                    ...
                    _context_menu(
```

The bpy.types.VIEW3D_MT_object is the **Object** menu menu in the 3D View top bar; most of the other suggestions are its submenus. The right-click menu is available as VIEW3D_MT_pose_context_menu. We use this one in our example, but we could very well use any other menu.

The append() and remove() methods add and remove a draw function from a menu. That can be done in the register()/unregister() functions of our add-on, so it becomes the following:

```
def register():
    bpy.utils.register_class(OBJECT_OT_collector_types)
    menu = bpy.types.VIEW3D_MT_object_context_menu
    menu.append(draw_collector_item)
def unregister():
    bpy.utils.unregister_class(OBJECT_OT_collector_types)
    menu = bpy.types.VIEW3D_MT_object_context_menu
    menu.remove(draw_collector_item)
```

Reloading the scripts, and invoking the right-click menu while in **Object Mode** displays our option at the bottom. Now that there is a way to invoke our operator in the UI, we can consider our add-on complete and commit our changes.

Figure 3.16: Our operator added to the context menu

Summary

In this chapter, we have coded a complete add-on that expands Blender functionalities and integrates seamlessly into an application. We have also learned how to work on our code while it is being used and improve our tools through consecutive steps of refinement.

In *Chapter 4,* we will learn how to affect the position and rotation of Blender objects via Python, and we will add interactive properties to our operator.

Questions

1. What is the difference between a Python script and a Blender add-on?
2. Which advantages does an add-on provide over sparse code?
3. What do operators do?
4. How do we define the conditions under which an operator can be executed?
5. Can we work on an add-on while it is being used? How do we update it?
6. How do we ignore bytecode (`.pyc`) files in Git version control?
7. How do we avoid creating duplicates?

4
Exploring Object Transformations

The ability to change an object's location, rotation, and dimension in a space is a tenet of any animation software.

Artists are used to changing the values of transform channels to carry out these operations. More technical users are aware of the geometric implications of such actions.

In this chapter, we will learn how Object Transformations work and how to implement them in our script. We will also learn how to add object constraints programmatically and how Blender can carry out the more difficult operations for us.

Finally, we will implement a new command that affects the transformation of more objects at once and accepts user input.

This chapter will cover the following key topics:

- Transforming objects, using coordinate notations, and avoiding pitfalls
- Applying object constraints and hierarchies
- Using matrix representation
- Adding interactive operators to our add-ons

Technical requirements

We will use Blender and **Visual Studio Code (VS Code)**.

The examples created in this chapter can be found at the following URL: `https://github.com/PacktPublishing/Python-Scripting-in-Blender/tree/main/ch4`.

Moving objects in space

Three-dimensional objects can be moved, rotated, and scaled. Since they do not change the geometry of an object, location and rotation are considered **rigid transformations**. Technically, changing the size of an object using its scale value applies a non-rigid transformation, but since the vertex geometry doesn't change, scale is considered an object-level transformation and is displayed alongside location and rotation.

In this section, we will use Python to transform objects in Blender.

Transforming objects

An object is transformed by changing the values of its Location, Rotation, and Scale channels. Location and scale coordinates are immediately associated with the X, Y, and Z of the Cartesian space; rotations have more options as they come with some implications.

Affecting an object's location

We have already met the `location` attribute in *Chapter 1* and *Chapter 2*. If we have an active object, such as the cube from Blender's default scene, the following lines will move it to the location with *x*, *y*, *z* coordinates 1.0, 2.0, and 3.0. These lines use **tuple assignment** to set all three coordinates at once:

```
import bpy
bpy.context.object.location = 1.0, 2.0, 3.0
```

Since Blender coordinates can also be assigned through letters, that expression is equivalent to the following:

```
import bpy
bpy.context.object.location.xyz = 1.0, 2.0, 3.0
```

Coordinates are stored inside **Vectors**. Vector components can be accessed separately:

```
import bpy
bpy.context.object.location[0] = 1.0
bpy.context.object.location[1] = 2.0
bpy.context.object.location[2] = 3.0
```

Alternatively, they can be accessed as follows:

```
import bpy
bpy.context.object.location.x = 1.0
bpy.context.object.location.y = 2.0
bpy.context.object.location.z = 3.0
```

Location and Scale are both stored as Vectors.

Affecting object scale

Like with location, the three dimensions of scale are accessed through the `Vector` coordinates:

```
>>> bpy.context.object.scale
Vector((1.0, 1.0, 1.0))
```

We can assign a non-uniform scale to an object, such as a different value for each axis:

```
import bpy
bpy.context.object.scale.xyz = 3.0, 2.0, 1.0
```

The scale of an object is more often uniform, meaning it is the same on each axis. Blender Vectors provide a convenient way for assigning uniform values:

```
import bpy
bpy.context.object.scale.xyz = 3.0
```

Like with `location`, `scale` coordinates can be set individually or together. The rest values are different, by the way: the scale at rest is [1.0, 1.0, 1.0] rather than [0.0, 0.0, 0.0]. That reflects how scaling is a multiplicative operation while location is additive.

Rotations are less immediate to combine. We will see that there are different ways to represent rotations in the first place.

Affecting object rotations

Using rotations, we can orient an object around the *x*, *y*, and *z* axes. Doing that will give objects an orientation of their own, with their own *x*, *y*, and *z* local axes.

We refer to these new axes, aligned with the object, as **Local Orientation**. Blender lets the user choose between different axes for transforming objects. The axes aligned with the viewport grid are the **Global Orientation** or **World Axes**:

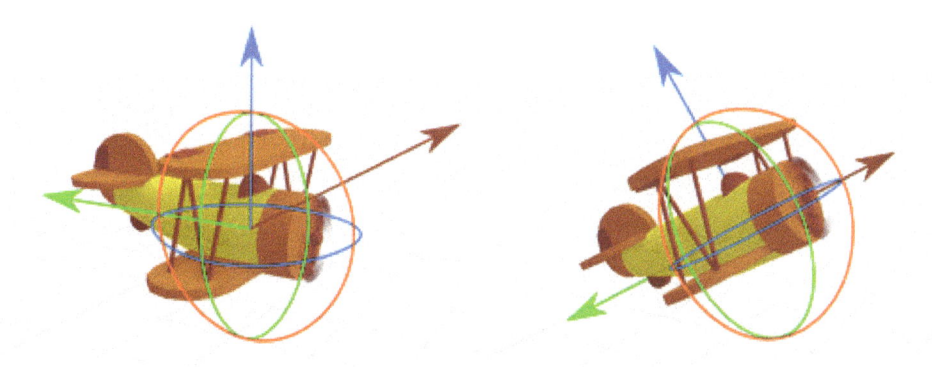

Figure 4.1: Rotation rings and axes of an object at rest and after a rotation

Even if an object was rotated, we can still change **Rotation Mode** in the viewport top bar and use *Global Orientation*:

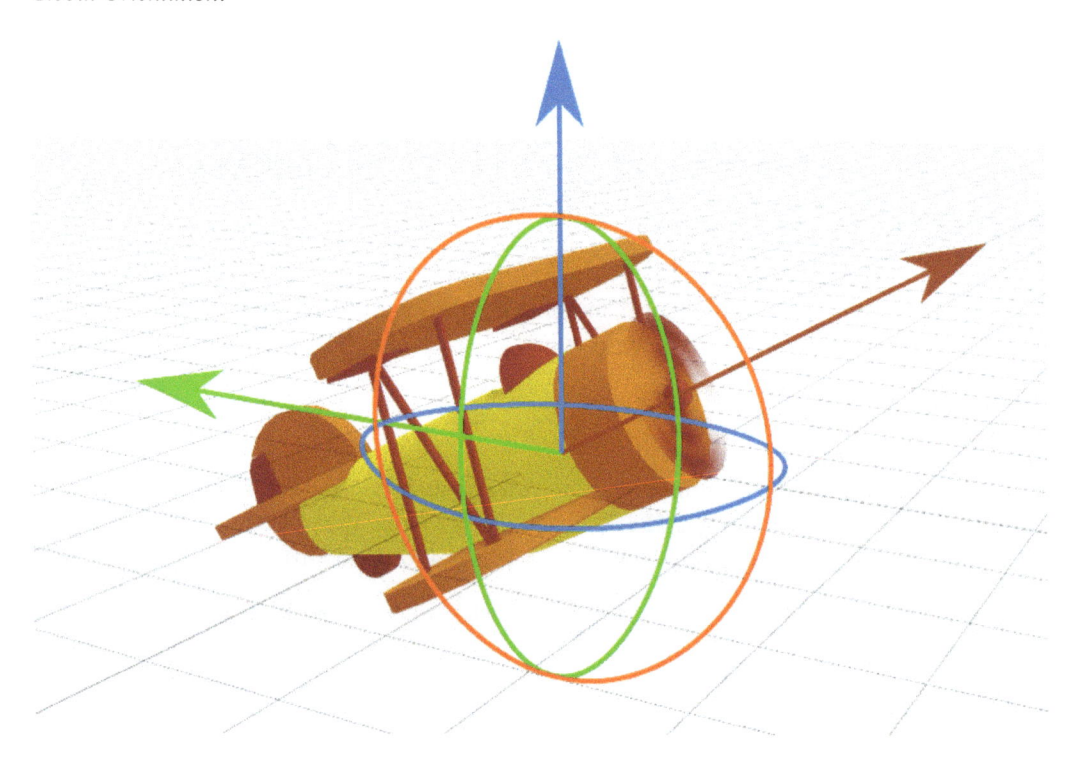

Figure 4.2: A rotated airplane still using Global Orientation

Rotations are more complex than translation and scale: by definition, a rotation involves a pivot and a constant distance. For that reason, rotations are affected by some minor issues that require extra consideration.

Issues related to rotations

Because of their composite nature, rotations around one axis can change the rotation value on another. To sum that up, rotation is described as a three-dimensional property with only two **degrees of freedom**, as no more than two channels have the chance to change freely.

Also, the order in which rotations are stacked together changes the result. To visualize a rotated object correctly, we need to know which axes were rotated first, that is, the **rotation order**.

We could just stick with one rotation order, say x, then y, and then z, but that would limit our options against another potential shortcoming: three-dimensional rotations that overlap one axis with another end up making one coordinate useless, a well-known problem known as **gimbal lock**.

Since different rotation orders lock at different angles, changing the order helps cope with the issue.

These problems aren't specific to Blender or any other animation software; they are inherent properties of three-dimensional spaces, up to and including the one that we inhabit.

To work around them, rotations provide a wider range of options. In addition to different orders for combining the three angles, there are also abstract representations such as quaternions. This terminology might sound scary at first, but it will become more familiar as we proceed with the chapter.

Changing rotation mode

The **Rotation Mode** box in **Transform Properties** displays the available options for rotating objects:

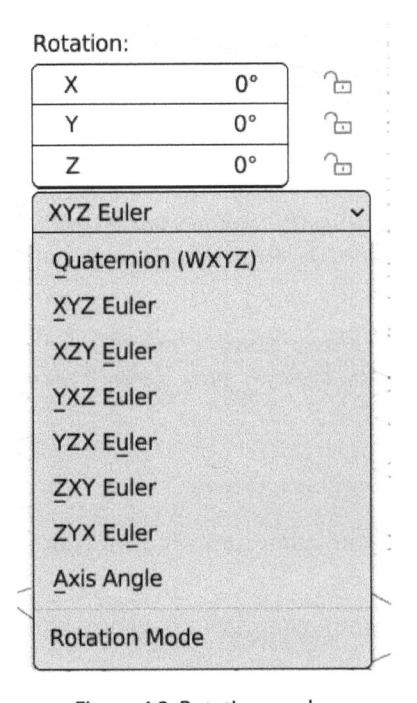

Figure 4.3: Rotation modes

We do not need to cover this topic in full here, but essentially the following provides a brief introduction:

- **Quaternions**: These are mathematic notations that use four coefficients: in Blender, **W**, **X**, **Y**, and **Z**. Quaternions do not suffer from gimbal lock.
- **Euler angles**: These list the angles on three rotation axes. It's the common acceptance of rotation and comes with two caveats: the result depends on the axis order, and one axis might end up overlapping another. To mitigate the perils of losing a channel to gimbal lock, more combinations of **X**, **Y**, and **Z** are allowed.

- **Axis Angle**: This uses **X**, **Y,** and **Z** to define a point as the rotation axis. The **W** attribute is the twisting angle in said direction.

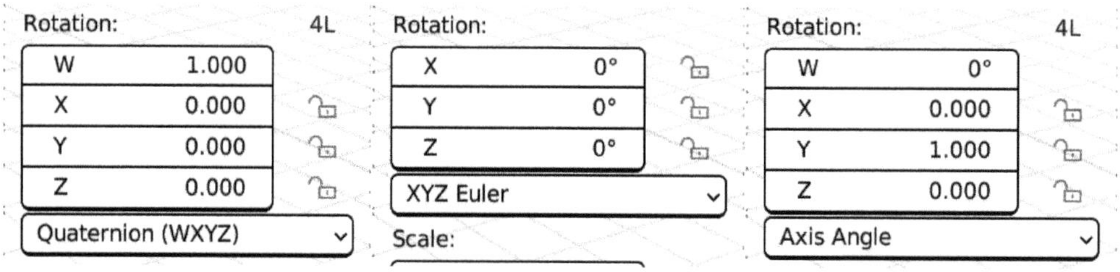

Figure 4.4: Rotation attributes for the Quaternion, Euler, and Axis Angle modes

Changing this property in the interface changes the displayed channels. In Python, we need to use different attributes depending on the current mode.

Accessing rotations in Python

The `rotation_mode` attribute specifies which system is being used to rotate an object. It is an **enum** attribute, that is, it contains a string that can only belong to a predefined set. Trying to assign an arbitrary string causes `TypeError`. The error message prints out the allowed keywords:

```
>>> import bpy
>>> bpy.context.object.rotation_mode = "this won't work"
TypeError: bpy_struct: item.attr = val: enum "this won't work" not
found in ('QUATERNION', 'XYZ', 'XZY', 'YXZ', 'YZX', 'ZXY', 'ZYX',
'AXIS_ANGLE')
```

Each mode provides its attributes for setting rotations:

- `QUATERNION`: To affect the quaternion coefficients *W*, *X*, *Y*, and *Z*, we use the following, respectively:
  - `rotation_quaternion.w` or `rotation_quaternion[0]`
  - `rotation_quaternion.x` or `rotation_quaternion[1]`
  - `rotation_quaternion.y` or `rotation_quaternion[2]`
  - `rotation_quaternion.z` or `rotation_quaternion[3]`
- XYZ, XZY, YXZ, YZX, ZXY, and ZYX are Euler angles evaluated in different orders. No matter which one we choose, the Euler attributes for these are the following:
  - `rotation_euler.x` or `rotation_euler[0]`
  - `rotation_euler.y` or `rotation_euler[1]`
  - `rotation_euler.z` or `rotation_euler[2]`

  We should set these values in radians.

- AXIS_ANGLE: *Axis Angle – Axis Angle (W+XYZ)*, defines a rotation around some axis defined by 3D-Vector. We can set the torsion angle in radians via the following:

  - `rotation_axis_angle[0]`

  We can set the axis vector x, y, z coordinates using the following:

  - `rotation_axis_angle[1]`
  - `rotation_axis_angle[2]`
  - `rotation_axis_angle[3]`

The `math` module provides some help in using radians as angular units.

Using radians and degrees

Blender's API describes angles of rotation using radians rather than degrees. Degrees express an angle using values between 0 and 360, while radians range between 0 and 2π. The Greek letter π (pi) refers to the ratio between a circle and its diameter. 2π (approximately 6.28) measures the arc of a full circle of radius 1.0.

In Python, we can use the `math` module's functions to convert between the two systems, `radians()` and `degrees()`, and the `pi` variable for quick access to the value of π.

Take the following example:

```
>>> from math import radians, degrees, pi
>>> degrees(2 * pi)
360.0
>>> radians(360)
6.283185307179586
```

With that in mind, when we set rotations, we can convert angular units on the fly.

Setting rotation attributes

Before we set a rotation in a script, we must ensure that we use the right rotation system. In the following snippet, we set the rotation mode beforehand:

```
import bpy
ob = bpy.context.object
# apply a 90 degrees on X axis rotation using Quaternions
ob.rotation_mode = 'QUATERNION'
ob.rotation_quaternion.w = 0.707107
ob.rotation_quaternion.x = 0.707107
ob.rotation_quaternion.y = 0.0
ob.rotation_quaternion.z = 0.0
# apply a 90 degrees on X axis rotation using Eulers
```

```
ob.rotation_mode = 'XYZ'
ob.rotation_euler.x = radians(90)
ob.rotation_euler.y = 0.0
ob.rotation_euler.z = 0.0
# apply a 90 degrees on X axis rotation using Axis Angle
ob.rotation_mode = 'AXIS_ANGLE'
ob.rotation_axis_angle[0] = radians(90)
ob.rotation_axis_angle[1] = 1
ob.rotation_axis_angle[1] = 0
ob.rotation_axis_angle[1] = 0
```

When we change `rotation_mode`, Blender converts the current state to the selected system. That prevents an object from suddenly changing its orientation in space and works for most cases, but there are a few exceptions. For instance, animations have values set for each keyframe, so switching the rotation type of animated controls ends up changing the visual rotation during playback. In that case, we can use conversion methods in our scripts, as we will see in the next Python snippet.

Converting between rotation systems

In the following snippet, we start with a `Euler` rotation and use conversion methods to change the rotation mode:

```
from mathutils import Euler
# create a 90 degrees rotation Euler
rot_90x_eu = Euler((radians(90), 0, 0))
# convert to quaternion
rot_90x_quat = rot_90x_eu.to_quaternion()
# convert to axis angle
rot_90x_aa = rot_90x_quat.to_axis_angle()
```

At the time of writing, the Euler representation doesn't have a `to_axis_angle()` method, so we convert to quaternion first. Using quaternions as a crossroad is common, as they are the most generic system for expressing rotations.

Rotations can also be written down as a **matrix**. The matrix form is how all the transforms are stored internally. We will get to that after we have learned more about indirect transforms, that is, moving an object without changing its channels.

Transforming objects indirectly

We have seen how to transform an object by altering its channels directly. There are two other ways to influence an object's position, rotation, and scale. **Object Constraints** are special utilities that affect the transformation either by limiting certain values or by copying them from another object.

Then there is the possibility to arrange more objects in a hierarchy via **Parenting**, that is, by making one object belong to another.

We will see how these operations are reflected in Python.

Using Object Constraints

Constraints can move, rotate, or scale an object without changing its transform properties. Some of them, such as **Copy Transforms**, override the object transform completely; others, such as **Limit Distance**, operate on top of them.

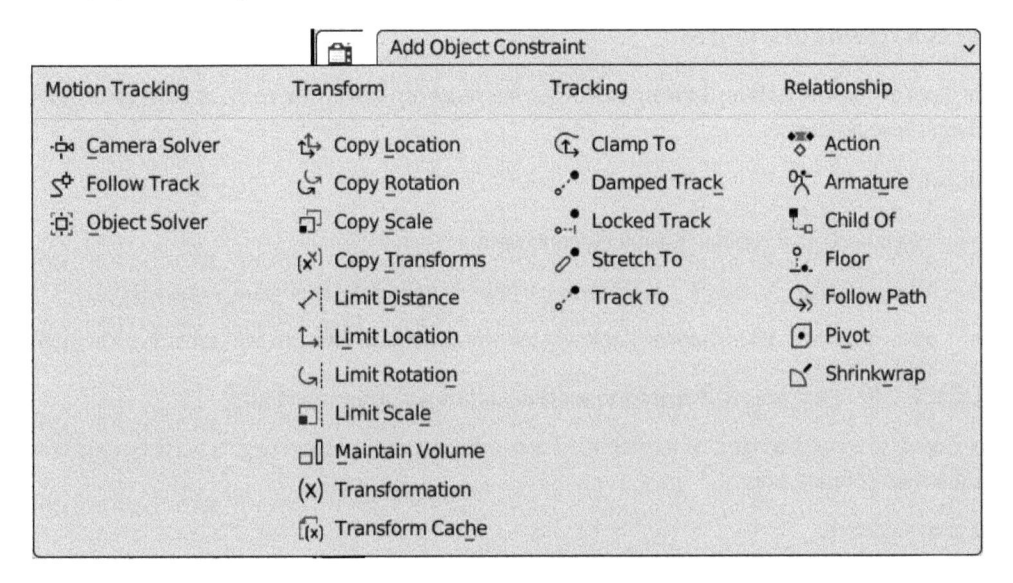

Figure 4.5: Blender constraints menu

Most constraints bind the transforms of more objects together, such as **Copy Location**, while others, such as **Limit Location**, have their own transform attributes.

An object can have an unspecified number of constraints. The steps to add them in Python are very similar to how they work in the graphic interface.

Adding constraints in Python

Constraints are exposed as a collection property of an object. They can be added by providing a constraint type to the `new(type)` method.

Much like with rotation mode, providing a wrong keyword will prompt an error and list the available options:

```
>>> import bpy
>>> bpy.context.object.constraints.new("this won't work")
TypeError: ObjectConstraints.new(): error with keyword argument "type"
 - enum " this won't work " not found in ('CAMERA_SOLVER', 'FOLLOW_
TRACK', 'OBJECT_SOLVER', 'COPY_LOCATION', 'COPY_ROTATION', 'COPY_
SCALE', 'COPY_TRANSFORMS', 'LIMIT_DISTANCE', 'LIMIT_LOCATION', ...
```

The new method returns the created constraint, so we can easily access its properties.

Setting constraint attributes

Different types of constraints have different attributes, but some common patterns exist. Most constraints will contain these properties:

Boolean switches:

- .enabled: This enables/disables a constraint
- .use_x, .use_y, .use_z: Use when available to enable/disable only one axis
- .use_offset: Use when available to sum the constraint effect to the transform channels

- Object: Use .target, if available, to set the bind target of the constraint
- String: Use .subtarget, if available, to use only part of the target (e.g., a vertex group) for the actual computation
- Enum switches:
  - .target_space: This makes the constraint act at the **Local**, **World**, or **Custom Object** level
  - .owner_space: This changes the constraint source data to the **Local**, **World,** or **Custom Object** level

Float number: Use .influence to convey only a fraction of the effect

Some properties are specific to each type, such as the distance attribute of the **Distance Constraint**. In that case, their path can be traced by hovering over or right-clicking in the graphic interface (see the *Copying the data path section in Chapter 2*) or from the API documentation (see the *Accessing Blender data* section in *Chapter 2*).

Limiting an object scale

The following snippet adds a **Limit Scale** constraint that limits the maximum height of the active object:

```
import bpy
ob = bpy.context.object
limit = ob.constraints.new(type='LIMIT_SCALE')
limit.use_max_z = True   # limit the height only
limit.max_z = 0.5
```

If applied to the default cube, it will halve its height as if a scale of [1.0, 1.0, 0.5] had been applied, despite its scale values still being [1.0, 1.0, 1.0].

Objects can be part of a hierarchy. In that case, they follow the objects that are higher in their hierarchical tree. We will explore this concept next.

Using object hierarchies

Objects in the viewport can be arranged as **children** of other objects. In that case, they will be affected by the translation, rotation, and scale of their **parent**.

We can access hierarchical relationships in Python via the parent, children, and children_recursive attributes. Only the parent attribute is writable; the other two are only for listing.

The difference between children and children_recursive is that the latter lists every affected object down the hierarchy, including children of children and all the *descendants*.

This snippet parents all the existing objects one under the other, then it prints a report:

```
import bpy
previous = bpy.data.objects[0]
for ob in bpy.data.objects[1:]:
    # parent each object under its predecessor
    ob.parent = previous
    previous = ob
for ob in bpy.data.objects:
    # now print out the children of each object
    print(ob.name)
    child_names = (c.name for c in ob.children)
    print("\tchildren:", ", ".join(child_names))
    child_names = (c.name for c in ob.children_recursive)
    print("\tchildren recursive:", ", ".join(child_names))
    print("")
```

Running that code in the default scene brings the following result:

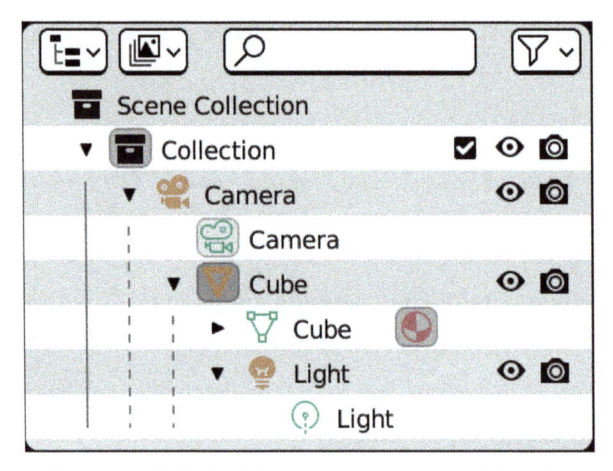

Figure 4.6: Default objects reparented in one hierarchy

This is reflected in the printout: the first object lists all the others as *grandchildren*, while `children_recursive` and `children` contain the same results for the last two, which have no other descendants:

```
Camera
        children: Cube
        children recursive: Cube, Light
Cube
        children: Light
        children recursive: Light
Light
        children:
        children recursive:
```

If we look at the viewport, we can see that the object positions have changed: parenting an object in Python applies a new reference system instantly. To replicate that behavior, we need to understand the transformation matrix.

Understanding the transform matrix

Three-dimensional transforms of Location, Rotation, and Scale are stored together inside a **matrix**. Matrices are, at large, tables of numbers arranged in rows and columns. Transformation matrices are combined using **linear algebra**. We will not go into the details here; we will just have a quick look at what a matrix means and how we can use it in our scripts.

Like with other representations, Blender provides a `Matrix` class in the `mathutils` module:

```
>>> from mathutils import Matrix
>>> Matrix()
Matrix(((1.0, 0.0, 0.0, 0.0),
        (0.0, 1.0, 0.0, 0.0),
        (0.0, 0.0, 1.0, 0.0),
        (0.0, 0.0, 0.0, 1.0)))
```

A matrix containing these default values, `1.0` in its *diagonal* entries and `0.0` everywhere else, represents the *rest* state. In other words, an object associated with this matrix was not moved, rotated, or scaled. It is known as an **identity matrix**, as it leaves an object in its *identical* state.

Whenever an object is moved, rotated, or scaled, the entries of its matrix change to different values.

Accessing matrices

Objects contain more than one matrix. Trying to reach an object matrix via autocompletion shows four different attributes:

```
>>> bpy.context.object.matrix_
                            basis
                            local
                            parent_inverse
                            world
```

Each of them covers a specific aspect:

- `matrix_basis`: This contains the local location, rotation, and scale of an object before it is transformed by object constraints. This matrix reflects the channels displayed in the object properties.

- `matrix_local`: This contains the local location, rotation, and scale of an object, omitting the transformation inherited by the parent object but not the one resulting from constraints.

- `matrix_parent_inverse`: Whenever we don't want an object at rest to match its parent exactly, we add an offset inside this matrix.

- `matrix_world`: This contains the final location, rotation, and scale in world coordinates, reflecting all the transformations to which an object is subject.

With that in mind, we can improve the *parent snippet* from the previous section and keep the object positions intact.

Storing object matrices

Assigning a parent relationship via Python previously has snapped every object to its parent positions.

We want them to maintain their visual transformation after the change in hierarchy. In matrix terms, we are saying that we want to keep their world matrix unchanged. To do that, we will learn how to store a matrix properly.

Copying matrices

Python variables containing single values store their own data. Variables with aggregate values such as lists, dictionaries, and Blender `mathutils` types point to shared references of their values.

Let's look at the following example. The b variable has the same value as a. After a is changed to 5, b is still 4:

```
>>> a = 4
>>> b = a
>>> a += 1
>>> print(b)
4
```

The same doesn't apply to lists, even if they consist of one single element:

```
>>> a = [4]
>>> b = a
>>> a[0] += 1
>>> print(b)
[5]
```

Despite being a different variable, the b list points to the same data as the a list. To free it from getting updates from the original, we must state explicitly that it is a copy.

Expert Python users know very well how to avert that using Python's `copy` module. Blender aggregate types provide a `.copy()` method for convenience.

In the following snippet, changes to `matrix_a` will also change `matrix_b`:

```
# two variables pointing to the same matrix
matrix_b = matrix_a   # matrix_b ALWAYS equals matrix_a
```

The following creates a **deep copy** of `matrix_a`, that is, all its values are copied:

```
# deep copy of a matrix
matrix_b = matrix_a.copy()   # matrix_b stores its values
```

We can now keep the object's world transformations and restore them after the hierarchy has changed.

Restoring transformations using the world matrix

Since `matrix_world` is writeable, it can be stored and reapplied after setting the parent.

To restore the matrix *as it was*, we need to store a copy of its value, like in the following snippet:

```
import bpy
previous = bpy.data.objects[0]
for ob in bpy.data.objects[1:]:
    # store a copy of the world mat
    w_mat = ob.matrix_world.copy()  # .copy() is important!
    # parent each object under its predecessor
    ob.parent = previous
    # restore world position
    ob.matrix_world = w_mat
    # set current object as parent of the next
    previous = ob
```

We can see that the objects maintain their position. If we look at the transform channels, we will find that they have changed.

Setting the world matrix affects the location/rotation/scale values. In their rest position, the objects still go back to their parent center.

If that is not what we want to achieve, we can use the `matrix_parent_inverse` attribute to offset the rest position.

Creating rest offsets with the parent inverse matrix

The `parent_matrix_inverse` attribute contains a transform that is hidden from the interface. It is used for setting a rest position away from the parent's origin.

The idea is to counter the inherited transform, adding its inverse to the transform. For instance, the inverse of moving an object to the [5.0, 5.0, 5.0] coordinates is moving it to [-5.0, -5.0, -5.0].

Inverting a rotation is a little bit more complicated, but in Blender, we can find the inverse of any transform using the `.inverted()` method of its matrix.

This is how the following snippet parents the objects in `bpy.data`, while keeping their transform and visual coordinates:

```
import bpy
previous = bpy.data.objects[0]
for ob in bpy.data.objects[1:]:
    # parent each object under its predecessor
```

```
    ob.parent = previous
    # set parent inverse offset
    offset_matrix = previous.matrix_world.inverted()
    ob.matrix_parent_inverse = offset_matrix
    # set current object as parent of the next
    previous = ob
```

The matrix system can be scary, as many people don't usually think of transformations in this form. But even this basic understanding of it provides a very powerful tool in our scripting bench.

In the next section, we put the skills learned throughout the chapter to use in a single add-on. This add-on changes the positions of many objects as one and can optionally work through constraints.

Writing the Elevator add-on

Now that we know how to transform objects in Python, we can write a new add-on that contains a transformation operator.

This add-on allows us to move all selected objects above a certain height. It can be useful whenever we want to set a minimum height, that is, a *floor*, for our scene. As we did in *Chapter 3*, we start with a basic implementation, and we will then proceed to refine it. As usual, we start our work by setting a folder for the code of the chapter.

Setting the environment

As we did at the beginning of *Chapter 3*, we create a folder for *Chapter 4* in our **VS Code** project; then, from Blender's menu bar, we can access the Blender **Preferences** window and then **File Paths** to set the ch4 folder as the **Scripts** folder:

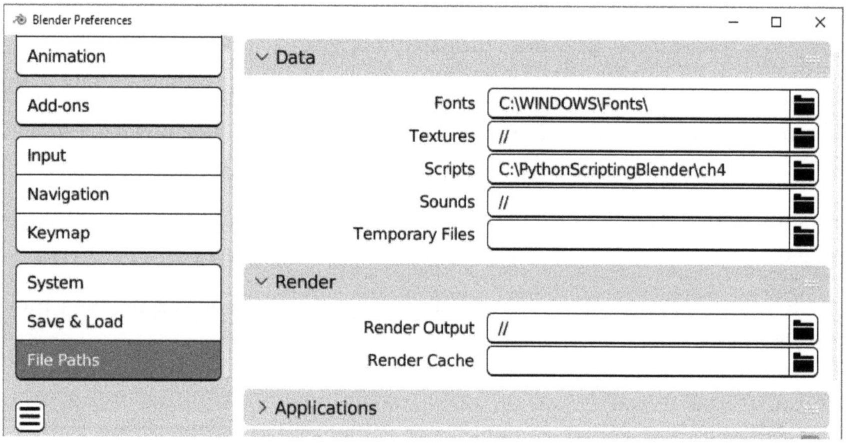

Figure 4.7: System folder for Chapter 4

Now it's time to add a new file to our project:

1. Select `PythonScriptingBlender/ch4/addons` in VS Code.
2. Create a new file by clicking the **New File** icon.
3. Name the new file `object_elevator.py`.
4. Open the file by double-clicking it.

We can now start writing our add-on.

Writing the first draft

As we have seen in the *Add-on requirements* section in *Chapter 3*, our add-on needs the following:

- The add-on *information* `bl_info` dictionary
- An *operator* that performs the desired action
- The `register`/`unregister` function for `enable`/`disable` operations

Let's begin writing the first draft by filling in the requirements; we can refine the add-on in the second step:

1. We write down the add-on information in the `bl_info` header. That also helps clarify the purpose and functionality of the tool:

object_elevator.py

```python
bl_info = {
    "name": "Elevator",
    "author": "John Doe",
    "version": (1, 0),
    "blender": (3, 00, 0),
    "description": "Move objects up to a minimum height",
    "category": "Object",
}
```

2. Now, let's nail down the main functionality: the add-on contains an operator that moves all the objects up to a given height. We store this height in the static variable floor, which, for now, is hardcoded and set to 5.0:

```python
class OBJECT_OT_elevator(bpy.types.Operator):
    """Move Objects up to a given height"""
    bl_idname = "object.pckt_floor_transform"
    bl_label = "Elevate Objects"
    floor = 5.0
```

3. Since it affects the selected objects, the condition to check in the `poll()` method is that the selection is not empty:

   ```
   @classmethod
   def poll(cls, context):
       return len(bpy.context.selected_objects) > 0
   ```

4. Here's the bulk of the code: the `execute` function checks for each object that its Z location is not less than `self.floor` (at the moment, `self.floor` equals 5.0). When all the objects have been processed, it returns a `'FINISHED'` status:

   ```
   def execute(self, context):
       for ob in context.selected_objects:
           if ob.location.z > self.floor:
               continue
           ob.location.z = self.floor
       return {'FINISHED'}
   ```

5. Now, we can add our operator to the object right-click menu; to do that, we need a `drawmenu` function:

   ```
   def draw_elevator_item(self, context):
       # Menu draw function
       row = self.layout.row()
       row.operator(OBJECT_OT_elevator.bl_idname)
   ```

6. All the elements of our add-on are ready; all that is left is to add them to the registration functions. This is how we do it:

   ```
   def register():
       # add operator and menu item
       bpy.utils.register_class(OBJECT_OT_elevator)
       object_menu = bpy.types.VIEW3D_MT_object_context_menu
       object_menu.append(draw_elevator_item)
   def unregister():
       # remove operator and menu item
       bpy.utils.unregister_class(OBJECT_OT_elevator)
       object_menu = bpy.types.VIEW3D_MT_object_context_menu
       object_menu.remove(draw_elevator_item)
   ```

Our add-on is ready for its test drive. We can find it in the **Add-ons** preferences:

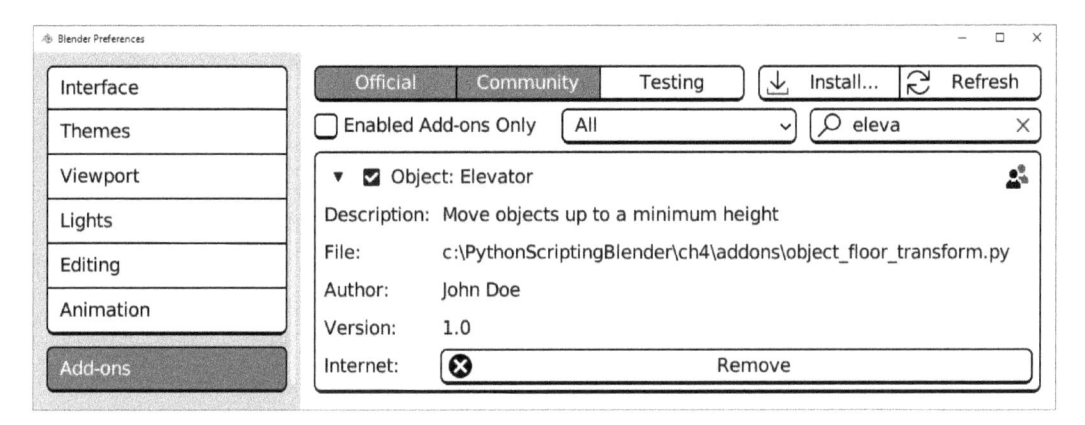

Figure 4.8: Object: Elevator enabled in the Add-ons preferences

When the add-on is enabled, a new entry is added to the object's *right-click* menu:

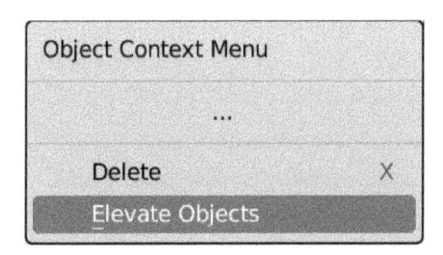

Figure 4.9: Right-clicking in the viewport shows our new menu entry

If we select some objects and open the context menu via right-clicking them, we will find **Elevate Objects** as an available action. Clicking on it sets `location.z` to `5.0` unless it already has a higher value.

Setting a minimum height for a scene can be useful when it contains a ground level, and we want to ensure that no object ends up below it. The static value of `OBJECT_OT_elevator.floor` doesn't help here, though, as it only applies to the case when the ground level equals `5.0`.

Luckily that was only for testing: the final version of the script makes use of an input parameter instead.

Using input properties

Replacing the static `floor` member in our operator with an editable value requires Blender to channel the user input to our Python script.

For that purpose, Blender's API provides special properties that show up as graphic elements in the interface and can be used as variables in Python scripts. These properties are part of the `bpy.props` module.

To make `floor` an editable property of our operator:

1. As `OBJECT_OT_elevator.floor` is a float number, so we need to use `FloatProperty`:

    ```
    import bpy
    from bpy.props import FloatProperty
    ```

2. Since we are forcing a specific type, we will use a Python **annotation** rather than a declaration, so we change `floor = 5.0` to `floor:FloatProperty(name="Floor", default=0)`.

> **Take note**
>
> Using an annotation in lieu of variables of a determined type is a best practice in Python, but it is required in Blender: the input property will not appear otherwise.

3. Then we must keep in mind that, because of how Blender works, operators that accept input values must be aware of the undo system. So, we add the `bl_options = {'REGISTER', 'UNDO'}` property.

    Here's how the header of our operator looks now:

    ```
    class OBJECT_OT_elevator(bpy.types.Operator):
        """Move Objects up or down by given offset"""
        bl_idname = "object.pckt_type_collector"
        bl_label = "Create Type Collections"
        bl_options = {'REGISTER', 'UNDO'}

        floor: FloatProperty(name="Floor", default=0)
    ```

4. Refreshing the operators by pressing *F3* + **Reload Scripts** and executing **Elevate Objects** again displays the input properties inside an expansion popup at the bottom left of the screen:

Figure 4.10: Our editable Floor property

Changing this property affects the minimum height of all selected objects.

So far, we have operated on the `location.z` attribute. This might not work if our object has a parent with a different orientation or scale. We can overcome that using the object world matrix instead.

Setting the height in the world matrix

Blender stores the object translation in the matrix's last column, as seen in *Figure 4.11*:

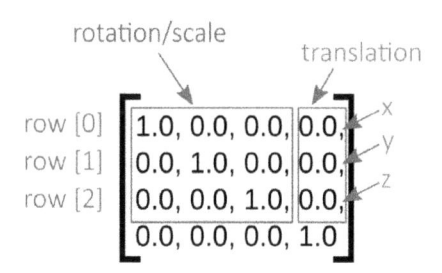

Figure 4.11: The entries of a transform matrix

The indices of `Matrix` point to its rows; so, to access location z, we need to get the third row and look for its fourth element. Since the enumeration starts with 0, the indices we are looking for are, respectively, `[2]` and `[3]`.

Our `execute` function now uses `matrix_world[2][3]` instead of `location.z`. Since matrix values are not automatically updated during script execution, we'll need to invoke `context.view_layer.update()` after the value is set:

```
def execute(self, context):
    selected_objects = context.selected_objects
    for ob in selected_objects:
        matrix_world = ob.matrix_world
        if matrix_world[2][3] > self.floor:
            continue
        matrix_world[2][3] = self.floor
        # make sure next object matrix will be updated
        context.view_layer.update()
    return {'FINISHED'}
```

This version of the script can handle the objects that inherit a parent transform, but what if the parent is also selected?

Moving a parent after a child has already been handled will change the positions of both, thus bringing the child to a wrong height.

We need to make sure that parent objects are always moved first.

Avoiding duplicate transformations

We need to reorder our list of objects, but with `context.selected_objects` being read-only, we cannot reorder it directly; we need to copy its content to a list.

Copying selected_objects to an editable list

We can use the `copy` module to create a **shallow copy** of that list. It will reference the same data but allow us to sort them at will:

```
from copy import copy
```

Then, in the `execute` method, locate the following code:

```
selected_objects = context.selected_objects
```

Replace it with this code:

```
selected_objects = copy(context.selected_objects)
```

Now we can order this list in a way that won't cause the same object to be moved twice.

Ordering by hierarchy

To sort a list, we need a function that returns each element's position in a new order.

We want to handle child objects only after their parents are already processed. Reordering the list so that objects with more ancestors are processed later will meet this condition.

We need a function that returns the number of ancestors: starting with an object, it checks whether it has a parent, and then whether that parent has a parent, until none is found. The `ancestors_count` function achieves that using a `while` loop:

```
def ancestors_count(ob):
    """Return number of objects up in the hierarchy"""
    ancestors = 0
    while ob.parent:
        ancestors += 1
        ob = ob.parent
    return ancestors
```

We add this function to our script and use it as the `key` argument of the `sort` method:

```
    def execute(self, context):
        # sort parent objects first
        selected_objects = copy(context.selected_objects)
        selected_objects.sort(key=ancestors_count)
        for ob in selected_objects:
```

```
            world_mat = ob.matrix_world
            if world_mat[2][3] > self.floor:
                continue

            # ensure update of next object's matrix
            world_mat[2][3] = self.floor
        return {'FINISHED'}
```

Our add-on is now able to raise all the selected objects to a minimum height and avoids summing the transforms in hierarchies.

We could consider it finished, but since we know how to add constraints, we can use them for the same purpose.

Adding the constraints switch

We can allow the user to use constraints and leave the transform channels unaffected. This is how we can do it:

1. Since we want to display a checkbox for using constraints, we need to add a Boolean property to our operator. We need to import `BoolProperty` as we did with `FloatProperty` earlier:

    ```
    from bpy.props import BoolProperty
    ```

2. Then we add a `BoolProperty` annotation to our operator:

    ```
    class OBJECT_OT_elevator(bpy.types.Operator):
        """Move Objects up or down by given offset"""
        bl_idname = "object.pckt_type_collector"
        bl_label = "Create Type Collections"
        bl_options = {'REGISTER', 'UNDO'}

        floor: FloatProperty(name="Floor", default=0)
        constr: BoolProperty(name="Constraints", default=False)
    ```

3. We will use constraints when the `constr` property is set to `True`. We set it to `False` by default so that a new option doesn't change the add-on's behavior.

4. Using constraints makes our job easier; we don't need to sort the objects and set their matrices. Our `execute` function now starts like this:

    ```
    def execute(self, context):
        if self.constr:
            for ob in context.selected_objects:
                limit = ob.constraints.new('LIMIT_LOCATION')
                limit.use_min_z = True
                limit.min_z = self.floor
    ```

```
        return {'FINISHED'}
    # affect coordinates directly
    # sort parent objects first
    ...
```

If we use constraints, we can just exit the function, returning a `{'FINISHED'}` set as soon as we are done setting them. If we don't, the `execute` function keeps going with the previous code.

The visual result is equivalent, but turning **Constraints** on doesn't affect the transform channels. There is one last caveat: if the operator is run multiple times on the same objects, a new constraint is added.

We will make **Elevate Objects** reuse an existing constraint when it is found. That avoids creating too many constraints for the same purpose. It also prevents the effects of previous constraints from interfering. When an object has more than one limit to its location, only the more restrictive one is effective.

Avoiding duplicate constraints

If **Limit Location** is found on an object, our operator uses it. We make this behavior optional in case the user wants to create new constraints anyway:

1. To do that, we add another Boolean property to our operator first:

   ```
   reuse: BoolProperty(name="Reuse Constraints", default=True)
   ```

2. Then, inside our loop, we check for an existing constraint that we can use. If it is not found, our script creates it.

   This behavior can be implemented in a function:

   ```
   def get_constraint(ob, constr_type, reuse=True):
       """Return first constraint of given type.
       If not found, a new one is created"""
       if reuse:
           for constr in ob.constraints:
               if constr.type == constr_type:
                   return constr
       return ob.constraints.new(constr_type)
   ```

3. That has made our `execute` method much cleaner:

   ```
   def execute(self, context):
       if self.constr:
           for ob in context.selected_objects:
               limit = get_constraint(ob,
                                       'LIMIT_LOCATION',
   ```

```
                                self.reuse)
        limit.use_min_z = True
        limit.min_z = self.floor
    return {'FINISHED'}
...
```

If we reload the scripts and run the operator, we will see all its properties in the execution panel:

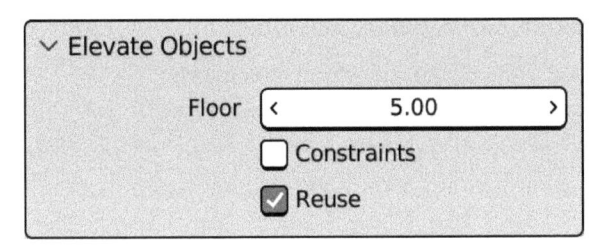

Figure 4.12: All the Elevate Objects options

Ideally, the **Reuse** property should be displayed only when **Constraints** is enabled, as it has no effect otherwise.

This is possible if we take care of drawing the user interface of our tools, which will be introduced in the next chapter.

For now, we have added a good deal of flexibility to a script that started as a very simple tool. This brings us to the end of the chapter, as we have covered most of the topics about writing custom tools.

Summary

In this chapter, we learned how to use `Vector`, `Quaternion`, and `Matrix` entities to our advantage, not to mention the different *rotation modes*. That gives us the elements for understanding and mastering the transformations in space and moving the objects in the scene.

We also learned how to create constraints in Python, which is very important in all set-up scripts.

Lastly, we learned how our operators can get user input and display their parameters inside the Blender user interface during their execution.

In *Chapter 5*, we will learn how to code our own panels for the graphic interface and make its options aware of the context.

Questions

1. What is a rigid transformation?
2. Can we convert coordinates between different rotation systems?
3. Can we convert coordinates between different rotation orders?
4. Why are quaternions useful for conversion?
5. In which form are transformations stored internally?
6. Are objects associated with only one transformation matrix?

5
Designing Graphical Interfaces

Many tools add their own elements to the graphical interface. In the previous chapters, we used existing menus, but we can also add new panels to the Blender window.

To design an interface, we must decide which elements to show and how to reach them, what information should be provided, and which actions should be allowed.

In this chapter, you will learn how to insert new panels into different regions of Blender, how to display information and icons, and how to add buttons that can invoke operators.

This chapter will cover the following topics:

- Understanding the Blender interface
- Drawing a custom panel
- Context and UI interaction

Technical requirements

We will use Blender and Visual Studio Code in this chapter. The examples created in this chapter can be found at https://github.com/PacktPublishing/Python-Scripting-in-Blender/tree/main/ch5.

The example files include 2D images to be used as icons. Optionally, any 2D software can be used to create custom .png images, and you can use them instead.

To implement our interface, we will have to learn how Blender is structured. Let's begin our journey into graphical interfaces with a deep dive into the Blender screen.

Areas, regions, and panels

The Blender window is split into **areas**. Each area can contain an **editor** of a different type, such as the *viewport* for 3D objects or the *sequencer* for editing videos. Each editor, or space, can contain one or more **regions**. The number and type of regions vary across different types of editors: for instance, some editors, such as the **Preferences** window, have a navigation sidebar, while others don't.

The Blender manual explains the interface in detail: `https://docs.blender.org/manual/en/3.1/interface/index.html`.

What we need to know for now is that regions can contain **panels**, and panels are the basic containers of graphical elements such as text, editable values, and buttons.

We can create new panels with Python, which makes it possible to customize any region with ease. A panel must contain information about the area and region to which it belongs:

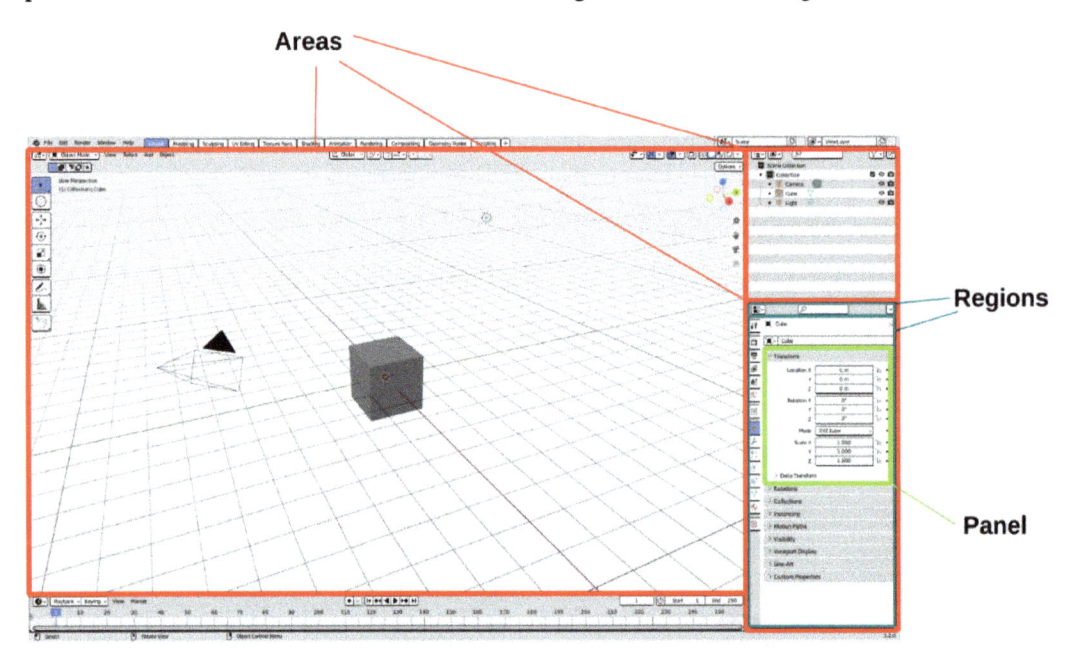

Figure 5.1: Areas, regions, and the panel in the Blender interface

Internally, panels can access information about Blender and the scene so that they can display the status and properties of the objects and execute operators. Now that we are more familiar with the anatomy of the screen, we are going to create a panel that helps us deal with 3D objects.

Creating a simple panel

We will start with a simple panel that contains some text and icons, and we will see how to expand this initial idea into a tool that can help manage the objects in the scene.

Our panel is a new class that derives from `bpy.types.Panel`. Like operators, panels require some static members to be set; otherwise, they will not work. Similar to operators, panels can have a `poll()` class method that states under which conditions the panel can be displayed.

Instead of using the `execute` function, panels set up and draw their content via the `draw(self, context)` function.

Since we are adding a new piece to the Blender interface, we will do that inside a new add-on. It's not mandatory, but it makes it easier to enable and disable our panel.

To keep our code orderly and clean, we will create a new folder for the scripts written for this chapter.

Setting the environment

Let's create a folder for *Chapter 5* in our **Visual Studio Code** project. Then, in the **Blender Preferences** area, set the `ch5` folder as a **Scripts Folder** and restart Blender.

Our add-on script contains a panel, much like the ones in the previous chapters contained operators:

1. Select `PythonScriptingBlender/ch5/addons` in **Visual Studio Code**.
2. Create a new file by clicking the **New File** icon.
3. Name the new file `simple_panel.py`.
4. Open the file by double-clicking on it.

We can now start writing the add-on for our panel.

Drafting our panel add-on

As we know from *Chapter 3*, three elements are required:

- A `bl_info` dictionary containing basic information
- An `import bpy` statement to access the Blender API
- The `register()` and `unregister()` methods for enabling/disabling add-ons, respectively

We also need a class for the graphical element that we want to add – in this case, a class that derives from `bpy.types.Panel`.

We will start with the information dictionary and add the stubs for the required elements to set a frame on which we can code a fully working UI add-on.

Writing the info dictionary

The `bl_info` dictionary will provide the name property of the add-on, its author and version, and the required blender version, plus a short description. We can also add a category under which the add-on is listed. Here's what the code will look like:

```
bl_info = {
    "name": "A Very Simple Panel",
    "author": "John Doe",
    "version": (1, 0),
    "blender": (3, 2, 0),
    "description": "Just show up a panel in the UI",
    "category": "Learning",
}
```

Now, we can proceed with the required import statements and the main class.

Drafting the Panel class

Now that we've imported the bpy module, we can write a class based on bpy.types.Panel.

We can use any name for our class, but Blender recommends some guidelines:

- Since our panel will be part of the object properties, the class name must begin with OBJECT
- The name contains _PT_ in the middle since this is a Panel Type

For now, our class will only contain a *docstring* and a pass statement:

```
import bpy
class OBJECT_PT_very_simple(bpy.types.Panel):
    """Creates a Panel in the object context of the
    properties editor"""
    # still a draft: actual code will be added later
    pass
```

Before adding methods and attributes, we will handle the class activation and dismissal through the registration functions.

Panel registration

The register and unregister functions add and remove this class to/from Blender when the add-on is enabled and disabled, respectively:

```
def register():
    bpy.utils.register_class(OBJECT_PT_very_simple)
def unregister():
    bpy.utils.unregister_class(OBJECT_PT_very_simple)
```

With that, we have created the initial structure of our panel add-on. We will now add the elements and attributes for displaying some text.

Setting display attributes

Blender looks for attributes that follow the bl_* pattern to determine where and how the panel is displayed. Panels have the same identification attributes as operators, as we saw in *Chapter 3*, when we introduced the Operator class:

- bl_label: The display name of the panel
- bl_idname: The unique name of the panel for internal usage

Then, there are attributes used only on classes that derive from bpy.types.Panels:

- bl_space_type: The editor to which the panel belongs
- bl_region_type: The region of the editor to use
- bl_context: The sub-region for specific objects/modes
- bl_category: The tab inside the region, when available

All of them are static strings, and bl_space_type, bl_region_type, and bl_context must match specific values known to Blender as regions of the screen.

The possible values encompass all the available editors in Blender. That might seem overwhelming at first, but once we have an idea of where to place our panel, we can look that up in the online documentation at https://docs.blender.org/api/3.2/bpy.types.Panel.html.

Since Blender contains many editors and each of them has its own sub-elements, we will have a look at the possible combinations.

Choosing our editor view via bl_space_type

First, we must decide which Blender editor we are adding our panel to. That depends mainly on the purpose of our tool and where it will be more convenient to find it. For instance, if our panel helps make videos, it will be part of the **Video Sequencer**; if it is a scripting utility, we might assign it to the *Python Console* or the *Text Editor*. Blender recognizes the following values for `bl_space_type`:

- `EMPTY`: This value is not used in scripts
- `VIEW_3D`: **3D Viewport** for manipulating *objects*
- `IMAGE_EDITOR`: **UV/Image Editor** to view and edit *images* and UV Maps
- `NODE_EDITOR`: **Node Editor** for node-based *shading* and *compositing* tools
- `SEQUENCE_EDITOR`: **Video Sequencer** *editing* tools
- `CLIP_EDITOR`: **Movie Clip Editor** for *motion tracking*
- `DOPESHEET_EDITOR`: **Dope Sheet** for adjusting the timing of *keyframes*
- `GRAPH_EDITOR`: **Graph Editor** for drivers and keyframe *interpolation*
- `NLA_EDITOR`: **Nonlinear Animation** to combine and layer *actions*
- `TEXT_EDITOR` **Text Editor** to edit *scripts* and in-file *documentation*
- `CONSOLE`: **Python Console** for interactive script *development*
- `INFO`: **Info** about operations, warnings, and error *messages*
- `TOPBAR`: **Topbar** for global, *per-window settings*
- `STATUSBAR`: **Status Bar** at the bottom of the screen for *general information*
- `OUTLINER`: **Outliner** overview of the *scene tree* and data blocks
- `PROPERTIES`: **Properties** to edit the *attributes* of active objects and data blocks
- `FILE_BROWSER`: **File Browser** to scroll through *files and assets*
- `SPREADSHEET`: **Spreadsheet** to explore *geometry data* in a table
- `PREFERENCES`: **Preferences** to edit persistent *configuration* settings

Once we have decided on the space type, we are ready to pick a region for it.

Selecting a region via bl_region_type

The kind of region depends on the *space* we chose in the previous step. Different editors have different regions. So, only the default value is always available. Here is a description of all the options for `bl_region_type`:

- `WINDOW`: The *main* region of a space area. This is the default value.
- `HEADER`: A small horizontal strip for *menus* and buttons.
- `CHANNELS`: Used in older versions of Blender, left for backward compatibility.
- `TEMPORARY`: *Poupps* detached from the main window.
- `UI`: Sidebar containing object settings (toggled with *N*).
- `TOOLS`: A toolbar containing a set of interactive tools (toggled with *T*).
- `TOOL_PROPS`: Settings in *modal windows*, such as **File Browser**.
- `PREVIEW`: The preview area of the **Video Sequencer**.
- `HUD`: The operator's **Redo** panel.
- `NAVIGATION_BAR`: *Sidebar* in the **Preferences** window.
- `EXECUTE`: *Bottom bar* in modal windows.
- `FOOTER`: A bar for displaying *information* about the current operation.
- `TOOL_HEADER`: A small horizontal strip for *tool settings*.
- `XR`: The interface for *virtual reality* controllers.

Picking a context via bl_context

Some areas change according to the current selection, active tool, or interaction mode. In that case, the `bl_context` attribute is required.

For instance, the **Properties** space changes when an entity of a different type is selected, so it is tabbed in `'SCENE'`, `'OBJECT'`, and `'CONSTRAINTS'`. If we are not sure about which one to use, we can just activate the tab we are interested in and check the **Info Log** area for a line stating `bpy.context.space_data.context = NAME_OF_CONTEXT`:

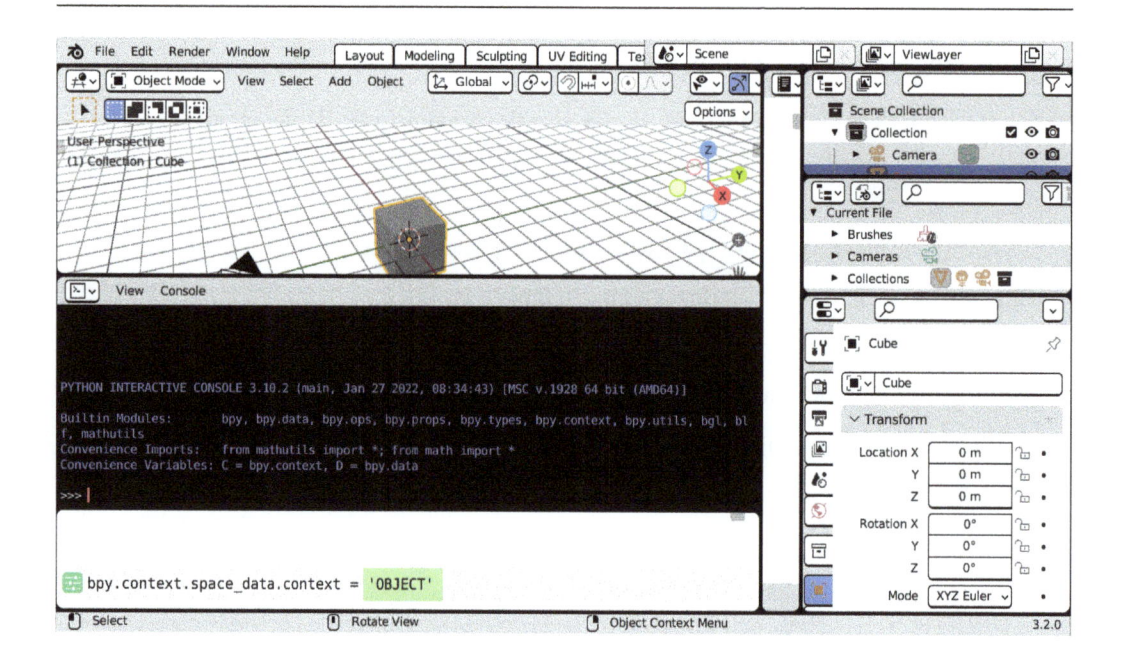

Figure 5.2: UI context name in the Info Log area, after Object Properties have been selected

Areas that do not follow the user context but still allow you to group their panels in tabs offer a *category* attribute instead.

Grouping in tabs using bl_category

Regions with arbitrary tabs will look at the `bl_category` variable to look up the correct label. If no value is given, the new panel will be added to the **Miscellaneous** tab. If no tab is named after that value, a new one will be created.

We are going to use the category attribute at the end of this chapter in conjunction with the `'VIEW_3D'` space type. We are going to start with the `'PROPERTIES'` editor, which does not have tabs.

Adding a panel to the Object Properties area

To add our panel to the **Object Properties** area, we must set its `bl_space_type` to `'PROPERTIES'` and `bl_context` to `'object'`.

`Panel` needs a `draw` function where the actual design takes place. At this stage, we can leave it blank:

```
import bpy
class OBJECT_PT_very_simple(bpy.types.Panel):
    """Creates a Panel in the object context of the
```

```
    properties space"""
    bl_label = "A Very Simple Panel"
    bl_idname = "VERYSIMPLE_PT_layout"
    bl_space_type = 'PROPERTIES'
    bl_region_type = 'WINDOW'
    bl_context = 'object'

    def draw(self, context):
        # add layout elements
        pass
```

Like most runtime functions of Blender classes, `draw` takes the `self` and `context` arguments. As per Python convention, `self` is the running instance of the class, while `context` contains information about the current state of the Blender scene.

Now, let's learn how the `draw` method is used to add elements to the panel's layout.

Drawing the panel's content

The `draw` function is executed continuously whenever a panel is used or updated. For this reason, it should not perform any computationally expensive task and just take care of the elements to display.

The elements of a panel are arranged according to its layout. Since the layout is a non-static member, it can be accessed inside the `draw` function using `self.layout`.

By default, all elements are stacked vertically in a `column`, but different types of layouts will provide a different way to arrange the widgets in a `row` or inside a `grid`.

Layouts can be also nested together for more complex arrangements. Let's learn how to access the main layout and add elements to it.

Working with layouts

All layout types derive from the `UILayout` class. They have methods to add child elements or sub-layouts. The full list of attributes and methods is reported in the API documentation at https://docs.blender.org/api/3.2/bpy.types.UILayout.html.

So, to display text, we can use the `UILayout.label` method. Here are the first few lines of code for our `draw` function:

```
    def draw(self, context):
        layout = self.layout
        layout.label(text="A Very Simple Label")
```

If we enable this add-on and reach for the **Object Properties** area, we will be able to see our new panel displaying some text:

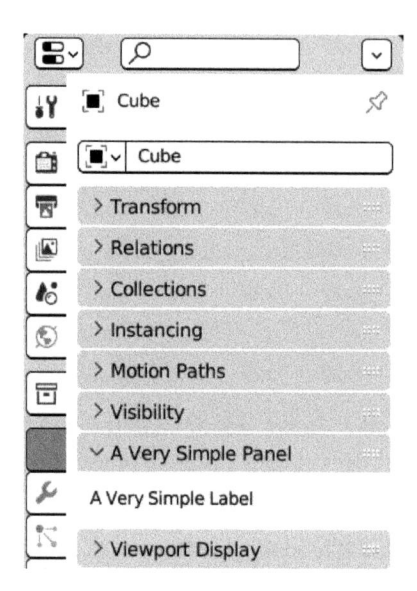

Figure 5.3: Our panel showing up in the Object Properties area

Displaying icons

Labels can display **icons** too. There are two types of icons:

- *Built-in* icons that come with Blender. The `label` method provides an `icon` keyword to use them.
- *External Images* can be used via the `icon_value` parameter.

Blender's native set of icons is used across the application. Each icon is identified with a keyword. For instance, `LIGHT` displays a lightbulb:

Figure 5.4: Blender icon for the LIGHT keyword

There are more than 800 built-in icons, so Blender includes an add-on for searching through them.

Looking for built-in icons with the Icon Viewer add-on

The **Icon Viewer** add-on comes with the Blender installation. It can be found in the **Development** category or by searching for `icon` in the **Search Bar** area:

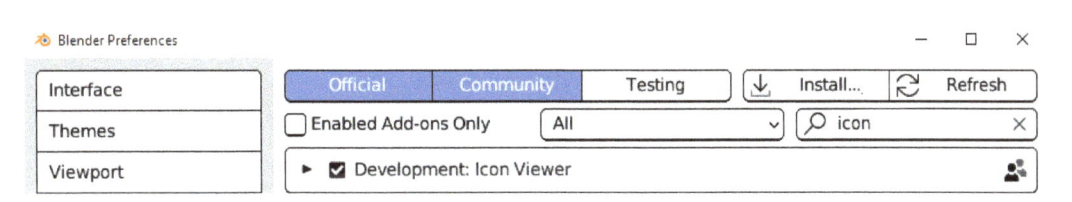

Figure 5.5: Activating the Icon Viewer add-on

Once the add-on has been enabled, the **Icon Viewer** button appears in the header of the **Python Console** header:

Figure 5.6: The Icon Viewer button in the Python Console header

Clicking this button opens a window that shows all native icons. We can select them by left-clicking:

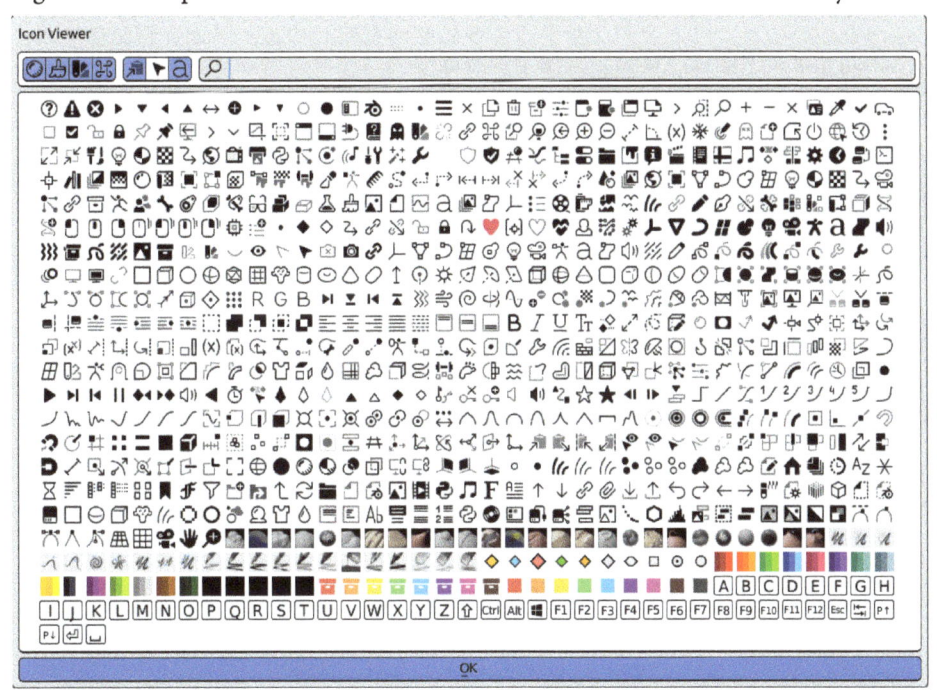

Figure 5.7: The Icon Viewer add-on window

Selecting an icon displays the associated keyword in the top-right corner. The keyword is also copied to the clipboard. For example, if we select the *question mark* icon, which is the first icon on the top left at the time of writing, the QUESTION keyword will be displayed, as shown in the following figure:

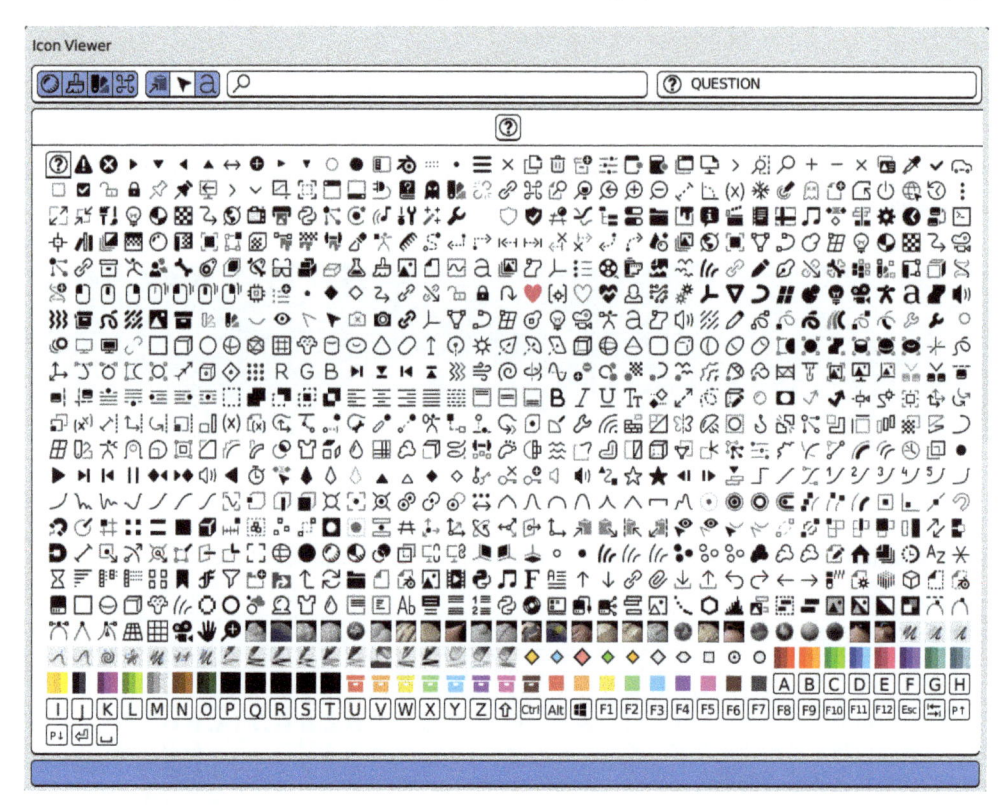

Figure 5.8: The QUESTION keyword is displayed in the top-right corner

We can type a search key in the filter field in the top middle, which is marked with a magnifier icon.

For instance, we can type "info" to show the 'INFO' icon only. Now that we know their keywords, we can display those icons in this way:

```
def draw(self, context):
    layout = self.layout
    layout.label(text="A Very Simple Label",
                 icon='INFO')
    layout.label(text="Isn't it great?",
                 icon='QUESTION')
```

Label icons are displayed before the text and are a good way to make it stand out:

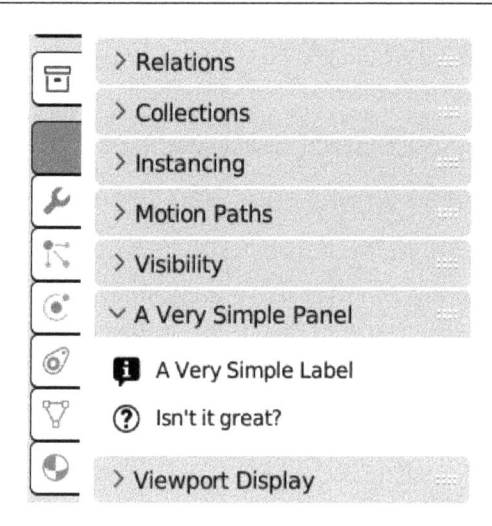

Figure 5.9: The 'INFO' and 'QUESTION' icons displayed in our custom panel

Built-in icons are always available and don't require external files to be distributed alongside our scripts. We can also use image files when needed. The `bpu.utils.previews` module can be used to load icons from image files and retrieve them using an index number.

Using custom image icons

In this example, we will add the icon of a smiling face to our panel. The image file is named `icon_smile_64.png` and can be found in this chapter's Git folder.

Alternatively, any image stored in `.png` format alongside the add-on's `.py` file will work. In that case, the image filename used in the script must be changed accordingly.

The resolution should not be too high: a 64-pixel-wide square picture is usually more than enough:

Figure 5.10: A 64x64 smiley face

To add custom icons to Blender, our script needs to import the following:

- The `os` Python module, to build the icon file path and make sure it will work on all platforms
- The `bpy.utils.previews` Blender module, to generate a Blender identifier for our icon

Here is what our `import` section will look like once we import them:

```
import bpy
from bpy.utils import previews
import os
```

Our icons must be accessible everywhere in the script. We can use a global variable, a static member, or a singleton for storage. In this example, we are using a global variable as it is the simpler option.

So, right after the `import` section, we must add the following lines:

```
# global variable for icon storage
custom_icons = None
```

We initialize the variable as None since we can load and clear it inside the `register/unregister` function. We can also add specific functions for that. This way, the code will be easier to follow:

```
def load_custom_icons():
    """Load icon from the add-on folder"""
    Addon_path = os.path.dirname(__file__)
    img_file = os.path.join(addon_path,
                "icon_smile_64.png")
    global custom_icons
    custom_icons = previews.new()
    custom_icons.load("smile_face",img_file, 'IMAGE')
```

Then, we need a function that clears `custom_icons` when the add-on is unregistered:

```
def remove_custom_icons():
    """Clear Icons loaded from file"""
    global custom_icons
    bpy.utils.previews.remove(custom_icons)
```

These functions are then invoked in the registration section:

```
def register():
    load_custom_icons()
    bpy.utils.register_class(VerySimplePanel)
def unregister():
    bpy.utils.unregister_class(VerySimplePanel)
    clear_custom_icons()
```

Once we read the image file, we used `"smile_face"` as the first argument of `custom_icons.load()`, so that is the keyword that will be used for retrieving its identifier. Here's the code to use in a label:

```
layout.label(text="Smile", icon_value=custom_icons['smile_face'].icon_id)
```

If we look up and execute **Reload Scripts** from the *F3* search panel, we will see our custom icon in the panel:

Figure 5.11: Smiley icon loaded from our file and displayed in our panel

For now, we have used the default column layout. We will learn how to use a different arrangement in the next section.

> **Where have my widgets gone?**
>
> Errors in the interface code fail "silently"; that is, Blender doesn't complain visibly and instead just stops drawing the buggy panel.
>
> This prevents the UI from crashing but makes our code more difficult to debug; we will only notice that some of our widgets are not displayed.
>
> When that happens, the best thing to do is check the console output or the **Info Log** area in the **Scripting** workspace. It will contain *traceback* information about which line of code is failing.

Using layouts in our panels

If we are not happy with the default stacking of the global layout, we can add a layout type of our choice to it and use that instead, and we'll get a different arrangement.

For instance, we can put two labels on the same line using a `row`. Also, even if we are happy with stacking our elements one under the other, it is good practice to create a `column` sub-layout anyway. This practice has at least two advantages:

- We preserve the panel's look, even if the default arrangement should change
- We do not pollute the original layout

Let's see how we can change the way our widgets are stacked.

Arranging in columns and rows

We can nest more layout types together inside our `draw` function. For instance, we can place the last two labels from the previous example side by side rather than arrange them vertically. To do that, we must do two things:

1. First, we must create a `column` and add the first label to it.

110   Designing Graphical Interfaces

2. Then, we must create a `row`. The two labels we will add to it will be next to each other:

```
def draw(self, context):
    col = self.layout.column()
    col.label(text="A Very Simple Label",
              icon='INFO')
    row = col.row()
    row.label(text="Isn't it great?",
              icon='QUESTION')
    icon_id = custom_icons["smile_face"].icon_id
    row.label(text="Smile", icon_value=icon_id)
```

Now, our panel consists of only two lines:

Figure 5.12: The second line consists of two labels

Adding frames with box layouts

Other types of sub-layouts provide additional effects. For instance, a box layout is like a column, but it is framed in a smoothed rectangle. Let's say we want to display some information from the add-on's `bl_info`. Here, we can add these lines to the `draw` function:

```
box = col.box()
row = box.row()
row.label(text="version:")
row.label(text=str(bl_info['version']))
```

After we call **Reload Scripts**, we will see a frame around that information:

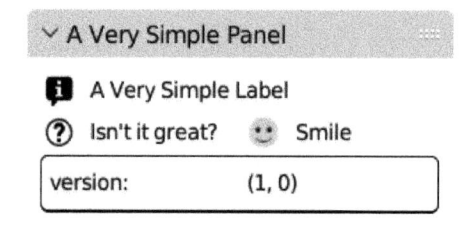

Figure 5.13: A box layout surrounds the version information

We have put a caption of "version" and some information stating bl_info['version'] in a row. That gives the same space to each element. To have more control over how much space is taken by the first element, we can use a split layout.

Using composite layouts

Some layouts consist of more rows or columns. A split layout distributes the available space across different columns, while a grid layout creates rows and columns automatically.

We are going to use them to build a more sophisticated panel.

Arranging in splits

We can use the split method to create a layout whose columns' width can be tweaked. The factor argument is optional and accepts values between 0.0 and 1.0. Leaving it to the default value of 0.0 computes the optimal width automatically; otherwise, it sets the percentage occupied by the first column.

In this example, we'll use a factor of 0.33 to give less space to the first column. Here, we will also create two columns so that we can fill them later and arrange more elements like we would in a table.

The following snippet displays two entries per line. The first column takes about one-third of the space:

```
# ...
box = col.box()
split = box.split(factor=0.33)
left_col = split.column()
left_col.label(text="author:")
left_col.label(text="version:")
right_col = split.column()
right_col.label(text=str(bl_info['author']))
right_col.label(text=str(bl_info['version']))
```

Upon reloading the scripts, we will see our captions taking up one-third of the space, leaving the rest to the relevant information:

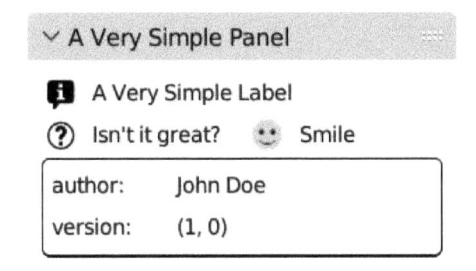

Figure 5.14: Author and version information taking one-third of the space

Designing Graphical Interfaces

We can take advantage of dictionary methods to add more information from `bl_info`. This way, we can populate our `split` layout using a `for` loop.

Populating with dictionaries

Since we have created the columns already, we can add more entries using a loop. This is ideal for displaying the entries in a dictionary.

Let's say that we want to show all the add-on information. In that case, we can iterate all the keyword/value pairs using the `items()` method:

```
# …
box = col.box()
split = box.split(factor=0.3)
left_col = split.column()
right_col = split.column()
for k, v in bl_info.items():
    if not v:
        # ignore empty entries
        continue
    left_col.label(text=k)
    right_col.label(text=str(v))
```

Here, we skip unset values of `bl_info` using `continue` when v is empty. In these few lines, we can display all the available add-on information:

Figure 5.15: A box layout displaying bl_info

If we are happy with leaving the column width to Blender, we can use a grid layout instead.

Arranging grids

A `grid_flow` layout is very convenient for arranging our elements into tables as it creates rows and columns automatically. For instance, we can display the object names from the scene on two columns by using `grid_flow(columns=2)` and adding labels to a `for` loop:

```
# ...
col.label(text="Scene Objects:")
grid = col.grid_flow(columns=2)
for ob in context.scene.objects:
    grid.label(text=ob.name)
```

This code will display the names of the objects in the current scene, arranged in a two-column grid:

Figure 5.16: Object names displayed in a grid

With that, we have seen that labels can display icons too. This means we can display an icon of the object's type beside each name, just like the outliner does.

Building icon keywords

A quick search in the **Icon Viewer** area confirms that the identifying string of object type icons, such as OUTLINER_OB_MESH and OUTLINER_OB_CURVE, follow this pattern:

```
OUTLINER_OB_[OBJECT_TYPE]
```

This is depicted in the following figure:

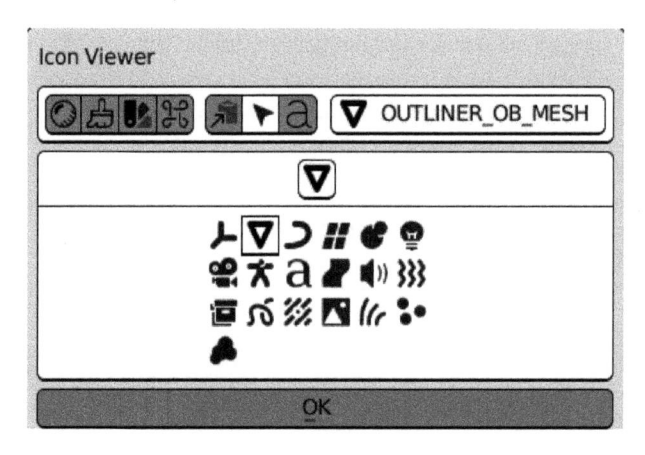

Figure 5.17: Object type icons as displayed in the Icon Viewer area

With that in mind, we can build those keywords using *string formatting*, a feature of Python 3 that makes combining strings and variables easier. To inform Python that we are using formatting, we must put an f character before the quote or apostrophe delimiters, then surround our variables with curly brackets inside the string. Here is an example:

```
>>> h = "Hello"
>>> print(f"{h}, World!")
Hello, World!
```

With that in mind, we get the string for the object type – for example, 'MESH', 'CURVE', or 'ARMATURE' – using the ob.type attribute, then build the icon keyword using the following line:

```
f'OUTLINER_OB_{ob.type}'
```

This result can be fed to the icon parameter inside our loop:

```
        col.label(text="Scene Objects:")
        grid = col.grid_flow(columns=2)
        for ob in context.scene.objects:
            grid.label(text=ob.name,
                       icon=f'OUTLINER_OB_{ob.type}')
```

We can reload the scripts and see how icons are displayed before names:

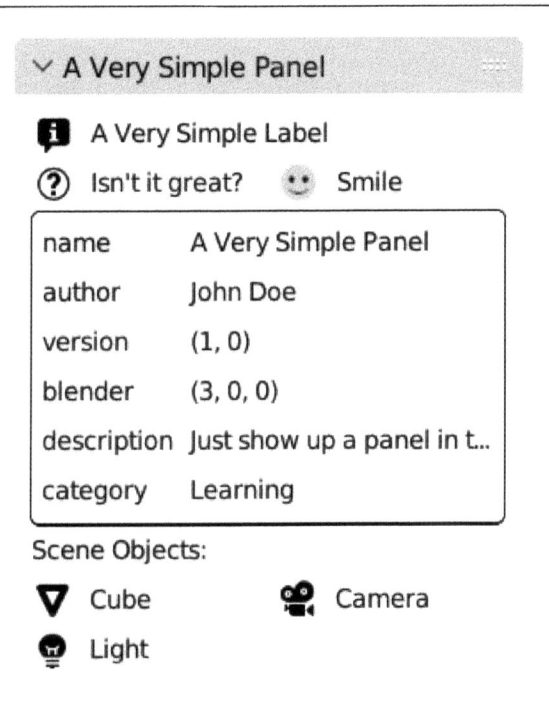

Figure 5.18: A custom panel listing the scene objects and their icons

We don't want this list to take up too much space on large scenes, so we will break the loop after a certain number of objects. For instance, we can stop listing objects and display an ellipsis after the fourth listed object.

Leaving the ellipsis on the last line implies filling the grid row by row. To do that, we must set the `row_major` argument to `True` for our `grid_flow`:

```
col.label(text="Scene Objects:")
grid = col.grid_flow(columns=2, row_major=True)
for i, ob in enumerate(context.scene.objects):
    if i > 3:   # stop after the third object
        grid.label(text"..")
        break
    grid.label(text=ob.name,
               icon=f'OUTLINER_OB_{ob.type}')
```

> **A (bad) kind of magic**
>
> Arbitrary digits appearing in the middle of the code, such as those in `i > 3`, are called **magic numbers**, and using them is considered bad practice as it makes it very difficult to find and change those values at a later stage.
>
> A better solution is to make those numbers members of the class and access them later.

Storing 3 as a static member makes it easier to display the number of remaining objects. String formatting also works with numeric variables, so we can compute how many objects are left and use the result in curly brackets:

```python
class OBJECT_PT_very_simple(bpy.types.Panel):
    #...
    bl_context = 'object'
    max_objects = 3

    def draw(self, context):
        # ...
        for i, ob in enumerate(context.scene.objects):
            if i > self.max_objects:
                objects_left = len(context.scene.objects)
                objects_left -= self.max_objects
                txt = f"... (more {objects_left} objects"
                grid.label(text=txt)
                break
```

Since `max_objects` is an attribute of the class, it can be changed via Python.

Blender considers these add-ons to be Python modules, so it is possible to execute these lines in the **Python Console** or **Text Editor** area:

```python
import very_simple_panel
very_simple_panel.OBJECT_PT_very_simple.max_objects = 10
```

The downside of this trick is that every reload of the add-on resets that value. A better way to change the settings in our add-on, which is by using `bpy.types.Preferences`, will be discussed in *Chapter 6*:

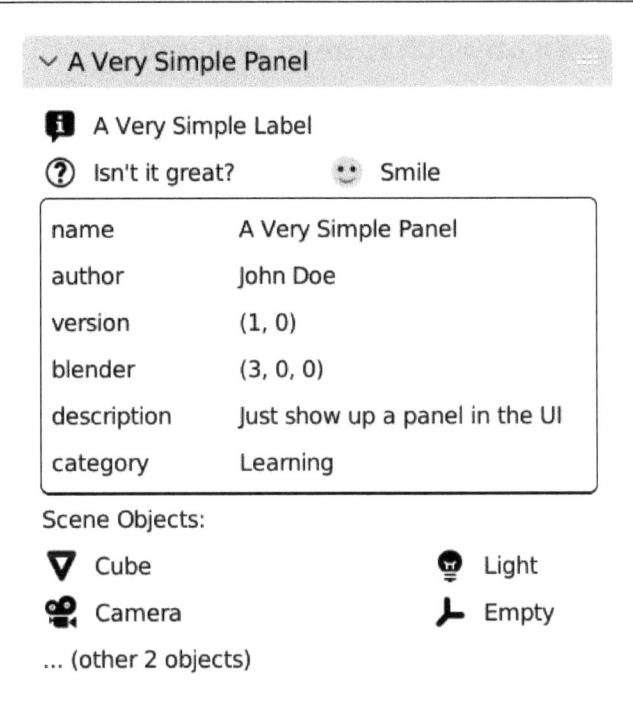

Figure 5.19: Changing the limit displays more than three objects

Using icons and informative text adds to the visual feedback of our UI. In the next section, we'll take advantage of the colors from layout states to convey status information.

Providing color feedback

Our object list will be much more useful if we can highlight which objects are selected and which are active. For instance, to reflect the selection status of an object in the color of its name, our script must perform two actions:

1. Check whether an object is selected.
2. If it's selected or active, display its name in a different color.

Let's learn how to perform these tasks using Blender's API.

Checking whether an object has been selected

We can get the selection status of an object using its `select_get()` method. For instance, if the `'Cube'` object is selected, its `selected_get` method will return `True`:

```
>>> import bpy
>>> bpy.data.objects['Cube'].select_get()
True
```

We already know from *Chapter 2*, that, unlike the selection status, `active` is not a flag of the object, so how we retrieve this information is a bit different.

Checking whether an object is active

To check whether an object is active, we can test whether it matches the one stored in `context.object`. Here's what happens when `'Cube'` is the active object:

```
>>> import bpy
>>> bpy.data.objects['Cube'] == bpy.context.object
True
```

Now that we know how to retrieve the activity status of an object, let's look at ways we can alter the color of its labels.

Drawing layouts in red or gray

Sometimes, painting text with a different color is useful to make an entry stand out. Blender doesn't allow us to set the color of a piece of text explicitly, but we can take advantage of two specific attributes that alter the way a UI layout is displayed:

- `UILayout.enabled = False` is meant to display an element without letting the user interact with it. This is very useful if we want to make the user aware that, even if an operation is not possible now, the interface for executing it is there to be found.
- `UILayout.alert = True` is useful for warning the user about something wrong, or potentially wrong.

Those are very specific purposes, but we can take advantage of how they affect the displayed color:

- UI layouts whose `enabled` attribute equals `False` are *gray*
- UI layouts whose `alert` attribute equals `True` are *red*

So, we can use that to change the color of an entire layout. Labels are not layouts, and the `label()` method returns a None type. Since we cannot set those attributes directly on the text labels, we need to create a new layout for each entry of the grid and use that when we create our text:

```
# ...
for i, ob in enumerate(context.scene.objects):
    # layout item to set entry color
    item_layout = grid.column()
    item_layout.label(text=ob.name,
                      icon=f'OUTLINER_OB_{ob.type}')
```

We can set `item_layout.enabled` to True for selected objects and False for the unselected ones with this line:

```
item_layout.enabled = ob.select_get()
```

Likewise, we can set `item_layout.alert` by assigning the result of the equality test (==) directly:

```
item_layout.alert = ob == context.object
```

As we can see, the list now provides information about which objects are active and/or selected:

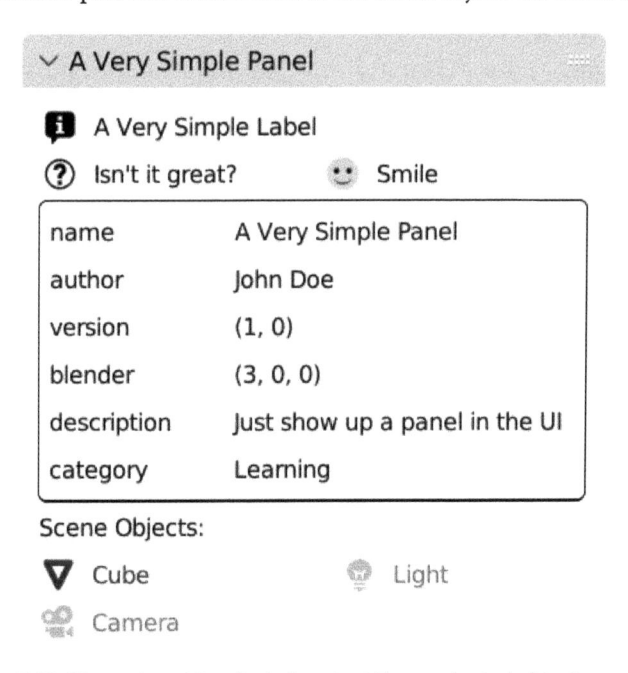

Figure 5.20: The active object is dark red, while unselected objects are gray

We can also add buttons to perform some operations, as we'll see in the next section.

Displaying buttons

Intuitively, pushing a button performs a transformative action. Since buttons take up space, the default interface displays only the more generic operations. When we write custom interfaces, we can add more buttons based on our specific needs. This is made easier by how Blender translates operators into buttons. In this section, we'll learn how buttons and operators are equivalent when it comes to the graphical interface.

Using the operator method

We can use the `UILayout.operator` method to display a button. In Blender, a button executes an operator. This operator is found through its identifier – that is, the `bl_idname` attribute, which we encountered in *Chapter 3* – and every operator must have it.

For instance, to add a button that deletes the selected objects, we must provide the identifier of the **Delete** operator.

If we use the **Delete** action from the **Object** menu or the *X* key and look into the **Scripting** workspace, we will find this new line in the **Info Log** area:

```
bpy.ops.object.delete(use_global=False)
```

The part before the parentheses, `bpy.ops.object.delete`, is the operator class. We must be careful as we must not use the class itself as the argument of the operator, but the identifier of that class. We can get the identifier using the `idname()` method:

```
>>> bpy.ops.object.delete.idname()
'OBJECT_OT_delete'
```

Using the `'OBJECT_OT_delete'` string as the argument of `operator()` will create a **Delete** button.

> **ID please**
>
> Using the `operator` class instead of an operator's identifier with `operator` causes `TypeError`: the operator and all the elements that follow it will not be displayed.
>
> We can either use the `idname()` function or the identifier string directly. The function is preferred as it guarantees compatibility in case of future changes.

To display a **Delete** button, we must add the following line to our `draw` function:

```
col.operator(bpy.ops.object.delete.idname())
```

Here's what we'll see:

Figure 5.21: The Delete button has been added to the panel

Pressing the **Delete** button deletes the selected object. It is equivalent to invoking **Object | Delete** from the menu.

Setting the operator's text and visibility

We can customize the button text or toggle the button's display. For instance, we can hide **Delete** if there are no selected objects. Like most information about the status, selected objects can be accessed from `context`:

```
num_selected = len(context.selected_objects)
```

We can reflect this information in the button label. The following snippet changes the button's text according to the number of objects that have been selected. It also adds an "s" to the word "object" at the end so that it can use the plural form when needed:

```
if num_selected > 0:
    op_txt = f"Delete {num_selected} object"
    if num_selected > 1:
        op_txt += "s"   # add plural 's'
    col.operator(bpy.ops.object.delete.idname(),
                 text=op_txt)
```

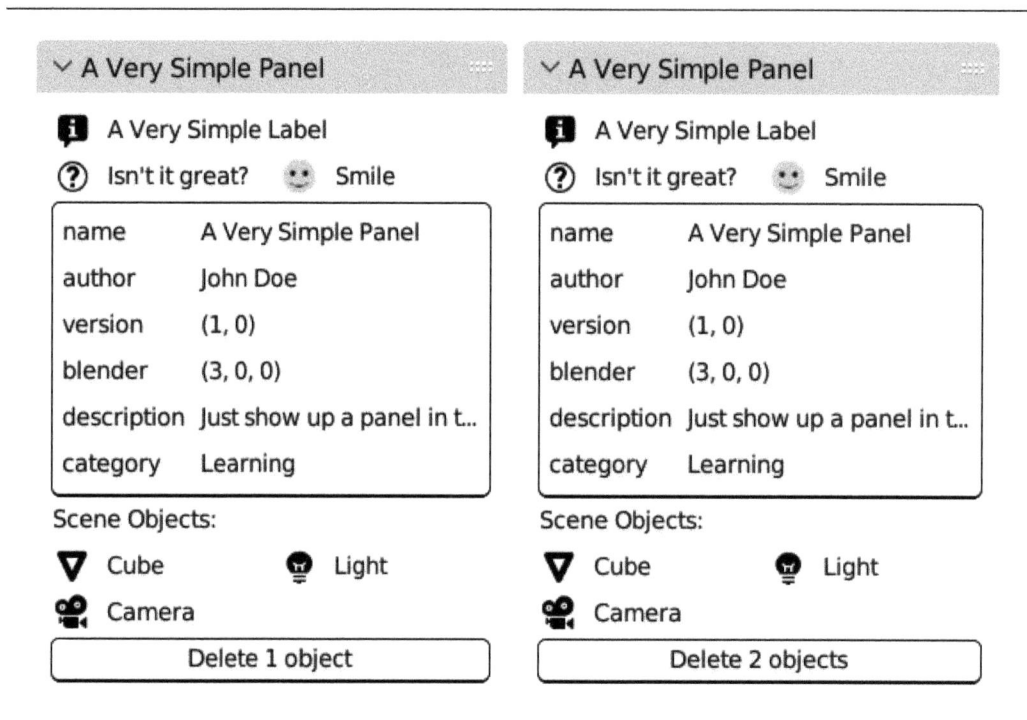

Figure 5.22: The text of the button changes according to the selection

> **Nothing to hide (usually)**
>
> It is often said that hiding pieces of the UI is generally wrong as it leaves the user with no knowledge of where a feature can be found once the conditions have been met. This is generally a valid point, even though for didactical purposes, a disappearing button was used in the preceding example.
>
> If we want to abide by the "no-hiding" rule, we can add an `else` statement containing a disabled layout:
>
> ```
> if (num_selected > 0):
>     # ...
> else:
>     to_disable = col.column()
>     to_disable.enabled = False
>     to_disable.operator(
>                 bpy.ops.object.delete.idname(),
>                 text="Delete Selected"
>                 )
> ```
>
> When coding, rules can be broken but not ignored!

Overriding an operator's settings

The `delete` operator prompts a confirm dialog before deleting an object. This is its default behavior, and it can be overridden:

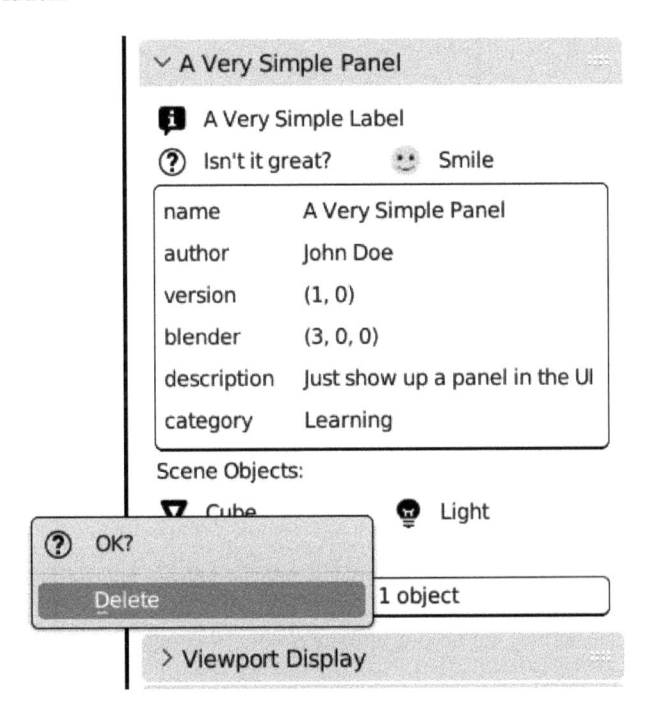

Figure 5.23: Clicking Delete opens a confirmation menu

This is reflected in the documented docstring. If we type the operator's address and press *Tab*, the autocomplete will display two optional arguments called `use_global` and `confirm`:

```
>>> bpy.ops.object.delete(
delete()
bpy.ops.object.delete(use_global=False, confirm=True)
Delete selected objects
>>> bpy.ops.object.delete(
```

You can learn more about this by looking at the API documentation. Right-clicking on the **Delete** button will display a menu containing a direct link:

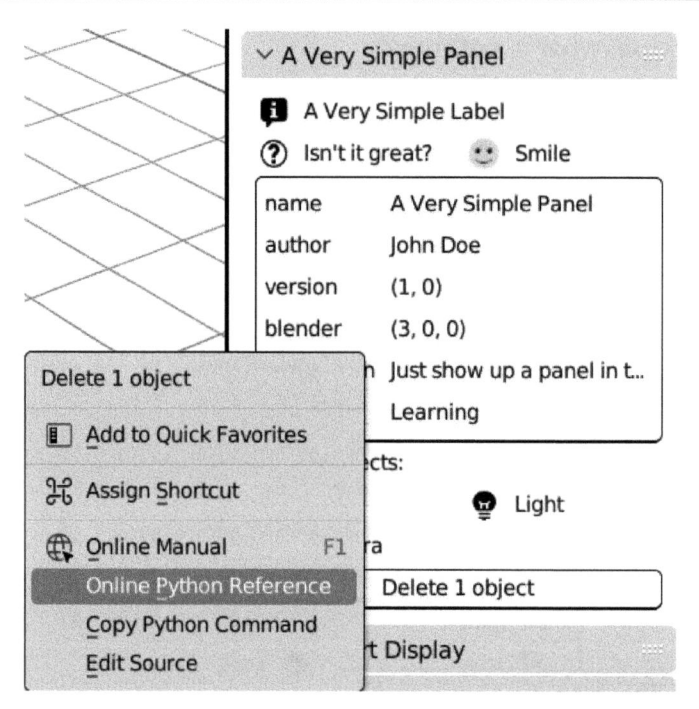

Figure 5.24: The right-click menu of our Delete button can open the online documentation

The documentation describes these Boolean arguments:

- `use_global` (Boolean, optional): Delete globally or remove the object from all scenes
- `confirm` (Boolean, optional): Confirm or prompt for confirmation

According to the documentation, setting `use_global` to `True` would remove the selected objects from all the currently opened scenes. We do not want that, so we are not changing the default value.

The `confirm` parameter, on the other hand, is `True` by default. We need to change that to `False`, and since the button takes care of invoking the operator, we need to change that in the button's properties.

Setting operator properties

The `operator` function returns an `OperatorProperties` object, which is a class containing the attributes that can be set. Typically, we use the following code:

```
col.operator(bpy.ops.object.delete.idname(),
             text=op_txt)
```

Instead, we will store the properties returned by `operator` in the `props` variable so that we can change them later:

```
props = col.operator(bpy.ops.object.delete.idname(),
        text=op_txt)
props.confirm = False
```

This button triggers the `delete` operator, which is native to Blender. Since the interface considers Python and built-in operators equivalent, we can display buttons for our operators too.

Adding buttons for our functions

We will add a button for displacing each of the selected objects randomly. This can be done to give a more "natural" look to our scene. To do that, we must write a new operator. Blender's operators transform all the selected objects in the same way. First, we must import the `random` module at the beginning of our script:

```
import bpy
from bpy.utils import previews
import os
import random
```

We proceed with our location function. It can be part of the operator class, but we can also write a function that stands on. The operator will call it inside its `execute` method. This function's arguments are as follows:

- The objects to dislocate
- The max number of units to add or subtract from each object's location
- Which axis should be affected

We will feed the amount of displacement to the `randint` function, which will return a random integer number between a `min` and `max` range. We'll do that for each of the three axes (*X*, *Y*, and *Z*), so long as their entries in `do_axis` are `True`. The amount and `do_axis` arguments are optional. We set their default values to `1` and `True, True, True` in the function's declaration:

```
def add_random_location(objects, amount=1,
                    do_axis=(True, True, True)):
    """Add units to the locations of given objects"""
    for ob in objects:
        for i in range(3):
            if do_axis[i]:
                loc = ob.location
                loc[i] += random.randint(-amount, amount)
```

Now, we need an operator to display in the interface. We will add properties for the `amount` and `do_axis` function arguments. To an operator, an integer and a tuple of Booleans are `IntProperty` and `BoolVectorProperty`, respectively:

```
class TRANSFORM_OT_random_location(bpy.types.Operator):
    """Add units to the locations of selected objects"""
    bl_idname = "transform.add_random_location"
    bl_label = "Add random Location"
    amount: bpy.props.IntProperty(name="Amount",
                                  default=1)
    axis: bpy.props.BoolVectorProperty(
                        name="Displace Axis",
                        default=(True, True, True)
                        )
```

The operator methods are straightforward; `poll` only makes sure that there are objects selected, while `execute` runs `add_random_location`:

```
    @classmethod
    def poll(cls, context):
        return context.selected_objects
    def execute(self, context):
        add_random_location(context.selected_objects,
                            self.amount,
                            self.axis)
        return {'FINISHED'}
```

Adding this operator to the layout displays a new button. As stated earlier, native and scripted operators are the same to the interfacee. In both cases, it looks for the operator's identifier when it comes to invoking it. Scripted operators offer one small advantage, though: we can refer to their `bl_idname` attribute directly since their classes and our graphical interface belong to the same module or package.

Here's our line for displaying the **Add random Location** button:

```
    col.operator(
            TRANSFORM_OT_random_location.bl_idname
            )
```

And of course, we mustn't neglect class registration and removal. Here's the line we should add to `register()`:

```
    bpy.utils.register_class(
                    TRANSFORM_OT_random_location
                    )
```

Likewise, the add-on's `unregister()` function should contain the following:

```
bpy.utils.unregister_class(
                    TRANSFORM_OT_random_location
                    )
```

After invoking **Reload Scripts**, a new button will appear:

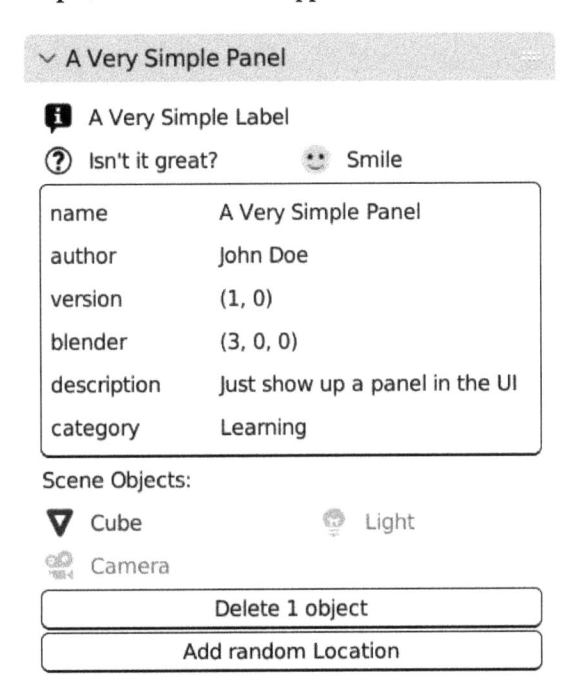

Figure 5.25: Our panel now displays two buttons

Pressing this button should add random variation to the positions of selected objects since the operator properties do not pop up at execution. Even adding the `bl_options = {'REGISTER', 'UNDO'}` operator property, which we learned about in the *Writing the Elevator add-on* section in *Chapter 4*, would not change that: operator properties must be displayed explicitly when they are not run from the **3D Viewport** area.

Displaying the operator properties

Besides `poll` and `execute`, Blender operators involve another method, named `invoke`. The `invoke` method is run internally right before `execute`. Usually, we don't need to define it, but in this case, we use it to tell Blender that we want to display and edit the operator properties – that is, our function arguments.

Besides `self` and `context`, `invoke` takes `event` as an argument. It contains information about what triggered the operator, but we don't need that now. We only tell `window_manager` to display the properties dialog. So, we must add a few lines of code after the `poll` method:

```
@classmethod
def poll(cls, context):
    return context.selected_objects
def invoke(self, context, event):
    wm = context.window_manager
    return wm.invoke_props_dialog(self)
```

Reloading the scripts and pressing the **Add random Location** button now allows us to change the **Amount** and Displace **Axis** properties given to the `add_random_location` function:

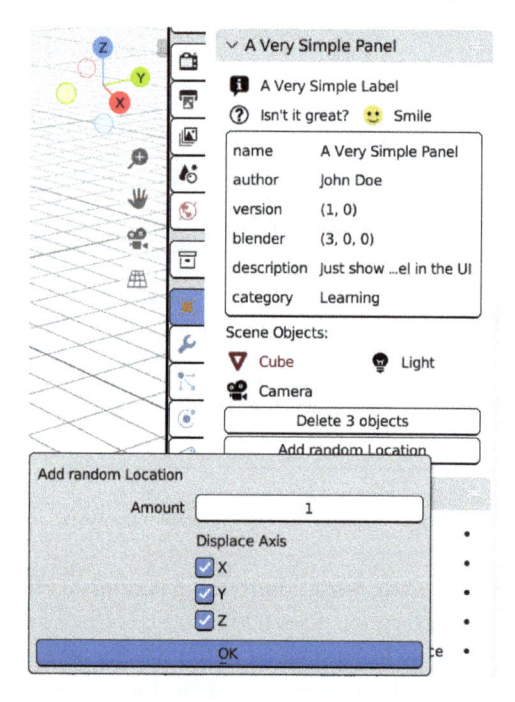

Figure 5.26: Using operator properties as function arguments

With that, our object panel is finished. As a bonus, next, we will learn how to move it to a different part of the UI.

Using different regions

Usually, panels can be moved freely to another part of the interface. There are a few exceptions where repositioning a panel would not make much sense. For instance, a tool that helps select the controls of a character would be of little help in the Video Editor, and its `poll()` method might be looking for attributes, such as animation bones, outside of the animation's `context`.

Outside of those cases, changing the `bl_*` attributes of a `Panel` class is enough to move our panel to a different place. Please refer to the *panel attributes* that we looked at in the *Creating a simple panel* section of this chapter.

So, to display our panel in the **3D Viewport** area, we can change the values of `bl_space_type` and `bl_region_type` as follows:

```
bl_space_type = 'VIEW_3D'
bl_region_type = 'UI'
```

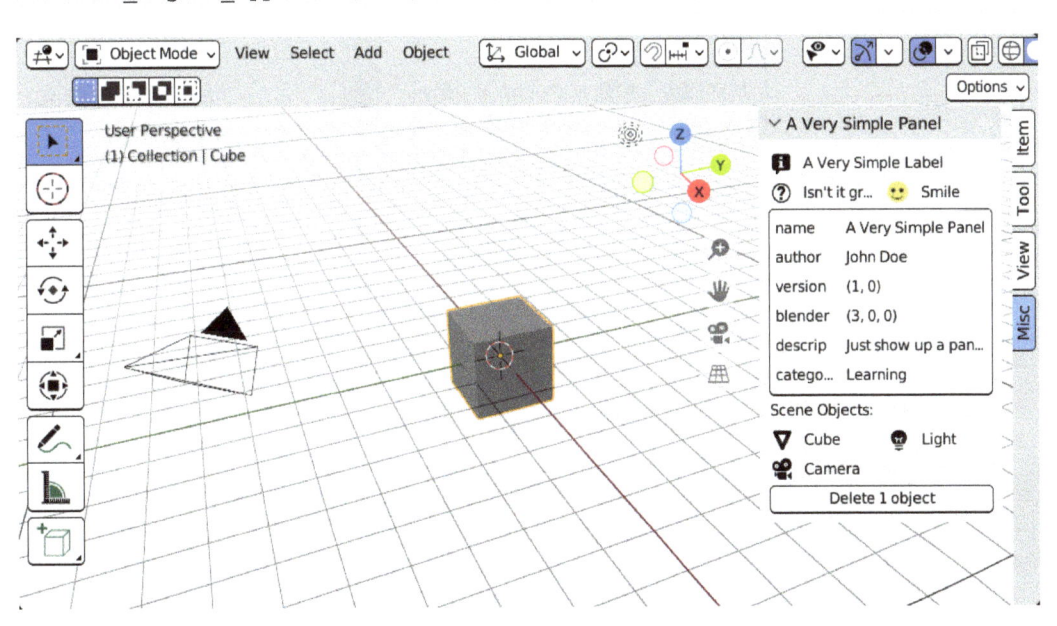

Figure 5.27: Our panel has been moved to the 3D Viewport area

By default, the **Misc** tab is used, but the `bl_category` attribute can be used to specify new or existing tabs:

```
class VerySimplePanel(bpy.types.Panel):
    """Creates a Panel in the viewport properties"""
    bl_label = "A Very Simple Panel"
    bl_idname = "VERYSIMPLE_PT_layout"
    bl_space_type = 'VIEW_3D'
```

```
    bl_region_type = 'UI'
    bl_category = "Our Panel"
```

If a Blender add-on contains more panels, putting them under the same tab is a good way to keep the interface neat:

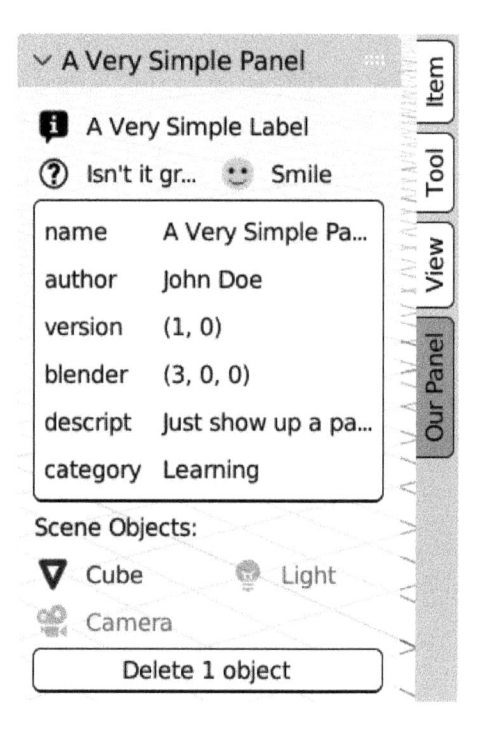

Figure 5.28: A Viewport tab created from the bl_category attribute

We have reached the end of our interface overview. There will be more UI insights in the next few chapters when we introduce lists and thumbnails, but for now, we have built a solid understanding of how to use layouts in Blender.

Summary

In this chapter, we learned how to create and populate a custom `UIPanel` via Python and how to integrate that into our add-on. That gave us insight into how the Blender interface works in general and which steps we must take to add our widgets to it.

We also nested layouts together for a more complex appearance and displayed both native and external icons.

Lastly, we learned how to change our panel's look according to the context without too much increase in complexity, as well as how to add functions to the UI.

This closes the first part of this book, where we gained an overall understanding of how Blender and Python work together and what Python scripts can do.

The add-on we have written relies on an external file called `icon_smile_64.png`. If we were to distribute it to the public, we would have to package it as a ZIP file. This is something we are going to do in *Chapter 6*, which marks the beginning of *Part 2, Interactive Tools and Animation*.

Questions

1. Is it possible for an area of the screen to host more than one editor?
2. Do all the editors consist of the same regions?
3. How do we set the editor, region, and context to which a panel belongs?
4. Must we always set a panel's category?
5. Are the elements of a panel static or can they change dynamically?
6. Can we alter the color of a piece of text?
7. How do we display buttons?

Part 2: Interactive Tools and Animation

This part exposes modular, structured add-ons that interact with the animation system. It also introduces modal tools that capture the user input and the different steps of an operator's execution.

This section comprises the following chapters:

- *Chapter 6, Structuring Our Code and Add-Ons*
- *Chapter 7, The Animation System*
- *Chapter 8, Animation Modifiers*
- *Chapter 9, Animation Drivers*
- *Chapter 10, Advanced and Modal Operators*

6
Structuring Our Code and Add-Ons

The add-ons we have created so far consist of single Python files. That's ok, but to deal with complexity, we can split our code into related modules contained in the same directory.

Writing modules that interact with each other rather than a single huge file makes design and maintenance easier, allowing us to shift our focus to single aspects of our task.

The presence of non-code files, such as images and other media, can be another reason for adopting a folder structure. This is because sharing one folder is more practical than handling the Python script and the data separately.

In this chapter, you will learn how to code across separate modules of a package and blend everything using the import system. The packaged add-on that we are going to create will be easier to distribute, read, and maintain, and it will be possible to grasp the functionality of its different parts by just looking at the filenames.

This chapter will cover the following topics:

- Creating a Python package
- Loading and refreshing code and assets
- Reading environment variables in your scripts
- Using the Preferences system

Technical requirements

We will use Blender and Visual Studio Code in this chapter. The examples created in this chapter can be found at `https://github.com/PacktPublishing/Python-Scripting-in-Blender/tree/main/ch6`.

Optionally, on Windows, we can use 7-Zip to create compressed archives. 7-Zip is a free application that can be downloaded from `https://www.7zip.org`.

Folders, packages, and add-ons

We know that an add-on consists of Python code accompanied by information for the Blender plugin system. While single-file Python scripts are called modules, a folder of scripts is called a package.

Writing an add-on folder implies that we will store the Blender information at the package level, so we will create a directory and create the package information first.

Creating a package folder and the init file

Let's create a folder for *this chapter* in our Python project. Then, in the **Blender Preferences** area, set the `ch6` folder as our **Scripts Folder** and restart Blender. To make a package, we need to create a new folder rather than a new file. We can do that using the file manager or, like in the following steps, use the files bar of our programmer editor:

1. Select `PythonScriptingBlender/ch6/addons`.
2. Create a new folder by clicking the **New Folder** icon:

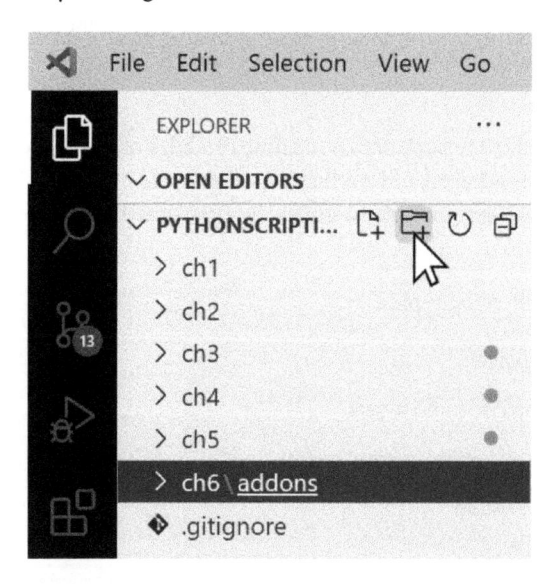

Figure 6.1: Creating folders in Visual Studio Code

3. Name the new folder `structured_addon`.

A Python package contains a file named __init__.py. This is the **entry point** of the folder and Python runs it automatically when it imports a package. To create it, follow these steps:

1. Select the .../ch6/addons/structured_addon folder.
2. Create a new file by clicking on the **New File** icon:

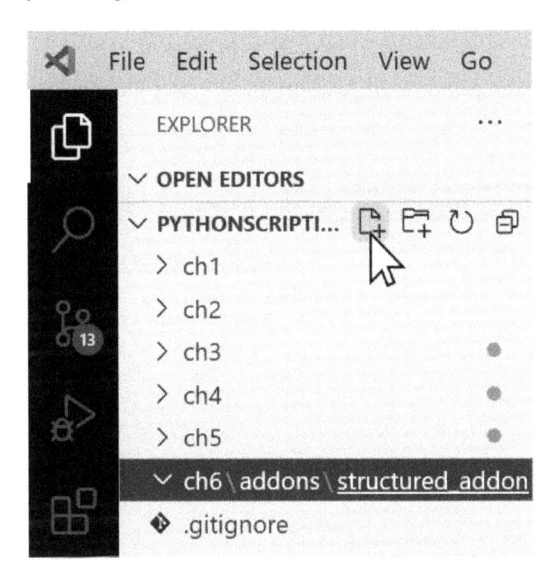

Figure 6.2: Creating a new file in Visual Studio Code

3. Name the new file __init__.py.
4. Open the file by double-clicking it.

When Blender searches for installed add-ons, it will look for the bl_info dictionary inside the __init__.py files of this folder. We will fill in this information in the usual way.

Writing the init file

This bl_info dictionary contains the usual attributes for add-on discovery:

```
bl_info = {
    "name": "A Structured Add-on",
    "author": "John Doe",
    "version": (1, 0),
    "blender": (3, 2, 0),
    "description": "Add-on consisting of multiple files",
    "category": "Learning",
}
```

Providing a `register()` and an `unregister()` function will allow us to enable and disable the add-on:

```
def register():
    pass
def unregister():
    pass
```

Now, we should be able to see our **Structured Add-on** if we restart Blender or refresh the add-ons list:

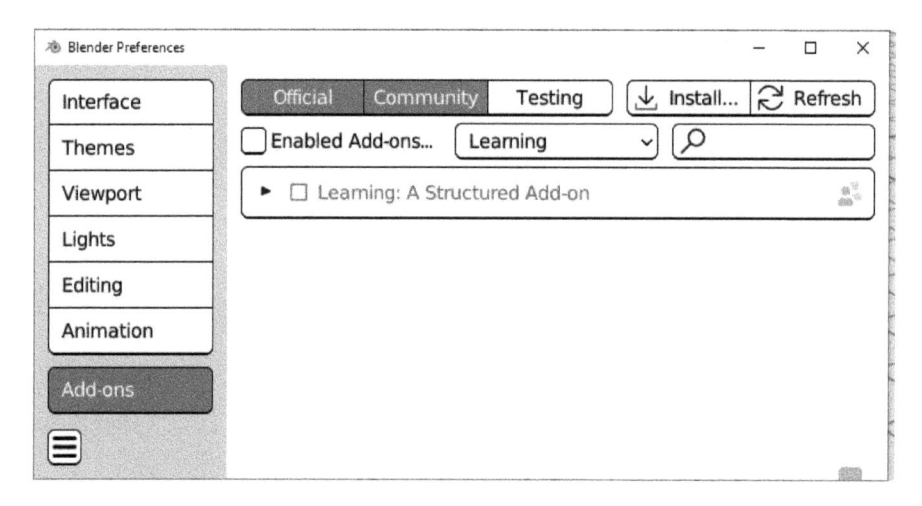

Figure 6.3: Structured Add-on listed in the "Learning" category

We are going to make it useful by adding some content using different `.py` files.

Guidelines for separating modules

There is a trade-off between partitioning and centralizing the code: excessively atomized code risks being unclear and hard to maintain. So, even if there are no fixed rules about splitting a program, there are general criteria for writing modular code:

- Non-Python files such as *media* (images, sounds, and so on) have their subfolders according to their types
- *Generic code* used by unrelated classes can be considered a utility module and used like a library
- *Specific code* relevant to a particular functionality should be a specific module
- *UI* classes, such as panels and menus, can be separated by non-UI code
- *Operators* can be separated from non-operator code and split per category

- *Import* statements relevant to only a part of a script might imply that entire sections could go to another file, thus reducing the number of imported libraries in one file

We will put these concepts into practice and see how, starting with an example we are familiar with, the package architecture makes our code clearer and more effective:

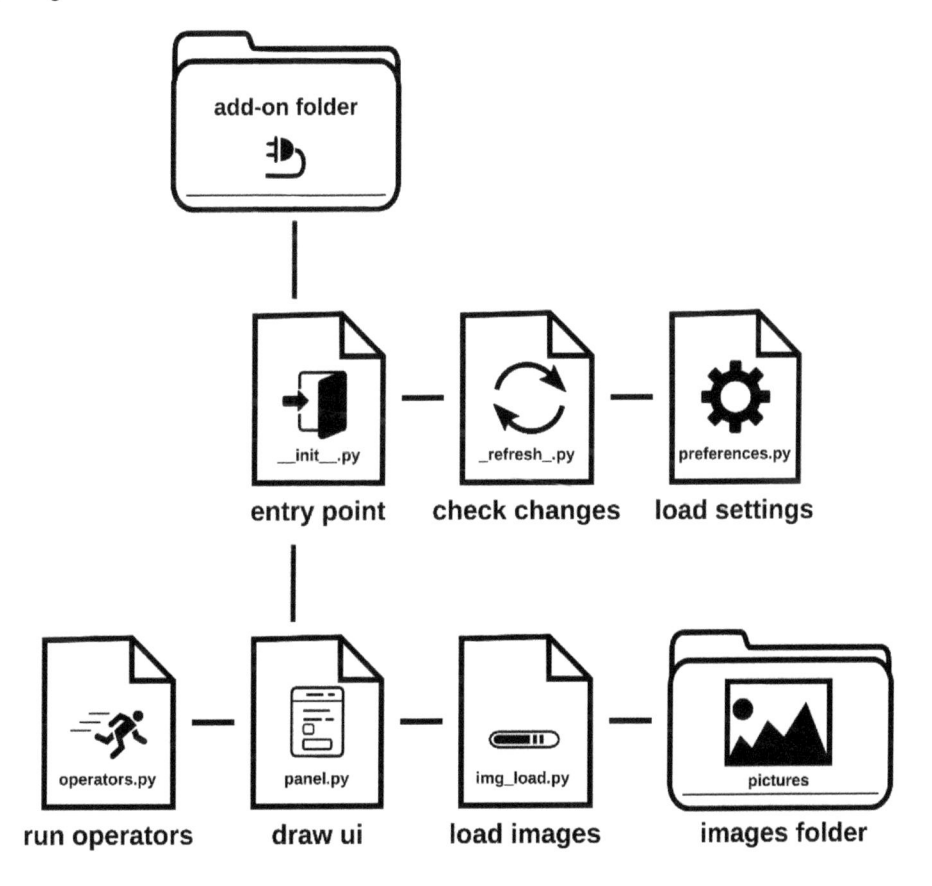

Figure 6.4: Execution of an add-on folder – __init__.py glues all the parts together

Writing the structured panel

We wrote a user interface in *Chapter 5*, that relied on an external .png file to display an icon. That makes the tool difficult to share because Blender can only install either one .py or .zip file.

140　Structuring Our Code and Add-Ons

We can bundle pictures and code together if we structure it all as a folder. According to the guidelines summed up earlier, we can create the following:

- A subfolder for the *icon storage* (media files) named `pictures`
- A module for *icon loading* (generic functionality) named `img_load.py`
- A module that contains the *panel* (UI separation) named `panel.py`
- A module for add-on *preferences* (specific functionality) named `preferences.py`
- A module to *reload* the import system (maintenance utility) named `_refresh_.py`

In the next section, we will create a folder for storing the image files and the code for loading them.

Packing external images

If we use image files for our add-on, we can create a folder in the `structured_addon` directory and name it `pictures`. Since we are going to write a module for loading icons, this folder can contain a collection of image files.

In the `ch6\addons\structured_addon\pictures` folder from the examples, we have `pack_64.png`, a clipart representing a package, and `smile_64.png`, the smiley face from the previous chapter:

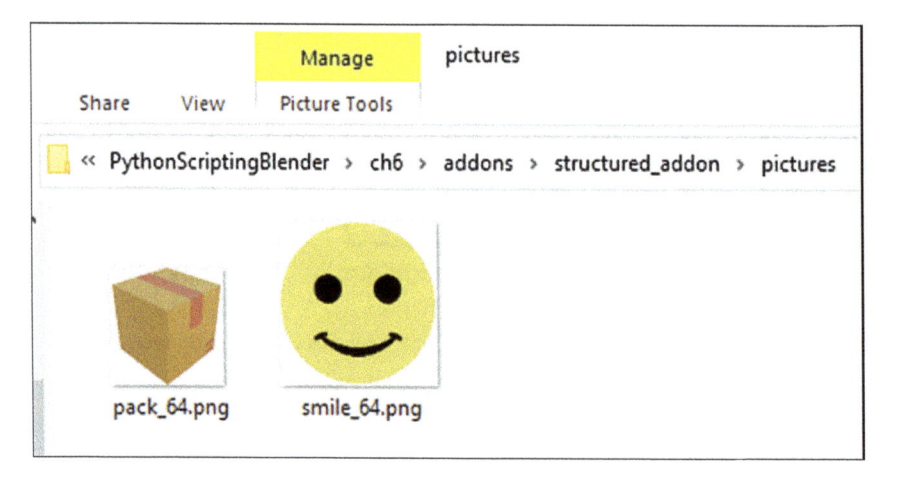

Figure 6.5: The pictures used for this add-on are stored in a folder

Once all our images are in this folder, we can write the code to load them.

Writing an icon library

In *Chapter 5*, we wrote a function that loads a specific image file from disk. That worked great. Now that we are loading two icons, we can just use the same routine twice.

But now that we have an entire module for loading images, we can write a more sophisticated solution that works for any number of icons since it doesn't rely on hardcoded full paths.

This new loader scans the pictures folder for images. We will make sure that loading times are not increased by multiple calls from other modules so that we end up with a more flexible, yet still reliable, loader for custom images. Let's create the module's file, following the same steps as before:

1. Select the .../ch6/addons/structured_addon folder.
2. Create a new file by clicking the **New File** icon.
3. Name the new file img_loader.py.
4. Open the file by double-clicking it.

This module will handle icon loading for the entire package.

Loading pictures from a folder

The img_loader module scrolls the image files from a folder, so we need to import the os package to access directories. And of course, bpy.utils.previews is needed for loading the images from the file and storing them as icons:

```
from bpy.utils import previews
import os
```

We use a global variable, a list, to store the Blender previews Collection. Following the Python naming convention, the variable name is uppercase since it's global. Also, it starts with an underscore because it is not meant to be used in any other module:

```
_CUSTOM_ICONS = None
```

We create the register_icons() function to load the icons from disk. It is like the load_custom_icons function from the first section of *Chapter 5*.

If _CUSTOM_ICONS tests True to the if condition, the return statement will exit the function immediately. That prevents it from loading the icons repeatedly every time that the module is used. Otherwise, we create a new collection of icons via previews.new():

```
def register_icons():
    """Load icons from the add-on folder"""
    global _CUSTOM_ICONS
    if _CUSTOM_ICONS:   # avoid loading icons twice
```

```
        return
collection = previews.new()
```

Rather than hardcoding filenames, we load all the images contained in the `pictures` folder. We don't want to load non-image files, so we store a list of our viable image extensions in the `img_extensions` variable. We are only using the `.png` and `.jpg` formats in this example but others, such as `.tif`, can be used:

```
img_extensions = ('.png', '.jpg')
```

We get the path to the pictures folder by adding `'pictures'` to the module's path. When dealing with files, path functions from the `os` utilities are preferred to string manipulation since they ensure multi-platform compatibility. So, we build the `picture_path` variable using the `os.path.join` function:

```
module_path = os.path.dirname(__file__)
picture_path = os.path.join(module_path, 'pictures')
```

The `os.listdir` function returns a list of all the filenames contained in a directory. We navigate the list with a `for` loop, and at each iteration, we separate the filename from the extension using the `os.path.splitext` function. Both lower and uppercase extensions are valid, but string comparison is a case-sensitive operation. We convert all file extensions into lowercase letters so that `.jpg` or `.png` files can be considered. When a file extension is not found in `img_extensions`, the file is skipped by the `continue` statement:

```
for img_file in os.listdir(picture_path):
    img_name, ext = os.path.splitext(img_file)
    if ext.lower() not in img_extensions:
        # skip non image files
        continue
```

> **Bail out quickly or stick to it!**
>
> Escaping one loop iteration using `continue`, an entire loop using `break`, or a function using `return` before it's over is a valid technique to interrupt a procedure as soon as its conditions are not met. It avoids nesting too many `if` statements, but it is recommended to do that only at the beginning of an execution: having exit points at seemingly random points in the code makes it hard to read.

`os.listdir` lists only the filenames and not their full disk paths. To get it, we must join `picture_path` and `img_file` together, using `os.path.join` again. We use `img_name` – that is, the filename without an extension – as the keyword for retrieving the icon from the collection:

```
    disk_path = os.path.join(picture_path, img_file)
    collection.load(img_name, disk_path, 'IMAGE')
```

Once the `for` loop is over, we can store the collection in the `_CUSTOM_ICONS` list:

```
_CUSTOM_ICONS = collection
```

Using filenames as keywords is convenient as, for instance, `'smile_64'` will be the keyword for the `smile_64.png` file, but it can be ambiguous when our folder contains files with the same name but different extensions, such as `smile_64.jpg`. Our script will assume that the picture folder doesn't contain pictures with the same filenames.

With that, we have created the `register_icons()` function, which initializes the icon collection. Now, we need to add a function to clean it up when the add-on is disabled; otherwise, the leftover thumbnails in our computer's RAM will interfere with subsequent executions.

Unregistering icons

When the add-on is disabled, we must discharge its icons from our computer's memory.

To do that, we must define the `unregister_icons` function. In this function, we invoke `previews.remove()` and use `_CUSTOM_ICONS` as its argument. We also need to make sure that `_CUSTOM_ICONS` is set to None at the end of the function; otherwise, Python will keep invalid references to deleted icons and cause Blender to crash:

```
def unregister_icons():
    global _CUSTOM_ICONS
    if _CUSTOM_ICONS:
        previews.remove(_CUSTOM_ICONS)
    _CUSTOM_ICONS = None
```

Now that `img_loader` can load and unload icons, what we need is a getter to access `_CUSTOM_ICONS` from the other modules.

Getting the collection

Python doesn't forbid access to module members, even if we mark them as *private* using a name with leading underscores. So, we could access the `_CUSTOM_ICONS` variable by typing the following:

```
>>> img_loader._CUSTOM_ICONS
```

Still, we can add more control if we use a function to get the loaded icons:

- In the future, we can change `_CUSTOM_ICONS` to a dictionary or list. That would have no repercussions for other modules using the data if the function used to get them is changed accordingly.

- It makes it easy to check that the conditions are met. In this case, our call to `register_icons()` makes sure that the icons are registered in case they weren't for some reason. This practice adheres to **defensive programming**, as it aims to make the script work even against unforeseen circumstances.
- It allows us to set *roadblocks* in case some vital condition was not met. For instance, we have added an `assert _CUSTOM_ICONS` statement that will cause an error if the variable has not been set, despite the recent call to `register_icons()`. This is an example of **offensive programming** because it stops the execution when something is wrong:

```
def get_icons_collection():
    """Get icons loaded from folder"""
    register_icons()   # load icons from disk
    assert _CUSTOM_ICONS  # if None something is wrong
    return _CUSTOM_ICONS
```

Now, the picture loader provides a code interface for loading, unloading, and getting all the icons from the pictures folder. The main module can import it via relative import.

Using relative imports

The `import` statement looks for modules installed in the Python search path, such as the built-in library or, in our case, the Blender API (bpy). Trying to import a module that is not in the search path halts the script with a `ModuleNotFoundError`.

For modules that belong to the same package, we use a slightly different syntax that gives access to the other modules of the same package: a **relative** import statement.

In relative imports, the package is represented with a dot (`.`), and modules are imported using the `from . import module` syntax.

So, in the import section of our `__init__.py` file, add the following:

```
from . import img_loader
```

The register and unregister functions will invoke the `register_icons()` and `unregister_icons()` functions contained in the `img_loader` namespace, respectively:

```
def register():
    img_loader.register_icons()
def unregister():
    img_loader.unregister_icons()
```

Now that the entire process of loading images is handled in one module, we can write the `.py` file of the *user interface*.

In the next section, we will see how, once we gain access to our icons system via a relative import of `img_loader`, we won't have to worry about loading icon files anymore.

Adding a user interface

We have already created the `panel.py` module, which will contain all the *user interface* classes and functions, so this file is going to contain our panel class.

Writing the UI module

We will start importing the bpy module and our collection of icons via a relative import of `img_loader`:

```
import bpy
from . import img_loader
```

The `OBJECT_PT_structured` class is derived from `Panel`. Like the one from *Chapter 5*, it contains the `bl_*` identifiers required by Blender in its static section:

```
class OBJECT_PT_structured(bpy.types.Panel):
    """Creates a Panel in the object context"""
    bl_label = "A Modular Panel"
    bl_idname = "MODULAR_PT_layout"
    bl_space_type = 'PROPERTIES'
    bl_region_type = 'WINDOW'
    bl_context = 'object'
```

For now, our `draw` function is a few lines of code that display an icon, followed by text:

```
    def draw(self, context):
        layout = self.layout
        icons = img_loader.get_icons_collection()
        layout.label(text="A Custom Icon",
                     icon_value=icons['pack_64'].icon_id)
```

Next, we must write the functions for registering and unregistering the class from this module:

```
def register_classes():
    bpy.utils.register_class(OBJECT_PT_structured)
def unregister_classes():
    bpy.utils.unregister_class(OBJECT_PT_structured)
```

Providing registration utilities inside the module relieves `__init__.py` from concerns about which classes are defined in `panel` and which ones should be registered/unregistered. It is like what we did in *Getting the collection* in section 2 of this chapter, *Packing external images*.

These designs fall under the practice of **encapsulation** – that is, restricting direct access to the components of a module or object. Adhering to it is not inherently better, but it can help in keeping the code flexible and clean.

Importing the UI

Inside `__init__.py`, we import `panel` from the `.` namespace, and invoke its `register_classes()` and `unregister_classes()` functions:

```
from . import img_loader
from . import panel

def register():
    img_loader.register_icons()
    panel.register_classes()
def unregister():
    panel.unregister_classes()
    img_loader.unregister_icons()
```

In this example, the `unregister` order is the reverse of the one in the `register` function. That is not relevant to the execution of the add-on, and it is followed here only for the sake of clarity.

We can test our code by enabling **Structured Panel** in the **Add-ons** list from the **Edit | Preferences** menu.

We can see the panel and our new icon in the object section:

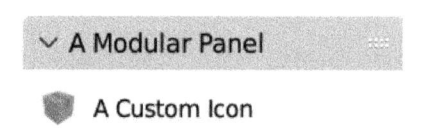

Figure 6.6: panel.py displays an icon via img_loader.py

Now, we will add other elements and complete the panel.

Completing the Objects panel

A slightly simpler version of the panel displayed in *Chapter 5*, uses pretty much the same code. The maximum number of displayed objects is still stored in the `max_objects` static member, but it would work better if implemented as a preference of the add-on. We will do that in the *Using addon preferences* section, a few pages ahead in this chapter:

```
class OBJECT_PT_structured(bpy.types.Panel):
    """Creates a Panel in the object context"""
    bl_label = "A Modular Panel"
    bl_idname = "MODULAR_PT_layout"
    bl_space_type = 'PROPERTIES'
    bl_region_type = 'WINDOW'
    bl_context = 'object'
    max_objects = 3   # limit displayed list to 3 objects
```

The `draw` function displays a list of the scene objects:

```
def draw(self, context):
    layout = self.layout
    icons = img_loader.get_icons_collection()
    row = layout.row(align=True)
    row.label(text="Scene Objects",
              icon_value=icons['pack_64'].icon_id)
    row.label(text=" ",
              icon_value=icons["smile_64"].icon_id)
    grid = layout.grid_flow(columns=2,
                            row_major=True)
    for i, ob in enumerate(context.scene.objects):
        if i > self.max_objects:
            grid.label(text="...")
            break
        # display object name and type icon
        grid.label(text=ob.name,
                   icon=f'OUTLINER_OB_{ob.type}')
```

This time, reloading the scripts does not reflect the changes in the preceding code: only the __init__. py file is refreshed on reload. We are going to cover explicitly reloading internal modules in the next section.

Reloading cached modules

When a module is imported, Python caches a copy of it for future access. Since the __init__.py file is the only one to be updated by the **Reload Scripts** operator, we are left with two options:

- Close and restart Blender
- Explicitly call the `reload` function inside __init__.py

The latter is preferred over restarting the application as it takes less time. The `reload` function is part of the `importlib` module.

Reloading via importlib

The utilities contained in the `importlib` library interact with the import system, and the `reload` function forces the Python interpreter to reload a module from disk.

If the `img_loader` module has changed and needs to be reloaded, we can use the following command:

```
from importlib import reload
reload(img_loader)
```

So, to make sure that the changes to our add-on .py files are always applied, we can add these lines of code to __init__.py:

```
from . import img_loader
from . import panel

from importlib import reload
reload(img_loader)
reload(panel)
```

Reloading every relative module soon after it is imported will work, but leaving `reload` statements in published code impacts performance and is considered bad practice. Next, we will learn how to refresh inside a specific module of the add-on.

Implementing a refresh module

Calling `reload` increases the loading time of an add-on and makes the code less readable. Many developers add reload calls while they work and remove them when they are finished. However, using packages, we can move the refresh logic to another module.

To do that, we need to create a file in our add-on package and name it _refresh_.py. This module doesn't contain any add-on functionality, but it helps while we edit our code by ensuring that all modules are reloaded from disk and are up to date.

Reloading the package modules

The refresh module makes use of the following elements:

- The `reload` function from the `importlib` module
- The `sys` module, which is used by `_refresh_` to reload an instance of itself
- The `bpy` module, to access Blender preferences
- All the modules contained in the add-on

Those requirements translate into the following `import` statements:

```
from importlib import reload
import sys
import bpy

from . import *
```

The wildcard character, `*`, stands for all the modules contained in the current package (`.`). Now, we can write a function that reloads the add-on modules if Blender is set for development. We encountered the **Developer Extras** setting in the *Useful features for Python* section, at the beginning of *Chapter 2*. They can be found by going to **Edit | Preferences** from the top menu bar in the **Interface** tab of the **Preferences** window:

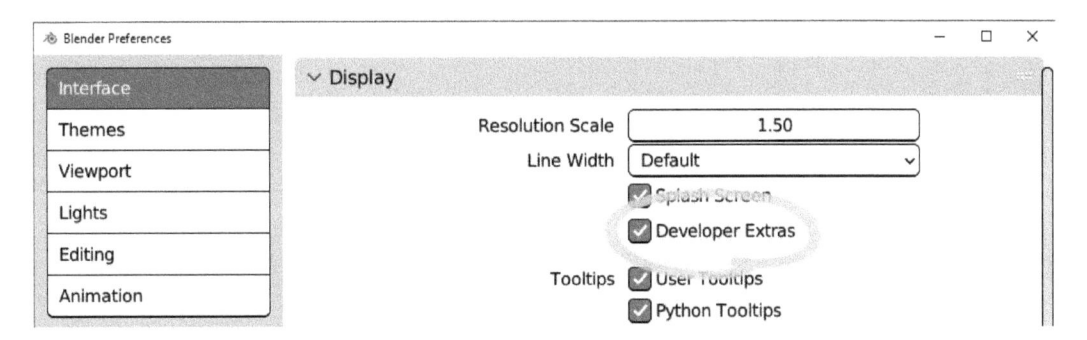

Figure 6.7: Enabling Developer Extras in the Preferences window

We can assume that when **Developer Extras** is on, we want the **Reload Scripts** operator to reload our submodules as well.

Using Developer Extras as a condition

We need to find the full Python path of **Developer Extras** to read its value. To do that, follow these steps:

1. Make sure that **Developer Extras** is enabled.
2. Also, make sure that **User Tooltips** and **Python Tooltips** are enabled.
3. Hover your mouse pointer over the **Developer Extras** checkbox or label.
4. Leaving your mouse still, without clicking or moving it, displays a tooltip:

```
Show options for developers (edit source in context …
Python: PreferencesView.show_developer_ui
```

According to the API reference, `PreferencesView` is the `view` member of the `Preferences` class, which can be found at `bpy.context.preferences`:

`https://docs.blender.org/api/3.3/bpy.types.Preferences.html`

`#bpy.types.Preferences.view`

So, the full path of the **Developer Extras** setting is as follows:

```
bpy.context.preferences.view.show_developer_ui
```

The value of `show_developer_ui` is either `True` or `False`. Using it as a condition, we exit `reload_modules` if **Developer Extras** is disabled:

```
def reload_modules():
    if not bpy.context.preferences.view.show_developer_ui:
        return
```

Then, we add a `reload` call for each `.py` file that we want to refresh. The first line reloads `_refresh_.py`, looking up the current filename in the system dictionary, `sys.modules`. This way, we can update changes in the `_refresh_` module itself. So, the full body of the `reload_modules` function looks like this:

```
def reload_modules():
    if not bpy.context.preferences.view.show_developer_ui:
        return

    reload(sys.modules[__name__])
    reload(img_loader)
    reload(panel)
```

Now, enabling **Developer Extras** in the preferences ensures the structured add-on modules are constantly updated. To make the reload happen, we need to call this function in `__init__.py`, as that is the only file to be executed when scripts are reloaded. We must invoke `_refresh_.reload_modules()` in the import section:

```
from . import img_loader
from . import panel
from . import _refresh_
_refresh_.reload_modules()
```

Calling **Reload Scripts** will now reflect the changes in `OBJECT_PT_structured`:

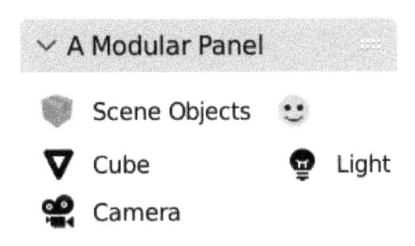

Figure 6.8: Our panel source code has been reloaded

The limitation of three objects can be set in the `max_objects = 3` static member. However, there is a better place for hosting our add-on setting. In the next section, we are going to implement proper preferences for our add-on.

Using add-on preferences

Besides using Blender preferences, we can use `bpy.types.AddonPreferences` to display the add-on-specific custom settings under the add-on activation checkbox. It's an interface, just like `bpy.types.Panel`, and we can add settings to its layout using its `draw` method.

The `bl_idname` attribute of `AddonPreferences` must match the Python name of the add-on. The usage of `__name__` for single files and `__package__` for folders makes our code easier to maintain: these variables always match the respective Python names, so changes in files and folders' names would have no consequences.

Creating preferences

Since we are using multiple files, we will create `preferences.py` inside the folder of our `structured_addon`. It contains the `StructuredPreferences` class:

```
import bpy

class StructuredPreferences(bpy.types.AddonPreferences):
    bl_idname = __package__
```

```
        def draw(self, context):
            layout = self.layout
            layout.label(text="Structured Add-On Preferences")
```

Then, we must add a `register_classes` and an `unregister_classes` function:

```
def register_classes():
    bpy.utils.register_class(StructuredPreferences)
def unregister_classes():
    bpy.utils.unregister_class(StructuredPreferences)
```

We can add `preferences` to the `import` section of `__init__.py`, which looks like this:

```
from . import panel
from . import img_loader
from . import preferences
from . import _refresh_
_refresh_.reload_modules()
```

Then, we must register the class from the preferences module alongside the others:

```
def register():
    img_loader.register_icons()
    preferences.register_classes()
    panel.register_classes()

def unregister():
    panel.unregister_classes()
    preferences.unregister_classes()
    img_loader.unregister_icons()
```

We must also make sure that the preferences will be reloaded in `_refresh_.py`. This is what the `_reload_modules` function will look like:

```
def _reload_modules():
    reload(sys.modules[__name__])
    reload(img_loader)
    reload(preferences)
    reload(panel)
```

If we use **Reload Scripts** now, we will see our preferences beneath the **Add-on** checkbox, in the **Add-Ons** list:

Using add-on preferences 153

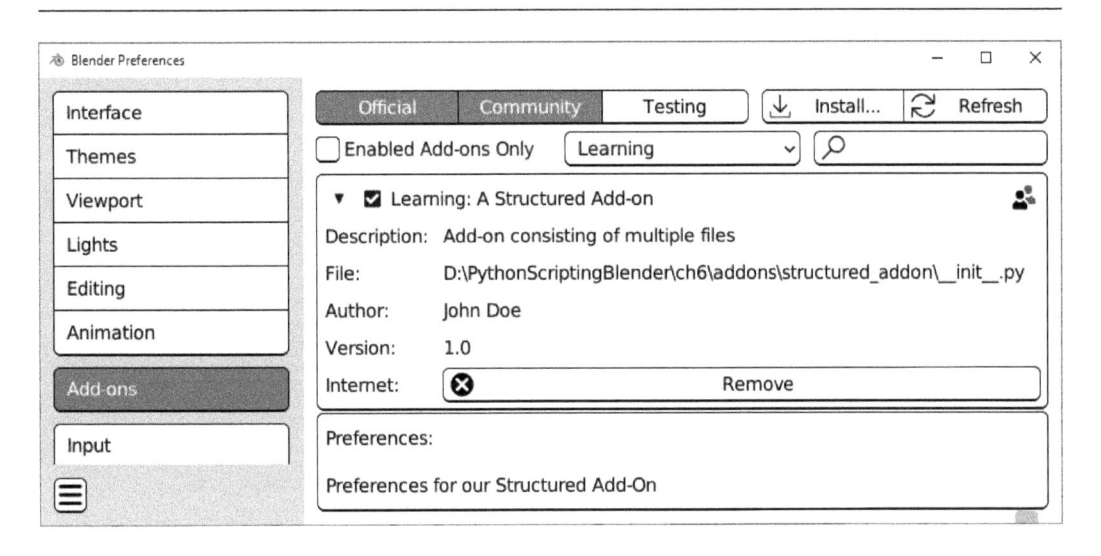

Figure 6.9: Add-ons settings displayed in the Preferences window

The preferences show up but are still empty. Next, we are going to add some values.

Populating the preferences

We want to replace `OBJECT_PT_structured .max_objects` with a setting. It's an integer number, so we will add an `IntProperty` to the `StructuredPreferences` class:

```
import bpy
from bpy.props import IntProperty
class StructuredPreferences(bpy.types.AddonPreferences):
    bl_idname = __package__
    max_objects: IntProperty(
        name="Maximum number of displayed objects",
        default=3
    )
```

Now that it contains an integer property, `StructuredPreferences` can store the maximum displayed objects setting. To display this property to the user, we will add it to the layout in the `draw` method. A simple `layout.prop` instruction will be enough:

```
self.layout.prop(self, max_objects)
```

But we can also use `split` for a nicer appearance. A split layout creates a column for each new entry. Adding an empty widget, a `separator`, as the first element, creates an indentation:

```
    def draw(self, context):
        layout = self.layout
```

```
                split = layout.split(factor=0.5)
                split.separator()
                split.label(text="Max Objects")
                split.prop(self, 'max_objects', text="")
```

Reloading the script will display **Max Objects** as an editable setting:

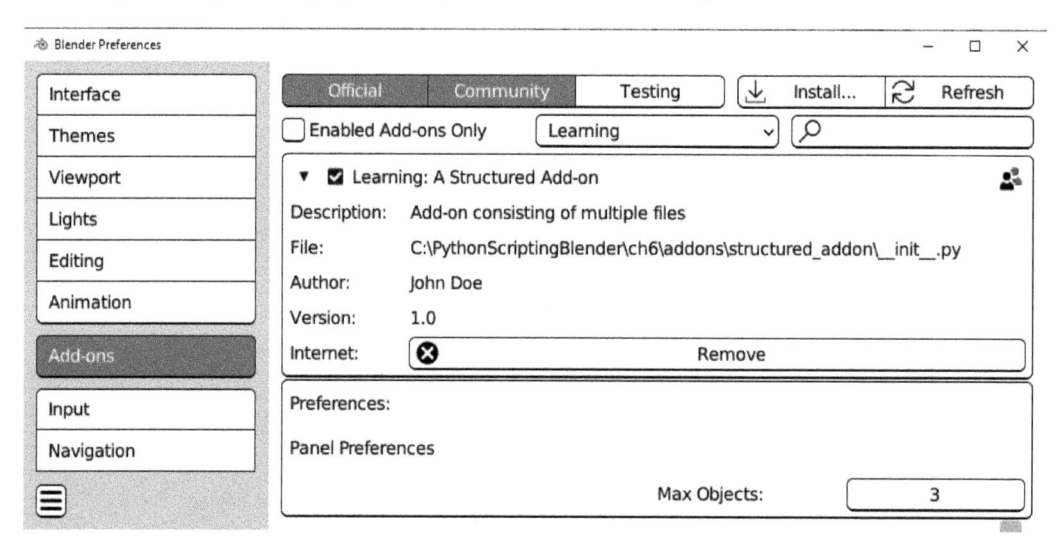

Figure 6.10: Max Objects as a Preferences setting

This value is saved along with the other user preferences, and Blender remembers its value when the application is restarted. We aren't using this setting yet: we need to adjust the code in our panel so that we can use it.

Using add-on preferences in code

Python scripts can access the preferences of an add-on using one line of code:

```
bpy.context.preferences.addons[ADDON_NAME].preferences
```

Notice how `preferences` is repeated at the end. It might seem redundant but it makes sense since `bpy.context.preferences.addons` refers to the application preferences, not the ones of the single add-on.

`bpy.context.preferences.addons[ADDON_NAME]` returns the add-on as a Python object.

With that in mind, we will go back to the `OBJECT_PT_structured` class in the *user interface's* `panel.py` module. Since we are going to use the value from the preferences, it should not have a `max_objects` static member anymore:

```
class OBJECT_PT_structured(bpy.types.Panel):
    """Creates a Panel in the object context"""
    bl_label = "A Modular Panel"
    bl_idname = "MODULAR_PT_layout"
    bl_space_type = 'PROPERTIES'
    bl_region_type = 'WINDOW'
    bl_context = 'object'
```

Now, before we iterate the scene objects in the `draw` function, we must get our `add_on` and `preferences` from the context. Using `enumerate`, so that we can keep count of the objects while they are displayed, we stop the loop when the amount stored in `preferences.max_objects` is reached:

```
add_on = context.preferences.addons[__package__]
preferences = add_on.preferences
for i, ob in enumerate(context.scene.objects):
    if i >= preferences.max_objects:
        grid.label(text="...")
        break
```

This time, we check `max_objects` with a greater or equal (`>=`) comparison because, since the enumeration starts from 0, breaking after `i > max_objects` would display one more object.

Just to be clear, using a separate module for the add-on preferences is not required – the entirety of the code written in this chapter could have been contained in a single, large `.py` file: we are just splitting the code for the sake of readability.

If our add-on contains operators, we can create modules for those as well.

Adding operators

Operators can be grouped into different files according to their purpose. For example, transform-related operators such as **Elevate Objects**, which we covered in *Chapter 4*, can be put into a file named `ops_transform.py`, while our first few operators, **Create Type Collections**, written in *Chapter 3*, can be put in an `ops_collections.py` file. All those classes would be then registered by `__init__.py` and, if needed, added to the add-on interface via relative import.

Another solution is creating one module for all the operators, which can be named `operators.py`. In this section, we will create an operators module for our add-on.

Writing the operators module

In the `structured _addon` folder, we will create the `operators.py` module. It will contain our operator class: we will reuse the **Add Random Location** operator from *Chapter 5*. Besides bpy, which is ubiquitous in Blender script, we will import the `random` module and use `randint` in the `add_random_location` function:

```python
import bpy
import random
def add_random_location(objects, amount=1,
                        do_axis=(True, True, True)):
    """Add units to the locations of given objects"""
    for ob in objects:
        for i in range(3):
            if do_axis[i]:
                loc = ob.location
                loc[i] += random.randint(-amount, amount)
```

Now, we can proceed with the add-on class. It's the same as in the *Displaying buttons* section in the previous chapter – `poll` returns `True` if there are selected objects, while `execute` runs `add_random_location`, with the operator's amount and axis as arguments:

```python
class TRANSFORM_OT_random_location(bpy.types.Operator):
    """Add units to the locations of selected objects"""
    bl_idname = "transform.add_random_location"
    bl_label = "Add random Location"
    amount: bpy.props.IntProperty(name="Amount",
                                  default=1)
    axis: bpy.props.BoolVectorProperty(
                              name="Displace Axis",
                              default=(True, True, True)
                              )
@classmethod
    def poll(cls, context):
        return context.selected_objects
    def execute(self, context):
        add_random_location(context.selected_objects,
                            self.amount,
                            self.axis)
        return {'FINISHED'}
```

Like in the case of `panel.py`, we must add functions for registering the module's classes:

```python
def register_classes():
    bpy.utils.register_class(TRANSFORM_OT_random_location)
def unregister_classes():
```

```
      bpy.utils.unregister_class(
                          TRANSFORM_OT_random_location
                          )
```

Now, we can import `operators.py` into the other modules of the script.

Registering operator classes

To use our operator, we must import `operators.py` in `__init__.py`, whose `import` section will look like this:

```
from . import operators
from . import img_load
from . import panel
from . import preferences
from . import _refresh_
```

Of course, we can add and remove our operators with `operator.register_class` and `operator.unregister_class`. Since operators might be used as buttons, we call `operators.register_classes` before `panel.register_classes`:

```
def register():
    preferences.unregister_classes()
    operators.register_classes()
    img_load.register_icons()
    panel.register_classes()
def unregister():
    panel.unregister_classes()
    img_load.unregister_icons()
    operators.register_classes()
    preferences.unregister_classes()
```

This will make **Add Random Location** available to Blender. However, if we want changes in `operators.py` to be effective when we reload the script, we must add `operators` to `_refresh_.reload_modules`.

Refreshing operators on reload

Thanks to the work we did in the *Reloading cached modules* section, adding operators to the refreshed modules is easy: we add `reload(operators)` to the `reload_modules` function. The whole `_refresh_.py` file now looks like this:

```
import sys
from importlib import reload
import bpy
```

Structuring Our Code and Add-Ons

```
from . import *
def reload_modules():
    if not bpy.context.preferences.view.show_developer_ui:
        return
    reload(sys.modules[__name__])
    reload(img_load)
    reload(preferences)
    reload(operators)
    reload(panel)
```

The only thing left to do is display the operator button in the panel.

Adding operator buttons

To add the **Add Random Location** button to the interface, we need to import our operators in `panel.py`, whose import section will look as follows:

```
import bpy
from . import img_loader
from . import operators
```

Now, our panel can access the `TRANSFORM_OT_random_location` class using `operators` as a namespace, so we will add a new element to the `draw` method:

```
        layout.operator(
            operators.TRANSFORM_OT_random_location.bl_idname
            )
```

Upon displaying the F3 **Search Bar** area to look up and run **Reload Scripts**, our panel will display the **Add random Location** button:

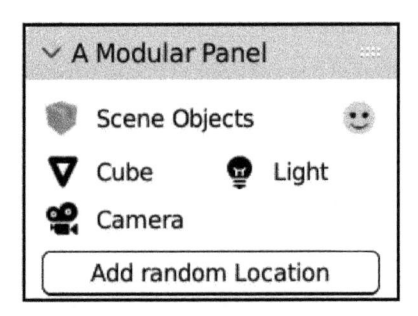

Figure 6.11: Modular panel displaying operators via relative import

Our add-on is finished. However, we could refine `panel.py` and add the same functionalities that we wrote for `VerySimplePanel` in *Chapter 5*, namely the following:

- Color-coded entries for selected/active objects
- A **Delete** button with a context-sensitive label

Implementing those is left as an exercise for you. In the next section, we will learn how to distribute our add-on folders to other users.

Packaging and installing add-ons

We learned how to install single `.py` add-ons in the *Installing our add-ons* section of *Chapter 3*. To distribute an add-on that consists of more files, we must create a `.zip` archive of it. Most of you will be familiar with how a `.zip` file is a compressed archive that can contain more files or folders.

Blender can install folders from a standard `.zip` archive, but there are two requirements:

- The `.zip` file must contain the add-on as a first-level folder
- The name of the first-level folder must not contain any dot (`.`) as it won't work with Python's import system

There are third-party tools, such as **7-Zip**, that provide a wide array of options, but it is possible to create `.zip` files using the file utilities of your operating system. In this section, we will learn how to compress an add-on folder on **Windows OSX**, and **Ubuntu** systems.

Cleaning up bytecode

If the `structured_addon.zip\structured_addon` folder contains a subfolder named `__pycache__`, make sure you delete it: you should not distribute the `.pyc` files it contains.

Creating a .zip file using 7-Zip

7-Zip is a free compression utility for Windows. It is very lightweight and integrates with the file manager. Here are the steps to use it for packaging our add-ons:

1. Download and install 7-Zip from `https://www.7-zip.org`.
2. Open **File Explorer**.
3. Navigate to the directory containing the `structured_addon` folder.
4. Right-click on the `structured_addon` folder to show the context menu.
5. Select **7-Zip | Add to "structured_addon.zip"**.

The `structured_addon.zip` file will be created alongside the original folder. If for some reason it is not possible to install 7-Zip or any other compression tool, we can still create `.zip` files using Windows File Explorer alone.

Creating a .zip file using Windows File Manager

1. Open **File Explorer**.
2. Navigate to a folder where we want to create the add-on.
3. Display the context menu by right-clicking on the background.
4. From the right-click menu, select **New | Compressed (zipped) Folder**. We will name it `structured_addon.zip`:

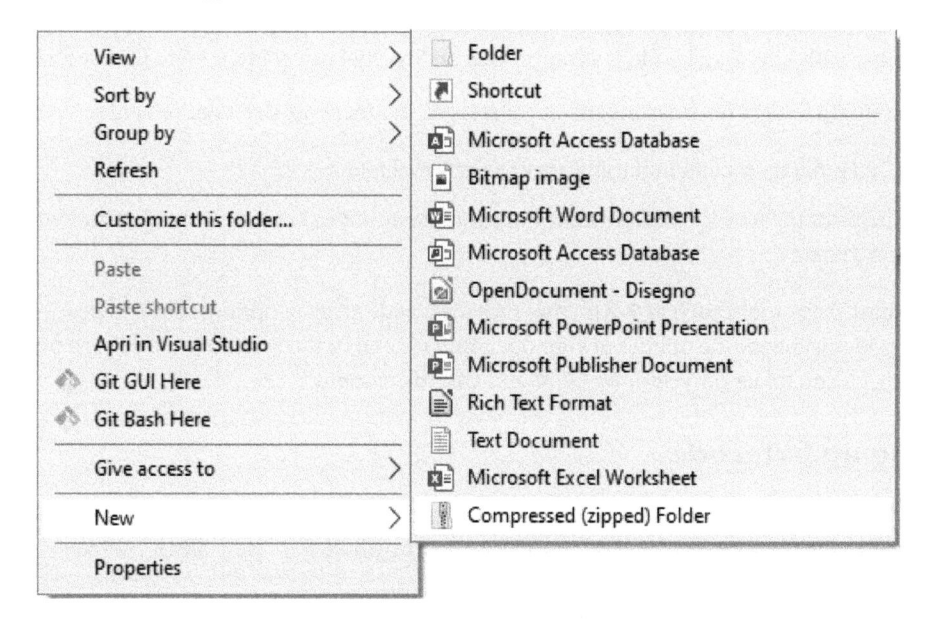

Figure 6.12: Creating empty .zip files using Windows File Explorer

So far, we have created a `.zip` file, but it is empty. Next, we will copy our add-on files there:

1. Copy the `ch6\addons\structured_addon` folder to the clipboard by using *Ctrl + C* or right-clicking and selecting **Copy**.
2. Double-click the `structured_addon.zip` archive to display its content.
3. Paste the `ch6\addons\structured_addon` folder into the archive via *Ctrl + V* or right-clicking and selecting **Paste**.

Creating a .zip file on Mac using Finder

Follow these steps:

1. Right-click on the `structure_addon` folder in **Finder** or left-click without releasing the button. A menu will appear.
2. Select **Compress "structured_addon"** from the menu:

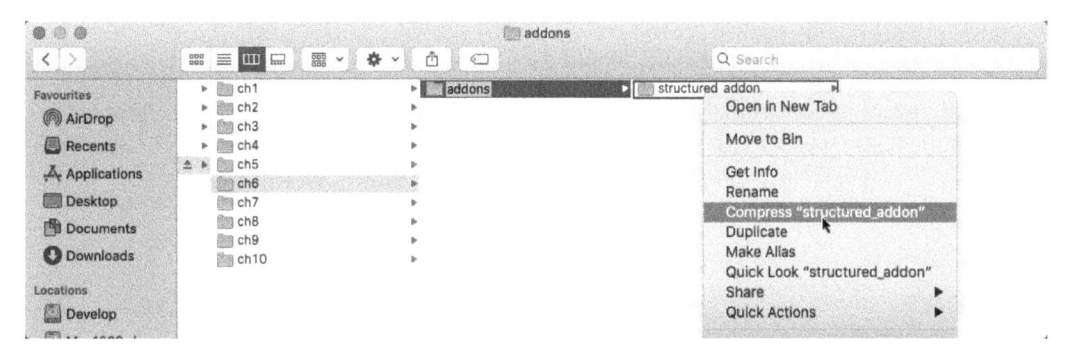

Figure 6.13: Compressing folders on a Mac computer

Creating a .zip file using Gnome

Gnome is the default environment for **Ubuntu** and other popular **Linux** distributions. Here's how to create a `.zip` file using Gnome:

1. Right-click on the `structure_addon` folder in the File Browser.
2. Choose the **Compress…** option from the menu.
3. Confirm the filename and `.zip` extension of the archive.
4. Click the **Create** button.

Installing .zip add-ons

The steps for installing a compressed add-on are the same as those we learned about in the *Expanding Blender by creating a simple add-on* section of *Chapter 3*:

1. Open the **Preferences** window via **Edit | Preferences** from the top menu.
2. Select the **Add-ons** tab in the left column.
3. Click on the **Install** button at the top right of **Add-ons Preferences**.
4. In the file browser, find the `structured_addon.zip` file.
5. Click the **Install Add-on** button at the bottom.

With that, we have gone through the complete development and release of our structured add-on. A modular approach is important in programming and works for relatively simple tools as well. Plus, it makes our scripts more manageable as they increase in complexity.

Summary

In this chapter, we learned how to set up a modular architecture for our code by splitting it into different files while keeping it coherent and clear. We also learned how to load files procedurally and how to write settings for our add-ons.

This approach confers interoperability and generical usefulness to our code and, by applying appropriate separation guidelines, eases our task in navigating the different parts of our tools.

In *Chapter 7*, we will learn how to animate with Python and change the animation settings with our scripts.

Questions

1. Can Blender add-ons consist of multiple files?
2. Which file of an add-on folder contains the info dictionary?
3. How does relative import work?
4. Does reloading an add-on refresh all its modules?
5. Where do we store the settings of an add-on?
6. How do we show the add-on properties in the preferences?
7. How do we distribute multi-file add-ons?

7
The Animation System

3D owes much of its popularity to the production of animated content. Its many advantages in terms of performance, quality, and scalability made it ubiquitous in motion pictures, cartoons, feature animation, and video games. With that comes the need for custom tools to ease animation-related tasks.

Most applications handle animation similarly, in part inherited from hand-drawn workflows: a sequence is broken into frames, whose rapid succession creates the illusion of motion.

A programmer working in 3D will have to account for animated values changing over time, and how such data is stored.

That might change in the future, but at the time of writing, animation involves a huge amount of manual work, leaving much room for automation.

In this chapter, you will get acquainted with the Blender animation process, learn how to access animation data in Python, and build one tool that sets the playback range and another that animates objects.

This chapter will cover the following topics:

- Understanding the animation system
- Changing the playback settings
- Creating animations with Python

Technical requirements

We will use Blender and Visual Studio Code in this chapter. The examples created in this chapter can be found at `https://github.com/PacktPublishing/Python-Scripting-in-Blender/tree/main/ch7`.

Understanding the animation system

While animations consist of a sequence of frames, only one frame is displayed on the screen at one time. Animators can scroll through these frames and play their animation like a video:

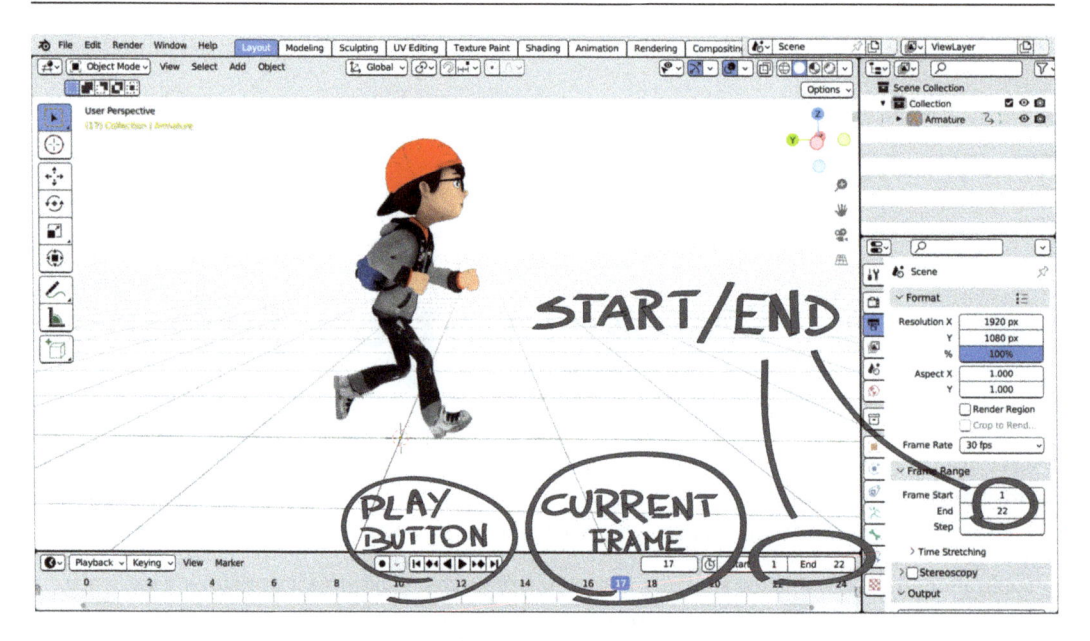

Figure 7.1: Playing an animation in Blender

The animation **Timeline**, at the bottom of the screen in the **Layout** workspace, controls and displays the current frame and the start/end of the sequence. It provides immediate visual feedback and is essential to animation.

Timeline and Current Frame

A **Timeline** is a Blender area for playing animations and changing the playback settings. It is marked with a clock icon and, because of its importance, is in more than one workspace: **Animation**, **Layout**, **Rendering**, and **Compositing** display a timeline.

In addition to the frame **Start** and **End** values, there is a slider for the **Current Frame** area and a button bar with **Media Controls**:

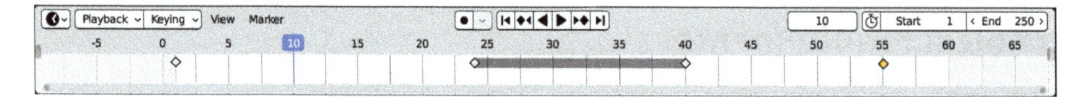

Figure 7.2: Blender's animation Timeline

Besides frame range and controls, the timeline displays the **keyframes** – that is, frames that contain changes in the object properties.

The frame range information, which is relevant to other tasks, such as **Rendering**, is an attribute of the scene that can be also set in the scene properties.

Duration and Frame Rate

The duration of the current scene can be set in the **Format** and **Frame Range** panels in the **Output** properties, the second tab starting from above, marked with a printer icon.

> **One scene, four tabs!**
>
> There are so many scene properties that they span the first four tabs. It can be confusing because all of them read **Scene** in their headers.
>
> These four categories are as follows:
>
> - **Render**, marked with a TV icon
> - **Output**, with a printer icon
> - **View Layers**, whose icon is a stack of pictures
> - **Scene**, whose icon represents a cone and a sphere
>
> Only the **Output** properties contain animation-related settings.

The **Frame Rate** property displays how many frames are contained in 1 second of animation and is also known as **frames per second (FPS)**.

The default value is 24 FPS, the historical rate for feature films. Because of the frequency of the power grid, footage for American TV is usually shot at 30 FPS, while European TVs use 25 FPS. Motion capture or video game animations may have higher rates, such as 60 FPS:

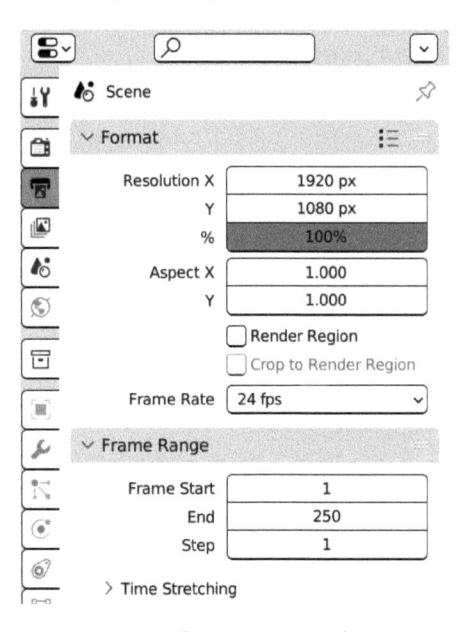

Figure 7.3: Scene range attributes

Raising the **Frame Rate** value makes the animation play more frames per second, so it shortens the playback duration as more frames are spent in less time.

While the graphic interface allows the animator to either pick a frame rate from a list of presets or display an additional property for custom values, in Python, `fps` is a numeric attribute of the `scene.render` properties:

```
>>> import bpy
>>> bpy.context.scene.render.fps
24
```

By default, the first frame of a scene, **Frame Start**, is set to 1 while the last frame, **Frame End**, is set to 250. These values are arbitrary and are changed to the planned duration of a specific shot.

The first and last frame of the scene can be accessed in Python as scene attributes:

```
>>> import bpy
>>> bpy.context.scene.frame_start
1
>>> bpy.context.scene.frame_end
250
```

Frame Step is the gap between one rendered frame and the next and is usually set to 1. It can be increased so that not all frames are rendered, a feature used by render managers to test the overall state of a sequence:

```
>>> import bpy
>>> bpy.context.scene.frame_step
1
```

While the start, end, and step of the sequence are available in the **Output** properties as well, the **current frame** and the **preview range** are displayed only in the **Timeline** view.

Current frame and preview range

Like `frame_start`, `frame_end`, and `frame_step`, the current frame is exposed as a Python attribute of the scene:

```
>>> import bpy
>>> bpy.context.scene.frame_current
1
```

In the **Timeline** view, the button with a stopwatch icon on the left of **Start/End** toggles the preview range. It displays an alternate range, different from the render settings:

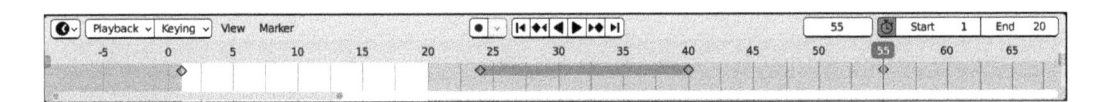

Figure 7.4: Enabling the preview range in the Timeline view

The region outside the preview range is marked in dark orange. Animators turn on the preview range to restrict the playback when they are working on a part of their assigned sequence.

In Python, we can access `frame_preview_start` and `frame_preview_end` like so:

```
>>> import bpy
>>> bpy.context.scene.frame_preview_start
1
>>> bpy.context.scene.frame_preview_end
250
```

All the frames between `start` and `end` make the animated sequence, but not all frames must store information. Those that do are the keyframes of the animation.

Animation keyframes

The position of objects at a certain moment is stored as **keyframes**. In this section, we will provide a brief overview of how keyframes are created and retrieved in the user interface, as well as with Python instructions.

Adding keyframes in Blender

There are at least two ways to set keyframes in Blender:

- Right-click on a property, then click on **Insert Keyframe(s)** from the context menu
- Press *I* in the Viewport to display the **Insert Keyframe Menu** area and select a property to animate

We can make changes and insert keyframes at different times to create an animation.

Animating objects

To get more familiar with animations, we can open Blender and add keyframes for the location of the default cube:

1. Open Blender and select an object. If there are none in the scene, we can use **Add | Mesh | Cube** from the top menu.
2. Press the *N* key to display the properties of the active object.
3. Right-click on any of the **Location** attributes.
4. Select **Insert Keyframes**.

However, one keyframe is not enough to make the cube move on the screen. To create a proper animation, we need to do the following:

1. Set a new value for the **Current Frame** field – for instance, 24.
2. Move the cube to a new location by pressing the *G* key and panning the mouse.
3. Confirm the new position by left-clicking or pressing the *Enter* key.
4. Press *I* to insert a **Location** keyframe.

We can play our animation by pressing the *spacebar* or clicking the **Play** button. In some instances, we might want to restrict the frame range to watch our animation in loops. We can set the sequence's **Start** and **End** manually, or we can write an add-on that sets them for us.

Writing the Action to Range add-on

Animators set the first and last frames of the scene according to the duration of the shot. If there are animated objects, this add-on can set the playback range automatically.

This operator will allow you to choose between the render and preview range.

Setting the environment

Let's create a folder for this chapter in our project. Then, in the **Blender Preferences** area, we need to set the `ch7` folder as our **Scripts Folder**. We must restart Blender to update its search paths.

Our add-on contains an operator, like the ones from *Chapter 3*, and *Chapter 4*:

1. Select `PythonScriptingBlender/ch7/addons`.
2. Create a new file by clicking the **New File** icon.
3. Name the new file `action_to_range.py`.
4. Open the file by double-clicking it.

We can now start writing our first animation add-on.

Writing the Action to Range information

The operator will be invoked from the **View** menu of the **Timeline** view, as reported in the location information:

```
bl_info = {
    "name": "Action to Range",
    "author": "John Packt",
    "version": (1, 0),
    "blender": (3, 00, 0),
```

```
        "location": "Timeline > View > Action to Scene Range"
        "description": " Action Duration to Scene Range",
        "category": "Learning",
}
```

The next steps are as follows:

1. Writing the operator.
2. Writing its menu entry.
3. Registering the classes and user interface.

Let's start with the operator class and its information.

Writing the Action to Range operator

As usual, the `ActionToSceneRange` operator derives from `bpy.types.Operator` and starts with the `bl_*` identifiers:

```
import bpy
class ActionToSceneRange(bpy.types.Operator):
    """Set Playback range to current action Start/End"""
    bl_idname = "anim.action_to_range"
    bl_label = "Action Range to Scene"
    bl_description = "Transfer action range to scene range"
    bl_options = {'REGISTER', 'UNDO'}
```

As noted in the *Understanding the animation system* section, there are two frame range settings in the scene: the main one affects the scene render, while the preview range only affects the Viewport playback.

We want a parameter to switch between the two. We will use a `BooleanProperty` so that we can affect either the main or preview range:

```
    use_preview: bpy.props.BoolProperty(default=False)
```

That's all for the static part of the operator. Adding a `poll` and an `execute` method will allow the operator to run.

Writing the operator methods

As we learned in *Chapter 3*, the `poll` method returns `False` when the conditions for running the operator are not met; it's `True` otherwise. We need to determine the operator requirements and put them in Python form.

Checking the requirements in the poll() method

To get the range of the active animation, we must verify the following conditions:

- There should be an active object
- The active object must be animated

When an object is animated, its keyframes are grouped into an **action**, which, in turn, becomes the active action in the object's **animation data**.

We will explore these entities in more depth in the next section, *Accessing animation data in Python*. For now, we can just test their existence in the following code:

```
@classmethod
def poll(cls, context):
    obj = context.object
    if not obj:
        return False
    if not obj.animation_data:
        return False
    if not obj.animation_data.action:
        return False
    return True
```

When any of the `not` conditions are met, the operator is grayed out in the interface. Otherwise, the operator can be launched, and that will run its `execute` method.

Writing the execute method

The `execute` method performs the operator activity. It does the following:

1. Finds the frame range of the current action
2. Sets the first and last frame of the scene accordingly
3. Fits the new frame range in the timeline visually

We already know how to access the active object's action. Its `frame_range` attribute contains the first and last frame of the action:

```
def execute(self, context):
    anim_data = context.object.animation_data
    first, last = anim_data.action.frame_range
```

Writing the Action to Range add-on   171

We get the current `scene` and perform *step 2*. If the timeline preview range is used, we should set the preview start/end frames. Frame values are stored as decimal floats, and we need to convert them into integers before using them for the `frame*` attributes:

```
scn = context.scene
if self.use_preview:
    scn.frame_preview_start = int(first)
    scn.frame_preview_end = int(last)
```

Otherwise, we must set the standard `frame_start` and `frame_end` of the scene:

```
else:
    scn.frame_start = int(first)
    scn.frame_end = int(last)
```

Now that we have set our values, we can invoke `ops.action.view_all()` to fit the **Timeline** view to the new range, and finish the execution:

```
bpy.ops.action.view_all()
return {'FINISHED'}
```

We need to add `'UNDO'` to `bl_options` to affect the operator attributes after the execution, as we learned in *Chapter 4*:

```
bl_options = {'REGISTER', 'UNDO'}
```

Unfortunately, operators that are launched outside of the **3D Viewport** area or the **Graph Editor** area don't display the **Operator Panel** area, thus preventing the user from switching `use_preview` to `False`.

To work around that, we can create two entries in the **Timeline | View** menu.

Writing the menu function

In *Chapter 3*, we learned that adding a function to a menu class allows us to add elements to its layout.

Also, in *Chapter 5*, we learned that operator properties are returned by the `layout.operator` function and can be set programmatically.

Combining these two techniques, we can create two menu entries that invoke the same operator, but we only enable `use_preview` on one of the two. This way, we end up with two menu items. They execute the same operator but with different settings and outcomes.

To make sure that the difference is reflected in the operator label, we can change it using the `text=` parameter:

```
def view_menu_items(self, context):
    props = self.layout.operator(
                    ActionToSceneRange.bl_idname,
                    text=ActionToSceneRange.bl_label +
                        " (preview) ")
    props.use_preview = True
```

We have added " (preview) " to the operator label so that it's clear that this is a variant of the `ActionToSceneRange` operator.

The default entry affects the actual scene range, so there is no need to specify the text label explicitly:

```
    props = self.layout.operator(
                    ActionToSceneRange.bl_idname
                    )
    props.use_preview = False
```

Menu entries are displayed with a **Last In First Out (LIFO)** policy. We added the (preview) item first, so it will be displayed after the default **Action to Scene Range** entry.

> **It won't default forever!**
>
> `ActionToSceneRange.use_preview` is already `False` by default, but we set `props.use_preview` to `False` anyway in `view_menu_items`.
>
> Unless `is_skip_save` is used for a property, the default value only affects the first execution of an operator. From then on, the last user choice becomes the new default.
>
> If an element of the interface matches specific operator settings, then we should set them explicitly in the code.

Now that we've created the elements of the add-on, we need to register the operator and menu entries. Then, it will be ready to go.

Finishing the add-on

We need the class name of the **Timeline | View** menu. To find it, we can look up the Python source of the Blender interface.

Finding a menu's Python class

We can right-click the **Timeline | View** menu and select **Edit Source** to find its Python name:

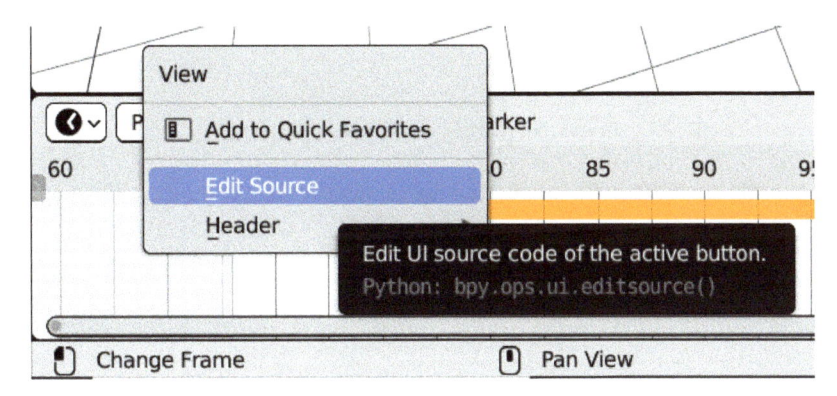

Figure 7.5: Opening Timeline | View

Then, in the **Scripting** workspace, select `space_time.py` in the **Text Editor** area:

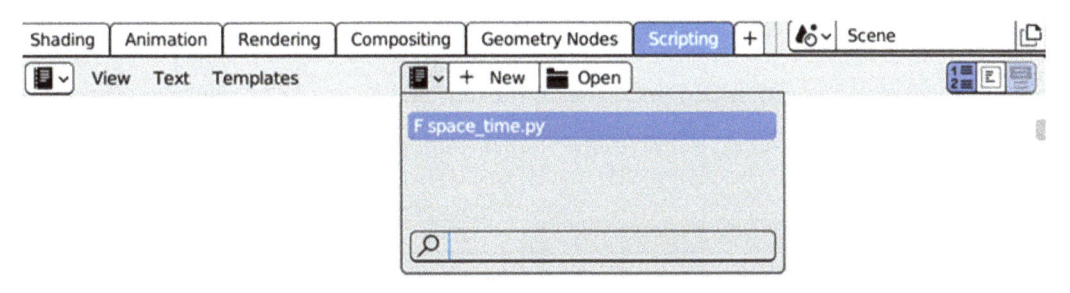

Figure 7.6: space_time.py as a loaded text block

The script found in the **Text Editor** area contains the instructions for the **Timeline** interface. Since we have loaded it by right-clicking on its element, in the editor, the text has been scrolled down to the part where the **Timeline | View** menu was added. The argument of the `menu()` function is the class name we are looking for:

```
sub.menu("TIME_MT_view")
```

We can use this name in our `register()` function.

Writing the register/unregister functions

We can use `register_class` to add `ActionToSceneRange` to the Blender operators, and we can append our items to `TIME_MT_view` to display our new entries in the **Timeline | View** menu:

```
def register():
    bpy.utils.register_class(ActionToSceneRange)
    bpy.types.TIME_MT_view.append(view_menu_items)
```

Likewise, when the add-on is disabled, `unregister()` removes our items from the menu and the operator from Blender:

```
def unregister():
    bpy.types.TIME_MT_view.remove(view_menu_items)
    bpy.utils.unregister_class(ActionToSceneRange)
```

Now, the operator is ready. We can use it on the cube we animated earlier in this chapter or open one of the files contained in `ch7/_scenes_`.

Enabling and running

If the `PythonScriptingBlender/ch7` folder was added to the `scripts` path, we can find and enable **Action to Range** in the **Add-ons** preferences:

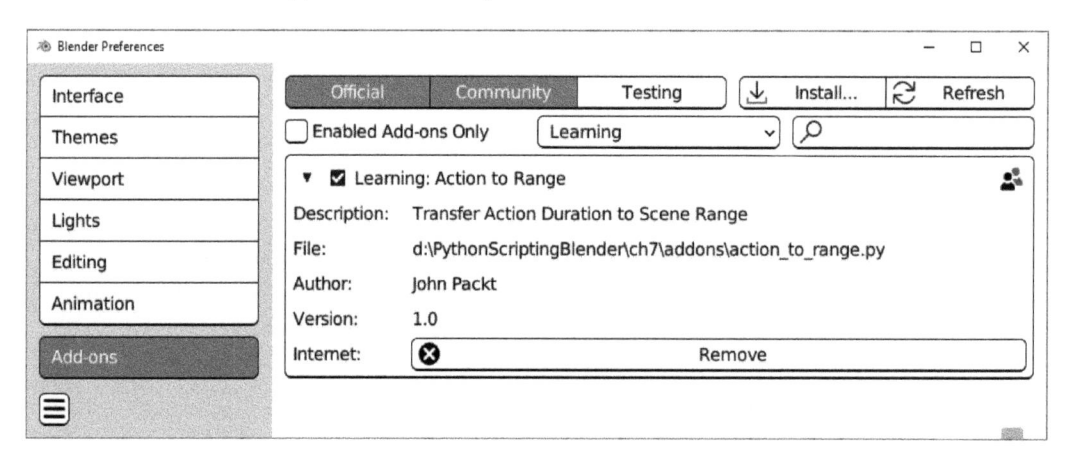

Figure 7.7: Enabling the Action to Range add-on

If the add-on was installed correctly, we will find two new entries in **Timeline | View**:

Writing the Action to Range add-on   175

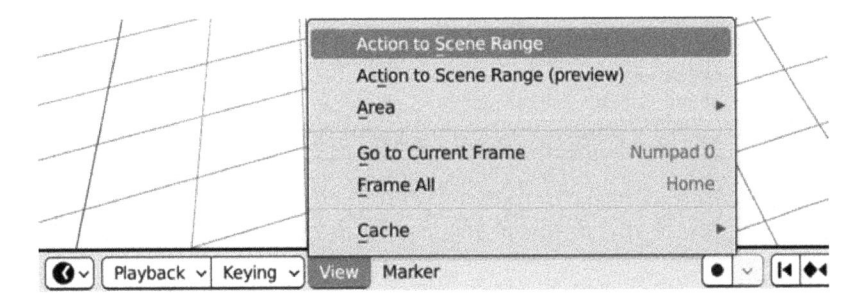

Figure 7.8: Action to Scene Range and its "preview" variant

Clicking **Action to Scene Range** sets the scene range to 1-24, while **Action to Scene Range (preview)** sets the preview range.

Since we have set `bl_options = {'REGISTER', 'UNDO'}` in the properties, we'll look at how this operator supports the **Adjust Last Operation** window.

Changing the parameters of the last operation

We can use **Edit | Adjust Last Operation** from the top menu bar to change the options in the last execution retroactively:

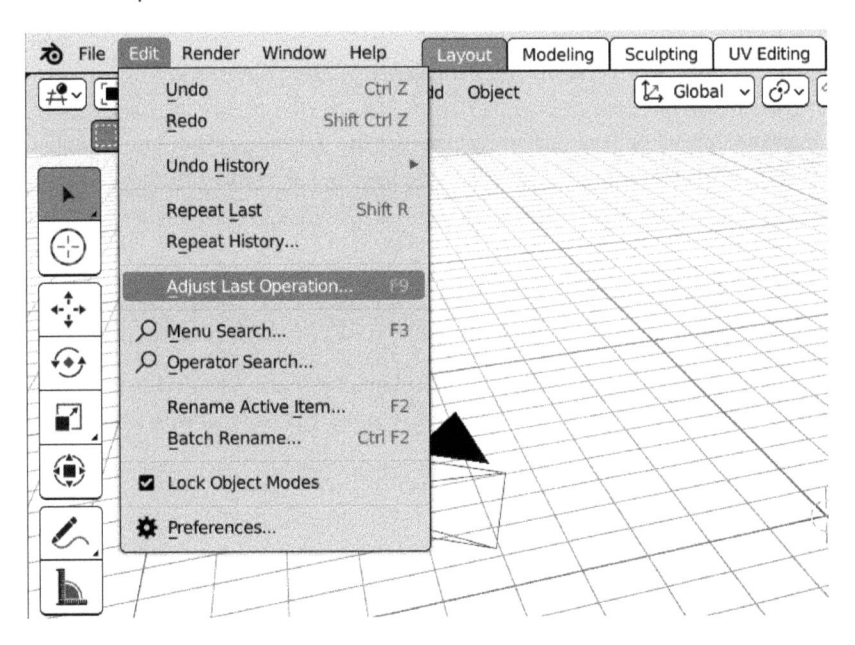

Figure 7.9: Changing the outcome of the last operation

A small window will appear, displaying the operator properties. Turning `use_preview` on and off changes the result of the operation:

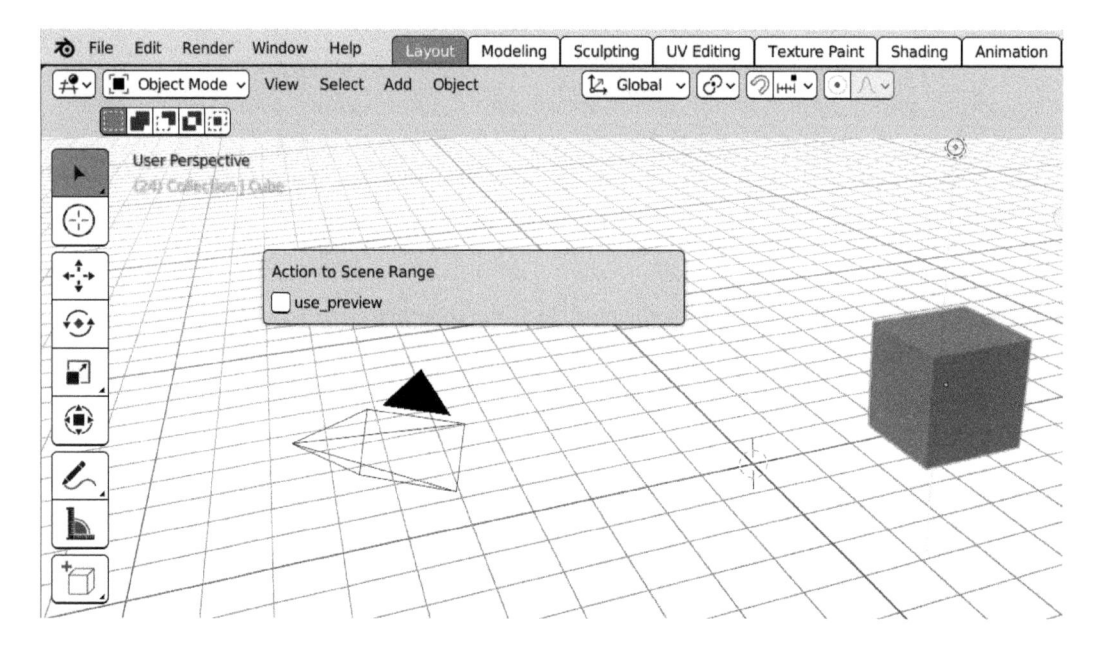

Figure 7.10: The Action to Scene Range properties window

The add-on is finished, but when it comes to recentering the **Timeline** view, our execute function calls `bpy.ops.action.view_all()`, a timeline operator. It is fine to call other operators in `execute`, but they can place additional restrictions on the validity of the context, so we must consider that their `poll` method might halt our script's execution.

For instance, by adding our operator to the **Timeline | View** menu, we could think that a timeline will always be present and that resorting to `action.view_all()`, which requires it, will never fail.

But what if the `F3` **Search Bar** area is used, and the user launches **Action to Frame Range** even if the **Timeline** view is not displayed in the interface? In that case, our script will halt with a `RuntimeError`:

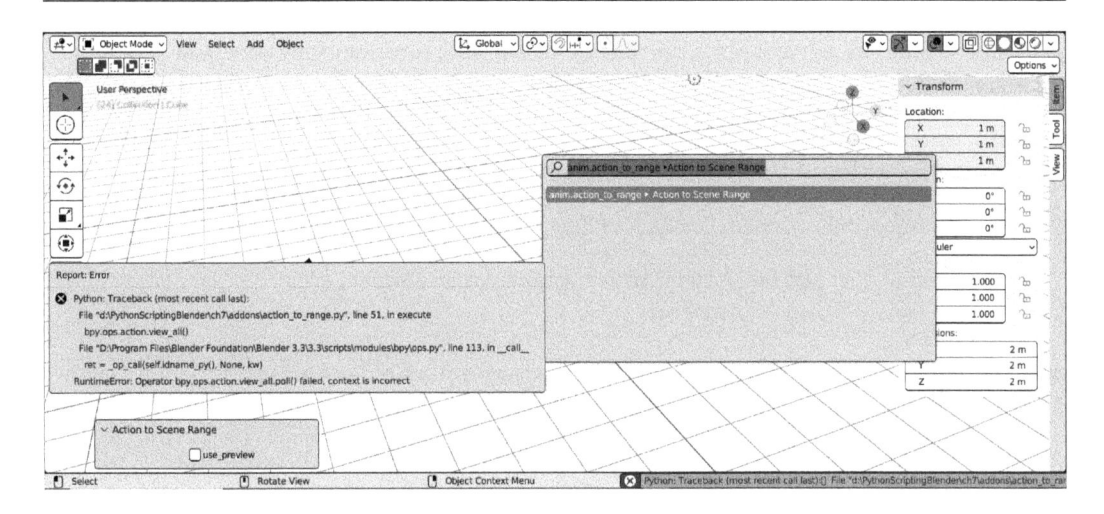

Figure 7.11: Our script causes an error if the timeline is not displayed

We can just warn the user or check the presence timelines in our `poll` method, but usually, the best practice is as follows:

- Use a `try` statement when calling other operators
- If possible, if a `RuntimeError` occurs, create an alternate `context` for running the other operator

This way, even if something goes wrong, our operator will carry on with its task.

Fixing context for other operators

We can prevent a Python script from stopping in case of errors by using `try` and `catch` statements. The code that risks causing errors goes under the `try` indent block, while the code to execute in case a specific error happens goes under the `except ErrorType` indent.

In our case, the error message was raised when **Action to Range** ran with no **Timeline** in view. This specifies a `RuntimeError`:

```
RuntimeError: Operator bpy.ops.action.view_all.poll() failed, context
is incorrect
```

To get past this issue, we must provide a plan B inside an `except RuntimeError` block. If we don't want to do anything, we can use the empty `pass` instruction:

```
try:
    bpy.ops.action.view_all()
except RuntimeError:
    pass
```

But we can do better: we can look for a timeline in the window, override `context`, and pass it to the operator.

In *Chapter 5*, we learned that a Blender window is split into `screen`, `areas`, and `regions`. From the documentation, we know that timeline editors are of the `'DOPESHEET_EDITOR'` type.

There might be more windows open. For each of them, we can get the screen attribute:

```
for window in context.window_manager.windows:
    screen = window.screen
```

Then, we must look for a `'DOPESHEET_EDITOR'` among `areas` of the screen:

```
for area in screen.areas:
    if area.type != 'DOPESHEET_EDITOR':
        continue
```

By skipping every area that is *not* a `'DOPESHEET_EDITOR'`, we can ensure that the following lines are executed only if the area is a timeline. We need to look for its main region, which is of the `'WINDOW'` type:

```
for region in area.regions:
    if region.type == 'WINDOW':
```

The timeline's `window`, `area`, and `region` are fed to `context.temp_override` inside a `with` statement.

In Python, `with` sets a condition that stays valid inside its scope – that is, indented lines of code. There, we can call `bpy.ops.action.view_all()`:

```
            with context.temp_override(
                                    window=window,
                                    area=area,
                                    region=region):
                bpy.ops.action.view_all()
            break
        break
return {'FINISHED'}
```

The two `break` statements stop the search after a timeline is found. We have made sure that `view_all` is called only if its conditions are met.

Our add-on automated a tedious operation by checking the action frame range, without looking into the keyframes it contains. To understand how we can access and manipulate the animation data, next, we will learn how keyframes are displayed and edited.

Editing keyframes

Animation software gives visual cues of keyframe distribution. In Blender, keyframes are displayed with special colors in the interface and as diamond widgets in the animation editors.

Animated properties have colored backgrounds. If the current frame is a keyframe, the background is yellow; otherwise, it is green:

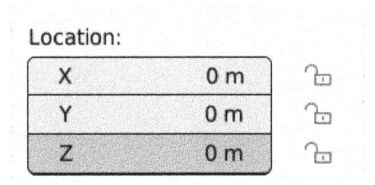

Figure 7.12: Location is animated; the current frame is the keyframe for X and Y

Keyframes of the selected objects are displayed as diamonds in the **Timeline** editor:

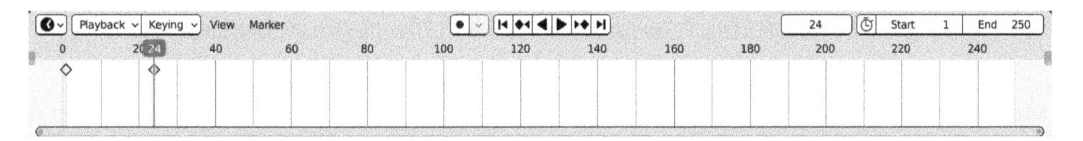

Figure 7.13: The animation Timeline. Frames 1 and 24 have keyframes

Blender transitions from one keyframe to the other by tracing a graph between them. These graphs are referred to as **animation curves** or **f-curves**.

Animation curves and the Graph Editor

Like most animation software, Blender generates a transition between two animated values by inbetweening two or more keyframes. A keyframe contains two elements – a moment in time and the value of a property at that moment.

These changes in value over time are represented in the **Graph Editor** area, a coordinate system where the horizontal axis is the frame number and the vertical axis is the animated value at each frame:

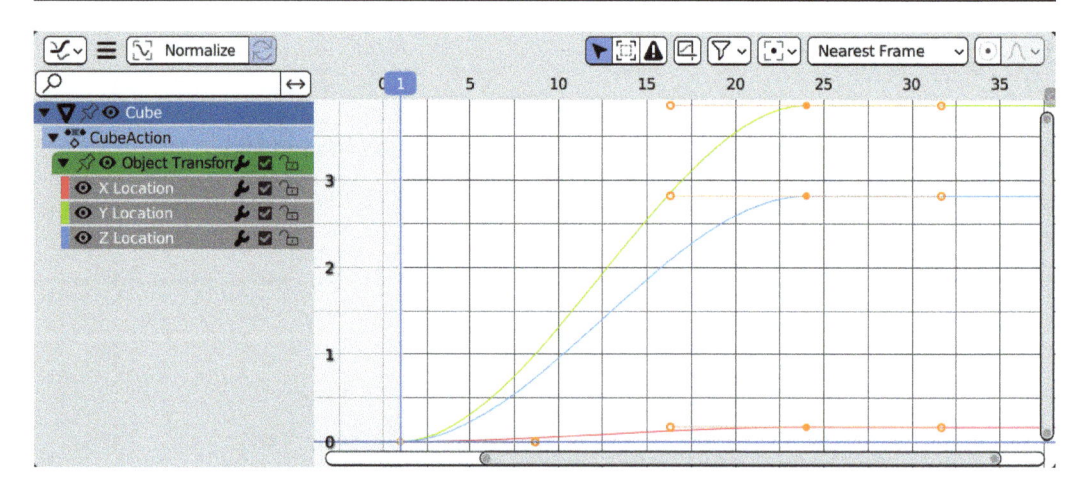

Figure 7.14: Values over time as animation curves in the Graph Editor

A keyframe created at frame 1 that sets a property to 0 is displayed as a dot with coordinates of (1, 0).

Blender interpolates the transition between one keyframe and another. The transition between a keyframe and its neighbors is an **F-Curve** – that is, a continuous graph that connects two keyframes smoothly.

> **Say his F-name!**
>
> F-curves are named after James Ferguson, a researcher at The Boeing Company who, in 1964, published a paper named *Multivariable Curve Interpolation*. His interpolation formulas have fueled the advancements in modern computer graphics.

This way, every *animation curve*, or *F-Curve*, contains both the keyframes set by the animator and the transition generated by Blender, acting both as storage for the animation data and the interpolator that fills the parts where they are missing.

Interpolations can make use of straight lines connecting the points, or curve lines with tangent handles – that is, **Bezier** curves.

Setting a **Location** keyframe creates curves for the **X**, **Y**, and **Z** channels.

Animation curves are displayed in the **Graph Editor** area. We can select **Graph Editor** from the drop-down list on the left of any area header:

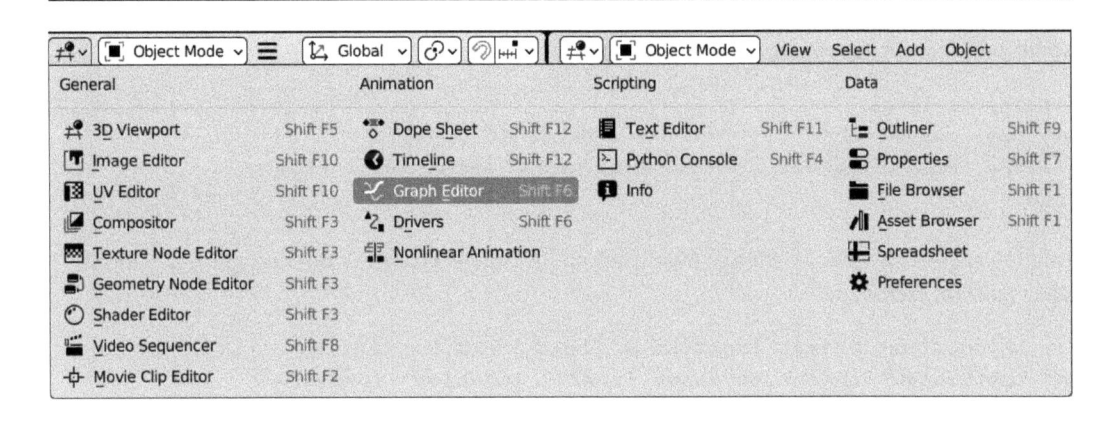

Figure 7.15: Selecting the Graph Editor as the content of a Blender area

The f-curves of an animation are stored in **actions**, which are the top containers in the animation data.

The structure of the animation data can be summed up as **Action | F-Curves | Keyframes**.

Traversing this hierarchy is done differently via Python, where we can retrieve the animation values in our scripts.

Accessing animation data in Python

Let's switch to the **Scripting Workspace** area to familiarize ourselves with the animation system API.

Adding keyframes in Python

The Python class of every animatable object provides a method that we can use to insert keyframes, named `keyframe_insert`. It is very similar to the **Insert Keyframe** menu and requires a `data_path` string for specifying which property to animate. Optional parameters such as `index` and `frame` allow us to specify one of the channels of an aggregate property or a frame different from the current one:

```
keyframe_insert(data_path,
                index=- 1,
                frame=bpy.context.scene.frame_current,
    […]
    Returns
            Success of keyframe insertion.
```

The following lines set a keyframe for the active object's location to `10.0`, `10.0`, `10.0` at frame 1:

```
>>> import bpy
>>> bpy.context.object.location = 10.0, 10.0, 10.0
>>> bpy.context.object.keyframe_insert('location', frame=1)
True
```

Animation requires a value to change over time, so just one keyframe is not enough. We will set another value for frame 24:

```
>>> bpy.context.object.location = -10.0, -10.0, -10.0
>>> bpy.context.object.keyframe_insert('location',frame=24)
True
```

We have only set a keyframe at the start and one at the end of our animation, but by default, Blender generates a transition between two neighbor keyframes so that the object will move a little bit at each of the frames between 1 and 24.

Our object starts at the `10.0`, `10.0`, `10.0` coordinates of the **x**, **y**, and **z** space and transitions smoothly toward `-10.0`, `-10.0`, `-10.0`.

Geometrically speaking, these coordinates mark the front top-right corner and bottom-left corner of a cube, implying that the motion happened along the diagonal of the three-dimensional space.

Retrieving keyframes in Python

If the active object has keyframes, we can traverse its `animation_data`:

```
>>> bpy.context.object.animation_data
bpy.data.objects['Cube']...AnimData
```

Since `animation_data` contains the current action, all its f-curves, and keyframes, we are going to use this container a lot. It can be convenient to store it as a variable as this way, we can avoid long lines of code while we gather the data. Here's how we get the current `action`:

```
>>> anim_data = bpy.context.object.animation_data
>>> anim_data.action
bpy.data.actions['CubeAction']
```

From the action, we can retrieve the list of animation `fcurves`:

```
>>> action = anim_data.action
>>> anim_data.action.fcurves
bpy.data.actions['CubeAction'].fcurves
```

For each curve, we can get the animated `data_path`. A data path identifies where a property is stored in Blender, but some properties, such as `location`, require an animation curve for each channel – for example, one curve for the *x*, one for *y*, and one for the *z* coordinate. For that reason, f-curves also have the `array_index` attribute, a number that designates the animated channel of an aggregate property. If we animate the three channels of `location` and scroll through the f-curves using Python, we will find three curves with the same path, `'location'`, each with a different index:

```
>>> fcurves = anim_data.action.fcurves
>>> for fc in fcurves:
...     print(fc.data_path, fc.array_index)
...
location 0
location 1
location 2
```

Every `keyframe_point` stores two coordinates in the `co` attribute. The first is the frame number, while the second is the value of that frame:

```
>>> for fc in fcurves:
...     print(fc.data_path, fc.array_index)
...     for kf in fc.keyframe_points:
...         frame, value = kf.co
...         print("\t frame", frame, "value", value)
location 0
     frame 1.0 value 0.0
     frame 24.0 value 0.2
location 1
     frame 1.0 value 0.0
     frame 24.0 value 4.0
location 2
     frame 1.0 value 0.0
     frame 24.0 value 3.0
```

While the current, first, and last frames of the scene are stored as integers, `co[0]` is a `float`. This allows us to insert animations between adjacent frames (subframe animation).

The curve interpolation mode is stored in the keyframe's `interpolation` attribute. The most used interpolations are as follows:

- `'CONSTANT'`: No interpolation
- `'LINEAR'`: Interpolation using straight lines
- `'BEZIER'`: Interpolation using curves, weighted with *handles*

Bezier curves, named after the French engineer Pierre Bèzier, are widely used in computer graphics because of their smooth and controllable behavior. They are the default interpolation in Blender. The current `interpolation` between a keyframe and its neighbors is stored as an attribute of the keyframe:

```
>>> kf.interpolation
'BEZIER'
```

Points of a Bezier curve have two additional coordinates – a left handle and a right one, both of which affect the interpolated path. To support curve interpolation, Blender keyframes contain two additional coordinates stored as the `handle_left` and `handle_right` attributes. Exactly like the `co` attribute, the curve handles are two-dimensional points:

```
>>> kf.handle_left
Vector((16.0, 10.0))
>>> kf.handle_right
Vector((31.0, 10.0))
```

Blender supports other interpolations. They cover very specific cases and at the time of writing, they are not much used in animation. They are named after the mathematical function used in their computation, and they are described in the API documentation at https://docs.blender.org/api/3.2/bpy.types.Keyframe.html and #bpy.types.Keyframe.interpolation:

- `QUAD`: Quadratic easing
- `CUBIC`: Cubic easing
- `QUART`: Quartic easing
- `QUINT`: Quintic easing
- `SINE`: Sinusoidal easing (weakest, almost linear but with a slight curvature)
- `EXPO`: Exponential easing (dramatic)
- `CIRC`: Circular easing (strongest and most dynamic)
- `BACK`: Cubic easing with overshoot and settle
- `BOUNCE`: Exponentially decaying parabolic bounce, like when objects collide
- `ELASTIC`: Exponentially decaying sine wave, like an elastic band

We will get back to keyframes at the end of this chapter; in the meantime, we will build a tool that sets the scene playback based on the duration of the current animation.

In these examples, our script uses the attributes of existing animations. In the next section, we are going to create animations with Python.

Writing the Vert Runner add-on

In this section, we will write an add-on that animates the selected objects along the geometry of the active object. The animation will trace a path that connects the vertices of a mesh, hence the name *Vert Runner*:

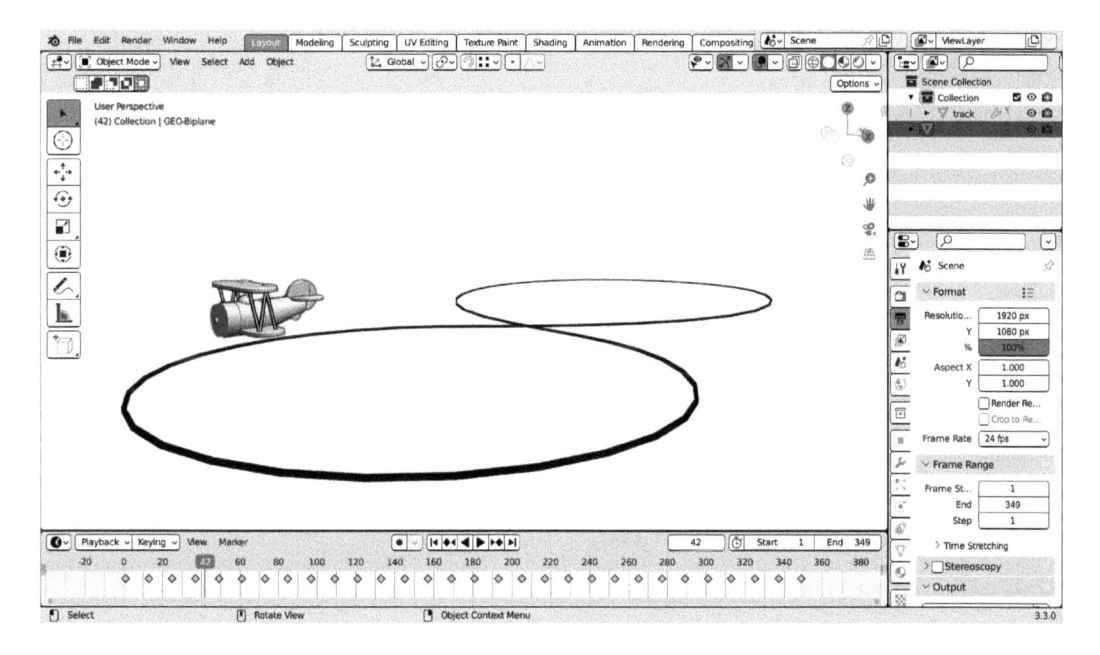

Figure 7.16: Animating a toy along the vertices of a path

This can be a basis for procedural walks or patrols, motion effects, or any other case where we have a geometrical path.

In this operator, the selected objects and the active ones are treated differently: the active object is the reference geometry on which the selected objects are moved.

Setting the environment

Let's start by adding a new script to our add-ons directory:

1. Select `PythonScriptingBlender/ch7/addons` in **VS Code**.
2. Create a new file by clicking on the **New File** icon.
3. Name the new file `vert_runner.py`.
4. Open the file by double-clicking it.

As usual, we will start with the add-on information.

Writing the Vert Runner information

Our new operator can be invoked by selecting **Object** | **Animation** | **Vert Runner** from the menu bar of the **3D Viewport** area. This will be our `location` information:

```
bl_info = {
    "name": "Vert Runner",
    "author": "John Packt",
    "version": (1, 0),
    "blender": (3, 00, 0),
    "location": "Object > Animation > Vert Runner"
    "description": "Run on vertices of the active object",
    "category": "Learning",
}
```

We will proceed with the usual steps:

1. Writing the operator
2. Writing the menu entry
3. Registering the classes and interface

Writing the Vert Runner operator

After the `import` section, we must create the `VertRunner` class and its `bl_*` identifiers:

```
import bpy
class VertRunner(bpy.types.Operator):
    """Run over vertices of the active object"""
    bl_idname = "object.vert_runner"
    bl_label = "Vertex Runner"
    bl_description = "Animate along verts of active object"
    bl_options = {'REGISTER', 'UNDO'}
```

We set the distance between each keyframe with an `Integer` property:

```
    step: bpy.props.IntProperty(default=12)
```

The next step is writing the `poll` and `execute` methods of this operator.

Writing the operator methods

We will write the `poll` method based on what is needed to run the desired operations.

Requirements to check in the poll() method

To animate the selected objects over the geometry of the active object, we need the following:

- An active object
- Mesh data
- Selected objects

Using these conditions, to have the `poll()` method return `False`, they translate to the following:

```
@classmethod
def poll(cls, context):
    obj = context.object
    if not obj:
        return False
    if not obj.type == 'MESH':
        return False
    if not len(context.selected_objects) > 1:
        return False
    return True
```

If none of the `return False` conditions are met, the poll is successful. In that case, the operator can run its execute method.

Writing the execute() method

Breaking the operator's goal into steps, we should do the following:

1. Get a list of patrol points; in this case, the vertices of the active object.
2. Scroll through the selected objects.
3. Move them through the patrol points and set the keyframes.

We will start by storing the active object's vertices in a `list`:

```
def execute(self, context):
    verts = list(context.object.data.vertices)
```

When we iterate through the selected objects, we should make sure to skip the active one, which is likely selected:

```
for ob in context.selected_objects:
    if ob == context.active_object:
        continue
```

Then, we must iterate through the vertices list and set keyframes for each coordinate, starting with the current frame. We must advance the `frame` number at every iteration:

```
        frame = context.scene.frame_current
        for vert in verts:
            ob.location = vert.co
            ob.keyframe_insert('location', frame=frame)
            frame += self.step
        return {'FINISHED'}
```

When the for loop is over, we must return a `'FINISHED'` state and exit the operator. Now that the VertRunner class is complete, we can work on its menu entry.

Writing the menu and register functions

Since menu elements are displayed in reverse order, we must add a `separator` first:

```
def anim_menu_func(self, context):
    self.layout.separator()
    self.layout.operator(VertRunner.bl_idname,
                         text=VertRunner.bl_label)
```

Now, it's time to register the operator and menu so that it can run from the interface:

```
def register():
    bpy.utils.register_class(VertRunner)
    bpy.types.VIEW3D_MT_object_animation.append(
                                            anim_menu_func)
def unregister():
    bpy.types.VIEW3D_MT_object_animation.remove(
                                            anim_menu_func)
    bpy.utils.unregister_class(VertRunner)
```

If we refresh the **Add-ons** list, we will see **Vert Runner** in the **Learning** category. Enabling it adds **Vert Runner** to the **Object | Animation** menu:

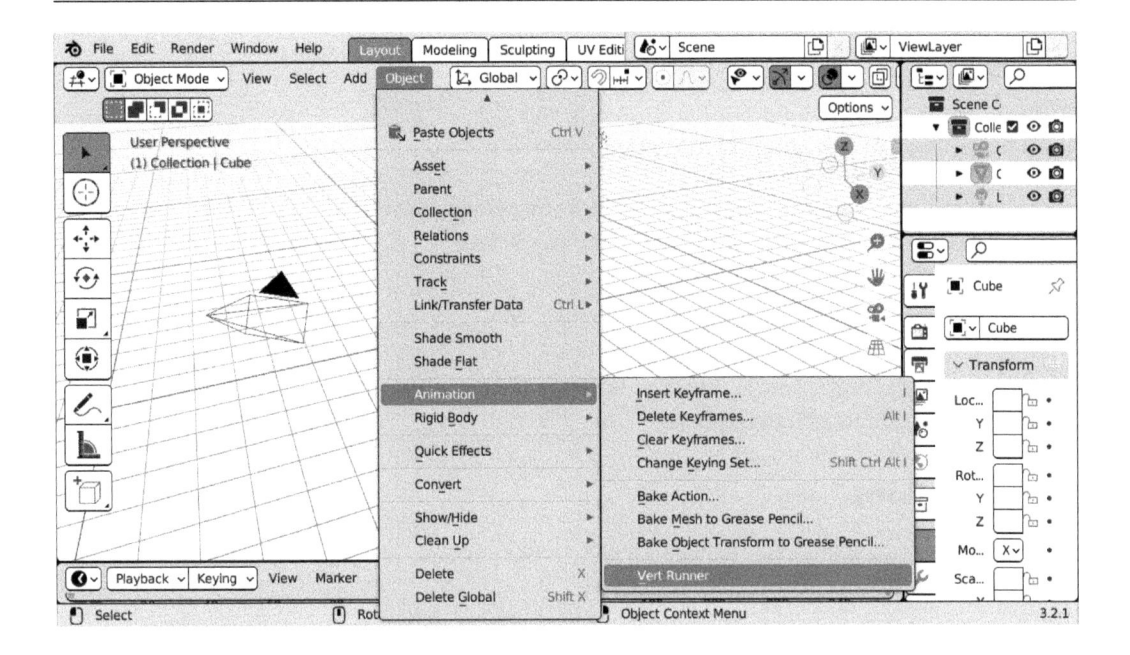

Figure 7.17: Object | Animation | Vert Runner animates the selected objects

Using **Vert Runner** after selecting at least two objects will animate the selected objects along the vertices of the active object. We can add an option to make the animation cyclic and animate the object rotation.

Creating cyclic animations

Sometimes, we want the first and last frame of an animation to match so that we can watch it in loops – for instance, an endless clip of a character running in circles.

In our case, an object passes through all the points of a mesh, starting with the first and ending with the last vertex, so the first and last frames of the animation will differ.

To create an animation cycle, we need to add the extra step of going back to the first coordinates after we have passed the last vertex.

The user must be able to choose whether they want a cyclic animation or not, so we will add an option to our operator. The `loop` attribute is a Boolean property – it can be enabled and disabled when the operator is run:

```
class VertRunner(bpy.types.Operator):
    """Run over the vertices of the active object"""
    bl_idname = "object.vert_runner"
    bl_label = "Vert Runner"
```

```
        bl_description = "Animate along verts of active object"
        bl_options = {'REGISTER', 'UNDO'}
        step: bpy.props.IntProperty(default=12)
        loop: bpy.props.BoolProperty(default=True)
```

The implementation is very easy: adding a copy of its first element at the end of `verts` brings the objects back to their initial position at the end of the animation:

```
        if self.loop:
            verts.append(verts[0])
```

Animating rotations is slightly more complex. With the help of a little math, at each frame, we can orient the object toward its next destination.

Adding rotations

The math behind rotations can be challenging at first, but since we just want to rotate the objects around their *Z*-axes, we can use basic **trigonometry**.

In trigonometry, angles can be represented as arcs of a circle of radius 1 and consequently, maximum length equal to two times π. The letter π (spelled pi) is the ratio between a circle and its diameter. Its approximate value is 3.14.

Trigonometry is a framework that contains many useful functions regarding the relationships between angles, segments, and rotations. Among them, there is a function that answers the question we are posing – that is, how do we rotate an object so that it faces toward a point?

Representing rotation arcs

Imagine rotating an object toward a point of known *X* and *Y* coordinates. If the rotation traces an arc over an imaginary circle, we can consider the y coordinate of our point as the *height* of that arc. This dimension is called the **sine** of the angle, and it is very useful when comparing angles and lengths.

The inverse of *sine* is called **arcsine**. It is of interest to us because it is the rotation associated with a sine. In other words, if we want to measure an angle and we know its *sine*, we can find the rotation using the following expression:

```
    rotation = arcsin(sine)
```

We know the sine, which is the y coordinate of the point we want to look at:

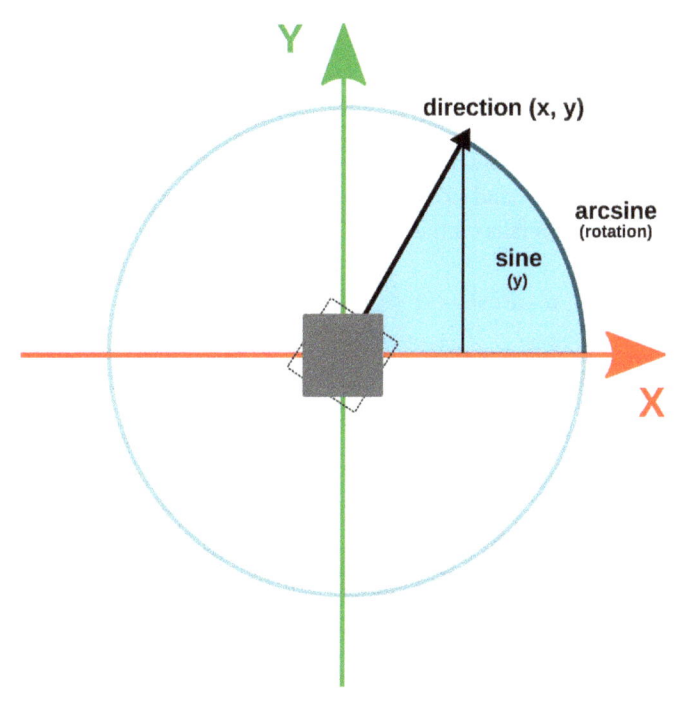

Figure 7.18: Trigonometric representation of a look-at rotation

So, *arcsine* is the trigonometric function we are looking for. It is shortened as `asin` in Python, and to use it, we must import it from the `math` module.

Implementing rotation

In trigonometry, we express rotations in **radians** – that is, arc lengths that are multiples of π. Rather than writing down our approximation of π as 3.14 in our code, we can import the `pi` constant from the `math` module. So, besides `asin`, we need `pi` as well so that our import section looks like this:

```
import bpy
from math import asin
from math import pi
```

We will write the `VertRunner.aim_to_point` method to address object rotations separately. The first step to do that is subtracting the current position from the target coordinates so that we can get a direction:

```
def aim_to_point(self, ob, point_co):
    """Orient object to look at coordinates"""
    direction = point_co - ob.location
```

Then, we must normalize the direction so that the result is not affected by distance:

```
direction.normalize()
```

The look-at rotation is returned by `asin(direction.y)`, but there is a catch: arcsine always assumes that it must cover the right-hand side of the circle – that is, positive values of `direction.x`. What happens when our direction falls on the other side?

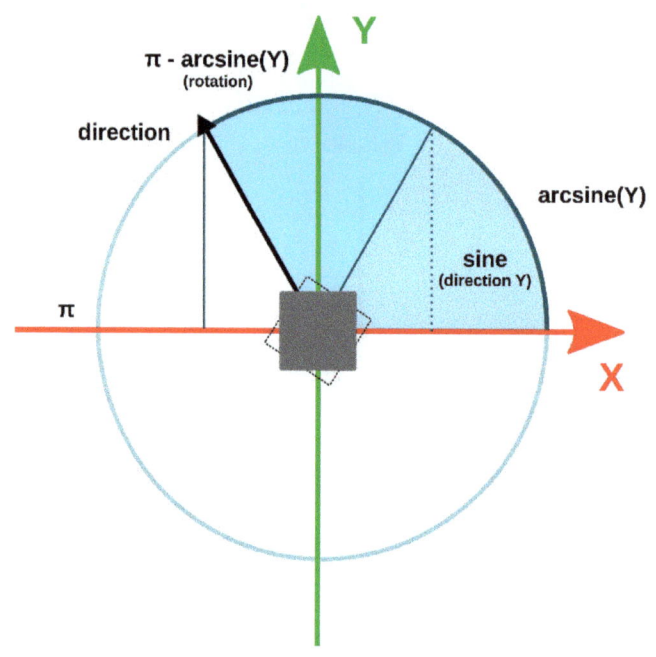

Figure 7.19: Look-at rotation for negative values of x

In that case, we can get to the other side of the circle by subtracting `pi` from the `asin` result since `pi` measures half of a unitary circumference length:

```
arc = asin(direction.y)
if direction.x < 0:
    arc = pi - arc
```

We must also account for the fact that, in Blender, objects at rest look in the opposite direction of the Y-axis, so we must add a 90 degrees clockwise rotation to the result.

In radians, that's `pi / 2`:

```
arc += pi / 2
```

At this point, `arc` contains the rotation we are looking for. We could use it right away, but there is still a problem: there are two ways to interpolate from one rotation to another.

Finding the shortest arc

Imagine rotating an object from 30° to 330°. The quickest way to do this is via a counterclockwise rotation that passes through 0° and stops at -30°, which is equivalent to 330°. The longest way is by passing clockwise from 30° to 180° and then, finally, 330°:

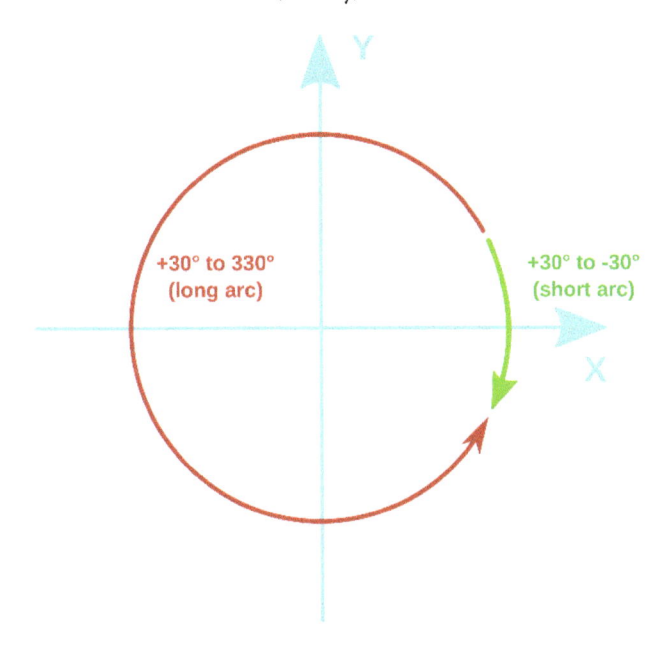

Figure 7.20: Short and long arcs of rotation from 30 to 330 degrees

Both are a valid transition from 30° to 330°, but we might want to prefer the shortest rotation: doing otherwise would cause an object to spin on itself.

To find the shortest arc away from the current rotation, we must store three possibilities in a tuple – the target orient, the same value after a complete clockwise rotation, and the same value rotated counterclockwise:

```
arcs = (arc, arc + 2*pi, arc - 2*pi)
```

Then, we must store the absolute rotational differences using a list comprehension. From there, we can get the shortest arc using `min`:

```
diffs = [abs(ob.rotation_euler.z - a) for a in arcs]
shortest = min(diffs)
```

We must use the arc associated with the minimum difference. Using that as a condition of the `next` statement, we can find it and assign it to `rotation_euler.z`:

```
res = next(a for i, a in enumerate(arcs)
           if diffs[i] == shortest)
ob.rotation_euler.z = res
```

We can now animate rotations using the `aim_to_point` method inside `execute`.

Putting everything together

The final version of `execute` is only slightly different. It starts in the same way: gathering the list of vertices, adding the first vertex again if we are animating a cycle, and skipping the active object:

```
def execute(self, context):
    verts = list(context.object.data.vertices)
    if self.loop:
        verts.append(verts[0])
    for ob in context.selected_objects:
        if ob == context.active_object:
            continue
```

Our orient method is based on the current object position, so before we start animating, we must move the object to the end of the path:

```
ob.location = context.object.data.vertices[-1].co
```

This way, when the animation starts, `aim_to_point` orients the object toward the first vertex. Now, we must insert keyframes for `rotation_euler.z` as well and repeat the process until all the points have been reached. After that, we can finish the execution:

```
        frame = context.scene.frame_current
        for vert in verts:
            self.aim_to_point(ob, vert.co)
            ob.keyframe_insert('rotation_euler',
                               frame=frame, index=2)
            ob.location = vert.co
            ob.keyframe_insert('location', frame=frame)
            frame += self.step
    return {'FINISHED'}
```

By enabling **Vert Runner** in the add-ons list or updating the scripts if it was enabled already, we can test our add-on on any pair of objects.

Using Vert Runner

We can use this operator on every couple of objects. There is a peculiar entry among the solids available in Blender – a stylized head of a **Monkey** jokingly inserted among more common shapes such as **Cube**, **Plane**, **Sphere**, and so on. The monkey's head, affectionately named **Suzanne**, makes rotations easier to visualize because of its obvious front side, so using it to test our add-on is a natural choice:

1. Add a monkey head to the scene via **Add** | **Mesh** | **Monkey** from the Viewport menu bar.
2. Add any other mesh to the scene or use the Cube shape from the default scene if present.
3. Keeping *Shift* pressed (multiple selection), select the monkey, then select the object to use as an animation guide.
4. From the Viewport menu bar, select **Object** | **Animation** | **Vert Runner**.
5. Play the animation with *Alt + A* or by clicking the media control button.

The cube will pass through each vertex of the active object. Speed and cyclic animation can be toggled in the options.

Though relatively simple, this tool can be expanded and generate motion for vehicles or even articulated characters.

Programming for animation generally comes down to converting an intuitive concept, such as looking toward a direction, into mathematical terms, like we did when extrapolating rotations. Plus, we have investigated the geometry structure and gained access to the vertex coordinates.

This brings us to the end of this chapter, where we learned how to affect the animation settings and the animation of objects.

Summary

In this chapter, we became familiar with object animation, learned how animations are created and stored, and looked at which scene settings are directly related to the animation system. We also learned how animation can be partly automated and approached from a geometric perspective, with a glimpse at the trigonometric representation of rotation angles.

Being able to automate part of the animation process is a valuable skill. Sometimes, the math involved might emerge and require solving, but we should not fear that, as math usually comes with a set of ready-to-use solutions for most ordinary use cases.

We have just started our journey into generated animation, which will continue in *Chapter 8*, where we will learn how to enrich animation curves with procedural effects.

Questions

1. How are animated values stored?
2. Can one animation curve contain the keyframes of an entire Vector property?
3. How are animation curves grouped?
4. The current frame number is 1. Without changing that setting, can we insert a keyframe at frame 4 using the user interface?
5. The current frame number is 1. Without changing that setting, can we insert a keyframe at frame 4 using the Python API?
6. Does a smooth motion require a keyframe on every frame?
7. How are keyframes interpolated?
8. Are there more ways to interpolate two rotations?

8
Animation Modifiers

Animation curves, or F-Curves, can be altered by modifiers without having their keyframes changed. This way, cinematic or motion effects can replace the initial curve completely or add to its original value.

The output of a modifier can be the input of another modifier, which, when combined, allows us to build complex results on top of simple animations.

Python scripts can be used to help automate this and streamline the workflow.

Changing a parameter affects the modifier's result, while its overall **Influence** can be reduced using the slider in the modifier interface.

In this chapter, you will learn how to add modifiers to animation F-Curves with your scripts and how to change their parameters.

This chapter will cover the following topics:

- Understanding F-Curve Modifiers in the Blender UI
- Adding F-Curve Modifiers via Python
- Using F-Curve Modifiers in our add-ons

Technical requirements

We will use Blender and Visual Studio Code in this chapter. The examples created in this chapter can be found at `https://github.com/PacktPublishing/Python-Scripting-in-Blender/tree/main/ch8`.

Using F-Curve Modifiers

Modifiers for animation curves, called **F-Curve Modifiers** or **F-Modifiers**, add non-destructive changes to animations while preserving their original data. We examined similar functionality in **Object Constraints** in *Chapter 4*, where we learned how to affect an object's position without changing the values stored in its channels.

Like object constraints, F-Modifiers are exposed to Python scripts through a collection property.

Before we delve into how F-Modifiers are scripted, we will have a look at how to create them in the **Graph Editor**.

Adding F-Curve Modifiers in the Graph Editor

We will now look at how to add variation to an animated object using F-Curve Modifiers.

For this example, we will use the `ani_loop.blend` scene, from the accompanying `PythonScriptingBlender/ch8/_scenes_` folder, but you can use any scene.

The animation along the 8-shaped path in `ani_loop.blend` wasn't created by hand: it was generated using the **Vert Runner** add-on developed in *Chapter 7*.

We will add some variation to the path of an animated object by creating an F-Curve Modifier in **Graph Editor**:

1. Select an animated object.
2. Change one of the UI areas to **Graph Editor**. A good place is the left Viewport in the **Animation Workspace**.
3. In the **Graph Editor** left panel, select the **X Location** channel.
4. Press *N* to display the property tabs. Make sure that the **Graph Editor** has focus and is large enough, or the tabs will not show up.
5. In the right panel of the **Graph Editor**, select the **Modifiers** tab.
6. From the **Modifiers** tab, select a modifier from the **Add Modifier** menu. In this example, we will use the **Stepped Interpolation** modifier.

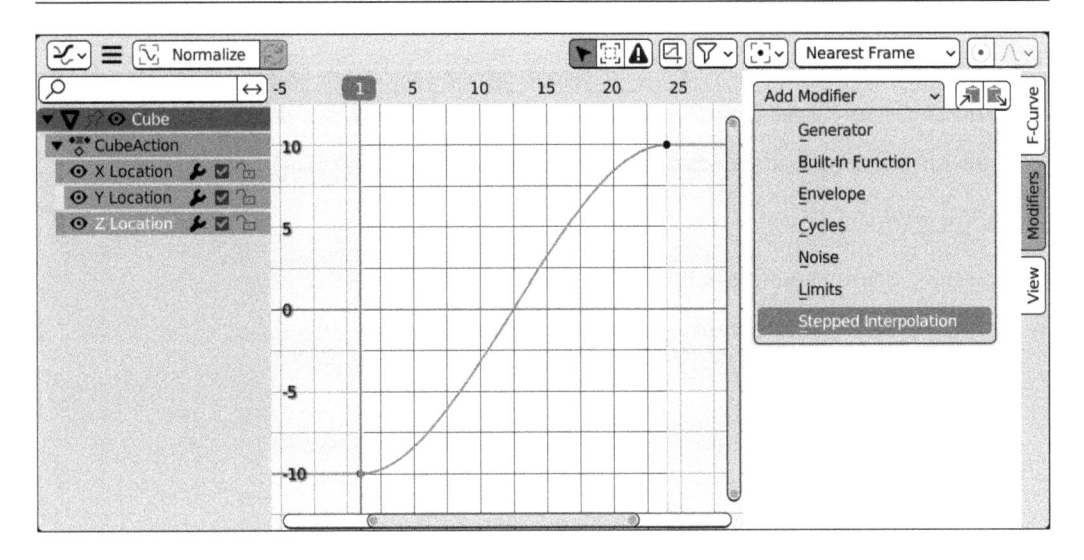

Figure 8.1: Adding curve modifiers in the Graph Editor

The animation curve for **Z Location** changes to a stepped graph. If we play the animation now, we will see the object proceeding in little jumps rather than smoothly, as before.

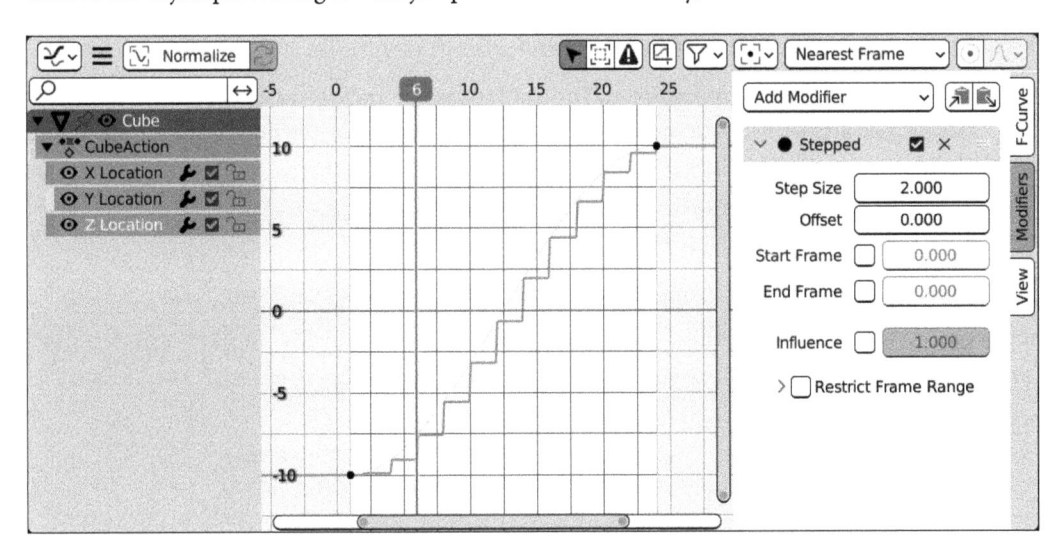

Figure 8.2: Stepped modifier applied on a smooth curve

The Blender manual describes modifiers in detail on the **F-Curve Modifiers** page:

```
docs.blender.org/manual/en/3.2/editors/graph_editor/fcurves/modifiers.
html
```

There are seven available types. The first two generate curves based on mathematical formulas:

- **Generator**: Expressions for lines, parabolas, and curves of higher degrees
- **Built-in**: Trigonometric and logarithmic formulas

The other five cover some basic animation tasks:

- **Envelope**: Control points for editing the overall shape of the curve
- **Cyclic**: To repeat animations in loops after their last frame
- **Noise**: Adds random jitter to the animation
- **Limits**: Limits the animation values to a range
- **Stepped Interpolation**: Converts smooth animation to jerky motion

Like constraints, modifiers of an F-Curve are exposed to Python as a collection. We can use the `fcurve.modifiers.new` method to add new modifiers via scripting.

Adding F-Curve Modifiers in Python

The `fcurve.modifiers.new(type)` method creates a new modifier according to the type provided in the argument. It returns the new modifier.

With the exception of **Built-in** and **Stepped Interpolation**, the respective keywords for which are `FNGENERATOR` and `STEPPED`, modifiers of a given type are created using the type name in uppercase letters:

```
type (enum in ['GENERATOR', 'FNGENERATOR', 'ENVELOPE', 'CYCLES',
'NOISE', 'LIMITS', 'STEPPED'])
```

So, to add a `'STEPPED'` modifier to the **Z Location** curve, that is, the third F-Curve of an animated object (index 2), we use the following:

```
>>> import bpy
>>> anim_data = bpy.context.object.animation_data
>>> m = anim_data.action.fcurves[2].modifiers.new('STEPPED')
```

Likewise, a modifier can be removed using the `fcurve.modifiers.remove` method. This time, the Python instance of the modifier must be used as an argument:

```
>>> anim_data.action.fcurves[2].modifiers.remove(m)
```

Now that we have learned where F-Modifiers can be found, how they work, and how to add more of them, both in the user interface and the Python Console, we can use this knowledge in our scripts.

The add-on we will write in the next section allows us to create shaky animations using F-Modifiers.

Writing the Shaker add-on

The **Shaker** add-on creates a shaky effect on the active object by adding noise modifiers to its animation curves.

There are cases when we want to add some shaking to a motion. For instance, directors often use a *camera shake* to suggest an object being bumped or hit. Another use case is the bumpy motion of a vehicle, or hairs and feathers in a windy environment. The Python script we are going to write will contain an operator and a menu function for quick execution.

Setting up the environment

We first create a Python script for our add-on:

1. Create the `PythonScriptingBlender/ch8/addons` folder. We can use the file manager or the **File** tab of our code editor, such as **VS Code**.
2. Create a new file in that folder and name it `object_shaker.py`. We can use the file manager or the **New File** button of our code editor.
3. Open the file in your editor of choice.
4. Set the **Scripts** path to `PythonScriptingBlender/ch8` in the Blender **File Paths** preferences.

Now, we will start writing the add-on code as usual.

Writing the Shaker add-on info

We will add our new operator, **Object Shaker**, to the right-click object menu. We can write the instructions on how to run the operator in the `location` attribute of the add-on info:

```
bl_info = {
    "name": "Object Shaker",
    "author": "Packt Man",
    "version": (1, 0),
    "blender": (3, 00, 0),
    "description": "Add Shaky motion to active object",
    "location": "Object Right Click -> Add Object Shake",
    "category": "Learning",
}
```

Writing the Add Object Shake operator class

We import the bpy module, then write the bl_* identifiers of Object Shaker:

```
import bpy
class ObjectShaker(bpy.types.Operator):
    """Set Playback range to current action Start/End"""
    bl_idname = "object.shaker_animation"
    bl_label = "Add Object Shake"
    bl_description = "Add Shake Motion to Active Object"
    bl_options = {'REGISTER', 'UNDO'}
```

This operator needs two float parameters:

- Noise duration in seconds
- Noise strength, that is, how much this modifier contributes to the animation

duration should be a positive number: there is no such thing as a negative amount of time. So, we set 0.0 as the property minimum. The amount of shaking, on the other hand, could benefit from values below 0.0 or above 1.0. It's a more peculiar circumstance in which we still want to set the range of values from 0.0 to 1.0 as the ordinary condition, but we don't want to prevent the user from going beyond those limits if they want to. We can set limits that apply to the slider but accept an out-of-range numerical input using the soft_min and soft_max parameters.

Adding limits and soft limits to properties

Normally, the influence, or strength, of the modifier, should range between 0.0 and 1.0 (meaning no influence and full influence, respectively) but using values outside that range has a multiplicative effect. For instance, an influence of 2.0 doubles the modifier's contribution.

Soft limits for Blender properties are useful in this case: min, max, soft_min, and soft_max limit the range of the slider in the interface, but while min and max never accept any number exceeding their range, soft_min and soft_max allow the user to click on the slider and type any value they wish using the keyboard.

Values exceeding the initial soft_min and soft_max parameters are considered valid input and become the new range of the slider:

```
duration: bpy.props.FloatProperty(default=1.0, min=0)
strenght: bpy.props.FloatProperty(default=1.0,
                                  soft_min=0,
                                  soft_max=1.0)
```

Now, we can write the poll method for verifying the conditions and the execute method to perform the action of adding noise.

Writing the operator methods

Besides the usual `poll` and `execute` methods, we will write a utility function for finding the F-Curve of a given property.

Writing the poll method

The condition for the `poll` method is very simple – the operator can be invoked if there is an active object:

```
@classmethod
def poll(cls, context):
    return bool(context.object)
```

We need an animated property to add a noise modifier. If it is already animated, we pick the existing animation curve, otherwise, we create a new one. This operation can be implemented as a separate function, named `get_fcurve`, which takes `data_path` as an argument and returns its animation curve. It creates a new curve if it doesn't exist yet.

Writing the get_fcurve method

We delegate the task of finding or creating a property animation curve to the `get_fcurve` function. Since it will be used by the `ObjectShaker` operator alone, we write it as a class method, with `self` as its first argument. We might want to use it on more than one property and object, so we also pass the object to inspect and `data_path` of the property to animate. In case of vector properties, we pass the `index` component as well. We use `obj` rather than `object` as a parameter name because the latter represents the Python basic class, a term we don't want to override.

We know from *Chapter 7*, that F-Curves belong to an action, and our operator adds noise to the current action, so this function will look for the `action` attribute of the object's animation data. Before we run `get_fcurve`, we should make sure that such an action exists, so, in line with the *Defensive Programming* practice learned in *Chapter 6*, we use `assert` to halt the script if, for unforeseen reasons, no current action is found:

```
def get_fcurve(self, obj, data_path, index):
    """Returns F-Curve of given data_path/index"""
    action = obj.animation_data.action
    assert action
```

Now we need to return the F-Curve that animates the `data_path` instance provided as an argument, and create it if it doesn't exist. We can attempt its creation using `try`, a statement learned in the *Improving our code* section of *Chapter 3*.

Trying to create two F-Curves with the same path causes a `RuntimeError` error, which, in a `try` statement, triggers the `except` clause. By looking for existing curves only if we need to, our code will be leaner and slightly faster.

Under the `except` statement, we use the `next` function on a conditional *iterator*, that is, a sequence of objects that satisfy our criteria, in this case, a matching `data_path` and `index`:

```
try:
    crv = action.fcurves.new(data_path,index=index)
except RuntimeError:
    crv = next(fc for fc in action.fcurves
                if fc.data_path == data_path and
                   fc.array_index == index)
```

In either case, we will end up with the `crv` variable containing the F-Curve we are looking for. We could have used a `for` loop to iterate `action.fcurves`, but the `next` function provides a valid and compact alternative.

Scrolling through collections efficiently

The `next` function returns the first valid element of a sequence. For example, typing `next(action.fcurves)` simply gives the first curve of an action. The argument of `next` can be any iterator, though, not just a list or a collection. Since iterators can contain conditional statements such as `if`, `next` can be a concise and performant alternative to `for` loops.

While `fc for fc in action.fcurves` scrolls all the elements of `fcurves`, the conditions on `fc.data_path` and `fc.array_index` ensure that the first curve that complies with those requirements is returned.

If no curve is found, `next` fails with a `StopIteration` error, but we know that it will not happen: an existing curve brought us to the `except` block of this `try` statement in the first place. So, either under the `try` block or under `except`, the `crv` variable now contains the F-Curve we are looking for. Before we add a modifier to it, we must make sure that it contains at least one keyframe.

Ensuring the presence of keyframes

At this point, we have stored an animation curve in the `crv` variable, but we must look for its keyframe points, or it will not be evaluated. If the `keyframe_points` collection is empty, we add keyframes to it by using `keyframe_points.insert`. We will use the current frame and value as arguments:

```
if not crv.keyframe_points:
    crv.keyframe_points.insert(
                frame=context.scene.frame_current,
                value=getattr(obj,
                        data_path)[index])
```

Now that we have an animation curve and it is guaranteed to support modifiers, we can return the `crv` variable and exit the `get_fcurve` function:

```
return crv
```

Writing the Shaker add-on

This function will be called in the `execute` method, the last missing piece of the operator.

Writing the execute method

If our object has not been animated yet, we create new `animation_data`, otherwise, we store the existing data in the `anim` variable:

```
def execute(self, context):
    if not context.object.animation_data:
        anim = context.object.animation_data_create()
    else:
        anim = context.object.animation_data
```

Likewise, we should create a new action if there isn't one yet or get the current one. In either case, it is going to be stored in the `action` variable:

```
if not anim.action:
    action = bpy.data.actions.new('ShakeMotion')
    anim.action = action
else:
    action = anim_data.action
```

Now, it's finally time to add some shaking motion. First, we need to express the duration of the effect in frames, rather than seconds. To do that, we multiply the `duration` parameter by the frames-per-second of the scene. Once we have the duration in frames, we divide it by half to center the object shake around the current frame; half of the frames will be played before it, while the second half will be played afterward:

```
fps = context.scene.render.fps
duration_frames = self.duration * fps / 2
current = context.scene.frame_current
start = current - duration_frames
end = current + duration_frames
```

The next step is looking for the animation curves that we want to alter: location Z, rotation_euler X, and rotation_euler Y. We need these ones specifically as they represent the up-down shake, yaw shake, and pitch shake of a camera, respectively.

If they don't exist, our `get_fcurve` method creates and returns them:

```
        z_loc_crv = self.get_fcurve(context,
                                    'location',
                                    index=2)
        x_rot_crv = self.get_fcurve(context,
                                    'rotation_euler',
                                    index=0)
```

```
                y_rot_crv = self.get_fcurve(context,
                                            'rotation_euler',
                                            index=1)
```

Since F-Modifiers are specific to each curve, we create a `NOISE` modifier for each of them. We use a `for` loop to create all three at once. The noise `strength` value, a float attribute, can be set directly from the `strength` parameter of the operator, while we computed the `start` and `end` values for the noise earlier:

```
        for crv in z_loc_crv, y_rot_crv, x_rot_crv:
            noise = crv.modifiers.new('NOISE')
            noise.strength = self.strenght
            noise.use_restricted_range = True
            noise.frame_start = start
            noise.frame_end = end
        return {'FINISHED'}
```

We have turned `use_restricted_range` on to limit the noise in our `start` and `end` frames: the `frame_start` and `frame_end` attributes would have no effect otherwise. Once we have set F-Modifiers for the three curves, we can finally exit the method.

Now that our operator is complete, we can add a menu item to the interface and the `register/unregister` functions.

Adding menu items

As we learned when writing interfaces, a menu function takes `self` and `context` as arguments.

Inside the menu function, we add a separator and the `ObjectShaker` operator to `self.layout`:

```
def m_items(self, context):
    self.layout.separator()
    self.layout.operator(ObjectShaker.bl_idname)
```

This function can then be added to any menu, but since our operator affects the animation of object transforms, we can use the right-click menu displayed by the Viewport in **Object Mode**.

Finding the class names of context menus

The API documentation doesn't contain a list of all menus. We can look for them in `bpy.types`, which contains all the Blender classes, and keep in mind that the class name we are looking for starts with `VIEW3D_MT` and ends with `_context_menu`.

We can use these criteria in a *list comprehension*, that is, a list-like object delimited by square brackets that, like the `next` function we have met earlier in this section, is built with a conditional iterator. We can run it in Blender's **Python Console**:

```
>>> [c for c in dir(bpy.types) if
    c.endswith('context_menu')]
```

Among the listed context menus, we find `VIEW3D_MT_object_context_menu`:

```
['ASSETBROWSER_MT_context_menu',
...
['VIEW3D_MT_edit_metaball_context_menu', 'VIEW3D_MT_gpencil_edit_
context_menu', 'VIEW3D_MT_object_context_menu', 'VIEW3D_MT_particle_
context_menu',
...
```

In returning the results that match the `context_menu` suffix, our list comprehension acted almost like a small search engine. To filter the result even further, we can add an `"object"` string as a requirement to filter the output to one result:

```
[c for c in dir(bpy.types) if c.endswith('context_menu')
                   and 'object' in c]
```

This list comprehension narrows the results down to the object context menu only:

```
>>> [c for c in dir(bpy.types) if c.endswith('context_menu')
...                    and 'object' in c]
['VIEW3D_MT_object_context_menu']
```

Now that we know which menu class to use, we can move to registering the add-on.

Registering the Shaker add-on

Enabling the add-on produces these two results:

- Adds the `ObjectShaker` class to Blender
- Adds the `m_items` function to the object right-click menu

Each of those tasks happen in the `register` function:

```
def register():
    bpy.utils.register_class(ObjectShaker)
    bpy.types.VIEW3D_MT_object_context_menu.append(m_items)
```

Following the same logic, when the add-on is disabled, its code is purged from Blender, upon which `m_items` should be removed from the menu and `ObjectShaker` from the registered classes. Failing to do so would leave orphan entities in Blender. The `unregister` function takes care of that:

```
def unregister():
    bpy.types.VIEW3D_MT_object_context_menu.remove(m_items)
    bpy.utils.unregister_class(ObjectShaker)
```

We can refresh the add-ons using the **Refresh** button in the **Add-ons** preferences and enable **Object Shaker** from the **Learning** category. When the add-on is enabled, the **Add Object Shake** option appears in the given object's right-click menu.

Using the Shaker add-on

Using our add-on, we can add a shaking motion to any object by following these steps:

1. Make the object active.
2. Right-click (or press W if **Select with Mouse Button** was set to **Right** in **Preferences | Keymap**).
3. Select **Add Object Shake** from the menu.
4. Adjust the **duration** and **strength** values in the **Execution** panel.

Like with the *Action Range add-on* from *Chapter 7*, the selected amount of **duration** and **strength** can be changed after execution using **Edit | Adjust Last Operation** from the top bar.

We have created a tool that adds a procedural behavior to an object using animation modifiers. This is a valuable shortcut when animating with Python. Moreover, it introduces us to the concept of a non-destructive modifier, that is, adding parametric changes that can be removed or edited at will.

Summary

We have learned how to create animation effects for our scenes and have seen how we can convert an idea into a procedural tool. Artists and technical animators can come up with convoluted conceptual configurations, which we can turn into quick-setup operators following the process outlined in this chapter.

Using the animation system is a convenient way to implement parametric behaviors, as it relies on the application update logic and produces fast, reliable outputs.

We will explore a similar but more powerful technique in *Chapter 9*, thus completing our overview of the animation system.

Questions

1. What do we mean by non-destructive modifiers?
2. Do modifiers change the keyframe points of a curve?
3. Can we add animation modifiers to non-animated objects?
4. How do we make sure that a property is animated?
5. What is a parameter soft limit?
6. In which cases do we use soft rather than strong limits?
7. How can we look for a class name in Python?

9
Animation Drivers

A **driver** is a function that controls the value of a property. It can take the value of other properties as input, creating a connection between two or more properties. For example, a driver might set the X location of an object based on the rotation of another object.

Drivers are similar to animations, with which they share the update system and f-curve data but are way more flexible and can be combined with Python to create custom setups.

They are an essential part of technical animation and are used for creating simple controls or complex mechanics. Drivers don't have a specific purpose: they are designed to create custom behaviors. For that reason, they are ubiquitous in rigging and help connect properties, even between entities of different types, such as objects and shaders.

In this chapter, you will learn how to create and test your Python drivers easily, as well as how to script their creation. Besides helping with automating rig mechanics, this knowledge will also make it easier for you to understand formulas and implement them in Blender.

This chapter will cover the following topics:

- Creating drivers
- Using Python expressions in drivers
- Scripting mathematic formulas
- Automating the driver setup

Technical requirements

We will use Blender and **Visual Studio Code** in this chapter, but any IDE will do. The examples that were created for this chapter can be found at `https://github.com/PacktPublishing/Python-Scripting-in-Blender/tree/main/ch9`.

Creating drivers

The procedure for creating **drivers** is very similar to the one for creating animations. While the animation time is the only input of animation curves, drivers can depend on one or more of the following:

- The result of Python expressions
- Any property that can be animated
- The transform channels of objects
- The difference in rotations between objects
- The distance between objects

When we create a driver, we must specify at least one input. In this section, we will learn how to set up a simple wheel by creating new drivers with the user interface.

Creating quick drivers via the right-click menu

There are a few shortcuts for creating drivers quickly.

Let's take a look at an example to understand these shortcuts. Suppose that, to animate a wheel, we want an object's **Location Y** to drive its **Rotation X** channel. We can set this up for Blender's default cube:

1. Open Blender or go back to the default scene via **File | New | General**.
2. Select the default **Cube** to make it active.
3. Press *N* to display the Transform properties.

Location Y is our input. Rather than look for its data path, we will copy it to the clipboard:

1. Right-click on **Location Y** to display the **Y:** menu.
2. From the menu, pick **Copy As New Driver**.

The driver doesn't exist yet, so we must create it for the property we want to affect:

1. Right-click on **Rotation X** to display the **X:** menu.
2. From the menu, pick **Paste Driver**.

The **Rotation X** channel will be colored purple, which is the color that's used for driven properties. Moving the **Cube** object along its **Y**-axis will also make it roll:

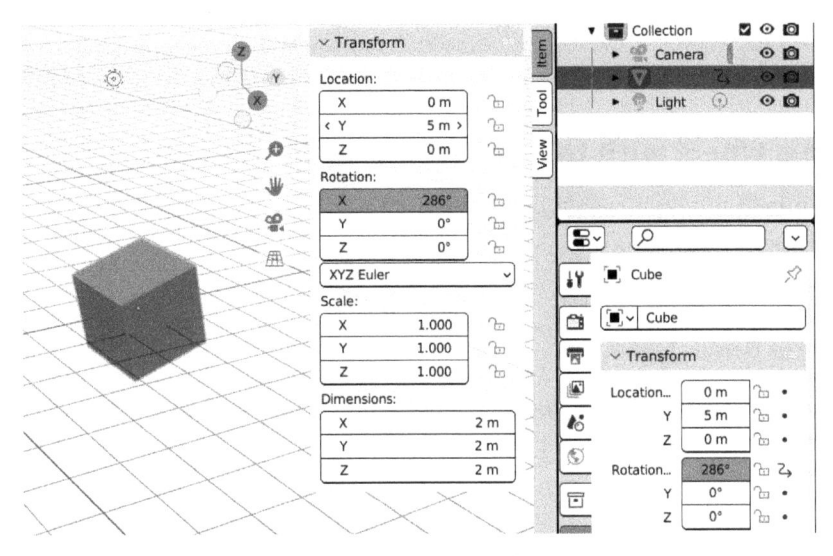

Figure 9.1: The Y location drives the X rotation

The driver that's using **Copy As New Driver** is a one-to-one connection driver, in that it copies the exact amount from one property to another. It is less evident in a location-to-rotation connection because, as we know from *Chapter 4*, rotations are stored as radians but displayed in degrees by default. A value of 5 radians is equivalent to about 286 degrees of rotation, as reflected in the values we can see in *Figure 9.1*.

Switching **Rotation Unit** to **Radians**, as shown in *Figure 9.2*, makes a one-to-one relationship between **Location Y** and **Rotation X** evident:

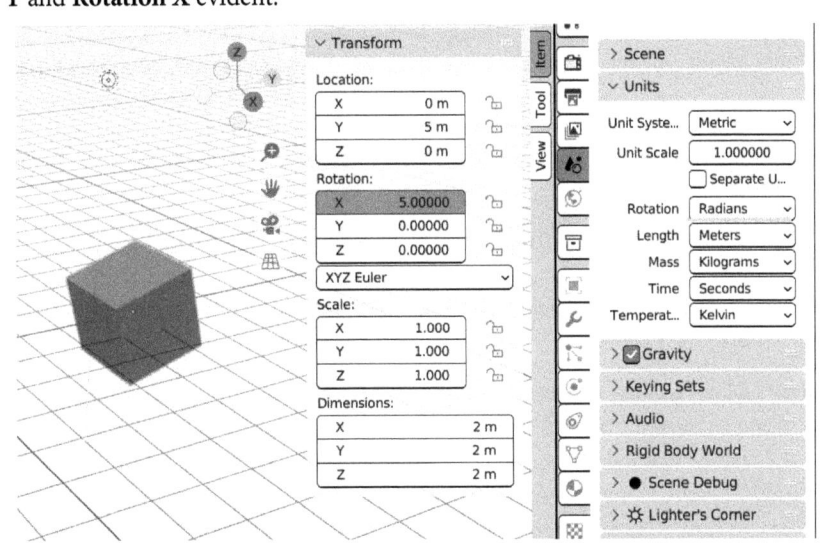

Figure 9.2: Location X and Rotation X display the same value using radians

Animation Drivers

Even if the cube rolls when it is moved, it doesn't look like a wheel: a wheel rotates the other way around. We can set that up using the **Drivers Editor** area.

Setting up a wheel with the Drivers Editor

In the **Drivers Editor** area, we can display and edit the drivers of the objects present in the scene. It can be brought up following these steps:

1. Right-click on a **Driven Property**.
2. Select **Open Drivers Editor**.

It's very similar to the **Graph Editor** area that we looked at in first *section* of *Chapter 7*, except it displays drivers rather than animation curves:

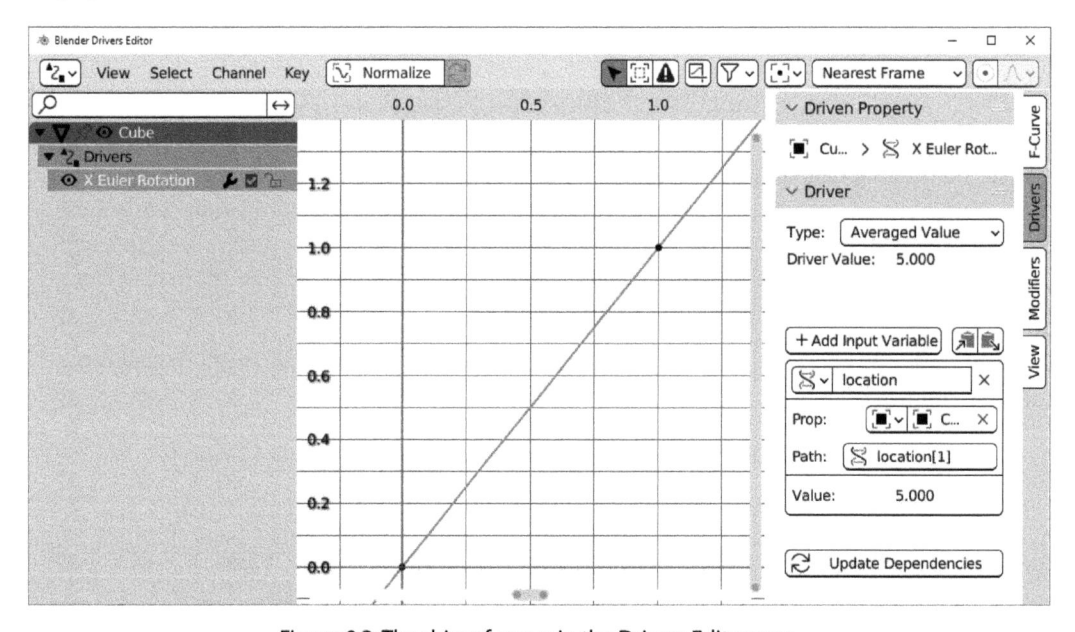

Figure 9.3: The driver f-curve in the Drivers Editor area

We can get a better view of the curve by selecting **View** | **Frame All** from the **Drivers Editor** menu bar or pressing *Home* on the keyboard.

The default driver's f-curve is the diagonal of the positive cartesian plane, with control points at coordinates (0.0, 0.0) and (1.0, 1.0). We can see that the result of the curve, displayed in the **Driver** panel as the **Driver Value** property, equals 5.0, the same value as the **location** input variable.

Since the rotation of a wheel is opposite to its motion, we need to invert that result by changing the curve. To do that, follow these steps:

1. In the **Drivers Editor** properties, select the **F-Curve** tab.
2. Select the top-right point of the f-curve by left-clicking.
3. In the **Active Keyframe** properties, change **Value** from `1.0` to `-1.0`:

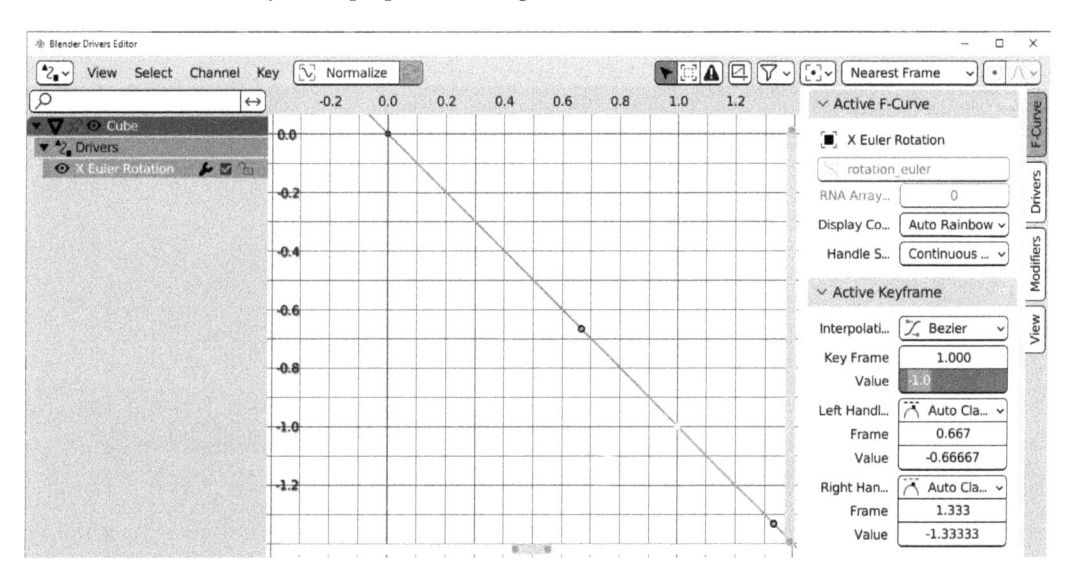

Figure 9.4: The driver's f-curve pointing downwards

Now, moving the cube over its **Y**-axis makes it roll in the right direction. If you look carefully, something will still be off: this driver is rolling slightly too slowly.

The ratio between a circle of size 1 and the length it covers in one round is π, the mathematical constant pi, which is approximately 3.14.

That distance only takes a half round to a wheel twice as large, like our default cube of size 2 x 2 x 2, so typing `pi/2` in the **Key Frame** field sets the ratio between **Location** and **Rotation** to approximately `1.571`, a multiplier slightly faster than `1`. Translating the cube on its **Y**-axis now makes it roll like a wheel, albeit a square one.

We used a division to get that result, but we can also use Python formulas in drivers. We can also create drivers by just typing a formula.

Creating driver expressions in properties

A different type of driver, one that relies on Python math formulas, can be created by typing a hash symbol (#) in a property field. Here are the steps for creating a driver expression:

1. Open Blender or go back to the default scene via **File | New | General**.
2. Select the default cube to make it active.
3. Left-click on the `rotation_euler.x` property to edit its value.
4. Type `#sin(frame)` and press *Enter*.

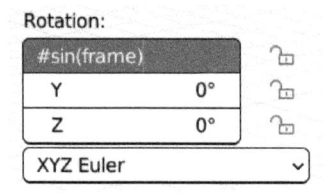

Figure 9. 5: Typing Python expressions in object properties

The expression we have just written is already active. If we start the playback by pressing the triangular **Play** button in the **media controls** area, or with *Alt + A*, the cube will jitter quickly on its **X**-axis.

The `sin(frame)` expression depends on time, as animations do, but the value per frame is the output of a Python instruction, and we can enrich it for more complex results.

In the next section, we will combine the `frame` variable, the `sin` function, and the driver inputs to create a procedural, parametric animation of a pendulum.

> We DON'T want results!
>
> Omitting the # symbol will set the result of the expression rather than creating a driver. Typing `frame` sets the property to the numeric value of the current frame, such as 1 or 24. If we type `#frame`, the value will change as we play the animation.

Driving a cyclic motion

A pendulum is a weight suspended from a fixed point, free to swing back and forth. It has many real-life applications in time, gravity, and geographic measurements, while in 3D, an oscillating motion is used for displaying clock mechanisms, hanging props, and other cyclic motions. The trigonometric function **sine** is commonly used to simulate this kind of motion.

The `sin` function from the `math` module is the Python syntax for *sine*. We encountered *sine* in *Chapter 7*, where we used its inverse, *arcsine*, to orient objects using Python. Sine is a periodic wave function – it repeats itself at fixed intervals:

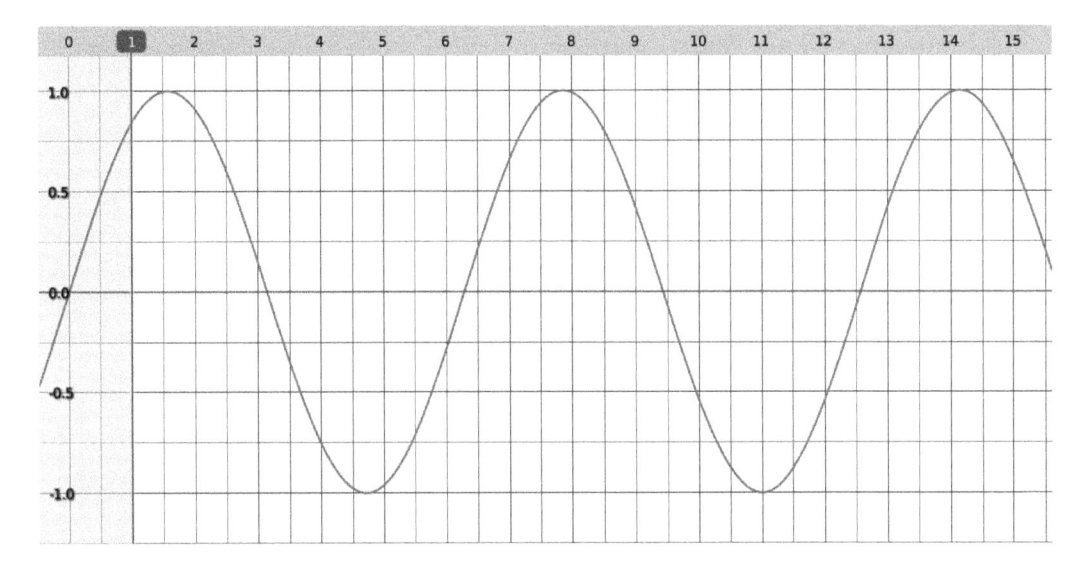

Figure 9.6: The sine function

Playing the animation will make the cube jitter very fast. To slow it down, we can click **Driven Property** and give the formula a slower pace.

For instance, we can change it to `sin(frame/10)` and it will slow down tenfold. Now, the cube rocks back and forth gently. We can do even better and set up a rotation pivot for a proper swing.

Changing the rotation pivot via constraints

The easier way to affect an object's pivot is by using **constraints**. We came across constraints in *Chapter 4*, and used them to change an object's position without altering its transform properties. This time, we will use a **Pivot Constraint** to alter the center of rotation.

Adding a Pivot Constraint in Blender

A **Pivot Constraint** moves an object's center of rotation to a different object's position or specific coordinates. We are going to use an **Empty**, a Blender object that doesn't contain any geometry:

1. Add an empty to the scene via **Add | Empty | Plain Axes** from the **3D View** area. This object will be the new rotation pivot.
2. Move this **Empty** somewhere above the **Cube** object so that it can act as a suspension point.

218   Animation Drivers

Now, we can create the constraint:

1. Select the **Cube** object and reach its **Constraints** tab in the properties. It is marked with the icon of a connection rod.
2. Select **Pivot** from the **Add Object Constraint** drop-down. A new constraint will be created:

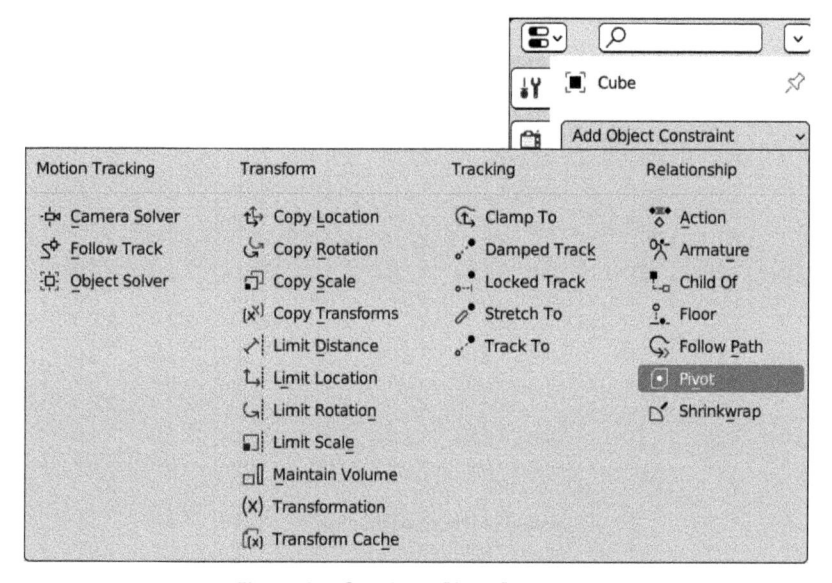

Figure 9.7: Creating a Pivot Constraint

3. Click the **Target** field in the **Pivot Constraint** panel, and select **Empty** among the list of objects.
4. Now, click the **Rotation Range** property and change it to **Always** so that rotations in all directions are affected.

If we play the animation, the cube oscillates left and right:

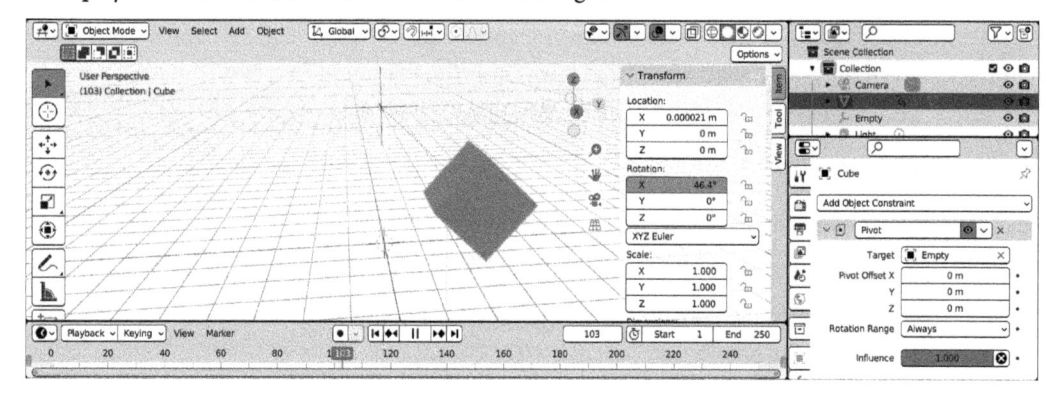

Figure 9.8: The Pivot Constraint changing the rotation center of the Cube object

It starts to look like a pendulum, but the speed of a swinging motion should depend on the length of the cord, which we are not considering in our formula. To improve our driver, we must learn how the sine function works and how to control its period. Then, we must study pendulum physics and write an expression that takes the cord length into account.

Controlling the period of the sin function

To have better control of the sine period, we need to observe its graph, as shown in *Figure 9.9*. Its value is 0 at frame 0, and after rising between frames 1 and 2, it goes back to zero just a little bit after frame 3:

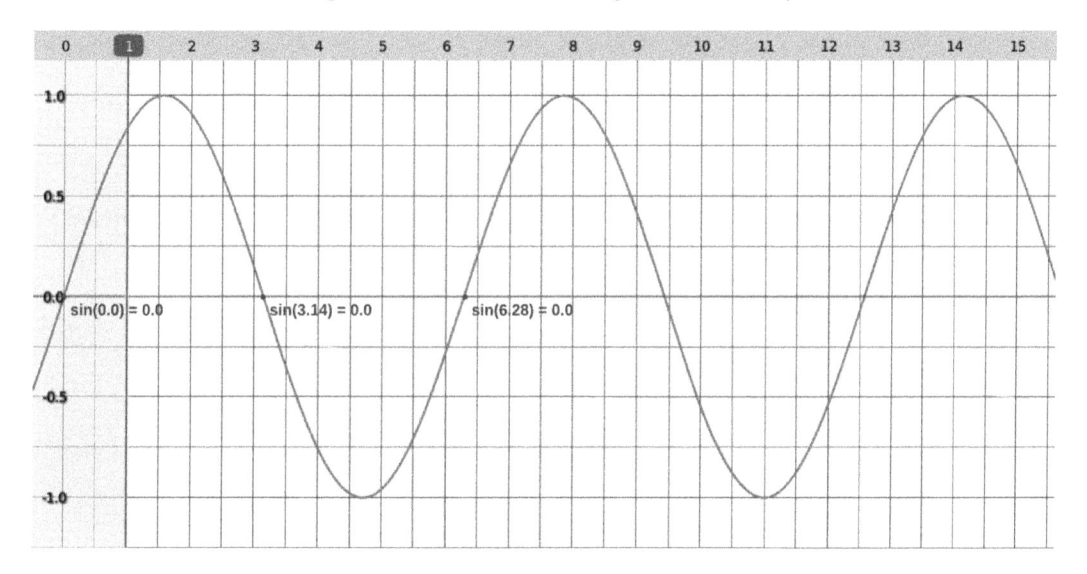

Figure 9.9: The sine function

This happens because sine, an angle-related function, depends on the mathematical constant π, and its value is zero at points 3.14, 6.28, and so on. The relationship between angles and circles is due to how angles describe circular arcs.

If the sine function repeats at every full circle, and a full circle measures 2 * π radians, we can say that the period of the `sin(frame)` formula is 2 * pi frames.

By using 2 * pi as an argument of `sin`, we get a formula whose period is just one frame:

```
sin(frame * 2 * pi)
```

The result of this formula is always 0, but that's more useful than it seems: dividing `frame * 2 * pi` by a specific number of frames, we can set how much it takes for the formula to repeat – that is, we now have control over the period.

For instance, the result of the following formula repeats every 10 frames:

```
sin(frame * 2 * pi / 10)
```

Now, we can look up the pendulum formula and set up a physically correct oscillation.

Implementing the pendulum equation

According to Wikipedia (en.wikipedia.org/wiki/Pendulum), the period of a pendulum depends on the length of its cord, and is approximated with the following formula:

$$2\pi\sqrt{L/g}$$

It reads 2 times pi times the **square root** of length over gravity. In Python, this looks as follows:

```
2 * pi * sqrt(length / 9.8)
```

Here, sqrt is the square root operation and 9.8 is the gravity on Earth following the **International System of Units (SI)**. The time unit is seconds in this system, so we need to express the formulas in our driver in seconds.

The expression for repeating sin in one frame was as follows:

```
sin(frame * 2 * pi)
```

And since we need to apply a period in seconds, we divide that expression by the frames per second:

```
sin(frame/fps * 2 * pi)
```

This slows down our expression to a period of 1 second.

We aim to end up with a period of 2 * pi * sqrt(length / 9.8) seconds, so we divide the argument of sin by that amount.

After the division, we end up with a function of two variables, fps and length:

```
sin((frame / fps) * 2 * pi / (2 * pi * sqrt(length/9.8)))
```

The value of 2 * pi / 2 *pi is 1 and can be removed from the multiplication. Now, our formula looks much better:

```
sin(frame / fps / sqrt(length/9.8))
```

Typing it inside **Rotation X** creates a *driver*:

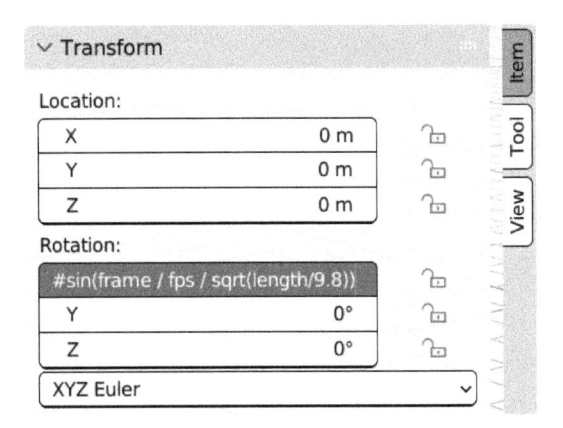

Figure 9.10: Implementation of the pendulum formula

The driver won't work yet, though – the `frame` variable is already defined by Blender, but `length` and `fps` do not exist and cause an error. We need to add these two variables to the driver properties.

Adding variables to drivers

We could perform this operation in the **Drivers Editor** area we used in the *Creating drivers* section of this chapter, but since we don't need to edit the *f-curve*, we can use a simpler interface.

Displaying the Driven Property window

The **Driven Property** window displays the details of a single driver. It is quick to access, and its content is the same as the **Drivers** tab in the **Drivers Editor** area.

The steps for displaying and editing a driven property are as follows:

1. Right-click on a driven property.
2. Select **Edit Driver** from the context menu.

The **Driven Property** window recaps the path of the affected property, which **Type** of driver it is, if there are errors in the driver, and which variables have been created:

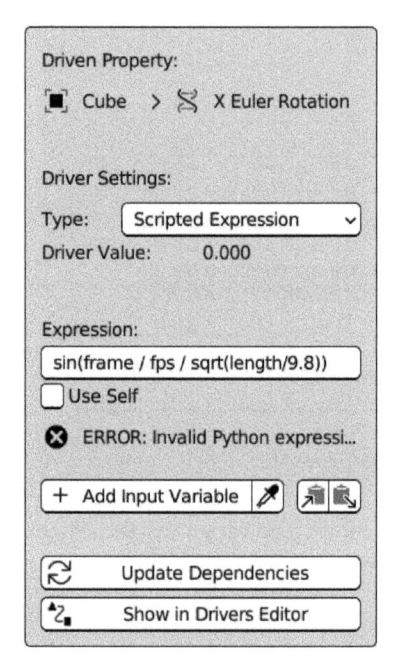

Figure 9.11: Properties of a scripted expression driver

At this stage, the driver type will be set to **Scripted Expression**; the **Expression** field contains our pendulum formula, while the error label informs us that something went wrong with the Python expression.

This error is caused by the missing `fps` and `length` variables. Adding them will fix it.

> **Hold on to your window!**
>
> **Driven Property** is a popover window that disappears when the mouse pointer moves back outside of its borders. Don't worry, though; every change will still be there when you open the window again.

Getting the frame per seconds property

Clicking the + **Add Input Variable** button adds a new variable to the driver. By default, this variable's name is `var`, and it's an **RNA property** variable – that is, it reads the value from another property in Blender. To get that value, we need to specify the following:

- The type of the entity (object, scene, action, and so on)
- The name of the entity
- The name of the property

These properties can be set in the **Variable** panel:

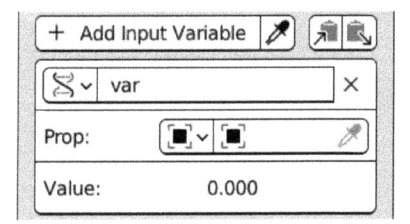

Figure 9.12: A newly created variable

Here are the steps to get the **Frames Per Second** render setting of the scene through this variable:

1. Select **Scene** from the property type list, which is displayed with the left button below the variable's name:

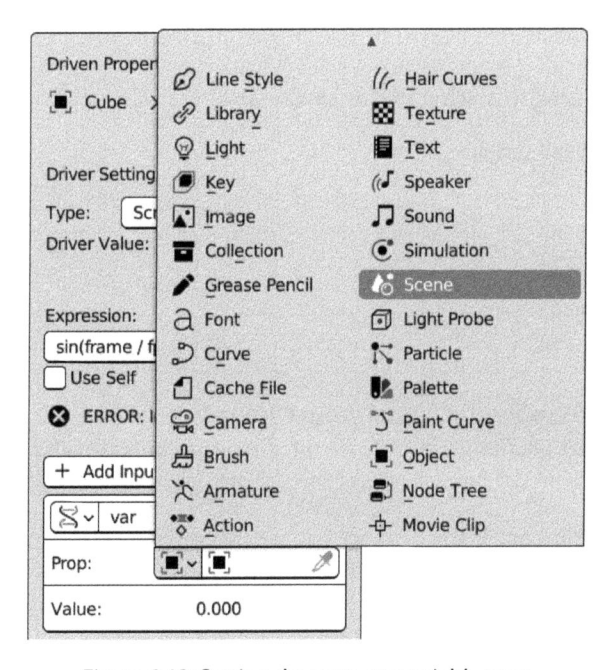

Figure 9.13: Setting the property variable type

2. A Blender file can contain more than one scene. We can display a list of them with the right list button and pick one. The name of the default scene is **Scene**.

3. Now that a scene has been selected, another field, **Path**, will appear. Here, we can set the attribute that can be accessed by the variable. Typing `render.fps` gets the frame per second, as set in the render settings.

4. We must rename the variable from `var` to `fps` by clicking the current name just right of the genetic code (RNA) icon:

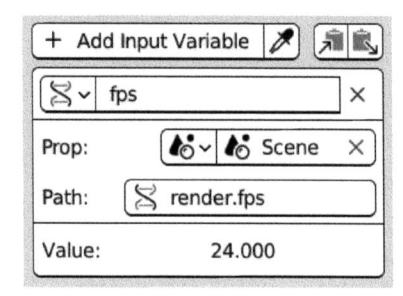

Figure 9.14: The fps variable in the render settings

Now, the variable name matches the one used in the driver expression so that `frame/fps` is the time at the current frame, in seconds. This allows the next variable, `length`, to influence the period with a seconds-based formula.

Getting the pendulum length with a distance variable

There are four types of driver variables:

- **Single Property**
- **Transform Channel**
- **Rotational Difference**
- **Distance**

While the first two, **Single Property** and **Transform Channel**, depend on the value of a property, **Rotational Difference** and **Distance** result from the difference between the transformations of two objects.

In this case, the length of the cord is the distance between the driven object and its pivot – that is, between **Cube** and **Empty**. So, we will use their **Distance** for `length`:

1. Add a new variable by clicking the **+ Add Input Variable** button.
2. Click the RNA icon to change the type to **Distance**. The panel will change, allowing you to select two objects:

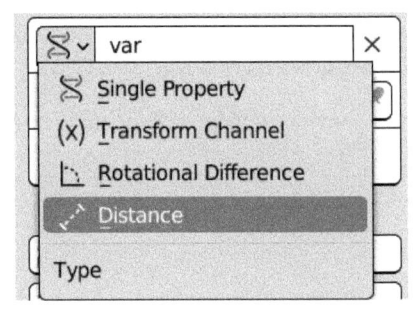

Figure 9.15: Changing the variable type

3. Select **Cube** and **Empty** and change the name of the variable to `length`:

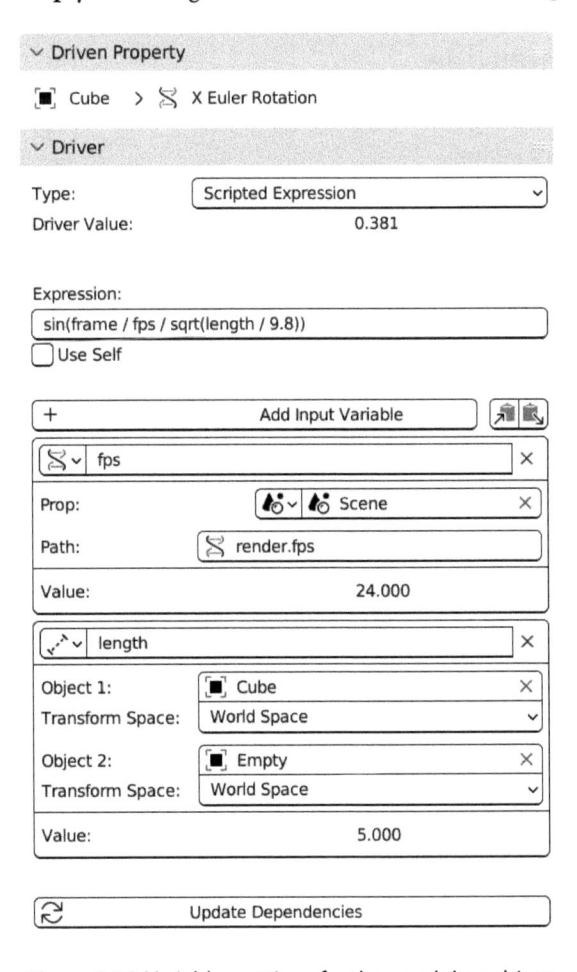

Figure 9.16: Variables settings for the pendulum driver

Moving the **Empty** or **Cube** object closer to each other while the animation plays makes the swing becomes faster, while setting them apart slows them down.

The maximum value of sin is 1, which, converted from *radians*, gives us the maximum angle reached by this driver:

```
>>> degrees(1)
57.29577951308232
```

This value is the amplitude of the oscillation. The amplitude of a pendulum depends on its initial position. In real life, the amplitude decreases progressively because of the friction of air, until the pendulum reaches its resting position and stops. We are not implementing air drag in our driver, but we can still add a control to influence the amplitude of the motion.

Controlling the amplitude

While the term **amplitude** has a specific meaning when dealing with wave graphs, for our goal, we can consider it a multiplier of motion.

Since we are programming for animation, it's more important for our amplitude control to make sense visually rather than physically.

Adding a custom property

We already control the pivot's position with an object of the **empty** type. Since moving **Empty** already alters the periodic motion, we can add a new property to it, to control the amplitude of the oscillation. This way, we can affect the behavior of the pendulum by selecting a single object.

The procedure for adding a property to an object is as follows:

1. Select the **Empty** object that we are using as a pivot.
2. In the **Object Properties** panel, find the **Custom Properties** section.
3. Click the **+ New** button to add a property. It will be named **prop** by default:

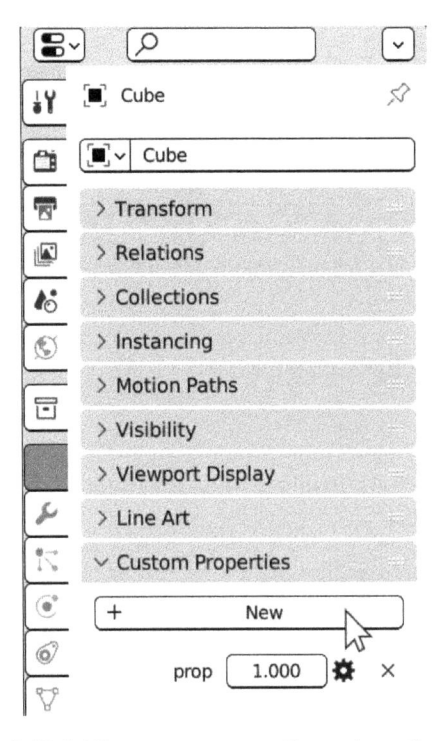

Figure 9.17: Adding custom properties to the active object

4. Click the cog icon and change **Property Name** to **amplitude**.
5. Right-click on the value (the default, 1.00, is good) and select **Copy Data Path**.

This copies the path of the property to the clipboard. This will be useful when we add the next driver variable.

Using custom properties in drivers

Multiplying the driver expression by the amp variable affects its result and allows us to modulate its amplitude. To do that, follow these steps:

1. Select the oscillating **Cube**.
2. Right-click on the driven rotation channel and select **Edit Driver** to bring up the **Driven Property** editor.
3. Click + **Add Input Variable** and name the new variable amp.
4. Click the **Prop:** field on the right and pick **Empty** as the property object.
5. Click the **Path:** field and paste the data path stored in the *clipboard* using *Ctrl + V*, or type ["amplitude"]. The square brackets are part of the *custom properties* Python path:

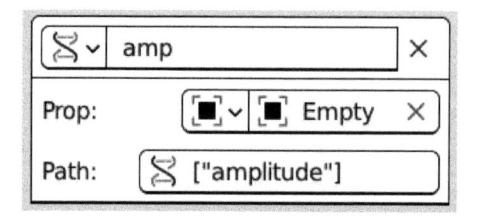

Figure 9.18: Custom property as a driver variable

We could just add `* amp` to the driver expression, but we can do even better: since the driver affects a rotation, we can add `pi` to the multiplication too:

```
sin(frame / fps / sqrt(length/9.8)) * amp * pi
```

The `sin` function oscillates between `-1.0` and `1.0`, so the result of our driver when **amplitude** is set to `1.0` ranges between `-pi` to `pi`.

Keeping in mind that a full circle arc measures `2 * pi`, it's fair to expect a value of `pi` to describe a half-circle rotation in radians. If we play the animation now, we'll see the pendulum oscillate up to its vertical direction – that is, rotate half circle to the left, go back, and then rotate half circle to the right: an amplitude of `1.0` makes the pendulum describe a full circle.

If we select the **Empty** object and change its amplitude to `0.5`, the pendulum will swing through a half-circle arc. An amplitude equal to `0.25` gives better results: a 45-degree maximum rotation on each side; a value of `0.0` would stop the pendulum.

A control ranging from `0.0` for a still pendulum to `1.0` for an entire rotation has an immediate meaning to animators and 3D users because it allows them to set up the fraction of the circle that they wish by changing the amplitude.

We used a Python formula in our driver, but we created the entire setup manually. In the next section, we will write a Python add-on to automate this procedure.

Writing the pendulum add-on

Using what we have learned so far, we can write an add-on that sets up a pendulum for the active object.

We will start with the steps from *Chapter 3*, and create a `.py` file for our add-on.

Setting the environment

Let's create a folder for *Chapter 9* in our **PythonScriptingBlender** project. In the **Blender Preferences** area, set the `ch9` folder as the **Scripts Folder** property and restart the application. We can create our new files and folder in our IDE (VS Code in this book) so that we can start editing:

1. Select `PythonScriptingBlender/ch9/addons` in **VS Code**.
2. Create a new file by clicking the **New File** icon.
3. Name the new file `pendulum.py`.
4. Open the file by double-clicking it.

We can now add the standard elements of most add-ons:

- Add-on information
- The `Operator` class
- The menu function
- Registration functions

Next, we'll learn how to write this information.

Writing the information

As usual, the information about our add-on goes into the `bl_info` dictionary:

```
bl_info = {
    "name": "Object Pendulum",
    "author": "John Packt",
    "version": (1, 0),
    "blender": (3, 00, 0),
    "description": "Add swing motion to active object",
    "category": "Learning",
}
```

This dictionary is just for Blender to display the add-on's name and description in the list. The next step is writing the `Operator` class.

Writing the Operator class

The `Operator` class carries on the actual work. We derive `bpy.types.Operator` and fill in the information in the static section of the class:

```
import bpy
class ObjectPendulum(bpy.types.Operator):
    """Set up swinging motion on active object"""
    bl_idname = "object.shaker_animation"
    bl_label = "Make Pendulum"
    bl_description = "Add swinging motion to Active Object"
    bl_options = {'REGISTER', 'UNDO'}
```

`bl_idname` starts with `object.` so that it will be added to the `bpy.ops.object` operators. We are doing that because everything we do in this operator affects the scene at the object level.

Now, we must add the oscillation parameters to the static attributes:

```
    amplitude: bpy.props.FloatProperty(default=0.25,
                                       min=0.0)
    length: bpy.props.FloatProperty(default=5.0, min=0.0)
```

They will determine the `amplitude` and `length` variables of the motion. By using `'REGISTER'` and `'UNDO'` as `bl_options`, the operator will allow live changes:

```
    bl_options = {'REGISTER', 'UNDO'}
```

Now, it's the `poll` method's turn, where the conditions for running the operator are checked. It must return `True` if there is an active object. We can use the `bool` function to convert `context.object` on the fly:

```
    @classmethod
    def poll(cls, context):
        return bool(context.object)
```

Finally, we have the `execute` method. It performs all the operations from the previous section of this chapter:

- Creates the pivot object
- Adds a custom property for the amplitude
- Creates a driver with the pendulum formula and variables

At the start of the function, we store the active object in the `ob` variable, then create a new object that will be the pivot. In *Chapter 2*, we learned that new objects can be created in two steps:

1. Get a new object via `bpy.data.objects.new`.
2. Link the object to a `Collection` present in the scene.

We will use `context.collection` and link the pivot to the active collection:

```
def execute(self, context):
    ob = context.object
    pivot_name = f"EMP-{ob.name}_pivot"
    pivot = bpy.data.objects.new(pivot_name, None)
    context.collection.objects.link(pivot)
```

Using `None` as the second argument of `new` creates a transform with no geometry data – that is, an **Empty**. As we know from *Chapter 4*, we can copy the world location from the active object's `matrix_world`. The pivot should be placed above the active object, and since `location` is stored in the fourth column of the transform matrix, we can raise the value of **Location Z** by increasing the fourth element of the third row (index `[2][3]`):

```
pivot.matrix_world = ob.matrix_world
pivot.matrix_world[2][3] += self.length
```

Now, it's time for the custom properties. We have seen how the data path to our *amplitude* property was `["amplitude"]`. That's because Python's access to custom properties follows the same syntax as Python dictionaries.

In Python dictionaries, the `dictionary["new_key"] = new_value` syntax adds a new item. Likewise, the Python code for creating the `amplitude` float property and assigning it the value of the operator's parameter of the same name is as follows:

```
pivot["amplitude"] = self.amplitude
```

`amplitude` will now appear under our pivot object. We will use that later in the driver. For now, we will add a **Pivot Constraint** to the active object:

```
constr = ob.constraints.new('PIVOT')
constr.target = pivot
constr.rotation_range = 'ALWAYS_ACTIVE'
```

Now, it's time to create our driver. Drivers, as objects, are slightly more complex than constraints as they contain other entities, such as the f-curve, and are part of the animation data. So, rather than using the `drivers.new` method from `animation_data`, we will resort to the `driver_add` method of the object, which sets up all the requirements. It returns the driver curve:

```
driver_crv = ob.driver_add('rotation_euler', 0)
driver = driver_crv.driver
```

> **Who drives the driver?**
>
> The `driver_add` method returns the f-curve rather than the driver itself. The actual driver can be accessed via the `curve.driver` attribute. This makes it easier to access the new curve, but it would have been reasonable to expect that `driver_add` would return the driver instead.

Our driver uses a Python expression, so must we set the `type` and `expression` attributes:

```
driver.type = "SCRIPTED"
xpr = "sin(frame/fps/sqrt(length/9.8)) * amp * pi"
driver.expression = xpr
```

The `fps`, `length`, and `amp` variables can be added using `variables.new`.

Once we've created a variable, we can set its targets. The current **Frames Per Seconds** rate is the `render.fps` property of `context.scene`, so it's only one target. We will set the variable type to a single property and fill `id_type`, `id`, and `data_path` of `targets[0]`:

```
fps = driver.variables.new()
fps.name = "fps"
fps.type = "SINGLE_PROP"
fps.targets[0].id_type = 'SCENE'
fps.targets[0].id = context.scene
fps.targets[0].data_path = "render.fps"
```

Our pendulum length is the distance between `pivot` and `ob`, so it has two targets:

```
len = driver.variables.new()
len.name = "length"
len.type = "LOC_DIFF"
len.targets[0].id = pivot
len.targets[1].id = ob
```

Finally, we can look at the amplitude. It's a custom property of the pivot and the variable is of the `'SINGLE_PROP'` type, but this time, `id_type` is a Blender object. Once the driver setup is complete, we can exit the function by returning the `'FINISHED'` state:

```
amp = driver.variables.new()
amp.name = "amp"
amp.type = "SINGLE_PROP"
amp.targets[0].id_type = "OBJECT"
amp.targets[0].id = pivot
amp.targets[0].data_path = "[\"amplitude\"]"
return {'FINISHED'}
```

The `ObjectPendulum` class is complete as it now covers the entire setup process. As usual, we must also add an entry to one of the Blender menus to make it easier to launch.

Writing the menu and registering the class

In *Chapter 3*, we learned that we can add our items to menus by writing a menu function. The argument self and context are, respectively, the menu instance and the application context. We must add the operator's `bl_idname` to the menu's `layout`:

```
def menu_func(self, context):
    self.layout.separator()
    self.layout.operator(ObjectPendulum.bl_idname)
```

Then, in the register function, we must add `menu_func` to one of Blender's menus. In this example, we will use the right-click menu that's available in object mode. We learned how to look for menu class names in *Chapter 8*, and the object context menu class is `VIEW3D_MT_object_context_menu`. We must also register the operator class, `ObjectPendulum`:

```
def register():
    bpy.utils.register_class(ObjectPendulum)
    ob_menu = bpy.types.VIEW3D_MT_object_context_menu
    ob_menu.append(menu_func)
```

This adds our new functionality to Blender when the **Object Pendulum** add-on is enabled. Of course, we must reverse those operations to clean up our add-on elements when it is disabled:

```
def unregister():
    ob_menu = bpy.types.VIEW3D_MT_object_context_menu
    ob_menu.remove(menu_func)
    bpy.utils.unregister_class(ObjectPendulum)
```

Now that our add-on is ready, the steps for setting up a pendulum instantly are as follows:

1. In **Object Mode**, select an object to make it active.
2. Right-click and choose **Make Pendulum** to invoke the add-on.
3. Set values for `length` and `amplitude` in the operator properties.

Writing this add-on put many of the techniques you learned in the previous chapters to use. Drivers are a very creative area of scripting, and this was just a taste of what we can do with them.

Summary

Drivers are powerful tools that sit at a crossroads between animation, rigging, and programming. On one hand, they can contain Python expressions and implement custom mechanics on their own, while on the other hand, the entire driver setup process can be automated via scripting.

The tool we wrote in this chapter is a small **auto-rig** that replicates the same mechanism, with editable parameters, on any Blender object.

The ability to combine drivers, constraints, and custom properties, as well as automate the whole procedure, is an essential part of 3D production as it allows non-technical users to carry on with technical tasks.

As a plus, by using Python, we converted a formula from physics into a working driver expression, a task that can sometimes be intimidating but can be carried out with observation and a little ingenuity.

This topic ends our tour of the animation system. In the next chapter, *Chapter 10*, we will learn how our operators can interact with the user and listen to events.

Questions

1. What color is used for driven properties in the interface?
2. Can we set keyframes for purple properties?
3. Can a metric property, such as **Location**, drive an angular property, such as **Rotation**?
4. Can we change the ratio between the driving and driven properties?
5. Can we type Python expressions when we set values in the interface?
6. How do we tell Blender that the expressions we have typed should be a driver?
7. How do we edit a driver property in the user interface? Is there only one way?
8. Can we add custom properties to an object and use them to control other objects?

9. In Python, can we create new drivers using the `collection.new` method, as we do with constraints? If yes, why do we use `object.driver_add` instead?

10. Why is the `targets` attribute of driver variables a list? Which type of variable has more than one target?

10
Advanced and Modal Operators

Since *Chapter 3*, we have resorted to operators to implement our features in Blender.

Operators have already proved to be incredibly flexible, with custom properties and looks. They can be even more powerful once we learn how to override all their methods.

The operators encountered in the previous chapters run as soon as they are launched and finish immediately. If we need to, we can make the execution modal and let the operator listen to input events.

In this chapter, you will learn how to control the execution of an operator, and how you can write fully interactive operators.

This chapter will cover the following topics:

- Understanding the operator flow
- Setting properties programmatically
- Writing modal operators

Technical requirements

We will use Blender and Visual Studio Code in this chapter, but any other programmer text editor can be used. The examples created in this chapter can be found at https://github.com/PacktPublishing/Python-Scripting-in-Blender/tree/main/ch10.

Understanding the operator flow

We dealt with operators since *Chapter 3*, and we learned how their `poll` method checks whether the operator can be executed, while `execute` performs the operation and exits.

Then in *Chapter 4*, we added editable parameters to the *Elevator* operator, thanks to the `'REGISTER'` and `'UNDO'` options.

We also learned about the clever trick to change a result in real time when a user changes a parameter – Blender secretly undoes the last operation and performs it again with the new options, hence the need for `'UNDO'`.

That became more evident in *Chapter 7*, when we learned how using **Edit | Adjust Last Operation** from the menu bar changes the result of the last operation.

While those solutions allow us to get input parameters with ease, they don't give access to the actual input events, such as the pressure of a key or the movement of a mouse.

That would require a **listener** – that is, code that waits for device inputs and is executed continuously. Normally, launching an operator runs its `execute` method instantly, so it couldn't possibly wait for inputs; therefore, the events must be handled by another method.

Another thing we cannot do in `execute` is set the operator's editable parameters. Since Blender runs `execute` again when a parameter is changed, the user would find themselves unable to set a property, as it would be overridden immediately.

Capturing events and initializing operator parameters are two tasks that cannot be performed by `execute`. Luckily, `execute` is not the only method involved when an operator is launched; we will see that an operator's lifetime encompasses a set of methods, each of them with a specific purpose.

Steps of execution

We know from *Chapter 3*, that the operator `poll` and `execute` methods are required, respectively, for validation and execution. In *Chapter 5*, we used `invoke` to make sure that the operator properties are displayed before it runs.

Now, we will take a closer look at how operators are displayed and run:

1. Blender checks the return value of `poll`. If the result is `False`, the operator is grayed out; otherwise, the operator can be launched.

2. The operator is launched, and it runs the `invoke` method. This method is optional; if we don't write it, its step is skipped, and Blender runs `execute` directly.

    One common use of `invoke` is the initialization of the operator's variables or internal value; unlike conventional Python classes, operators don't implement the traditional `__init__` method.

    Like `execute`, `invoke` must return an exit status, which can be `'FINISHED'`, `'CANCELLED'`, or `'RUNNING_MODAL'`.

3. If our operator is meant to listen for mouse and keyboard events, in `invoke`, we add it to the application **event handlers**, and then return the exit status to `'RUNNING_MODAL'`.

4. If the operator is part of the handlers, its `modal` method is executed at every trigger event (when a mouse cursor moves, a key is pressed, etc.), until the modal returns `'CANCELLED'` or `'FINISHED'`. Otherwise, to continue listening, it should return `'RUNNING_MODAL'`.
5. If `bl_options` is `{'REGISTER', 'UNDO'}`, the operator properties are displayed in a panel at the bottom left of the screen. The panel relies on the operator's `draw` method.
6. By default, all the operator properties that are not flagged with `hidden` upon declaration are displayed in the panel. Reimplementing this method allows us to implement a custom design using the techniques learned in *Chapter 5*.
7. Changing a value in the operator panel runs `execute` again, with updated properties.

The execution flow is summed up in *Figure 10.1*, which helps us understand how the methods in the execution flow add up when an operator is launched.

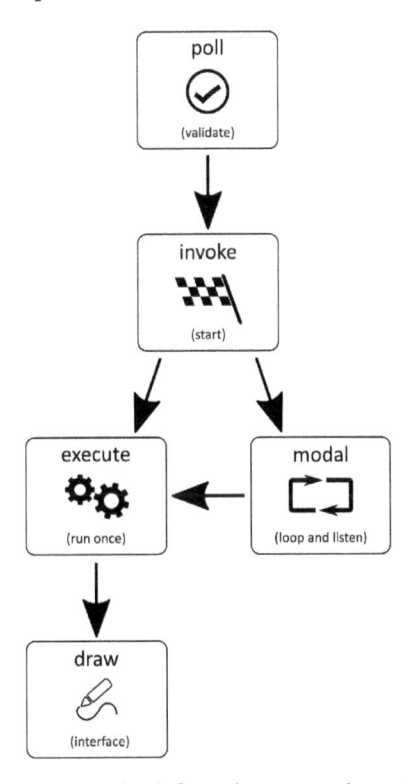

Figure 10.1: The operator methods from the start to the end of the evaluation

While `poll` is run by the interface every time that the operator is displayed, `invoke` is the first step of an operator flow, so we can use it to set the operator's parameters programmatically and, from there, move to `execute` or `modal`. In the next section, we will use `invoke` to initialize the operator parameters according to the time of the day.

Writing the "PunchClock" add-on

Some tools can require the current date and time from the operating system clock. In Python, we can use the `datetime` module to get them in our scripts, generally for versioning or logging purposes. There are no Blender properties designed specifically for time units, but an hour and a minute can be stored as two separate integer properties of an operator.

We know how to use the `default` argument to declare the initial value of a property, but what if that value is not always the same? For example, the current hour and minute change during the day, but `default` only sets static values.

But since `invoke` is executed before all the other methods, we can set our default values programmatically in there.

To demonstrate that, we will create an add-on to create a time format text in the current scene. By default, the text displays the current time of the day, but the user can change that.

Creating the add-on script

Let's create the `ch10` folder in our Python project, and then in **Blender Preferences**, we set it as the **Scripts** folder and restart Blender:

1. Select `PythonScriptingBlender/ch10/addons` in your file browser or programmer editor – for instance, **VS Code**.
2. Create a new file by clicking on the **New File** icon.
3. Name the new file `punch_clock.py`.
4. Open the file for editing.
5. Set the **Scripts** path to `PythonScriptingBlender/ch10` in the Blender **File Paths** preferences and restart Blender.

We store the add-on information in the `bl_info` dictionary, as usual:

```
bl_info = {
    "name": "Text PunchClock",
    "author": "Packt Man",
    "version": (1, 0),
    "blender": (3, 00, 0),
    "description": "Create an Hour/Minutes text object",
    "category": "Learning",
}
```

This add-on contains an operator, which will be available in the **Add** menu of the 3D Viewport.

We start with an operator that creates a text in the *HH:MM* format, like digital clocks, where *HH* stands for a 2-digit hour number and *MM* for the minutes.

Hours and minutes are stored as `IntProperty`, ranging between 0 and 23 for the hours and 0 and 59 for the minutes. The operator's code starts as follows:

```
import bpy
class PunchClock(bpy.types.Operator):
    """Create Hour/Minutes text"""
    bl_idname = "text.punch_clock"
    bl_label = "Create Hour/Minutes Text"
    bl_description = "Create Hour Minutes Text"
    bl_options = {'REGISTER', 'UNDO'}
    hour: bpy.props.IntProperty(default=0, min=0, max=23)
    mins: bpy.props.IntProperty(default=0, min=0, max=59)
```

We can add a new object if Blender is in **Object** mode, so the condition for `poll` is as follows:

```
    @classmethod
    def poll(cls, context):
        return context.mode == 'OBJECT'
```

In `execute`, we create new text data and set it to `{hour}:{min}`. The Blender type for text is named `FONT`, and its displayed text is stored in the `body` attribute.

We use **string formatting**, which we learned about in *Chapter 5*. Adding `:02` after a variable specifies that we want to display a 2-digit number – for instance, `f"{3:02}"` becomes `"03"`:

```
    def execute(self, context):
        txt_crv = bpy.data.curves.new(type="FONT",
                                      name="TXT-clock")
        txt_crv.body = f"{self.hour:02}:{self.mins:02}"
```

We create an object to link it to the current collection and see the text in the scene:

```
        txt_obj = bpy.data.objects.new(name="Font Object",
                                       object_data=txt_crv)
```

After that, we return `FINISHED` as execution state:

```
        context.collection.objects.link(txt_obj)
        return {'FINISHED'}
```

The first draft of our operator is ready, and now we create a menu function to add to the interface. We can use **Icon Viewer**, as we did in *Chapter 5*, and look for an icon that suits our operator. By typing `time` in the search field, we end up with three relevant icons – `TIME`, `MOD_TIME`, and `SORTTIME`. Any of those will do; we will pick `TIME` in this example.

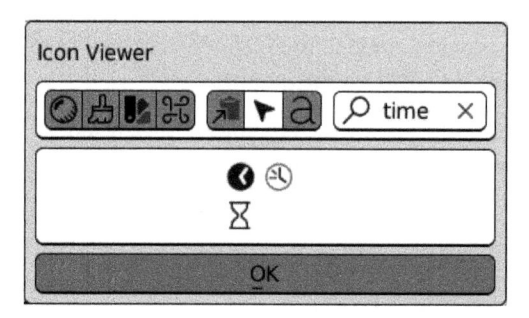

Figure 10.2: The time-related default icons in Icon Viewer

We start `menu_func` with a `separator` to set our operator apart, and then we add our entry for `PunchClock` via `Layout.operator`:

```
def menu_func(self, context):
    self.layout.separator()
    self.layout.operator(PunchClock.bl_idname, icon='TIME')
```

Finally, we add and remove our operator and menu item in the `register` and `unregister` functions:

```
def register():
    bpy.utils.register_class(PunchClock)
    bpy.types.VIEW3D_MT_add.append(menu_func)
def unregister():
    bpy.types.VIEW3D_MT_add.remove(menu_func)
    bpy.utils.unregister_class(PunchClock)
```

If we restart Blender or refresh the **Add-ons** list, we should be able to see the **PunchClock** add-on.

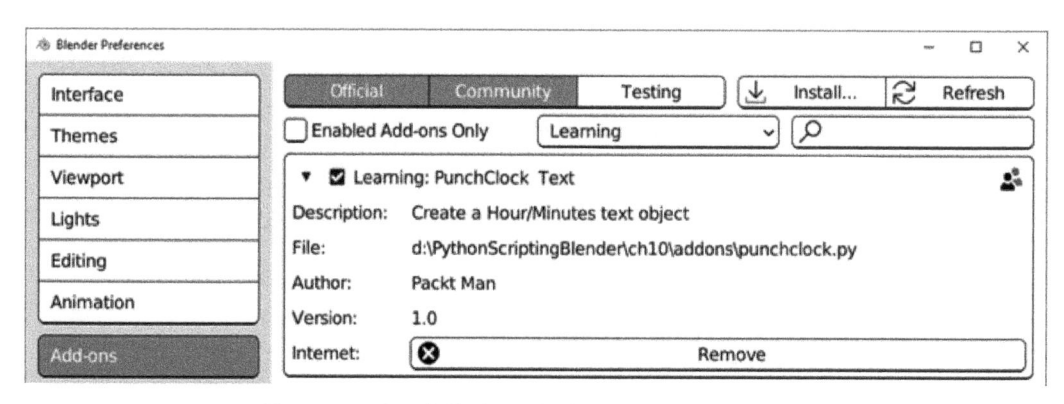

Figure 10.3: PunchClock, as displayed in the Add-ons list

At this stage, selecting **Add | Create Hour/Minutes Text** in the 3D Viewport top menu would add a text object displaying the time *00:00*.

We can get the current time from `datetime` and convert it to text, but we can do something even better – by setting `self.hour` and `self.mins` inside `invoke`, we will achieve the same result but also allow a user to change the displayed time.

Using invoke to initialize properties

To get the current time, we import `datetime` at the beginning of the script. The `import` section becomes the following:

```
import bpy
import datetime
```

Then, inside the operator class, we implement the `invoke` method. It can come right after `poll`, but any place under the `PunchClock` class will do:

```
    @classmethod
    def poll(cls, context):
        return context.mode == 'OBJECT'
    def invoke(self, context, event):
        now = datetime.datetime.now()
        self.hour = now.hour
        self.mins = now.minute
        return self.execute(context)
```

Now, the hour and minute of the operator are set up in `invoke`, and then `execute` is called to carry on the operation.

Finishing with `execute` is important, as that's what Blender expects when updating its operations chronology.

Launching **Create Hour/Minutes Text** now displays the current time in a new text object and allows us to change the hour and minute using the operator panel.

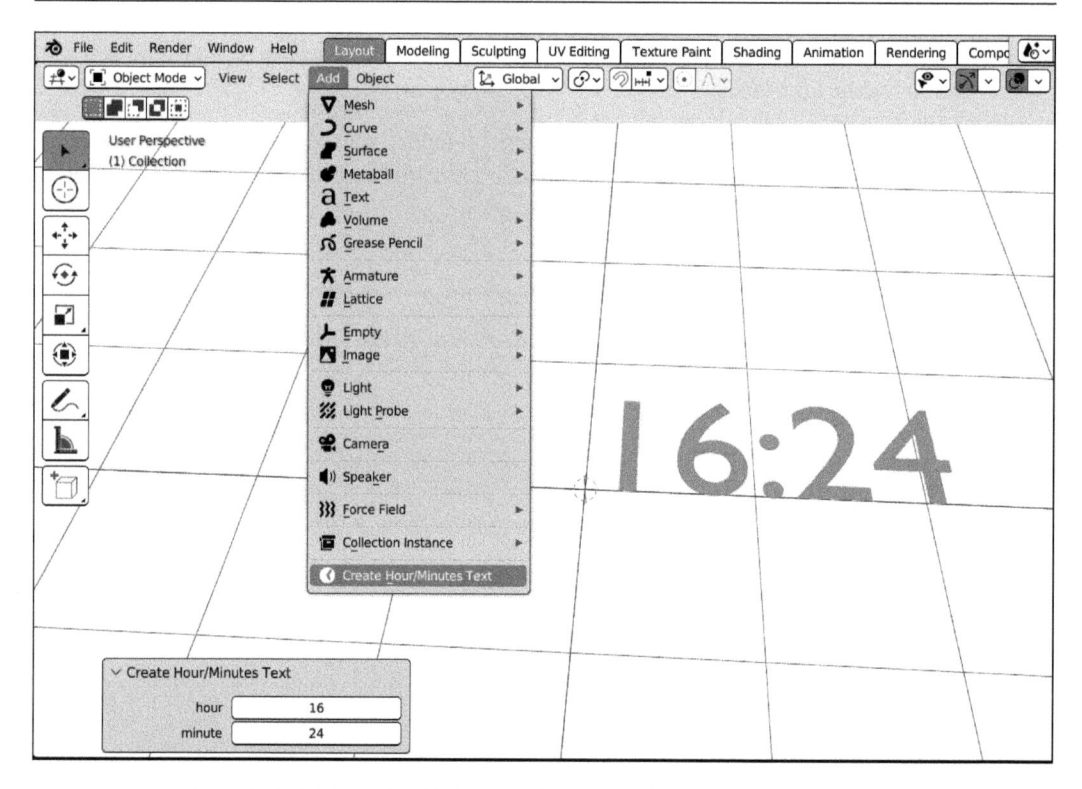

Figure 10.4: Adding editable hour and minute fields, set to the current time

By using `invoke`, we have set our default values programmatically. That's a common request in productions, since the desired defaults can change across projects, tasks, and departments.

We have added our operator to the **Add** menu, which is also displayed in a popup if called with the *Shift + A* key combination. It's a convenient shortcut, but pop-up menus have a different context that runs the operator's `execute` method directly.

To prevent the menu from skipping `invoke`, we need to override the layout's context in our menu function.

Ensuring default invoke in pop-up menus

Layout elements can pass a custom context and force a design choice on operators. For example, buttons displayed outside the viewport avoid displaying operator properties, and pop-up menus bypass the `invoke` method.

We have encountered this behavior in the *Displaying buttons* section of *Chapter 5*, and in the *Writing the Action to Range add-on* section in *Chapter 7*.

We worked around those issues, respectively, by calling a properties dialog in `invoke`, or by using **Edit | Adjust Last Operation**, but none of that would work in this case, because we want `invoke` to run even when the operator is launched from the **Add** menu and displayed with the *Shift + A* combination. Being a pop-up menu, it overrides the context and suppresses `invoke`.

Therefore, we will change the layout's `operator_context` to `"INVOKE_DEFAULT"`. We only need that for `PunchClock`, so, to minimize any potential impact on other menu entries, we add a new row and change only its `operator_context`.

Our menu function becomes the following:

```
def menu_func(self, context):
    self.layout.separator()
    row = self.layout.row()
    row.operator_context = "INVOKE_DEFAULT"
    row.operator(PunchClock.bl_idname, icon='TIME')
```

By executing `PunchClock` with its default context, we make sure that `invoke` is never skipped.

Now, the operator will always display its properties and let a user change them, but we can also implement a way to change the displayed time by just moving the mouse.

In the next section, we will add operator response to mouse and keyboard input, making our operator a modal application handler.

Adding modal behavior

In user interfaces, the term **modal** designates a sub-window or widget that takes all the user interaction for itself, until the operation is ended explicitly.

Usually, operators are designed to return to the main application immediately. If we don't want that, they should be added to the window manager's modal handlers.

The operator is then considered modal and will listen to the user inputs until it's closed manually.

We can make `PunchClock` modal and use mouse movement to set our clock. Modal operators have two requirements:

- `invoke` adds the operator to the handlers and returns `'RUNNING_MODAL'`.
- `modal` is implemented and returns `'RUNNING_MODAL'`. It returns `'FINISHED'` when a user ends it, or `'CANCELLED'` to exit with no changes.

We will start to implement the modal execution by changing `invoke` and its return value.

Adding the operator to the modal handlers

Instead of passing to `execute`, `invoke` now calls the `modal_handler_add` method of the current `window_manager`, and then it returns `{'RUNNING_MODAL'}`. The return status notifies that the operator is running in Blender and listens to events.

Since `modal` runs at every window update, we should keep it light and small. Adding objects to the scene is expensive, so we create and link the text in `invoke`, and only edit its body in `modal`. The `invoke` method stores `txt_crv` and `txt_obj` as operator member attributes:

```python
def invoke(self, context, event):
    now = datetime.datetime.now()
    self.hour = now.hour
    self.mins = now.minute
    self.txt_crv = bpy.data.curves.new(type="FONT",
                                       name="TXT-hhmm")
    self.txt_obj = bpy.data.objects.new(name="OB-Txt",
                                object_data=self.txt_crv)
    context.collection.objects.link(self.txt_obj)
    context.window_manager.modal_handler_add(self)
    return {'RUNNING_MODAL'}
```

The keywords that can be returned as status are listed in the API documentation (https://docs.blender.org/api/3.3/bpy_types_enum_items/operator_return_items.html) and are as follows:

- `RUNNING_MODAL`: Keeps the operator running with Blender
- `CANCELLED`: The operator exited without doing anything, so no undo entry should be pushed
- `FINISHED`: The operator exited after completing its action
- `PASS_THROUGH`: Do nothing and pass the event on
- `INTERFACE`: Handled but not executed (pop-up menus)

We have already dealt with `'RUNNING_MODAL'`, `'CANCELLED'`, and `'FINISHED'`, while `'PASS_THROUGH'` is useful to pass an event to the rest of an application, even if our script was listening to it. `'INTERFACE'` is used in pop-up menus, but usually, we don't need that for our scripts.

> **Status is not everything!**
>
> It's important to know that returning a status ratifies what was done in a method, but it doesn't perform anything.
>
> For instance, returning `'CANCELLED'` alone doesn't undo what was done in a method; we should undo all the changes programmatically – for example, remove the objects that our method might have created, and then return `'CANCELLED'`.

Now that the application handler will look for a `modal` method and run it, we can proceed with writing one for our operator.

Writing the modal method

Once an operator is added to the handlers, the window manager will run its `modal` method at every event of the user interface. As with `invoke`, besides `self` and `context`, this method takes a third argument – `event`.

The `event` argument contains information about what triggered any execution of `modal`. It can be a movement of a mouse or the press of a key.

The most relevant information is `type`, a string whose keywords are documented at https://docs.blender.org/api/3.3/bpy_types_enum_items/event_type_items.html.

Looking at `event.type`, we can find out what triggered the update, such as the following:

```
event.type == "MOUSEMOVE"
```

This means that the user did just move the mouse.

If the event was caused by the keyboard, `event.type` would be a letter, such as `"A"`, or a description of the key, such as `"LEFT_CTRL"`. The event type associated with numeric keys is the uppercase letters for that number – for example, `"THREE"`.

In this example, moving the mouse toward the right increases the current time, and moving it to the left decreases it.

Like with real clocks, we can set either the hours or minutes – we add a Boolean property to distinguish between the two. The properties section becomes the following:

```
hour: bpy.props.IntProperty(default=0, min=0, max=23)
mins: bpy.props.IntProperty(default=0, min=0, max=59)
set_hours: bpy.props.BoolProperty(default=True)
```

Now, we can finally write `PunchClock.modal`.

Moving the mouse updates the attributes associated with the cursor. For instance, the cursor position on the horizontal axis is stored as `mouse_x`, while the previous position is still available as `mouse_prev_x`. The difference between the two gives the movement direction.

We store that number as `delta` and divide it to slow the transition. A factor of 10 makes it slow enough for our purpose:

```
def modal(self, context, event):
    if event.type == 'MOUSEMOVE':
        delta = event.mouse_x - event.mouse_prev_x
        delta /= 10
```

`delta` is a float number, and as such, it cannot be summed with hour and mins, which are integers. For that reason, we round it to an integer value:

```
delta = round(delta)
```

We use `round` rather than `int` for this conversion. Since `int` approximates to the least or equal integer value, it would make the progress from one value to the next less smooth.

The value of `set_hours` decides whether `delta` is added to the hours or the minutes:

```
if self.set_hours:
    self.hour += delta
else:
    self.mins += delta
txt = f"{self.hour:02}:{self.mins:02}"
self.txt_crv.body = txt
```

To change `set_hours`, we resort to a key press. We make the user switch between hours and minutes by pressing the *Tab* key.

To get that key press, we ensure that `event.type` is `'TAB'` and `event.value` is `'PRESS'`:

```
if event.type == 'TAB' and event.value == 'PRESS':
    self.set_hours = not self.set_hours
```

Boolean variables can only be `True` or `False`, which are each other's negation. So, we have converted `set_hours` to its opposite by just using `not`.

> **Type is not enough!**
>
> A key that is pressed will also be released, and this action will generate another event, whose value is `'RELEASE'`. Checking only `event.type` without checking `event.value` puts our code at the risk of responding to keystrokes twice.

Lastly, when a user is happy with the displayed time, they can press *Return* and exit. Pressing *Return* triggers an event of type `'RET'`. We don't need to bother with `event.value` for exit events. Once we return `{'FINISHED'}`, the operator stops, so there are no risks of duplicate execution:

```
elif event.type == 'RET':
    return {'FINISHED'}
```

However, what if the user has second thoughts and wants to exit the tool without doing anything? We can allow the operation to be aborted at the press of `'ESC'`.

To do that, the operator must clean after itself by deleting the text created in `invoke`, and then return `{'CANCELLED'}` to avoid being added to the undo queue:

```
        elif event.type == 'ESC':
            bpy.data.objects.remove(self.txt_obj)
            return {'CANCELLED'}
```

That was the last event covered by our operator. We ignore any other event and, by default, return `{'RUNNING_MODAL'}` as status to keep listening.

So, the last line of `modal` is usually as follows:

```
        return {'RUNNING_MODAL'}
```

Calling **Reload Scripts**, and then **Add | Create Hour/Minutes Text**, creates a text of the current hour and starts listening to mouse/keyboard events. Moving the mouse left and right increases/decreases the current value, pressing *Tab* switches between hours and minutes, and pressing *Return* or *Esc* ends the operator.

Since all the action now takes place between `invoke` and `modal`, we could remove `execute`, but since `bl_options` is set to `{'REGISTER', 'UNDO'}`, Blender displays the operator properties. When a property is changed, the `execute` method is run.

We can see that after *Return* is pressed, **hour**, **min**, and **set_hours** can be changed in the operator panel.

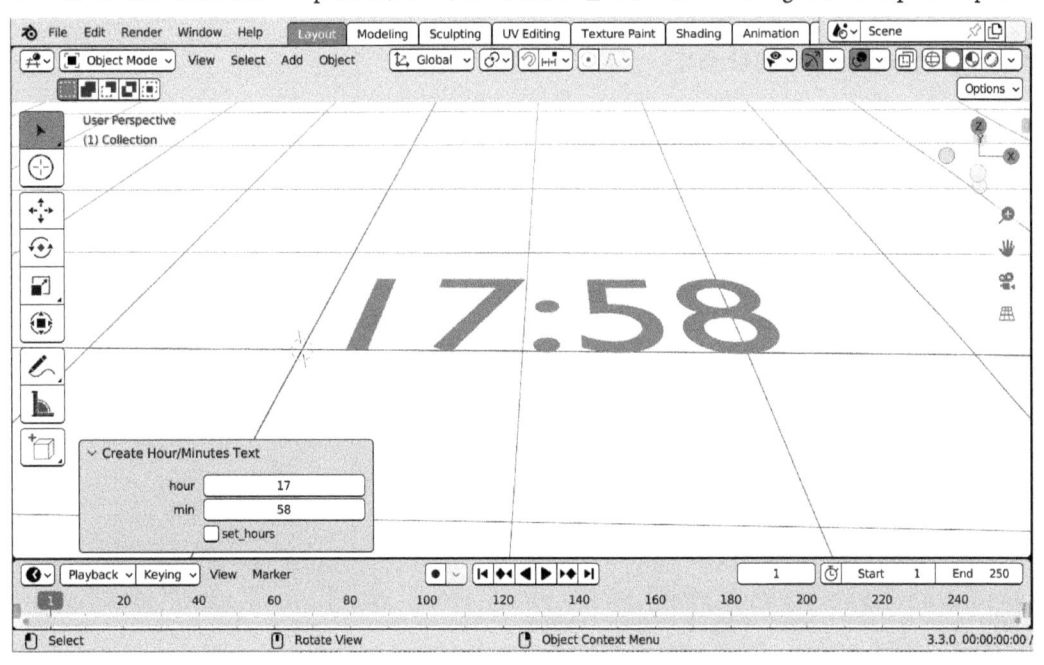

Figure 10.5: Operator properties after modal has exited

That panel can be customized – operators have a `draw` method that works in the same way as `Panel.draw`, which we learned about in *Chapter 5*.

So, rather than displaying hours and minutes in a column, we could show them in a time format in the operator panel. In the next section, we will implement the `draw` method and change the **Create Hour/Minutes Text** panel.

Styling the operator panel

We know that the operator panel is displayed in these circumstances:

- When `context.window_manager.invoke_props_dialog` is called explicitly.
- When `bl_options` is set to `{'REGISTER', 'UNDO'}` and the operator has finished.
- When **Edit | Adjust Last Operation** is called. This circumstance too requires the presence of `bl_options = {'REGISTER', 'UNDO'}`.

By default, all properties are displayed in a column layout. Most property types can be declared with a `hidden=True` flag, but that's not the case for `BoolProperty`, so we cannot do it with `set_hours`.

As a workaround, we could change `set_hours` to `IntProperty`, with a 0 to 1 range and `hidden` set to `True`, but by implementing the `draw` method for our operator, we can just omit the properties that we don't want to display.

Writing the draw method

We want to change two things in the **Create Hour/Minutes Text** panel:

- The hour and minutes should be in the same row
- The `set_hours` internal variable should not be displayed

Adding a `draw` method to an operator changes its layout. The method arguments are `self` and `context`, but we will only use the first. To display our properties on the same line, we will do the following:

1. Create a row to display hours and minutes.
2. Enable `align` for the new row.
3. Set the alignment to `'CENTER'`:

```
def draw(self, context):
    layout = self.layout
    row = layout.row(align=True)
    row.alignment = 'CENTER'
```

4. Use `row.prop` to display `self.hour`, `row.label` to display a semicolon, and `row.prop` again to display `self.mins`:

```
row.prop(self, 'hour', text="")
row.label(text=' :',)
row.prop(self, 'mins', text="")
```

We have set the text of `hour` and `mins` to `""` because no explanation is required. As intended, no checkbox is displayed for `set_hours`, since it's not mentioned in `draw`.

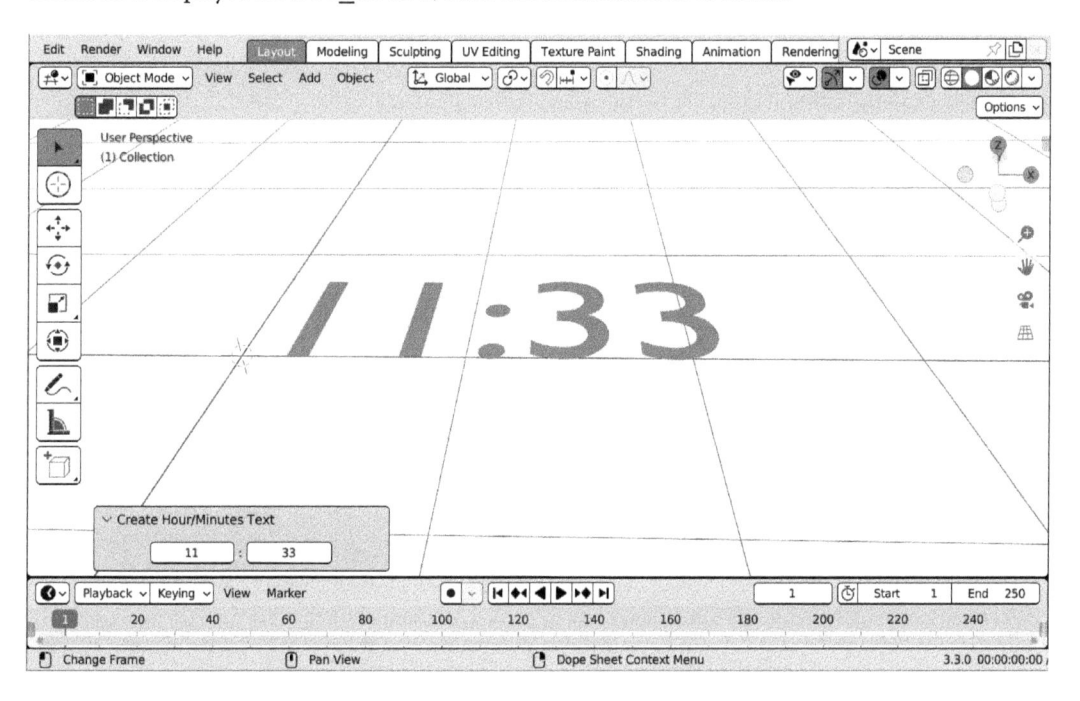

Figure 10.6: The custom hour/minutes operator panel

We could add more features, such as numeric input to set the hours, but since we have implemented all the operator methods, we can consider **PunchClock** finished.

Although we will discuss other operators in the rest of the book, this is the last chapter that covers them specifically, as we have learned how to customize every step of their execution.

Summary

We have gained a deep understanding of how operators are integrated in different parts of Blender and how we can manipulate their appearance and behavior. We have also learned how they can capture input and how they interact with the application event handler and interface.

This chapter marks the end of the second part of this book. The next chapter, *Object Modifiers*, is the start of *Part 3*, which deals with how the data of a scene is processed into the finished output.

Questions

1. Which operator method runs before the operator is launched?
2. Can a user launch an operator if its `poll` method returns `False`?
3. Can we set a default value on our operator parameters in a function?
4. The `modal` method can only return the `'RUNNING_MODAL'` status – true or false?
5. Does returning `'CANCELLED'` undo everything we did in a method?
6. Can we override the operator context of a menu or a panel layout?
7. Can we change the layout of an operator panel?

Part 3: Delivering Output

This part is centered on the final stages of the 3D pipeline: generating and deforming geometries and setting up the rendering and shading system. Automation of simple rigs and the construction of shader node trees are explored.

This section comprises the following chapters:

- *Chapter 11, Object Modifiers*
- *Chapter 12, Rendering and Shaders*

11
Object Modifiers

A major part of creating 3D content consists of editing geometries by adding and removing the vertices, edges, and faces of a model, or displacing the existing ones.

Object modifiers can perform these actions via non-destructive edits that affect the appearance of an object but not its internal data. They can be used for generative modeling, and without them, animation would be impossible, because deforming an object would require changing the geometric data at every frame.

Object modifiers are like the F-Modifiers treated in *Chapter 8*, but they present a greater variety in purpose and attributes.

In this chapter, we will cover the following:

- Understanding and using object modifiers
- Script deformation modifiers
- Generating armatures and meshes

Technical requirements

We will use Blender and Visual Studio Code in this chapter. The examples created in this chapter can be found at the following URL: `https://github.com/PacktPublishing/Python-Scripting-in-Blender/tree/main/ch11`.

Understanding object modifiers

Object modifiers change the displayed status of an object without altering its geometric data. We met something similar in *Chapter 8*, when we applied effects to animation F-Curves without changing their keyframes.

Like F-Modifiers, they can be stacked on each other and accessed in Python as a collection property.

Modifiers can be added manually, but their creation and setup can be scripted as well. Before we delve into the API, let's take a look at how to create them in the **Modifiers** properties.

Adding modifiers

Object modifiers are created in the **Modifiers** tab of **Properties** using the **Add Modifier** drop-down button. The tab is marked with the icon of a wrench.

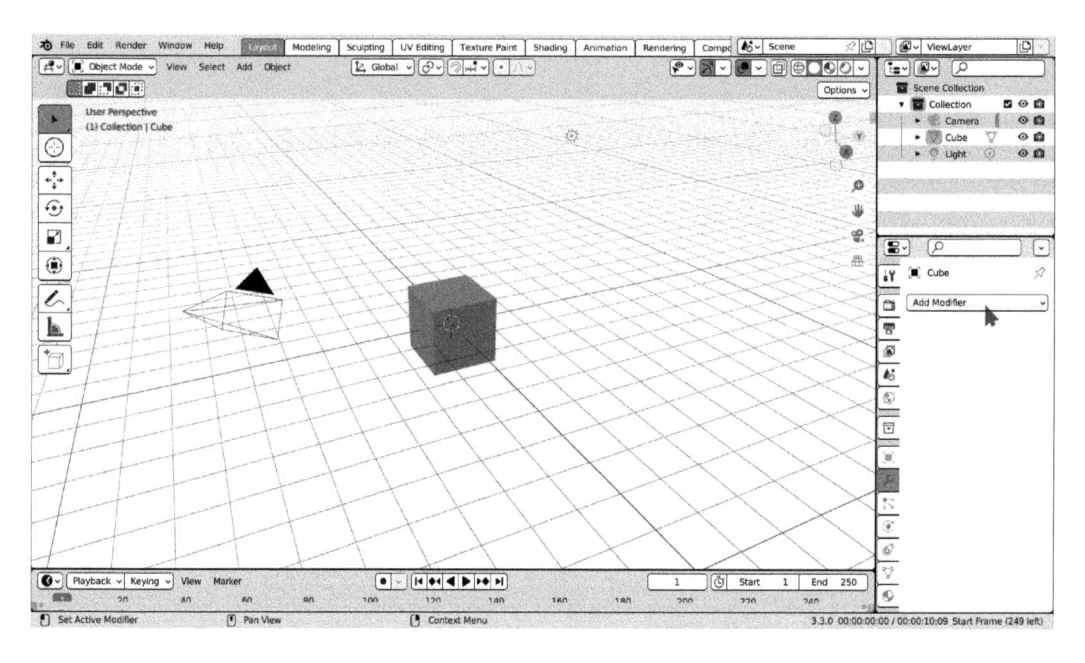

Figure 11.1: Adding modifiers in Blender

Clicking **Add Modifier** displays the available options. They change according to the object type: curves don't have as many modifiers as meshes, while nongeometric types such as empty or cameras can't have any modifiers at all.

Though their number has grown with time, all modifiers are grouped into four categories:

- **Modify** – Affects data that won't be displayed directly, such as vertex groups
- **Generate** – Adds or removes geometry to or from an object
- **Deform** – Changes the shape of an object without adding or removing vertices, edges, or faces
- **Physics** – Brings the result of physics simulations to the object

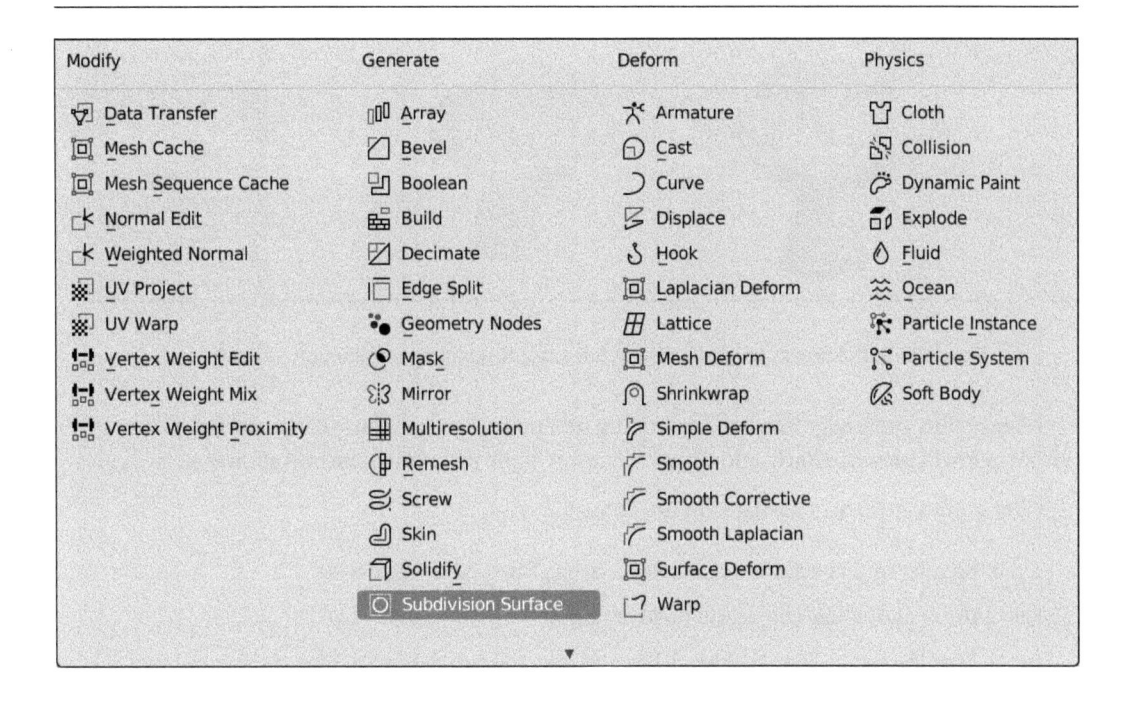

Modify	Generate	Deform	Physics
Data Transfer	Array	Armature	Cloth
Mesh Cache	Bevel	Cast	Collision
Mesh Sequence Cache	Boolean	Curve	Dynamic Paint
Normal Edit	Build	Displace	Explode
Weighted Normal	Decimate	Hook	Fluid
UV Project	Edge Split	Laplacian Deform	Ocean
UV Warp	Geometry Nodes	Lattice	Particle Instance
Vertex Weight Edit	Mask	Mesh Deform	Particle System
Vertex Weight Mix	Mirror	Shrinkwrap	Soft Body
Vertex Weight Proximity	Multiresolution	Simple Deform	
	Remesh	Smooth	
	Screw	Smooth Corrective	
	Skin	Smooth Laplacian	
	Solidify	Surface Deform	
	Subdivision Surface	Warp	

Figure 11.2: Clicking Add Modifier displays the available types

The interface displays one column per category, with several modifier types for each of the four. Even modifier types from the same category differ a lot from each other and present different sets of attributes.

To better understand how modifiers work, we can create one in the interface and see how that affects an object's geometry. For example, adding a **Subdivision Surface** modifier to an object makes it smoother by creating additional polygons.

Subdividing an object

Mesh objects are polygonal; that is, they consist of flat faces and sharp edges. That works well for simple solids like a cube, but not for smooth surfaces such as a sphere, or most real-life objects.

To give an illusion of smoothness, we subdivide the polygons of a mesh until they approximate a continuous surface.

The downside is that geometries that are too dense are problematic; they require more disk space and are not easy to model or edit. For that reason, rather than storing additional mesh data, we generate smooth geometry using the **Subdivision Surface** modifier.

258   Object Modifiers

Figure 11.3: The blocky model on the left is smoothed using Subdivision Surface

This modifier splits every edge into two, generating new polygons from those divisions. By default, an algorithm named **Catmull-Clark** smoothens the result while preserving the overall shape.

We can add a subdivision to a model with the following steps:

1. Open Blender or go back to the default scene via **File | New | General**.
2. Select the default **Cube** shape and make it active.
3. In the **Modifiers** tab, click **Add Modifier** and select **Subdivision Surface** at the bottom of the **Generate** column.
4. A new entry appears in the **Modifiers** properties. We can see the parameters of the **Subdivision** modifier.

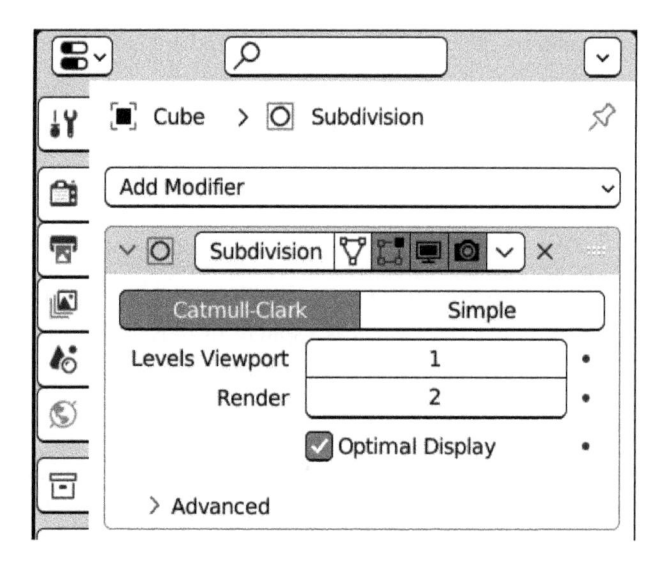

Figure 11.4: Subdivision Surface properties

5. Increasing the number in **Levels Viewport** adds subdivision to the object. Applying a **Catmull-Clark** division of 3 makes our **Cube** look much like a ball.
6. Clicking the **Simple** button disables the smoothing: the object is still subdivided, but its shape doesn't change.

Even if enabling **Simple** doesn't alter its shape, our object is still subdivided. That can be useful to other modifiers that can be added after **Subdivision**, as they will have more geometry to deform.

Now that our **Cube** has been subdivided, we will be able to alter its shape using a second modifier: **Cast**.

Changing the object's shape using Cast

With our **Subdivision** modifier still in place, we can add a new modifier to alter the object's shape:

1. In the **Modifiers** tab, click **Add Modifier** and select **Cast** at the top of the **Deform** column. Another modifier shows up under **Subdivision**.
2. Change the **Shape** property to `Cylinder` and the **Factor** to `1.0`. Our geometry is now a cylinder.

The two modifiers are displayed one on top of the other. Starting from the top, each modifier acts as the input of the next one. For this reason, the modifiers column is also called the **modifiers stack**.

Using modifiers, we have made our original object look like a cylinder, but that change can be reversed, or even animated. Moving the **Factor** slider between `0.0` and `1.0`, our object transitions from its original shape to the one set in **Cast**.

We can replicate the preceding steps in Python scripts using Blender's API.

Adding modifiers in Python

The Python class of Blender objects contains a `modifiers` attribute. Like all collections, `modifiers` provides the `new` method, which creates and returns new items. By using `new`, we can automate the setup of modifiers using Python.

Finding collection-type items

`Object.modifiers.new` takes two arguments: `name` and `type`. The first will be displayed in the modifier properties in the interface, while `type` specifies which kind of modifier we want to create. The `type` argument must belong to the list of available types, or it will cause an error. Available types are listed in the API documentation:

https://docs.blender.org/api/3.3/bpy_types_enum_items/object_modifier_type_items.html

But we can also get them from Blender itself. These commands will list the modifier keywords in Blender's Python console:

```
>>> import bpy
>>> mod_rna = bpy.types.ObjectModifiers.bl_rna
>>> mod_params = mod_rna.functions["new"].parameters
>>> mod_params["type"].enum_items.keys()
['DATA_TRANSFER', 'MESH_CACHE', 'MESH_SEQUENCE_CACHE', 'NORMAL_EDIT',
'WEIGHTED_NORMAL', 'UV_PROJECT', 'UV_WARP',
...
```

There's another way to get a modifier keyword:

1. Use the **Add Modifier** button in the interface.
2. Look for the argument of the `modifier_add` operator in the **Info** log. It's part of the **Scripting** workspace, as we know from *Chapter 1*.

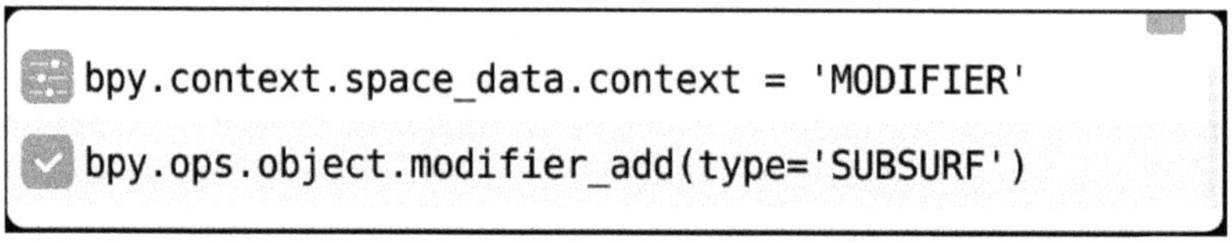

```
bpy.context.space_data.context = 'MODIFIER'
bpy.ops.object.modifier_add(type='SUBSURF')
```

Figure 11.5: Blender info log after adding Subdivision Surface

For instance, the keyword for the **Subdivision Surface** modifiers is `'SUBSURF'`.

Using modifiers.new

Since `modifiers.new` returns the created modifier, we can store the return value and replicate all the steps from the previous *Understanding object modifiers* section.

We'll see how to add a **Subdivision Surface** instance and a **Cast** modifier on the active object and how to reshape it into a cylinder using Python. First, our script needs to import bpy and add a subdivision to increase the available geometry:

```
import bpy
ob = bpy.context.object
subdiv = ob.modifiers.new('Subdivision', 'SUBSURF')
```

The `subdiv` variable contains the new **Subdivision Surface** modifier, so we can change the modifier's parameters by setting `subdiv`'s attributes.

If we are looking for the Python counterpart of an attribute we can see in the interface, we can resort to **Python Tooltips** and **Developer Extra**, the two options in **Edit** > **Preferences** from the top-bar menu. We learned about them in the *Useful features for Python* section in *Chapter 2*.

If tooltips are enabled, hovering the mouse on the **Levels Viewport** slider shows that its Python attribute is `levels`.

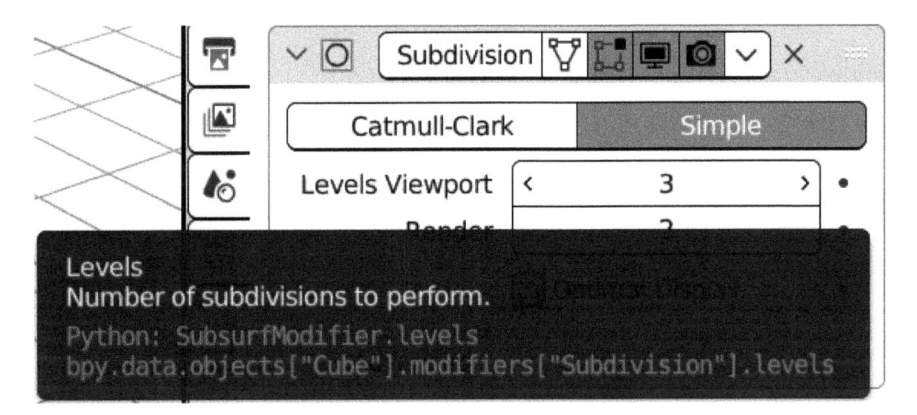

Figure 11.6: Subdivision attributes path displayed in tooltips

To increase the object's poly count without altering its shape, we set `subdiv.levels` to 3 and `subdivision_type` to `'SIMPLE'`:

```
subdiv.levels = 3
subdiv.subdivision_type = 'SIMPLE'
```

Now we have enough polygons to deform our object. We add a `'CAST'` modifier and reshape it to a cylinder:

```
cast = ob.modifiers.new('Cast', 'CAST')
cast.cast_type = 'CYLINDER'
cast.factor = 1.0
```

Subdivision Surface and **Cast** are self-sufficient, as they don't require other objects besides the one they are affecting. Other modifiers rely on data from ancillary objects.

In the next section, we will set up a modifier that depends on a deformer object.

Deformation objects

Many deformers translate a change from one object to another. That allows us to deform a complex object by manipulating a simpler one. Here are a few notable examples:

- **Curve** – Deforms a mesh along a curve object
- **Lattice** – Transfers the changes from a regular grid to a mesh
- **Armature** – Transfers the pose of an articulated structure to a mesh
- **Surface Deform** – Transfers the deformation from one mesh to another

The object used by a modifier can be set using the `modifier.object` attribute.

The **Armature** modifier reproduces the limb movements using a structure of **bones**, so it requires a special type of object that can be posed.

A **Lattice** modifier, on the other hand, relies on the internal coordinates of a grid, which are specific to **Lattice** object types.

As an example, we will see how to add lattice deformation to an object.

Using the Lattice modifier

To use lattice deformation, we need geometry to deform and an object of type lattice. We can use Blender's mascot, the monkey **Suzanne**:

1. Open Blender or go back to the default scene via **File | New | General**.
2. Delete the default **Cube** shape by pressing **Canc** or **X | Delete**.
3. Add a monkey head to the scene using **Add | Mesh | Monkey**.
4. Add a lattice to the scene by using **Add | Lattice**.

A lattice was added to the scene. By default, it is smaller than Suzanne, so we need to scale it up:

1. With the lattice still selected, press S to scale. Drag the mouse or press 2 to double its size.
2. Select Suzanne to add a modifier. In the **Modifiers** tab, Use **Add Modifier | Lattice**.
3. In the **Lattice** modifier, click the **Object** property and select the **Lattice** object from the options.

Editing the Lattice object changes Suzanne's shape:

1. Select **Lattice** in **3D Viewport**.
2. Press the *Tab* key to switch to **Edit Mode**.
3. Select one or more lattice vertices.
4. Press *G* and drag the mouse to move the selection: a lattice deformation is applied to Suzanne.

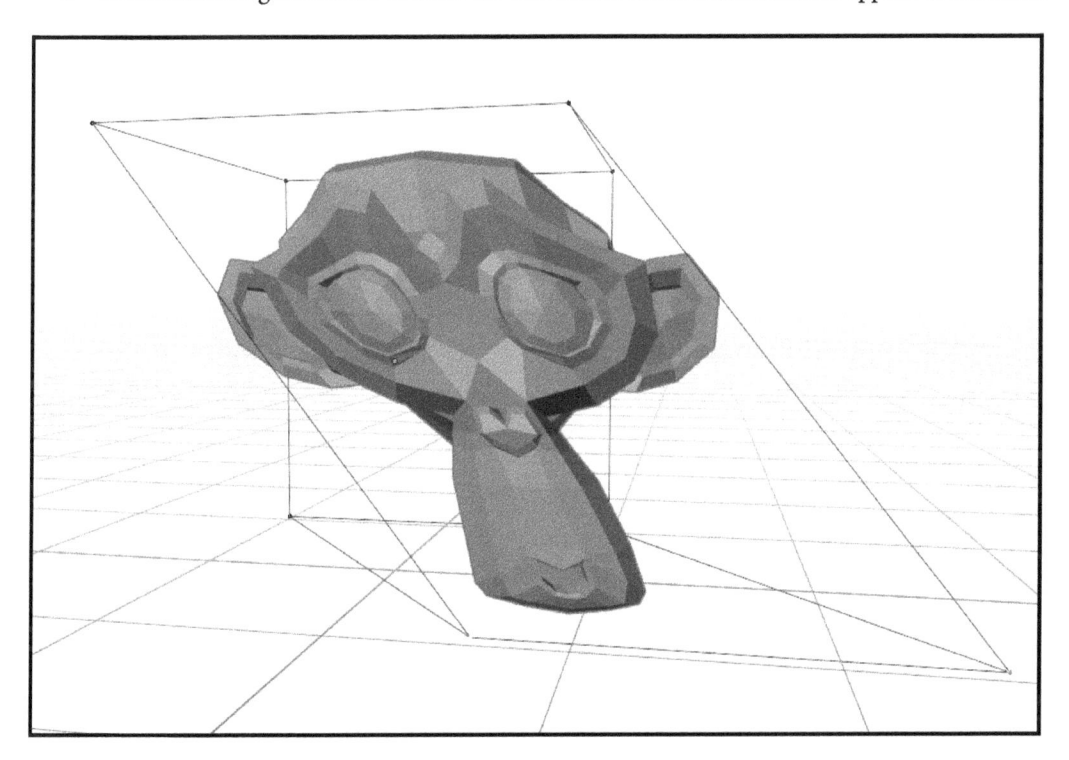

Figure 11.7: Mesh deformed by a lattice cage

Automating these steps with Python can make the process much easier. In the next section, we will write an operator that sets up a lattice deformation in one click.

Writing the Latte Express add-on

The **Latte Express** add-on creates a new lattice around the active object and sets up the modifier.

It's useful for creating basic rigs for cartoon deformation, or stylized objects. The add-on consists of an operator class and a menu entry.

Setting the environment

We create a Python script for our add-on:

1. Create a `PythonScriptingBlender/ch11/addons` folder. We can use the file manager or the file tab of our programmer editor, for example, **VS Code**.
2. Create a new file in that folder and name it `lattice_express.py`. We can do that using the file manager or the **New File** button in an IDE.
3. Open the file in your editor of choice.
4. Set the **Scripts** path to `PythonScriptingBlender/ch11` in the Blender **File Paths** preferences and restart Blender.

Now we can write the add-on and load it in Blender.

Writing the Latte Express information

Like other add-ons, Latte Express starts with a blank line, followed by the `bl_info` dictionary:

```
bl_info = {
    "name": "Latte Express",
    "author": "Packt Man",
    "version": (1, 0),
    "blender": (3, 00, 0),
    "description": "Create a Lattice on the active object",
    "category": "Learning",
}
```

Then we proceed with the add-on classes and interface, in this case, a simple operator.

Writing the Latte Express operator

We need to import the bpy module, so that we can create a new operator:

```
import bpy
class LatteExpress(bpy.types.Operator):
    """Set up Lattice Deformation"""
    bl_idname = "object.latte_expresso"
    bl_label = "Create Lattice on active object"
```

The operator requires an active object, so the condition in `poll` is as follows:

```
@classmethod
def poll(cls, context):
    return context.active_object
```

Creating a lattice object requires lattice data first, so inside `execute`, we call `bpy.data.lattices.new` and use its return value in `bpy.data.objects.new`. We name the new object and data after the active object, even if that's not required. Finally, we add the lattice to the scene by linking it to the current collection:

```
def execute(self, context):
    ob = context.object
    latt_data = bpy.data.lattices.new(f"LAT-{ob.name}")
    latt_obj = bpy.data.objects.new(
                        name=latt_data.name,
                        object_data=latt_data
                    )
    context.collection.objects.link(latt_obj)
```

Let's scale the lattice so that it fits our object. We can get its size from the `dimensions` attribute:

```
latt_obj.scale = ob.dimensions
```

We match the lattice position with the center of the active geometry. We can get the object location from the world matrix as we learned in *Chapter 4*:

```
ob_translation = ob.matrix_world.to_translation()
```

That alone would not work on objects that have their transform pivot away from their geometry center, so we must find the actual midpoint of our object.

Finding the center of a model

To create a lattice that matches the location and size of an object, we must find the median point of its vertices, but we don't have to look at all the components. We can find the center of the object's **bounding box**.

A bounding box is an imaginary parallelepiped that contains all the object geometry. We can display it by activating **Bound** in the **Object** properties.

266　Object Modifiers

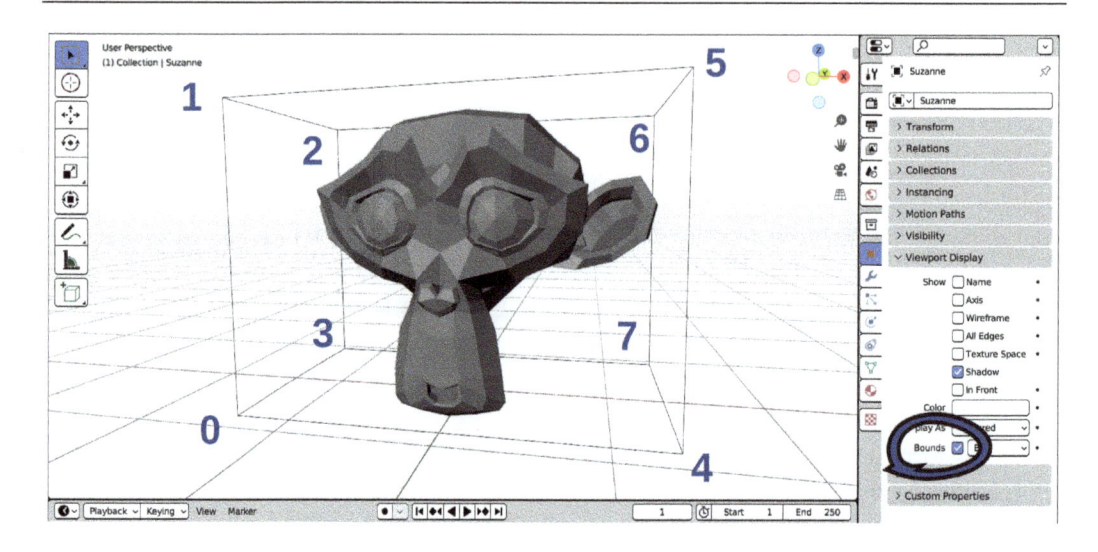

Figure 11.8: An object's bounding box with coordinate indices added on top

The bounding box is found in Python via the `bound_box` attribute. It's a list of eight coordinates, and we can find the center by interpolating two opposite corners.

The center of a box is found in the middle of its diagonals, so we want to mediate between the lower-left-back corner and the top-right-forward corner. We know the indices of those points from *Figure 11.8*. They are 0 and 6, respectively.

A better way to find those two corners is by using the `min` and `max` functions.

One of the two extremes has the lowest x, y, z values, and the other one has the highest. In other words, the components of the lower corner have the lowest sum, and those of the higher corner have the highest.

In Python, `min` and `max` return the lower and higher value in a list, but we can supply a different criterion, in this case, `sum`, using the `key` argument:

```
btm_left = min((c for c in ob.bound_box), key=sum)
top_right = max((c for c in ob.bound_box), key=sum)
```

To find the midpoint between two vectors, we can use the linear interpolation method (`lerp`) from the `Vector` class. In the `import` section, we need to add this line:

```
from mathutils import Vector
```

Then, in `execute`, we interpolate the two coordinates. The first argument of `lerp` can be any triplet, so we convert only one of the two corners to the `Vector` type. Since we are looking for the point sitting halfway between the two corners, we provide a factor of 0.5 as the second argument:

```
btm_left = Vector(btm_left)
ob_center = btm_left.lerp(top_right, 0.5)
```

We add `ob_center` to `ob_translation` to center the lattice to the geometry:

```
Ob_translation += ob_center
latt_obj.location = ob_translation
```

Our lattice, centered and scaled, can now be used to deform the object. We can use it inside a new modifier and return `{'FINISHED'}` to exit the operator:

```
mod = ob.modifiers.new("Lattice", 'LATTICE')
mod.object = latt_obj
return {'FINISHED'}
```

Now that the operator is finished, we can add a menu entry for using it.

Adding a Create Lattice menu item

We define a function to add `LatteExpress` to a menu. Using the **Icon Viewer** addon as in *Chapter 5*, we can find lattice-related icons such as MOD_LATTICE:

```
def menu_func(self, context):
    self.layout.operator(LatteExpress.bl_idname,
                         icon="MOD_LATTICE")
```

Of course, we need to register the new Blender class and function:

```
def register():
    bpy.utils.register_class(LatteExpress)
    ob_menu = bpy.types.VIEW3D_MT_object_context_menu
    ob_menu.append(menu_func)
def unregister():
    ob_menu = bpy.types.VIEW3D_MT_object_context_menu
    ob_menu.remove(menu_func)

    bpy.utils.unregister_class(LatteExpress)
```

We can refresh the add-on preferences and enable **Latte Express**.

Using the Latte Express add-on

Once we have set the **Scripts** path to the `ch11` folder, we will be able to activate **Latte Express** in the **Add-ons** preferences.

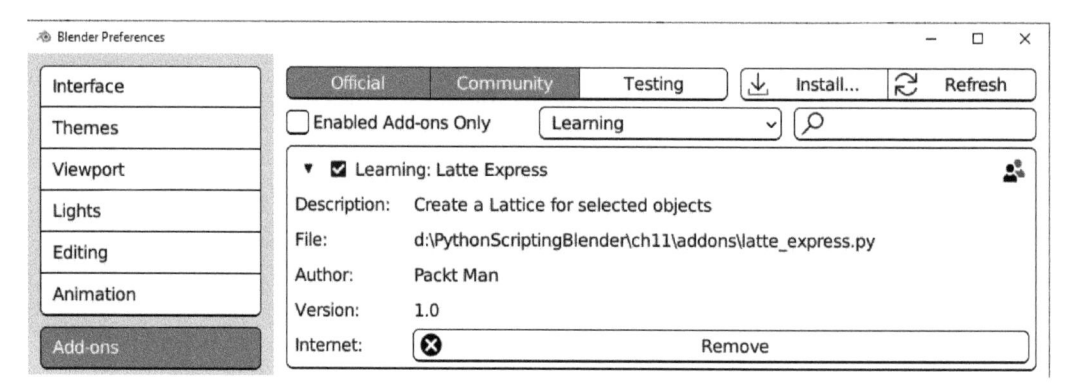

Figure 11.9: Enabling the Latte Express add-on

Our add-on makes the task of setting up a lattice deformation easier. Let's see how the workflow from the previous section, *Deformation objects*, has improved:

1. Open Blender or go back to the default scene via **File | New | General**.
2. Delete the default **Cube** shape by pressing **Canc** or **X | Delete**.
3. Add a monkey head to the scene using **Add | Mesh | Monkey**.
4. Use the mouse right-click to open the object menu in the **3D Viewport**.
5. Select **Create Lattice on Active Object**.

A lattice is created, centered, and scaled on the active object, while a modifier is set up. Besides automating the task, using this add-on gives better accuracy, as the lattice is scaled according to the object's exact dimensions.

In the next section, we will add more control over the geometry and lattice subdivision.

Improving Latte Express options

Some objects might not have enough polygons for the lattice deformation to work properly. We encountered a similar condition at the beginning of this chapter, in the *Understanding object modifiers* section, where we applied a **Subdivision Surface** modifier to our **Cube** shape before we could reshape it into a cylinder using a **Cast** modifier.

The resolution of lattice objects can also be increased to get more control over the deformation.

For those reasons, we will add object subdivision and lattice resolution options to our operator.

Adding object subdivisions

We add a subdivide option to **Latte Express** using `BoolProperty`. Since we will also set a `SUBSURF` modifier, we add `IntProperty` for the subdivision levels.

We add `bl_options = {'REGISTER', 'UNDO'}` to display the operator panel. The declaration of **LatteExpress** becomes as follows:

```
class LatteExpress(bpy.types.Operator):
    """Set up Lattice Deformation"""
    bl_idname = "object.latte_expresso"
    bl_label = "Create Lattice on active object"
    bl_options = {'REGISTER', 'UNDO'}
    add_subsurf: bpy.props.BoolProperty(default=True)
    subd_levels: bpy.props.IntProperty(default=2)
```

The `execute` method takes these options into account, creating a `SUBSURF` modifier if `add_subsurf` is True:

```
    def execute(self, context):
        ob = context.object
        if self.add_subsurf:
            subdiv = ob.modifiers.new("Subdivision",
                                     "SUBSURF")
            subdiv.levels = self.subd_levels
            subdiv.render_levels = self.subd_levels
            subdiv.subdivision_type = "SIMPLE"
```

Subdivision Surface has an additional attribute for rendering subdivision levels. We have set both to the same value to make sure that the Viewport and the rendered images look the same.

Changing lattice resolution

Lattices don't have polygons or subdivision modifiers, but they have resolution parameters to add more divisions along the three axes.

The `points_u`, `points_v`, and `points_w` attributes set the number of divisions across its *x*, *y*, and *z* axes.

We add a property to influence the grid resolution. We use `IntVectorProperty` for those three attributes and set its subtype to `'XYZ'` so that they are displayed like coordinates. The minimum value for resolution coordinates is 1, while we use 3 as default:

```
grid_levels: bpy.props.IntVectorProperty(
                                        default=(3, 3, 3),
                                        min=1,
                                        subtype='XYZ'
                                        )
```

Because of the way the lattice is implemented, changing the resolution before creating the lattice object changes the starting dimensions of a lattice. To avoid that, we only set `points_u`, `points_v`, and `points_w` after `latt_obj` is created.

So, the lattice section becomes as follows:

```
latt_data = bpy.data.lattices.new(f"LAT-{ob.name}")
latt_obj = bpy.data.objects.new(
                                name=latt_data.name,
                                object_data=latt_data
                                )
latt_data.points_u = self.grid_levels[0]
latt_data.points_v = self.grid_levels[1]
latt_data.points_w = self.grid_levels[2]
```

Now that we are adding subdivisions, the lattice grid will present internal vertices, that is, control points that end up being inside the lattice. We don't want that because we are using the lattice as an external cage.

So, we set `use_outside` of the lattice data to `True`:

```
latt_data.use_outside = False
```

After that, the `execute` method continues as before, linking `latt_obj` to `context.collection.objects`, setting its location and scale, and creating the object modifiers before it returns `{'FINISHED'}`.

If we save the script and use *F3* -> **Reload Scripts** and launch **Create Lattice on Active Object**, we'll see the options for the lattice resolution.

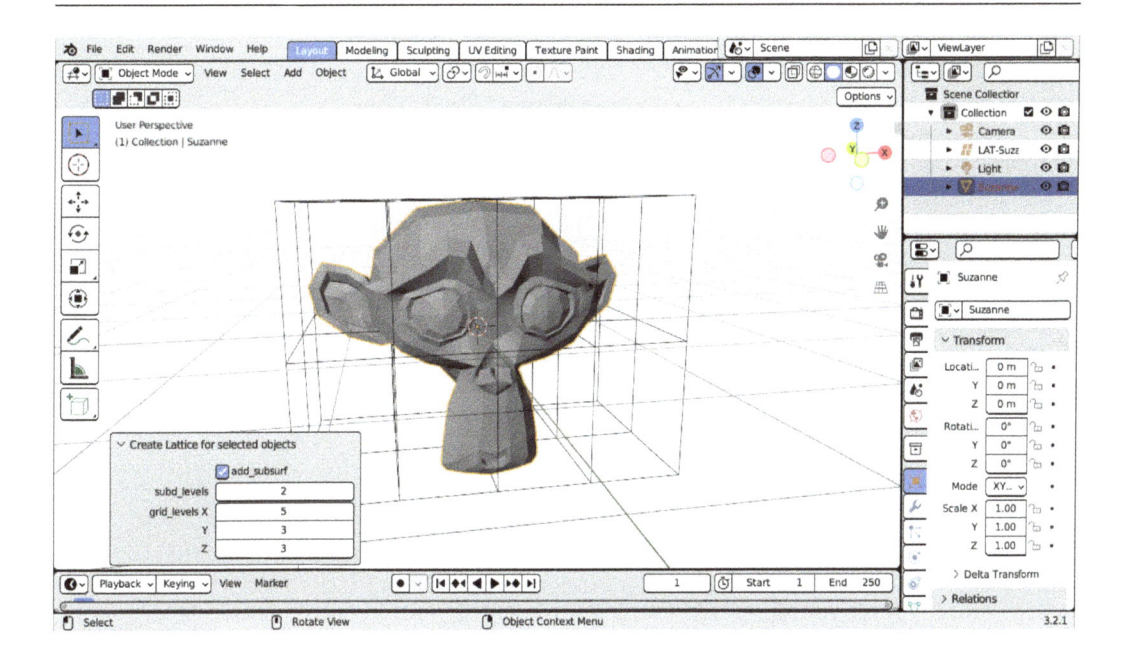

Figure 11.10: A 5x3x3 lattice created with Latte Express

Lattice grids add quick deformations without requiring additional data in the deformed object. Deformers such as **Armature**, the modifier used for articulated characters, require the assignment of **vertex groups** to work properly.

Using armature deformers

Armatures are deformation objects like lattices, but instead of using a grid, they rely on the translation, rotation, and scale of sub-objects called **bones**, in analogy with the human skeleton.

By default, bones are represented as octahedral sticks. Armatures can switch to **Pose Mode**, a special Blender mode in which bones can be animated individually using the techniques learned in *Chapter 7*.

The setup of an **Armature** modifier might take some extra steps but is similar to the one used for lattices.

Adding armature objects to the scene

To acquire familiarity with the bones, we will create a simple armature for **Suzanne**'s geometry:

1. Open Blender or go back to the default scene via **File | New | General**.
2. Delete the default **Cube** shape by pressing **Canc** or **X | Delete**.

3. Add a monkey head to the scene using **Add | Mesh | Monkey**.
4. Add an armature to the scene using **Add | Armature | Single Bone**.

At this point, we should see the tip of an octahedral bone on top of **Suzanne**'s head. Since most of the bone is hidden inside the model, we can press the Z key and switch to the wireframe display.

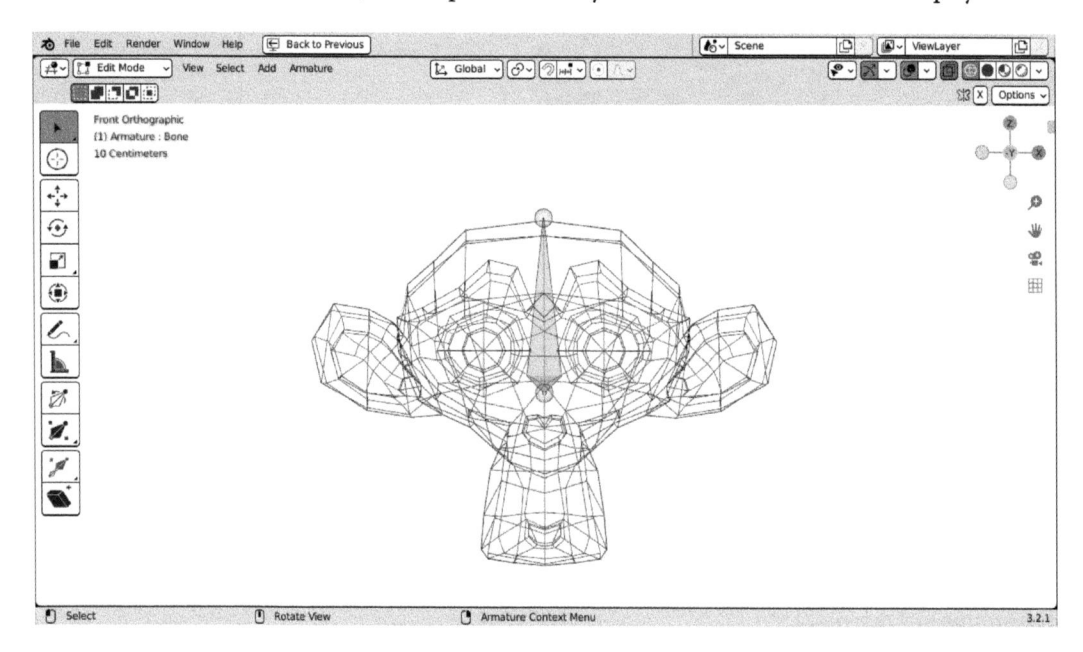

Figure 11.11: An armature bone inside a geometry, with a wireframe display

We could set up an **Armature** modifier right away, but armatures usually have more than one bone. For instance, we can add bones to the ears.

Adding armature bones

To have a better view while we create new bones, we can press the *1* key or use **View | Viewpoint | Front** from the top-bar menu, then we can press the . key, or **View | Frame Selected**, to center the view.

With the armature as the active object, we switch to **Edit Mode** by pressing *Tab* or using the drop-down box on the top left. Then, always in front view, we can add bone to the ears using the following steps:

1. Add a new bone using the *Shift + A* combination or **Add | Single Bone** from the top-bar menu. The new bone is added on top of the existing one.
2. Click on the bones to select one of them.
3. Press *R*, then type 50, and press *Enter* to rotate the bone toward the right-hand side of the screen.

4. Press *G*, then *X* to move it horizontally, and type 1. Then, press *Enter* to move the bone toward Suzanne's left ear.
5. Press *G*, then *Z* to move the bone vertically and type 0.2. Then, press *Enter* to move the bone slightly downward.
6. Blender has a naming convention for left and right bones. To add the .L suffix to the left ear bone, we select **Armature | Names | Auto-Name Left/Right** from the top-bar menu.
7. To create a bone for the other ear, we select **Armature | Symmetrize** from the top-bar menu.

The resulting armature should resemble a trident. The exact position of the bones is not important for the sake of this example.

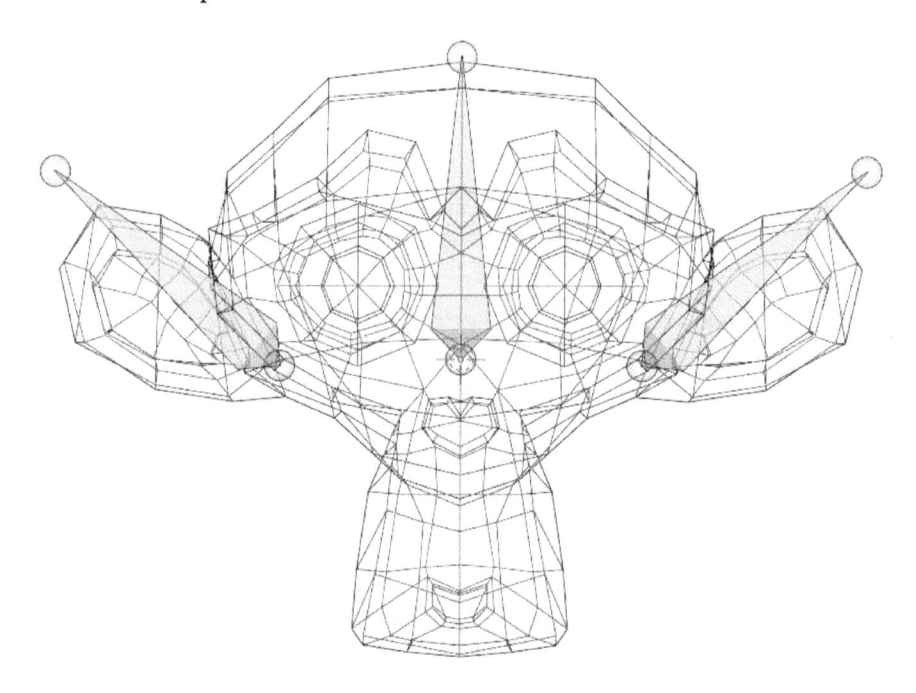

Figure 11.12: Ear bones for Blender's Suzanne

With three bones in place, we can go back to **Object Mode** by pressing *Tab* and go back to the **Solid** view by pressing *Z*. Now, we can bind our geometry to the armature.

Binding objects to armatures

As mentioned earlier, **Armature** deformers require additional information: each vertex should be assigned to one or more bones with a process called **weight painting**. It's a manual task for riggers, but we can use Blender automatic weights for a quick result:

1. In **Object Mode**, select the Suzanne object in **3D Viewport**, then keep the *Shift* key pressed and select the armature too.
2. Press *Ctrl + P* to open the **Set Parent** menu and pick **With Automatic Weights**. Or select **Object | Parent | With Automatic Weights** from the top-bar menu.

> **Beware the outliner**
>
> If you use **Outliner** for selecting objects, keep in mind that its policy is different:
>
> - In **Viewport**, the last selected of multiple objects is the active object
> - In **Outliner**, the first selected of multiple objects is the active object
>
> To parent an object to an armature, we either select the object and then the armature in **Viewport**, or first the armature and then the object in **Outliner**.

Now we can deform our mesh by posing the armature bones:

1. Select **Armature** and press *Ctrl + Tab*, or use the drop-down box on the top left of the screen and switch to **Pose Mode**.
2. Select any bone, then move, rotate, or scale it by using the *G, R,* and *S* keys.

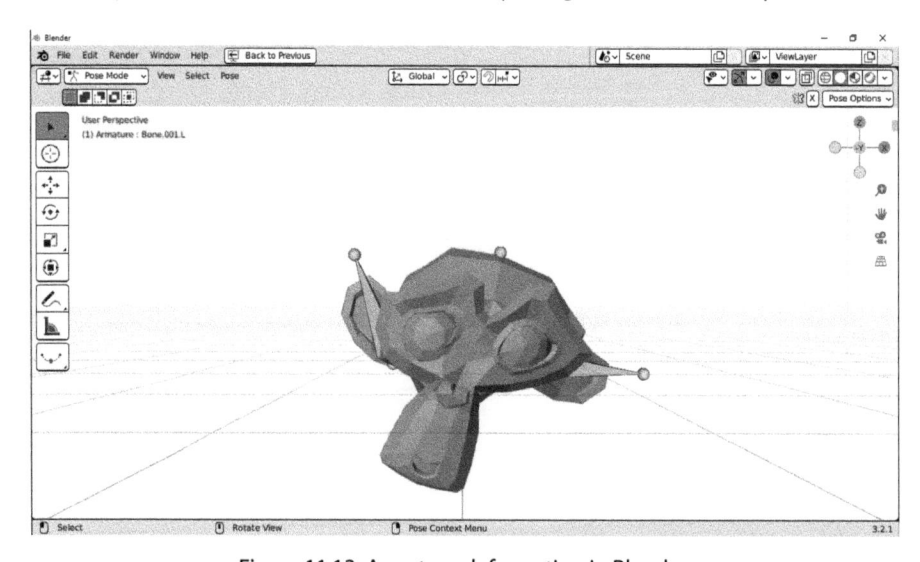

Figure 11.13: Armature deformation in Blender

Bones are a soft, controllable way to deform a model. Lattice grids can be deformed with armatures too, so we can create and set up an armature in **Latte Express**.

Scripting a lattice armature

Armatures are the recommended way for animating in Blender as they support linking across different `.blend` files and other advanced animation features.

Binding a lattice to an armature allows you to animate deformations without switching to **Edit Mode** to edit grid vertices.

Adding an armature condition

We want armatures to be an optional feature, so we can add another property for that. We set its default value to `True`, so an armature is created unless it's set otherwise:

```
add_armature: bpy.props.BoolProperty(default=True)
```

Inside the `execute` method, we check for this value and proceed accordingly.

Adding an armature to the scene

Armatures are created in the same way as lattices and other objects:

1. Create new data.
2. Create a new object using the data created.

Even if it is not strictly required, we set the new armature as the parent of the lattice to ensure consistency between their transforms.

If `add_armature` is `False`, we set the lattice location right away. Otherwise, we create a new armature. The underlying code takes over soon after we've got the object median point:

```
# …
ob_translation = ob.matrix_world.to_translation()
ob_translation += ob_center
if not self.add_armature:
    latt_obj.location = ob_translation
else:
    arm_data = bpy.data.armatures.new(
                        f"ARM-{ob.name}"
                    )
    arm_obj = bpy.data.objects.new(
```

```
                        name=arm_data.name,
                        object_data=arm_data
                        )
    context.collection.objects.link(arm_obj)
```

Once the armature is part of the scene, we can parent the lattice to it and move it to where the object is:

```
    latt_obj.parent = arm_obj
    arm_obj.location = ob_translation
```

It's common to have the armature's transform pivot under the affected geometry, so when an armature is at its resting position, the deformed character will be above ground level. Therefore, we move the armature to half the object height below the center, using the third coordinate of `dimensions`:

```
    half_height = ob.dimensions[2]/2
    arm_obj.location[2] -= half_height
```

The lattice, on the other hand, should be centered on the geometry, so we bring it up by the same amount:

```
    latt_obj.location[2] += half_height
```

Now that the armature and lattice are placed, we need to create some bones.

Creating edit bones

To create the bones manually, we select the armature and switch to **Edit Mode**. In Python, the same steps are performed with the following:

```
    context.view_layer.objects.active = arm_obj
    bpy.ops.object.mode_set(mode='EDIT',
                            toggle=False)
```

We pass `False` to the `toggle` argument of `mode_set`, because we are not switching back and forth between modes.

We will add as many bones as the lattice vertical sections. For instance, a lattice with a vertical resolution of 3 can be rigged with three bones.

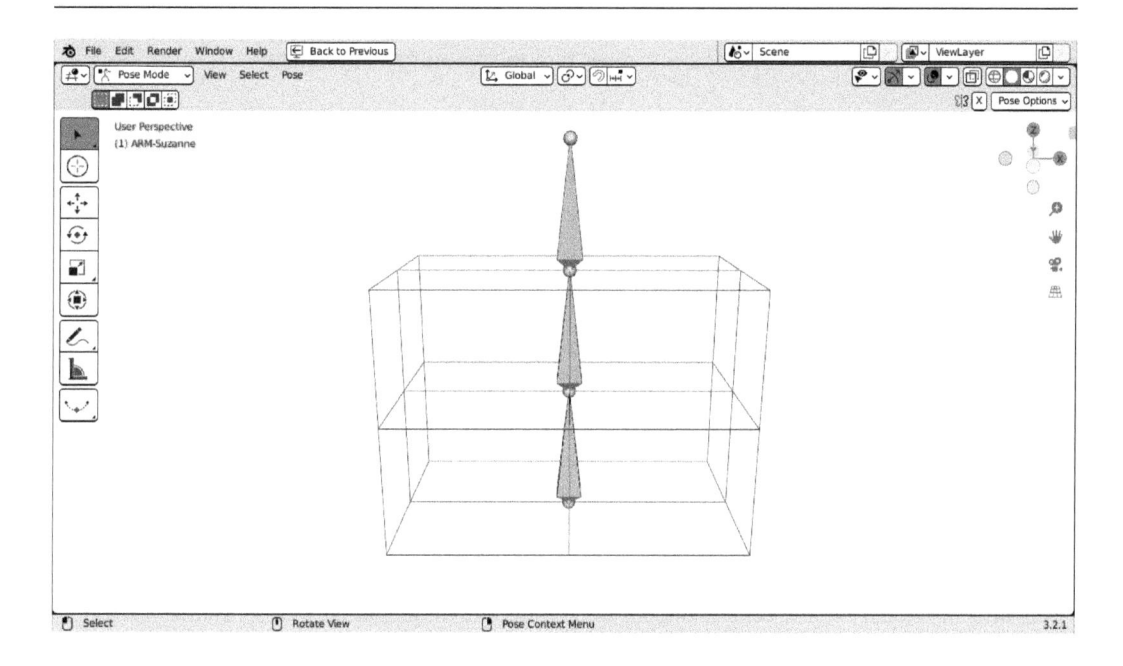

Figure 11.14: Rigging a lattice with armature bones

We get the number of levels from the `grid_levels` property. Each bone starts from the lower section and stops at the next. The last bone pops outside the lattice.

To get the optimal length, we divide the object height by the number of internal bones, i.e., one bone less than `grid_levels`:

```
grid_levels = self.grid_levels[2]
height = ob.dimensions[2]
bone_length = height / (grid_levels - 1)
```

We use a `for` loop to add an **edit bone** at each section. In Python, index-based loops use the `range` function. We add a two-digit suffix to each bone name:

```
for i in range(grid_levels):
    eb = arm_data.edit_bones.new(f"LAT_{i:02}")
```

Each bone has a start point (`head`) and an endpoint (`tail`). Since the armature's origin matches the first section of the lattice, the first bone has the coordinates 0, 0, 0.

The second bone should have a higher position to make room for the previous bone length, and so on, so the expression for each bone head is as follows:

```
eb.head = (0, 0, i * bone_length)
```

The `tail` part of the bone adds one `bone_length` to the `head[2]` coordinate:

```
eb.tail = (0, 0, eb.head[2] + bone_length)
```

To assign the lattice vertices to the bones, we must collect which vertices belong to the current level based on their Z coordinate.

Assigning vertices to bones

For each lattice point, we compare the third coordinate (`co[2]`) with the relative height of the current section. *Relative* means that the first section is at a height of 0.0, the last is at 1.0, the one in the middle is at 0.5, and so on.

Python indices start from 0, so the index of the last section is the number of sections minus 1. Keeping that in mind, here's how we can get the relative height of each level:

```
rel_height = i / (grid_levels-- 1)
```

Lattice points are relative to the center, and the size of one side of the lattice is 1.0, so the vertical coordinate of the lowest point is -0.5. For that reason, we lower `rel_height` by 0.5 units:

```
rel_height -= 0.5
```

To assign vertices, we need a list of their indices, which we store in the `vert_ids` list:

```
vert_ids = []
```

In this list, we need to store the identifier number of the lattice points, not their coordinates.

The lattice data points are an ordered collection, so their identifier is their ordinal index; that is, the first point is identified by index 1, the second point has index 2, and so on.

In Python, we can get the ordinal of the iterated items using `enumerate`:

```
for id, v in enumerate(latt_data.points):
    if v.co[2] == rel_height:
        vert_ids.append(id)
```

We can create a vertex group named after each bone and assign vertices using the `add` method. We also supply a weight of 1.0, because we are not blending the assignment between two groups, and set `'REPLACE'` as a condition, because we are not adding nor subtracting from a previous assignment:

```
vg = latt_obj.vertex_groups.new(
                    name=eb.name
                    )
vg.add(vert_ids, 1.0,'REPLACE')
```

Creating the bones and assigning their influence is the hard part of the process. Now we can create the modifiers.

Creating the Armature modifier

We add a new Armature modifier to `latt_obj` via the `modifiers.new` method, and we use `arm_obj` as its deformer object:

```
arm_mod = latt_obj.modifiers.new("Armature",
                                 "ARMATURE")
arm_mod.object = arm_obj
```

Finally, we leave **Edit Mode** and switch to `'POSE'`, so that the user can animate:

```
bpy.ops.object.mode_set(mode='POSE',
                        toggle=False)
```

At this point, `LattExpress` creates a lattice deformer and animation bones in one click. As an optional step, we can create custom shapes for displaying the bones.

Adding custom bone shapes

Armature bones are effective deformers, but we have experienced a major drawback for ourselves in the *Using armature deformers* section: bones tend to be hidden by the deformed geometry.

There are a few workarounds, such as activating the **In Front** attribute in the **Armature** properties and using **X-Ray** or **Wireframe** views.

Another gimmick consists in displaying special widgets by assigning mesh objects to the bone's **Custom Shape** attribute.

Creating mesh objects in Python

First, we must create a new mesh. A mesh consists of vertex coordinates, plus edges or faces that connect vertices.

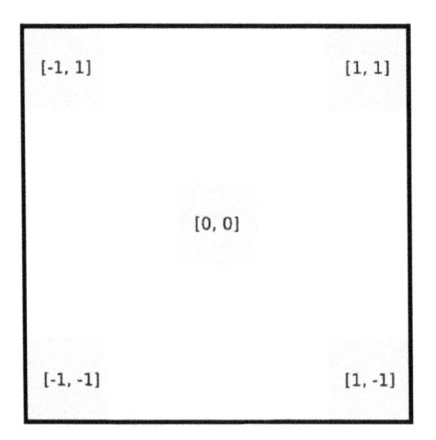

Figure 11.15: Vertex coordinates of a 2D square

In this example, we create a wireframe square and use it as a bone widget. Blender bones expand upon their Y axis, so the horizontal coordinates of our bones that are placed vertically are X and Z.

We build our list of vertices. We aim for a side length of 1.0, a measure easy to scale. For that reason, each side will go from a -0.5 to a 0.5 coordinate, or the other way around. If X and Z are the first and last coordinates, this is our vertex list:

```
v_cos = [
    [-0.5, 0.0, -0.5],
    [-0.5, 0.0, 0.5],
    [0.5, 0.0, 0.5],
    [0.5, 0.0, -0.5]
]
```

Next, we need a list of edges. An edge is a pair of vertex indices, each representing the two vertices that are going to connect. The four edges of a square connect vertex 0 to 1, 1 to 2, vertex 2 to 3, and 3 to 0:

```
edges = [
    [0, 1], [1, 2], [2, 3], [3, 0]
]
```

We can create new mesh data from Python lists using the `from_pydata` method. Since we don't need faces in a control widget, the third argument is an empty list:

```
mesh = bpy.data.meshes.new("WDG-square")
mesh.from_pydata(coords, edges, [])
```

We add the mesh to the scene:

```
wdg_obj = bpy.data.objects.new(mesh.name, mesh)
context.collection.objects.link(wdg_obj)
```

Now, we can assign the widget shape to the **pose bones** of our armature:

```
for pb in arm_obj.pose.bones:
    pb.custom_shape = wdg_obj
```

With a side length of `1.0`, our widget could be hidden as well, so we scale it to match the `dimensions` object.

Keeping in mind that a bone's up direction is the Y axis, but Blender's up direction is Z, we set the Z custom shape scale to the Y dimension:

```
pb_scale = pb.custom_shape_scale_xyz
pb_scale[0] = ob.dimensions[0]
pb_scale[2] = ob.dimensions[1]
```

Blender scales the displayed custom shape by the length of the bone, so we divide the scale by the bone length:

```
pb_scale[0] /= bone_length
pb_scale[2] /= bone_length
```

The armature created in our script is ready. We will tidy the scene and exit the operator.

> **Storing bones is bad for your variables!**
>
> Armature bones are represented by different Python entities depending on the current mode. When the armature is in **Edit Mode**, `EditBone` from the armature data `edit_bones` collection is used. When the armature is in **Pose Mode**, `PoseBone` from the `pose.bones` object is used.
>
> These collections are rebuilt every time the armature is updated, storing them in variables while they are changed can cause crashes.

Finalizing the setup

If an armature is created, we hide the widget mesh and the lattice:

```
wdg.hide_set(True)
latt_obj.hide_set(True)
```

The last steps of `execute` are the same as before: we create a lattice modifier for the deformed object, unselect the geometry, and finish:

```
mod = ob.modifiers.new("Lattice", "LATTICE")
mod.object = latt_obj
```

```
            ob.select_set(False)
        return {'FINISHED'}
```

Reloading the scripts and launching **Create Lattice on Active Object** will create a full animation setup complete with armature and bone shapes.

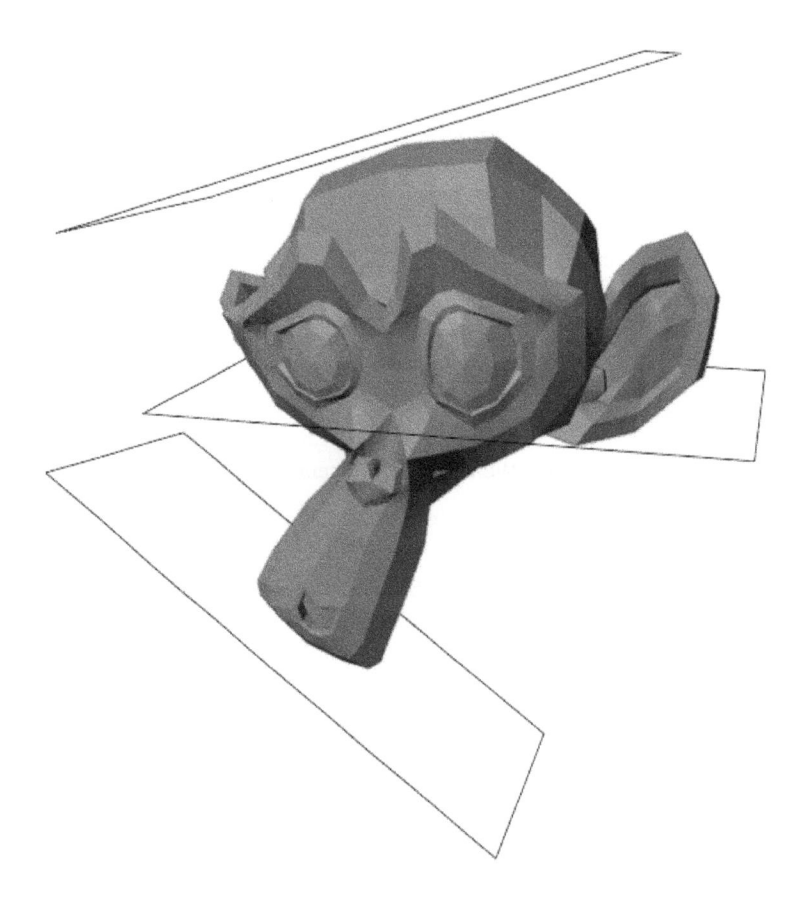

Figure 11.16: Suzanne deformed via animation controls

This add-on can still be improved. For instance, we could build oval shapes for our animation controls or tidy the `execute` method by moving some of the code to specific functions, but since it satisfies its initial purpose, we can consider it finished.

Summary

We have learned how to alter objects using modifiers and how to bind modifiers to animate objects. We have also gained a deeper understanding of how object data works and how objects of different types are created, linked to the scene, and integrated.

Using this knowledge, we have coded a production tool that can be used to deform any object.

In the next and final chapter of this book, *Chapter 12*, we will explore the last step of a 3D pipeline.

Questions

1. Do modifiers alter the object's data?
2. How do we add modifiers to an object?
3. Do modifiers rely on other objects besides the ones they deform?
4. True or false: We can change the resolution of lattice data before or after we create its lattice object with no consequences.
5. How do we add bones to an armature in Python?
6. True or false: There is only one bone collection property.
7. True or false: Only objects of type mesh can be deformed by armatures.
8. Blender has modes. Does the current mode have consequences on whether we can add or remove data in our script?
9. How do we create a mesh using Python?

12
Rendering and Shaders

A process called *rendering* generates the pixels of finished images by evaluating the geometries, lights, and camera of the scene.

The renderers, or Render Engines, that handle those computations can be external programs, independent from the 3D application, or fully integrated features of the animation package. All renderers have strong and weak points and can be grouped into two categories: real time, which assume a few approximations to achieve immediate visualization, and offline, which take more time to take more details into account.

To generate images, renderers rely on shaders – that is, instructions on how an object reacts to the light and position of the observer, and how that translates into the rendered pixels.

Shaders can be complex and are a discipline of their own, but the basic concept of how they work is not hard to grasp.

In this chapter, you will learn where to set the render properties, how to automate the creation of shaders using Python, and how to use the **File Browser** for loading images.

This chapter covers the following topics:

- Understanding the materials system
- Loading images in the Shader Editor
- Connecting and arranging shader nodes

Technical requirements

We will use Blender and Visual Studio Code in this chapter. The examples created for this chapter, along with the media files, can be found at `https://github.com/PacktPublishing/Python-Scripting-in-Blender/tree/main/ch12`.

Render and materials

Blender comes with two render engines: **Eevee**, the real-time renderer that can be used in the Viewport, and **Cycles**, an offline renderer. Additional engines, including most of the commercial offerings, can be installed in the form of render add-ons. A third option, **Workbench**, can be used for quickly and simply displaying renders in the Viewport.

Setting the Render Engine

The current **Render Engine**, along with other render settings, can be found in the scene **Render** properties. It's the first tab and is marked with an icon of a TV set:

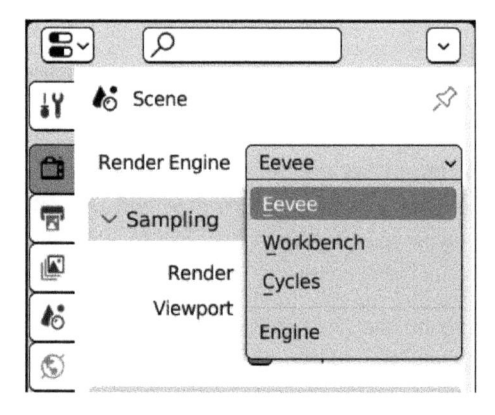

Figure 12.1: Selecting the current Render Engine

While **Workbench** is designed to have only a few render options and no shading system, **Eevee** and **Cycles** can combine images, colors, and attributes using a node-based system. This can be done in the **Shader Editor** area, available in the **Shading** workspace.

The Shading workspace

Shading involves disparate activities, such as accessing image files, checking the Viewport, and editing object properties. Once we set our **Render Engine** to Eeeve, Cycles, or an external engine that supports Blender's shading system, we can carry out those tasks in the **Shading** workspace. It contains the following:

- A **File Browser** for importing images
- The **3D Viewport** area for checking the materials
- An **Outliner**

Render and materials   287

- Data **Properties**; by default, the **World** settings tab is active
- The **Shaders Editor** area
- The **Image Editor** area:

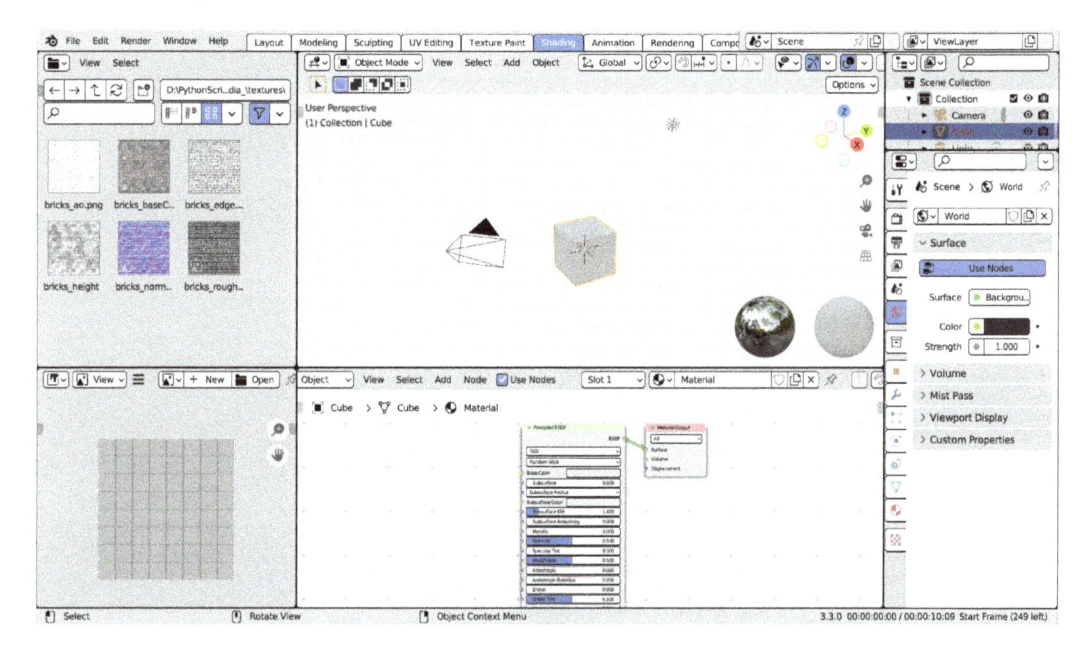

Figure 12.2: The Shading workspace

The default material presents a few color attributes that can be set in the **Material Properties** area. To understand how to script articulated materials with a proper layout, we will provide a brief overview of how the shader components come together in the shader graph.

Understanding object materials

We can change the overall look of an object by specifying its material. The term *material* follows the analogy of real-world objects, whose look is affected by the material of which they are made or coated.

Object materials can be edited in the **Material Properties** area. In version 3.3, it's the second-to-last property tab, marked with an icon of a sphere with a checkerboard pattern, as shown in *Figure 12.3*.

Setting Material Properties

Materials exist independently from objects. One material can be shared among multiple objects and an object can have more materials assigned to different sets of faces.

288　Rendering and Shaders

Scrolling down to the material **Settings**, we can edit how the material is processed by Blender – for instance, how its transparent parts are rendered over the background:

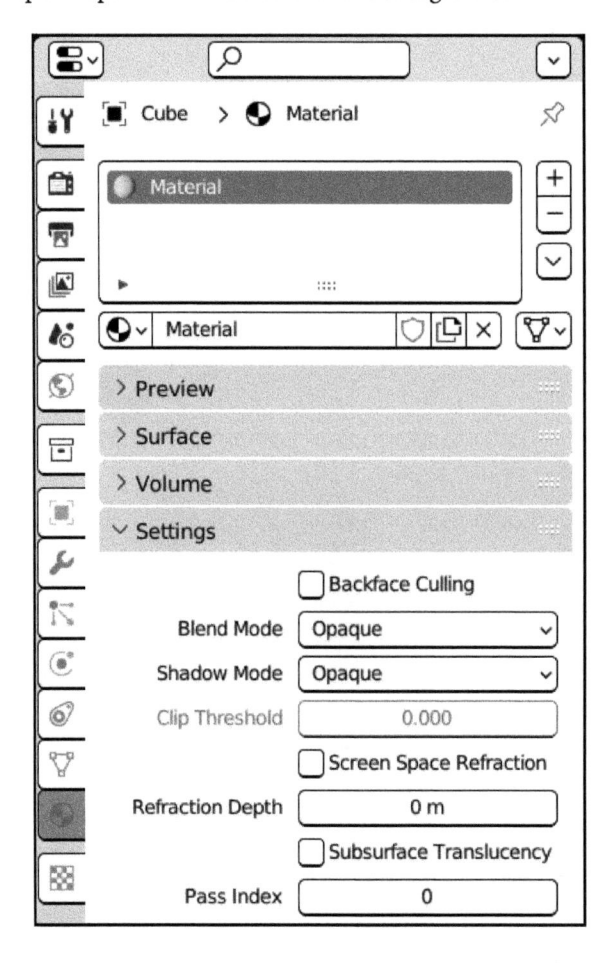

Figure 12.3: Settings in the Material Properties area

The properties commonly associated with actual materials, such as roughness, color, and transparency, are displayed in the **Surface** panel. Those properties are part of the **shader**, a generic algorithm used for computing how a surface should look. Every material has a shader associated with it.

Shaders introduce a new concept to this book: a visual framework known as the **nodes tree**. We can learn how it works by looking at the **Shader Editor** area.

The Shader Editor

The shading system supports different styles: realistic, cartoon, or technical drawings, to mention a few. Rather than providing a single interface with defined widgets, the functionalities of a renderer are scattered through interconnecting units called **nodes**.

Much like a function, a node performs a specific operation on one or more inputs and makes the results available through one or more outputs. Nodes are visual representations of functions, allowing non-programmers to combine logic blocks to get custom results.

Nodes are not unique to shading – they are used for **Compositing** and for generating meshes in the **Geometry Nodes** modifier.

By default, a Blender material presents a **Material Output** node in the **Shader Editor** area, with a **Principled BSDF** node as its **Surface** input. **Bidirectional Scattering Distribution Function (BSFD)** is a mathematical model of how a surface receives and reflects light rays. It is a form of **Physically-Based Rendering** (PBR), an approach based on how visual properties such as color, roughness, and permeability interact with light in the real world.

Material Output is the last node of the graph and transfers the shading to an object.

Only one output can be active at any time, so the shader graph is also called the **Node Tree**, with the output as the root from which all the other branches stem.

Understanding the Node Tree

The inputs and outputs of a node are displayed as colored circles called **sockets**. Input sockets are on the left-hand side of the node, while output sockets are on the right. Their color depends on the data type of the socket. For instance, the **Base Color** socket of a **Principled** node, which is yellow, assigns a color to a material, while **Roughness**, a gray socket, is a float number to denote how far from smooth it is.

Purple sockets, such as **Normal**, are vectors and can contain directional data.

Output sockets are on the right-hand side of a node, and can be connected, or linked, to the input sockets on the left-hand side of another node:

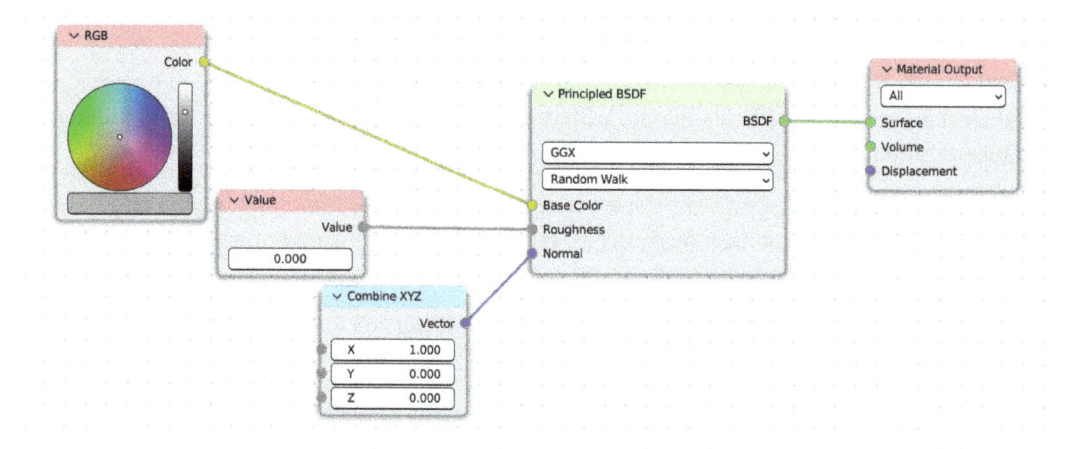

Figure 12.4: A principled node receiving color, roughness, and normal inputs

So, the color attribute of a **Base Color** is an input socket and can be connected to any color output from another node. For instance, the input of a **Principled** node's **Base Color** can come from an **RGB** node, as shown in *Figure 12.4*, but also from an **Image Texture**, as shown in *Figure 12.5*:

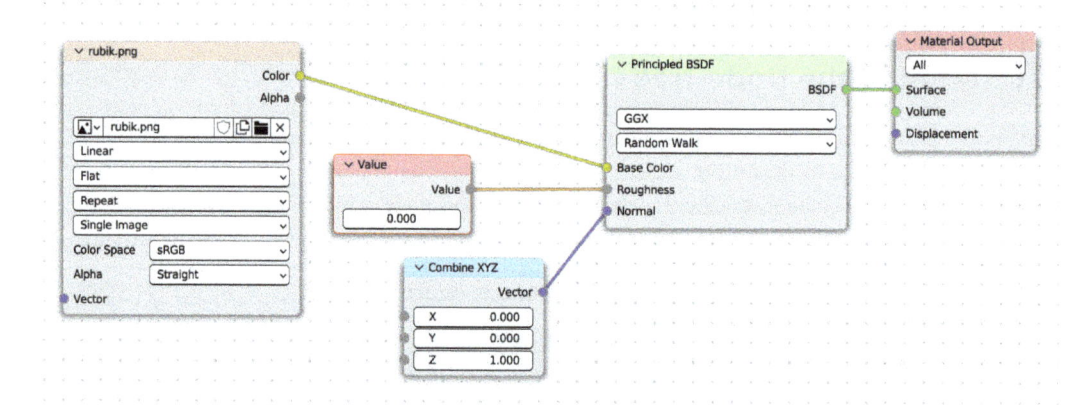

Figure 12.5: A principled node, with an image as the input of Base Color

> **Connection is conversion!**
>
> We can connect sockets of different types, such as vectors and colors; the data is converted automatically. The *X*, *Y*, and *Z* vector components are converted into the red, green, and blue elements of color, while the brightness of colors is converted into float values.

Now that we know how materials work, we will write a script that helps load **Image Textures**.

Writing the Textament add-on

While creating a shader can take time, we can automate some of the simpler operations. For instance, we can write an add-on to ease the task of loading images from disk and connecting them to the shader.

Using texture images

With the **Texture Image** node, we can use an image for coloring an object. That adds variation to how a material looks, as images can vary along the extension of an object and are not limited to a single color:

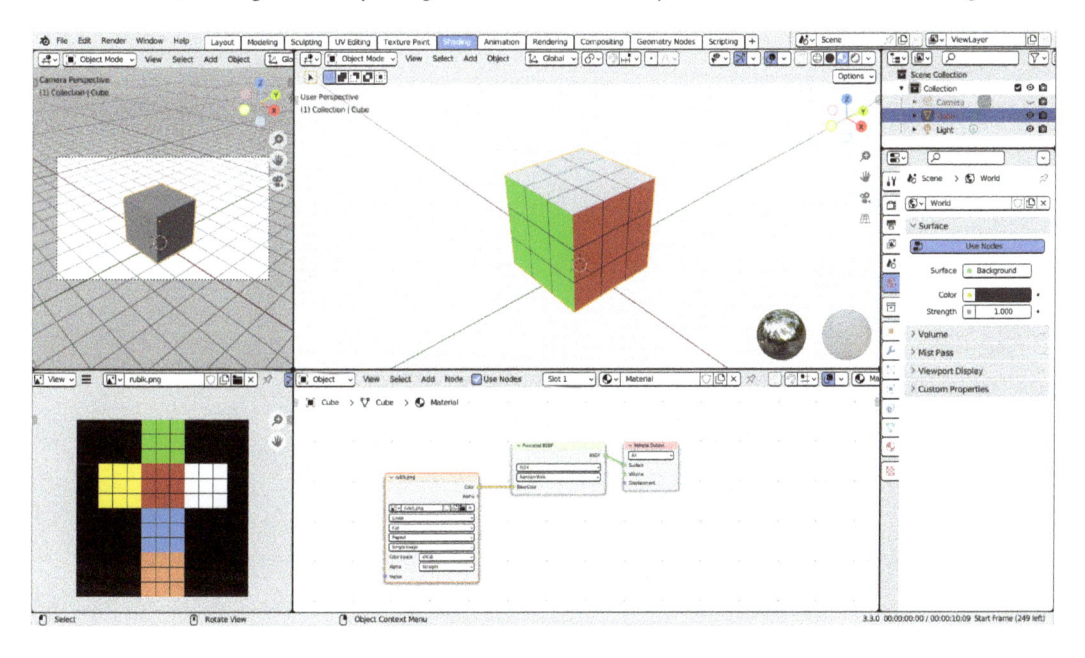

Figure 12.6: An image texture of a Rubik's cube, applied to a plain cube

The operator that we are going to write will load multiple images from disk and guess their usage from the image's filename. For instance, an image named `Metallic.png` would be loaded as a **Texture Image** and connected to the **Metallic** input of a **Principled** node.

As usual, we will set up an environment for developing a new add-on.

Setting up the environment

We will create a Python script for our add-on and make it known to Blender by performing these steps:

1. Create a folder called `PythonScriptingBlender/ch12/addons`. We can use the file manager or the file tab of our IDE for this, such as **VS Code**.
2. Create a new file in that folder and name it `textament.py`. We can use the file manager or the **New File** button of our IDE to do this.
3. Open the file in your editor of choice.
4. Set the **Scripts** path to `PythonScriptingBlender/ch12` in Blender's **File Paths** preferences.
5. Restart Blender to update the search paths.

Now, we will start writing the add-on information as usual.

Writing the Textament add-on information

In the information, we must specify what the add-on is for and where its tools can be found:

```
bl_info = {
    "name": "Textament",
    "author": "Packt Man",
    "version": (1, 0),
    "blender": (3, 00, 0),
    "description": "Load and connect node textures",
    "location": "Node-Graph header",
    "category": "Learning"
}
```

The add-on contains just one class – an import operator for loading images.

Writing an import operator

Our operator loads the image textures from disk, so we will need the `os` module to handle disk paths. Besides bpy, this operator will inherit from the `ImportHelper` utility class so that it can access Blender's **File Browser**

```
import os
import bpy
from bpy_extras.io_utils import ImportHelper
```

Operators that derive from `ImportHelper` store the selected file paths in a few extra properties.

Using Blender's File Browser

Like all operators, `AddTextures` is based on `bpy.types.Operator`, but since it operates on files, it inherits from the `ImportHelper` class too. By inheriting from both classes, when it is launched, `AddTextures` runs the `invoke` method of `ImportHelper`, which opens the **File Browser**. After a choice is made, our `execute` method runs as usual:

```
Class AddTextures(bpy.types.Operator, ImportHelper):
    """Load and connect material textures"""
    bl_idname = "texture.textament_load"
    bl_label = "Load and connect textures"
    bl_description = "Load and connect material textures"
```

Deriving from `ImportHelper` adds a `filepath` attribute to `AddTexture`, in which the path to the selected file is stored.

The `filepath` attribute stores the disk path to a single file, which is not enough in our case as we intend to load multiple files at once. For that reason, we need to store the selected `directory` in a `StringProperty`, and the selected `files` as a collection of `OperatorFileListElement`:

```
directory: bpy.props.StringProperty()
files: bpy.props.CollectionProperty(
            name="File Path",
            type=bpy.types.OperatorFileListElement,
        )
```

In another `StringProperty`, `filter_glob`, set the extensions of the files that should be displayed in the **File Browser** – in our case, `.png` and `.jpg` images. This property is `"HIDDEN"`: we don't want it to show up in the operator's options:

```
filter_glob: bpy.props.StringProperty(
                        default="*.png; *.jpg",
                        options={"HIDDEN"})
```

Now, we can write the operator method. We will start with `poll`, the method that checks if the operator can be launched.

Checking the existence of an active node

This operator works on the current node, so we need to check for the following:

- An active object exists
- There is an active material
- A material node tree has been found
- The material tree has an active node

So, the `poll` method returns `False` unless all the aforementioned conditions apply:

```
@classmethod
def poll(cls, context):
    ob = context.object
    if not ob:
        return False
    mat = ob.active_material
    if not ob:
        return False
    tree = mat.node_tree
    if not tree:
        return False
    return tree.nodes.active
```

If the operator is launched and files are selected, they will be stored to be used in the `execute` method.

Matching texture filenames

At the beginning of `execute`, we store the currently active node in a variable:

```
def execute(self, context):
    mat = context.object.active_material
    target_node = mat.node_tree.nodes.active
```

Operators that inherit from `ImportHelper` display the **File Browser** area when they are invoked and run their `execute` method after a choice in the **File Browser** is confirmed.

For that reason, at the time when `execute` is run, the `self.files` attribute will contain the file selection from the user. We can iterate `self.files` and compare each filename with the shader inputs. Rather than looking for an exact match, we will be happy to find a filename and an input name that are similar at large.

For instance, `"baseColor.png"` should connect with the `"Base Color"` socket. In other words, we want case-insensitive and space-insensitive matching.

A quick way to achieve this is by using a combination of the `lower` and `replace` methods. We can test this in any Python console; for example:

```
>>> "Base Color".lower().replace(" ", "")
'basecolor'
>>> "baseColor".lower().replace(" ", "")
'basecolor'
```

We will need to perform this operation for every file, on any input, so we should create a function for that.

The `lambda` statement is a quick way to create a function by just stating its arguments and one expression. For instance, putting an input, *x*, into lowercase and as a non-spaced string can be written in this form:

```
match_rule = lambda x : x.lower().replace(" ", "")
```

Unlike `def`, `lambda` doesn't assign a name to the function as names are not a requirement of the syntax:

lambda arguments : expression

Since we are storing its result in the `match_rule` variable, our example is equivalent to writing the following lines:

```
def match_rule(x):
    return x.lower().replace(" ", "")
```

`lambda` can be used to write more compact code, or if a function is required as an argument but is not supposed to be called directly.

We will use `match_rule` on every filename and every potential socket and compare the results while looking for a match.

Node sockets are stored in `inputs`, a dictionary-like collection attribute of every node. We can get a list of the socket names using the `keys` method:

```
input_names = target_node.inputs.keys()
```

Now, it's time to look for textures to link. We can combine two for loops and scroll all the inputs for each entry in `self.files`. If a match is found, the input/filename pair will be added to the `matching_names` dictionary:

```
matching_names = {}
for f in self.files:
    for inp in input_names:
        if match_rule(inp) in match_rule(f.name):
            matching_names[inp] = f.name
            break
```

The `break` statement aborts the `input_names` loop when a match is found so that we can proceed to the next file.

Once the `matching_names` dictionary contains the input for which textures were found and the relative filenames, we can load the images from disk and add them to the graph.

Loading image files

The elements of `self.file` are not full disk paths. We can build this from `directory` and `os.path.join` so that we can use `bpy.data.images.load`:

```
for inp, fname in matching_names.items():
    img_path = os.path.join(self.directory, fname)
    img = bpy.data.images.load(img_path,
                               check_existing=True)
```

The `check_existing` parameter avoids loading the same image more than once: if it is already present in `bpy.data.images`, the `load` method returns the existing entry.

We have mentioned that not all sockets are colors, but also that vectors, colors, and float sockets are converted automatically when they are connected. Therefore, non-color data such as metallic (a float number) or normal (a vector) can be stored in images.

One of the main points of a node graph is that we should be able to connect sockets of different, but broadly similar, types.

Getting non-color attributes from images

The colors of an image are not different from vectors in terms of their information, which consists of three channels or components: **red**, **green**, and **blue**.

Connecting a **Color** socket to a **Vector** socket will use the red, green, and blue channels as the *X*, *Y*, and *Z* coordinates of a three-dimensional vector, respectively.

If a color output is connected to a float socket, the brightness, also called its **luminance** or **value**, will be used as float input.

Whenever an image is used for storing values rather than colors, it's important to inform Blender about that; otherwise, color adjustments from the renderer would alter the image information.

We can do that by setting the image color space to `NonColor` if a socket is not of the `"RGBA"` type:

```
if target_node.inputs[inp].type != "RGBA":
    img.colorspace_settings.name = "Non-Color"
```

If we don't do that, even correct textures will produce render artifacts.

At this stage, the images have been loaded into Blender but they are not present in the node tree yet: we need to create an **Image Texture** for that.

Creating image texture nodes

New material nodes can be added to a material shading graph by accessing the `nodes` collection of its `node_tree`. The `new` collection method requires the node to be of the `argument` type. In this case, `ShaderNodeTexImage` is the type that we use for creating image textures, but we can find the Python type of every shading node by looking at the menu tooltips.

If **Python Tooltips** is enabled in **Edit | Preferences**, like we learned to do in *Chapter 2*, we can view the node type by hovering over the menu entry:

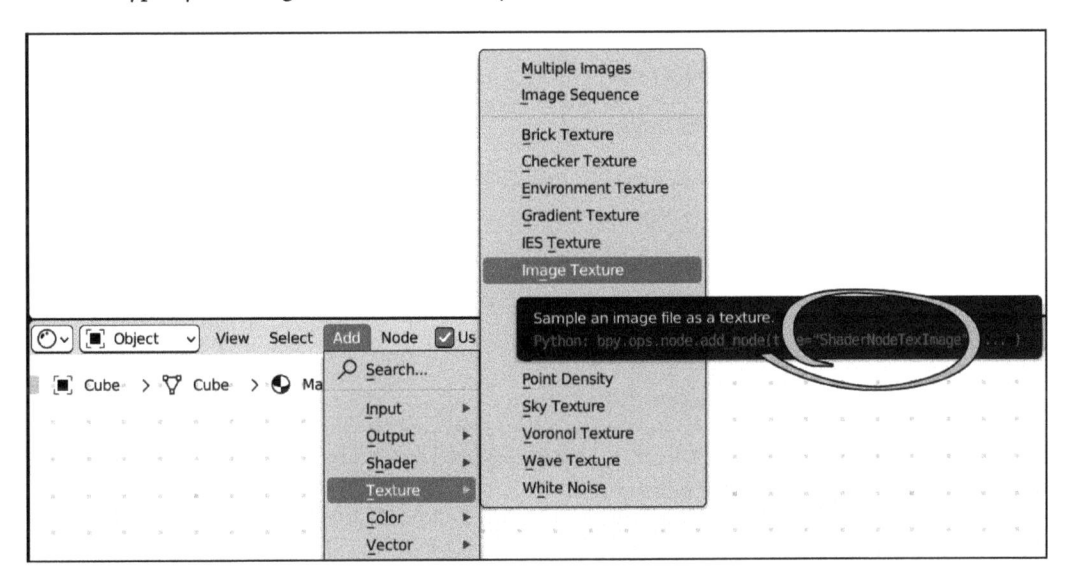

Figure 12.7: Hovering over the Add menu entries displays the node type in the tooltip

This way, we can create a new texture node and set its `image` attribute to the image that we have loaded from disk:

```
tree = mat.node_tree
tex_img = tree.nodes.new("ShaderNodeTexImage")
tex_img.image = img
```

The texture nodes added to the graph are now ready for connection links.

Connecting nodes

While most texture output can be connected directly to a shading node, some input types might require helper nodes in between. The most prominent case is that of detail, or **normal maps**. Before creating new connections, our code should check that no additional nodes are required.

Connecting image colors

Connection links can be created using the `node_tree.links.new` method. Its arguments are as follows:

- The output socket of the outgoing node
- The input socket of the receiving node

If we are not dealing with a normal map, we can connect the `"Color"` output of the texture to the input of the active node. No other action is required, so we can use `continue` to pass to the next input:

```
if inp != "Normal":
    tree.links.new(tex_img.outputs["Color"],
                   target_node.inputs[inp])
    continue
# normal map code follows
```

A `normal` input would not trigger `continue`, so we don't need an `else` statement for it: the normal map code follows, without additional indentation.

Connecting normal maps

Rendering a detailed surface using geometry alone would require so many polygons that the resulting model would be too heavy to store or display.

Normal mapping stores geometric details in the pixels of an image using the RGB-to-XYZ conversion.

Since the normals stored in this way must be merged with the original ones, a **Normal** texture should not connect directly to a shader node; instead, it should pass through a **NormalMap** node.

We can add a `"ShaderNodeNormalMap"` to the tree using new:

```
normal_map = tree.nodes.new(
                    "ShaderNodeNormalMap"
                    )
```

The `"Normal"` output of normal_map can be connected to the node input using the following code:

```
tree.links.new(normal_map.outputs["Normal"],
               target_node.inputs[inp])
```

Then, we must connect `tex_img` to the `normal_map` node:

```
tree.links.new(tex_img.outputs["Color"],
               normal_map.inputs["Color"])
```

Once the `inp, fname` loop is over, we can return the `'FINISHED'` status and exit:

```
return {'FINISHED'}
```

Since this script aims to make setting up the texture faster, we can add an operator button for quick execution.

Adding a header button

We have used menus for most of the operators in this book, but this time, we will add a button in the **Shader Editor** area's top bar – that is, its header. The steps are the same as those we used to add menu entries:

1. Create a function that accepts two arguments, `self` and `context`.
2. Append that function to the header type when the add-on registers.

Using **Icon Viewer**, which we introduced in *Chapter 5*, we can find an icon that suits our tool, such as NODE_TEXTURE. The `layout.operator` method will display `AddTextures` as a header button:

```
def shader_header_button(self, context):
    self.layout.operator(AddTextures.bl_idname,
                         icon="NODE_TEXTURE",
                         text="Load Textures")
```

Now, it's time to register the operator and the header function. We can find the header class we are looking for, `NODE_HT_header`, by looking in Blender's source file, `space_node.py`. This file can be loaded into Blender's text editor by right-clicking and choosing **Edit Source**. We can do this on any element of the **Shader Editor** area's header:

Figure 12.8: NODE_HT_header is the first class in space_node.py

Rendering and Shaders

As an alternative, we can print a list of all the header types using a `comprehension` in Blender's Python console. We learned how to do this in *Chapter 8*:

```
>>> [c for c in dir(bpy.types) if
    "header" in c]
['CLIP_HT_header', 'CONSOLE_HT_header', 'DOPESHEET_HT_header',
'FILEBROWSER_HT_header', 'GRAPH_HT_header', 'IMAGE_HT_header', 'IMAGE_
HT_tool_header', 'INFO_HT_header', 'NLA_HT_header', 'NODE_HT_header',
'OUTLINER_HT_header', 'PROPERTIES_HT_header', 'SEQUENCER_HT_header',
'SEQUENCER_HT_tool_header', 'SPREADSHEET_HT_header', 'STATUSBAR_HT_
header', 'TEXT_HT_header', 'USERPREF_HT_header', 'VIEW3D_HT_header',
'VIEW3D_HT_tool_header']
```

`NODE_HT_header` is in the middle of the list. We must append our entry to it inside the `register` function:

```
def register():
    bpy.utils.register_class(AddTextures)
    bpy.types.NODE_HT_header.append(shader_header_button)
```

In `unregister`, we must remove our interface and class when the add-on is disabled:

```
def unregister():
    bpy.types.NODE_HT_header.remove(shader_header_button)
    bpy.utils.unregiser_class(AddTextures)
```

Now that the add-on is ready, we can use it for loading textures instantly.

Using Load Textures

If the `ch12` folder was added to the **Scripts** path, we can enable **Textament** in the **Learning** category of the **Add-ons** preferences:

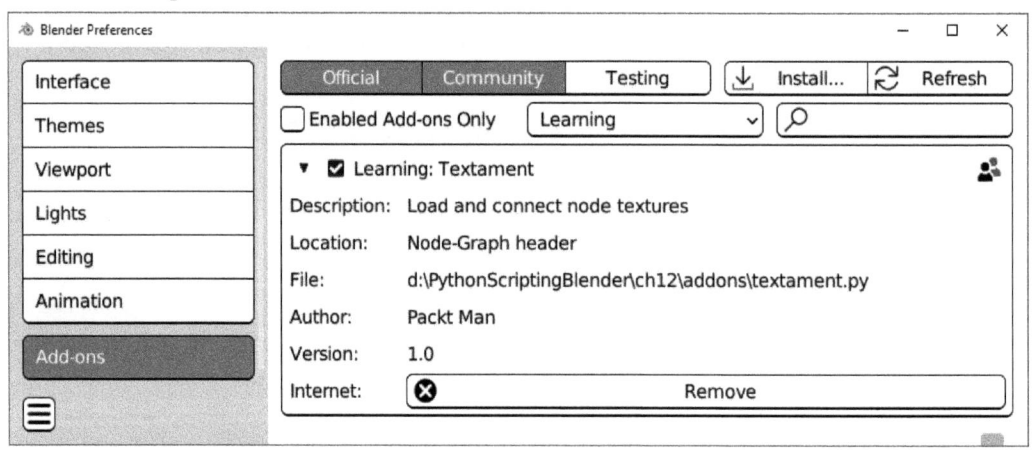

Figure 12.9: Enabling the "Textament" add-on

Once it's enabled, a button called **Load Textures** will be added to the **Shader Editor** header:

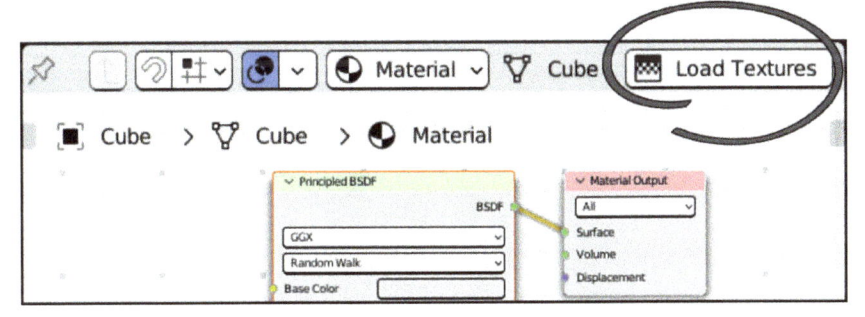

Figure 12.10: The Load Textures button in the Shader Editor header

Selecting a node allows you to click the **Load Textures** button, which opens the **File Browser** area.

To test this add-on on a simple model, we can apply a brick wall material to the default cube by following these steps:

1. Open Blender or go back to the default scene via **File** | **New** | **General**.
2. Switch to the **Shading** workspace using the tabs at the top of the window.
3. Click **Load Textures** in the **Shader Editor** area's header.
4. In the **File Browser** area, navigate to a folder containing images. The textures accompanying this chapter can be found at `https://github.com/PacktPublishing/Python-Scripting-in-Blender/tree/main/ch12/_media_/textures`.
5. Optionally, we can switch the **File Browser** area to **thumbnails** mode by clicking the thumbnails button on the top right. This is useful for looking for textures:

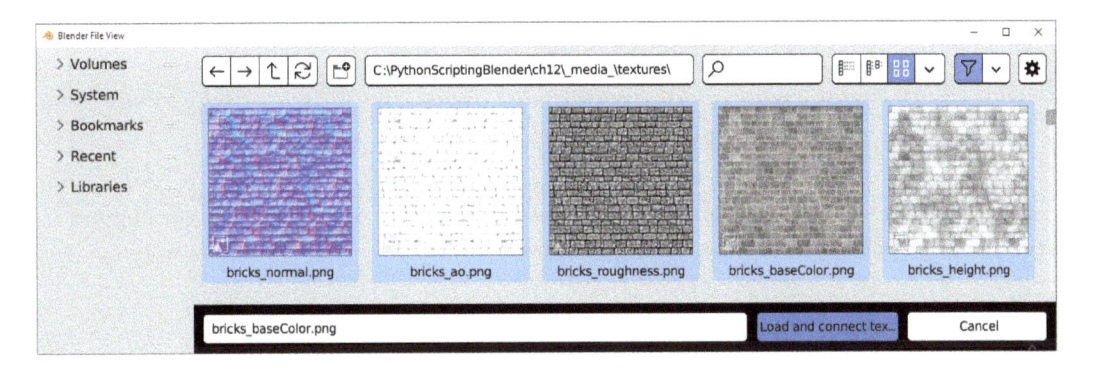

Figure 12.11: "Load and connect" thumbnails in the File Browser area

6. We can select multiple files by using the lasso, *Ctrl* + clicking, or pressing *A* to select all.
7. Press **Load and connect** to add the textures to the graph.

The `bricks_baseColor`, `bricks_normal`, and `bricks_roughness` textures are now the inputs of the material and make the cube look like a brick wall:

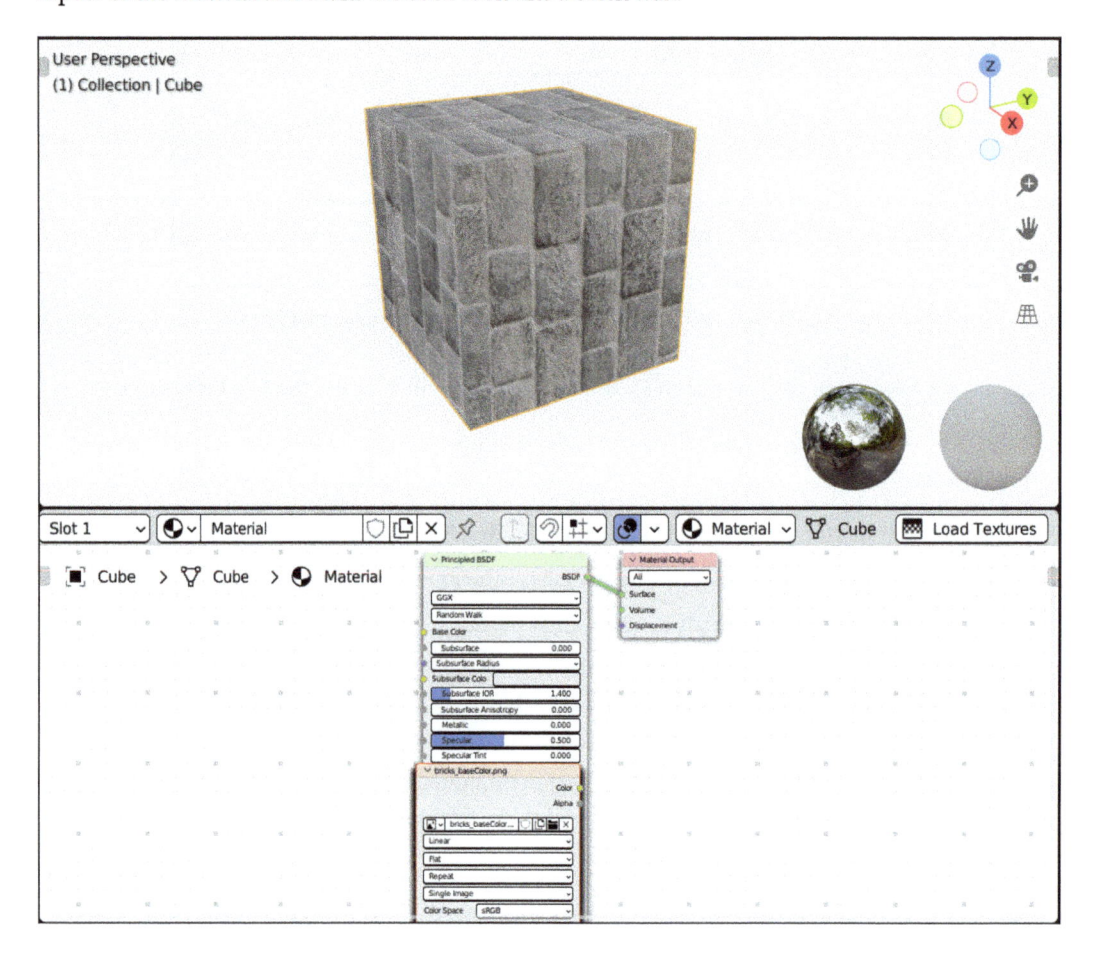

Figure 12.12: Brick textures loaded into the Shader Editor area

The operator was successful but all the nodes were created at the center of the graph. We can improve this considerably by adding code that rearranges the nodes.

Improving Load Textures

Nodes can be moved to a different position by setting the x and y attributes of their `location` property. This allows us to arrange them in our scripts.

Arranging shader nodes

Even if we can move our nodes freely, the API poses a few limitations:

- We can't access the exact location of the sockets
- The width and height of new nodes are not available in the scripts

One of those two issues at a time would be tolerable, as we could either move our nodes at the height of their inputs or get the space required by a new node on the fly. Since they occur together, we will resort to a workaround.

Assuming node spacing

We cannot get the size of new nodes in a script, but we can learn the default size of a texture node beforehand by looking at an existing shader tree. For instance, after we use **Load Texture**, we can switch to the **Scripting** workspace and get the `dimensions` property of an `'Image Texture'` node:

```
>>> node_tree = C.object.active_material.node_tree
>>> node_tree.nodes['Image Texture'].dimensions
Vector((360.0, 410.0))
```

The `Vector` property returned by `dimensions` contains the bounding box of the node, not the node's exact measures. We can verify that by querying the node's `width` instead:

```
>>> node_tree = C.object.active_material.node_tree
>>> node_tree.nodes['Image Texture'].width
240.0
```

Even if it is present, the `height` attribute does not help because it hasn't been updated and its value stays fixed at `100.0`.

Despite that weakness in the API, we have enough information to rearrange our tree: leaving `100.0` units between two nodes leaves enough room for connections, so we can use a spacing of `340.0` units between our textures and the initial node.

We must store that value in the declaration of our operator:

```
class AddTextures(bpy.types.Operator, ImportHelper):
    """Load and connect material textures"""
    bl_idname = "texture.textament_load"
    bl_label = "Load and connect textures"
    bl_description = "Load and connect material textures"
    _spacing = 340.0
```

To arrange our nodes vertically, we need to process them in the correct order.

Sorting the node creation

To space the nodes vertically in the correct way, we need to process them while following the sockets order in the target node layout; otherwise, the connection links will cross each other:

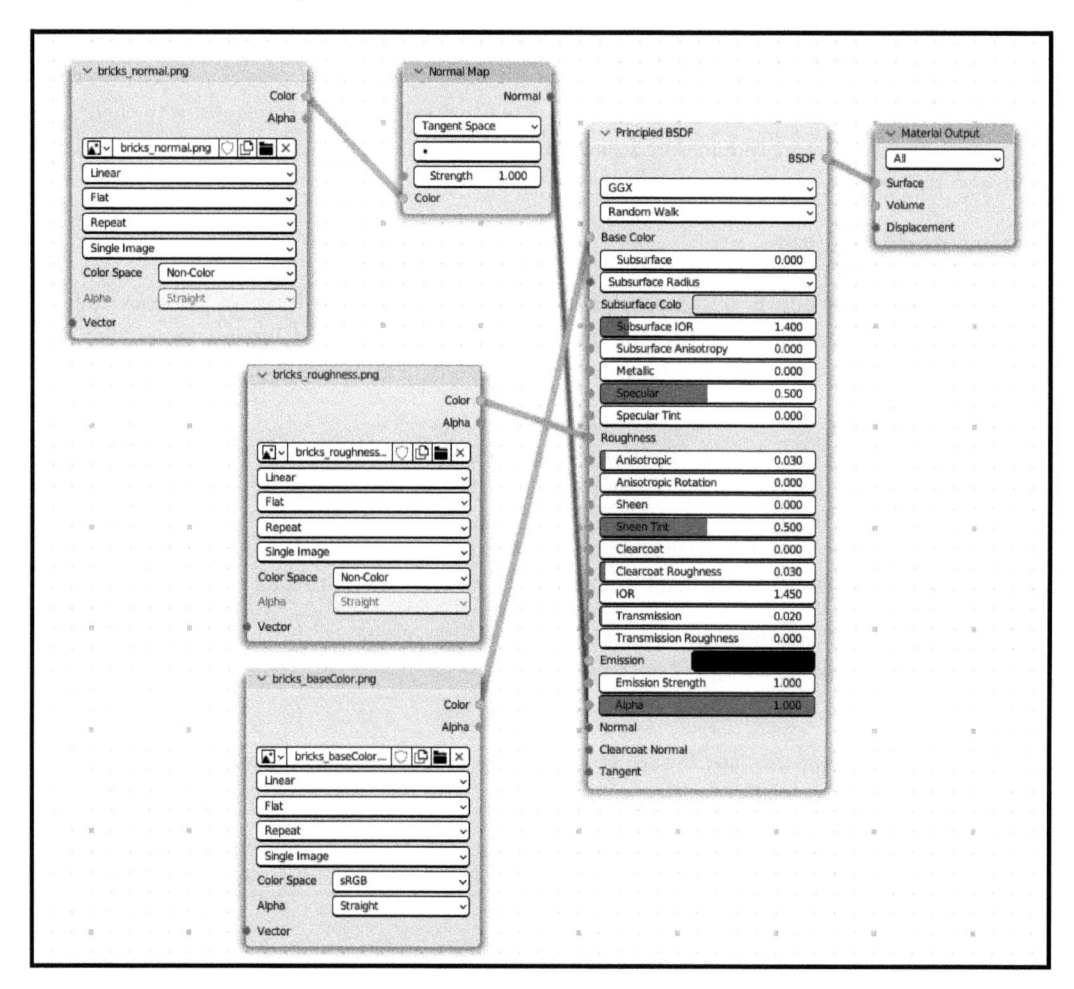

Figure 12.13: An unordered vertical arrangement leads to tangled, confusing links

Python dictionaries are unordered by design, so `matching_names` doesn't follow any order, but the `input_names` list does. This list contains the ordered names of all sockets. By filtering it with `matching_names`, we can obtain an ordered list of the matching inputs:

```
sorted_inputs = [
    i for i in input_names if i in matching_names
]
```

We must replace the `for inp, fname in matching_names.items()` loop with an iteration of `sorted_inputs`. Since we need an ordinal for vertical spacing, we must use `enumerate` to get the index of the current input. Here is the new image loop:

```
for i, inp in enumerate(sorted_inputs):
    img_path = os.path.join(self.directory,
                            matching_names[inp])
    img = bpy.data.images.load(img_path,
                               check_existing=True)
    if target_node.inputs[inp].type != 'RGBA':
        img.colorspace_settings.name = 'Non-Color'
    img_node = mat.node_tree.nodes.new(
                            "ShaderNodeTexImage")
    img_node.image = img
```

After a texture nodes is connected, we can change its location. We start with the same coordinates as `target_node`, then move the texture to the left by subtracting `_spacing` from `location.x`:

```
img_node.location = target_node.location
img_node.location.x -= self._spacing
```

We can move the texture nodes downwards by subtracting `self._spacing` from `location.y`. We are stacking the nodes vertically, so their y coordinates depend on their ordinal indexes. The first node, which has an index of 0, will not move at all from the initial position, the second node moves down by `self._spacing` times 1, the third by `self._spacing` times 2, and so on:

```
img_node.location.y -= i * self._spacing
```

Connecting `ShaderNodeNormalMap` requires horizontal space, so, after we align `normal_map` with its `img_node`, we must make some room by moving the texture to the left and `normal_map` to the right, by an amount of half `_spacing`:

```
normal_map = mat.node_tree.nodes.new(
                        "ShaderNodeNormalMap"
                        )
normal_map.location = img_node.location

img_node.location.x -= self._spacing / 2
normal_map.location.x += self._spacing / 2
```

Now, we must save the add-on and update it by clicking *F3* and choosing **Reload Scripts**. Launching **Load Textures** sets up a properly arranged node tree:

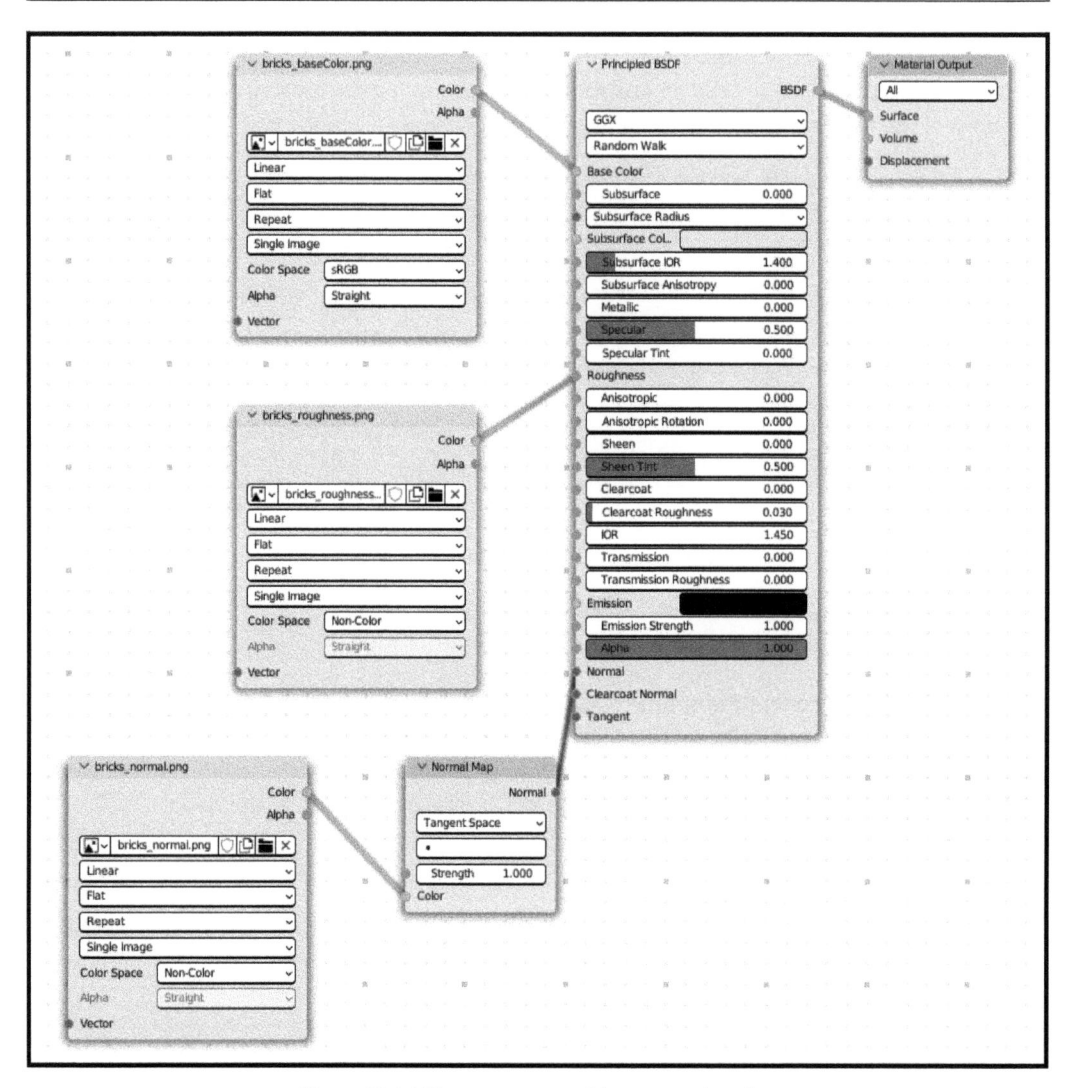

Figure 12.14: Texture set up, with arranged nodes

Now that the basic functionality is complete, we can implement an option for customizing the color of the material.

Mixing the Base Color

Sometimes, even if we are happy with our texture setup, we want to change the color while retaining the texture pattern. We can do that by adding a **MixRGB** node before the **Base Color** property of a principled node:

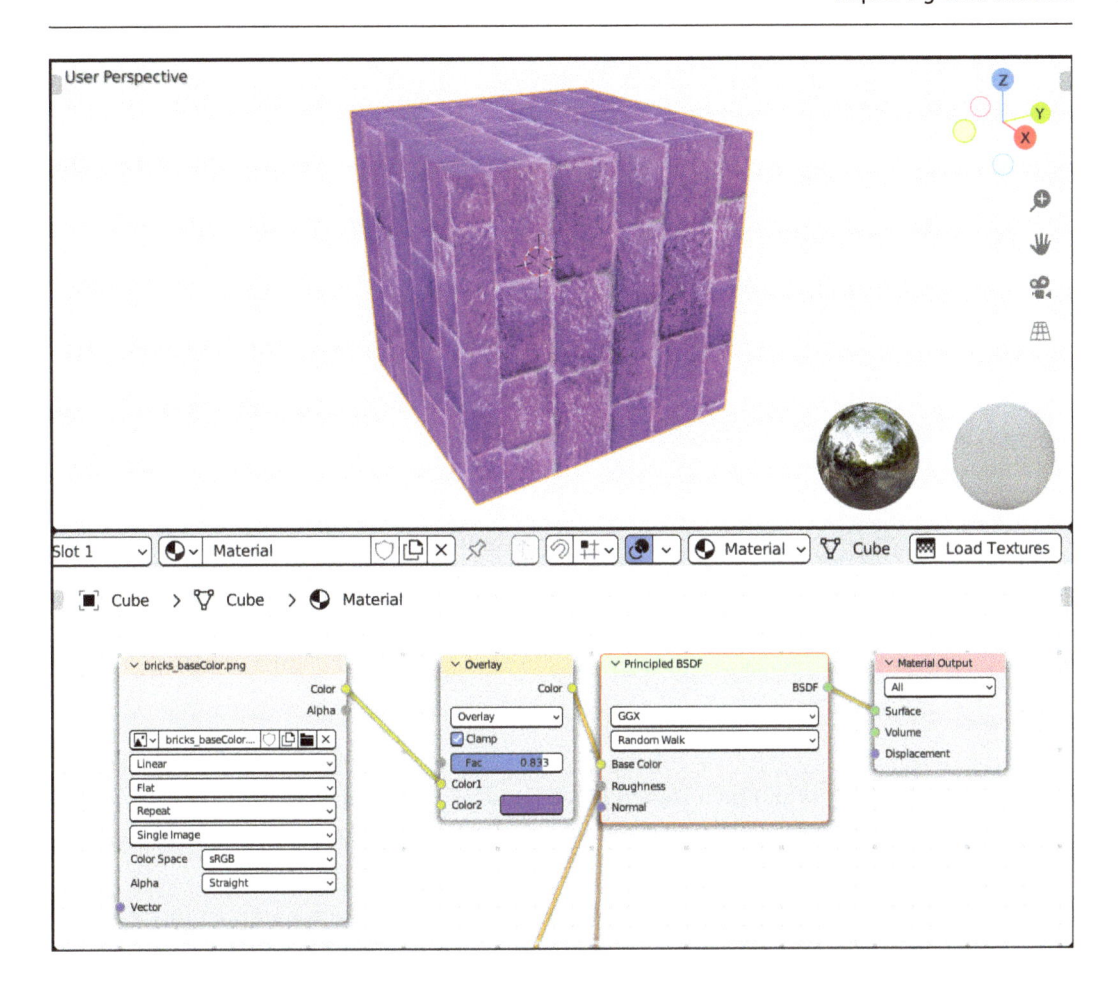

Figure 12.15: Affecting the material color with a MixRGB node

The **MixRGB** node features a factor slider (**Fac**) for blending two colors. The default blending type, **Mix**, replaces **Color1** with **Color2**, but other blending modes known in computer graphics, such as **Multiply**, **Overlay**, and **Color Dodge**, are also available.

The Python setup for a `ShaderNodeMixRGB` node is similar to that of a **Normal Map** node – when the input is `"Base Color"`, we create an intermediate node:

```
if inp == "Base Color":
    mix = mat.node_tree.nodes.new(
                            "ShaderNodeMixRGB")
```

Then, we align the image texture and the **Mix** node, and make room for additional connection links:

```
mix.location = img_node.location
img_node.location.x -= self._spacing / 2
mix.location.x += self._spacing / 2
```

We connect the image color to the `"Color1"` input of the **Mix** node:

```
mat.node_tree.links.new(
                 img_node.outputs["Color"],
                 mix.inputs["Color1"])
```

At this point, we would connect the **Mix** node to the color input, but we can store it in the `img_node` variable instead.

This way, the connection to `target_node` is made by the same line of code that connects all the other inputs except `"Normal"`:

```
    img_node = mix
if inp != "Normal":
    tree.links.new(tex_img.outputs["Color"],
                   target_node.inputs[inp])
    continue
```

If we execute **Reload Scripts** and then launch **Load Textures** again, a mixed layout like the one displayed in *Figure 12.15* is created. We can click on the **Color2** attribute and select a color from the picker or change the **Mix** node's **Blending Mode** from its drop-down menu.

We can also experiment with different solutions. For instance, we can use **Hue Saturation Value** rather than **MixRGB** by replacing `"ShaderNodeMixRGB"` with `"ShaderNodeHueSaturation"` and `"Color1"` with `"Color"`.

Node trees are interesting as they can be considered visual programming, but even the trivial operation of loading a few textures, if done manually, can take time.

This time, we didn't have to create an interface for manipulating the blended color as the mix node already provides it, so we could combine the best of two procedural approaches.

Summary

In this chapter, we learned how materials work and how nodes are created and connected in the **Shader Editor** area. We also learned how image textures can change the appearance of shaded objects and how they can store non-color data.

This was our first encounter with node trees, a generic visual programming approach that is not limited to shaders and is planned to expand to deformation and rigging in the future.

Node-based systems are flexible and powerful, but they benefit from scripted tools, like all other aspects of Blender.

Rendering is not the final step of production as compositing and editing follow in the computer graphics pipeline. But since this stage converts three-dimensional data into images, it's usually considered the last step of the 3D workflow.

That ends our journey into how Blender scripting works. We have covered object creation, deformation, animation, and rendering, but most importantly, how tools are designed and implemented, and how the software limitations can be overcome.

Those skills, combined with individual talent and experience, allow technical directors to bridge between artistic needs and software capabilities, empower their teams, and improve their abilities and understanding in the process.

Questions

1. How many render engines are present in Blender?
2. Do the words *material* and *shader* have the same meaning?
3. Are the shader nodes predefined values that determine how objects look or separate units performing independent operations?
4. Can we use images for coloring objects?
5. Can we make connections between different data types?
6. How do we arrange nodes in a graph?
7. In our shaders, can we alter the colors coming from an image?

Appendix

Blender and Python are so vast that even writing scripts for a shortlist of use cases encompasses a wide range of skills and disciplines. This book contains elements of animation, rigging, and shading and introduces programming techniques while exploring those processes.

This appendix contains a comprehensive summary that can be useful as a recap to help with the retention of the concepts explored in this book and help the reader navigate through the chapters.

Part 1: An Introduction to Python

This section covers the fundamentals of scripting and helps you become familiar with Blender's Python utilities. Besides providing a solid base for the chapters ahead, it contains all the information required for writing fully working tools.

Chapter 1, Python's Integration with Blender

This chapter introduces the tools used for scripting, internal and external text editors, and version control.

Here's a summary of the topics discussed in the chapter.

Installing multiple versions of Blender on the main operating systems

Blender 3.3 is the *long-term support* release used in the writing process. Although the content of this book is valid for all the 3. x series of blender, if you want to install version 3.3 alongside other versions, the following instructions are provided:

- Using Windows Installer
- Using the Microsoft Store
- Downloading a portable archive
- Installing on macOS

Using Python in Blender

The **Scripting** workspace is a Blender layout optimized for running Python quickly. It consists of an interactive console, a logger listing the commands of past actions, and a Text Editor that can run scripts. We will become familiar with it through these topics:

- Producing console output with the *"Hello World!"* example
- How to copy and paste Python instructions from the **Info Log**
- Checking the current version of Blender and Python using scripts
- An explanation of functions and arguments

Using external editors and version control tools

Even though the Text Editor is quick and useful, programmers usually take advantage of external code editors as well. **Visual Studio Code**, a multiplatform editor from **Microsoft**, is used in this book, but there are plenty of alternatives. **Version control** tools are useful tools that for storing the history of code changes. We learn how to use these tools by going through the following topics:

- Loading folders in Visual Studio Code
- Refreshing text files in the Blender Text Editor
- Initializing and using a **Git** repository

Chapter 2, Python Entities and API

This chapter explains how to interact with Blender using scripts, how to take advantage of features for developers, and how the **Application Programming Interface** (**API**) works.

The following sections are a summary of the topics discussed in the chapter.

User interface features for developers

There are two useful options in the **Interface** section of Blender's preferences:

- **Developer Extras:** This displays the **Edit Source** option when we right-click on an element of the interface so that we can easily access the Python source code of the **user interface** (**UI**). It also makes non-UI operators available in the search bar.
- **Python Tooltips:** This displays the Python property relative to the UI element under the mouse cursor.

Console features for developers

The interactive console provides two handy features for quick scripting:

- Code auto-completion by pressing the *Tab* key
- Commands history by pressing the Up-arrow key

Viewport features for developers

The **Math Vis (Console)** add-on included with Blender and available in the **3D View** section of the **Preferences** > **Add-ons** dialog displays three-dimensional mathematical entities such as *vectors* and *matrices* in the 3D Viewport. It can be useful when working with object location and rotation values.

Using Blender modules

Blender's Python module, `bpy`, is accessed in scripts using the `import` statement. Each of its components covers a specific aspect of the 3D app. Most notably, `data` contains all the objects available in the current session, while `context` contains the current state of the user interaction, such as the current selection. The API documentation is available online but can also be viewed using the `help()` function.

Using object collections

Lists of objects are accessed through `bpy_collection`, an aggregate type similar to a Python `dictionary`. Elements of a collection can be accessed with numeral indices or keywords and can be iterated in Python loops.

Operations such as renaming can reorder the elements of a collection, so a conversion to `list` is advised when the order is critical.

Blender collections don't have an `append()` method: the `new()` method is used for creating a new object, which is automatically appended. The `remove()` method removes an element from a collection and deletes it from Blender.

Context and user activity

Users can change the current state or context of Blender by adding or selecting objects. The last selected object is considered *active* and is the main target of object-related actions.

Context information is available as properties of `bpy.context`, is read-only, and can only be changed indirectly. For instance, `ob.select_set(True)` is used to select an object, as it's impossible to append to the `bpy.context.selected_objects` list.

Chapter 3, Creating Your Add-Ons

This chapter illustrates the process of creating Blender add-ons: Python scripts that can be installed as Blender plugins to add custom functions.

Here's a summary of the topics discussed in the chapter.

Writing scripts that are add-ons

Add-ons are Python modules or packages containing a dictionary named `bl_info`. This dictionary contains information such as the author and name of the add-on. Add-ons must provide two functions, `register()` and `unregister()`, used when an add-on is enabled or disabled.

Add-ons can be installed in Blender preferences, but setting the folder where they are developed as **Scripts** in **Preferences** > **File Paths** is more convenient for developers. Changes in our scripts are loaded by looking up `Reload Scripts` in the *F3* key search bar.

Writing Object Collector, an add-on that groups objects in the Outliner

Adding features to Blender involves the creation of an operator, that is, an instruction that can be launched from the user interface. The `bl_idname` and `bl_label` attributes determine how an operator is found and displayed in Blender, while the `poll()` and `execute()` functions regulate when it can be launched and what happens when it runs.

Add-ons add operators to Blender in their `register()` and `unregister()` functions.

Tips for working on add-ons

When using an external editor, enabling auto-save might help ensure that the Python script always includes the latest changes.

Enabling add-ons from the development folder might leave *bytecode*, that is, Python-compiled files in a folder named __pycache__. If we use Git version control, we can create a text file named `.gitignore` that contains __pycache__ to avoid bytecode files ever being versioned.

Avoiding duplicates using try and except

To prevent our script from creating the same collection twice, resulting in duplicates, we look for a collection inside a `try` statement and add an `except KeyError` block that is triggered when no collection is found. By creating new collections under the `except` statement, we ensure that collections with a given name are only created once. The try/except pattern is called *forgiveness rather than permission*, as it focuses on pulling back from non-allowed actions rather than checking whether an action is possible in the first place.

We use the `title()` string method for nicely formatted names with a capital first letter. We can create functions for adding our operator to Blender menus. They accept the `self` and `context` arguments and add operators to `self.layout`. Menu functions are added to Blender in the `register()` and `unregister()` functions of the add-on.

Chapter 4, Exploring Object Transformations

This chapter shows how to affect `location`, `rotation`, and `scale` of an object using Python and how the transform information is stored in Blender.

Here's a summary of the topics discussed in the chapter.

Moving and scaling objects with Python

`location` is stored as the x, y, and z coordinates of a three-dimensional vector. The coordinates of a vector can be changed individually or together, using tuple assignment.

`scale` is stored as an x, y, z vector too. While the rest value of `location` has the (0.0, 0.0, 0.0) coordinates, a non-scaled object's `scale` attribute is (1.0, 1.0, 1.0).

Peculiarities of rotations

Rotations are less straightforward than `location` and `scale`, as the `rotation` values over the three axes can affect each other, causing an issue known as *gimbal lock*.

There is more than one way to represent rotations; some involve multidimensional entities such as quaternions or rotation matrices, and two measure units for angles: *degrees* and *radians*. Blender objects have attributes for each notation system, which can be set via Python. Conversion utilities are provided for switching from one notation system to another.

Indirect transformations with parents and constraints

Objects can be arranged in hierarchies. Transformations of an object higher in the hierarchy (*parent*) affect all the objects under them (*children*).

Constraints are another way to transform an object without affecting its channels. They can be added using the `new()` method of the `constraints` collection.

Transforming objects with matrices

Setting values for the `location`, `rotation`, and `scale` channels affects the relative coordinates of an object. Assigning a transformation matrix allows us to use world-space coordinates instead. Matrix values are lazy-copied unless stated otherwise; if we store a matrix as a variable and don't want its values to change we need to use its `copy()` method.

Parenting to a transformed object in Python changes the object location unless a reverse transformation is set in the `matrix_parent_inverse` attribute.

Writing Elevator, an add-on that sets a floor for the selected objects

The operator from the **Elevator** add-on brings all the selected objects above a certain height. To do so, it implements `FloatProperty` that can be set when it's launched. Optional behaviors can be enabled by switching its `BoolProperty` members.

Editable properties must be added as *annotations*, Python arbitrary attributes.

Parent objects at the top of the hierarchy are moved first to avoid duplicate transformations. Constraints can be used optionally.

Chapter 5, Designing Graphical Interfaces

This chapter explains how to add custom panels and add them to the Blender interface.

Here's a summary of the topics discussed in the chapter.

Components of the UI

The Blender window is structured into areas, regions, and panels. Panels have a layout that is populated with text, icons, and buttons using Python.

Writing the Simple Panel add-on

This add-on registers a simple `Panel` class that displays text and icons in the **Object** properties. Arrangements can be created using the `row()` or `column()` methods, non-uniform columns using `split()`, and uniform tables using `grid_flow()`.

Blender icon names can be looked up using the **Icon Viewer** add-on or, in some cases, built using Python's string formatting.

Red and gray colors can be used to give visual feedback using the `alert` or `enabled` flags of a widget.

Operators added to a layout using the `operator()` method are displayed as buttons.

Part 2: Interactive Tools and Animation

This section explains how to write add-ons as folders rather than single files, interact with the animation system, and write modal operators that wait for user input. By the end of this section, you will be able to write advanced, interactive tools.

Chapter 6, Structuring Our Code and Add-Ons

This chapter explains how to write and distribute addons containing multiple files in a folder.

Here's a summary of the topics discussed in the chapter.

The relationship between modules, packages, and add-ons

While a single `.py` file is a Python module, a folder containing `.py` files is a Python package. Packages contain a file named `__init__.py`. If our package is an add-on, this file must contain the `bl_info` dictionary.

Guidelines for partitioning code

Some criteria for separating the code through different `.py` files are as follows:

- Media loaders
- Generic code versus specific code
- Interface code
- Operator modules
- Use of imported modules

For example, all the code used for loading custom icons, as explained in *Chapter 5*, can be moved to a module named `img_loader.py`.

Only `__init__.py` is reloaded by the **Reload Scripts** operator introduced in *Chapter 3*; the other files must be reloaded explicitly using Python's `importlib.reload()` function.

A panel to display the add-on preferences can be written in a `preferences.py` file, while `panel.py` and `operators.py` contain, respectively, the UI and the add-on operators.

Add-on folders compressed as `.zip` archives can be installed using the **Preferences | Addons | Install** button.

Chapter 7, The Animation System

This chapter explains how to animate objects in Blender and how to create and edit animations with Python.

Here's a summary of the topics discussed in the chapter.

The Animation system

The **Layout** and **Animation** Workspaces display animation keyframes on a **Timeline** including the scene actions, keyframes, and range. Keyframes establish the value of a property at a certain time.

Writing the Action to Range add-on

This add-on sets the start and end of the playback to the first and last frame of the current action of the active object. If a timeline is displayed onscreen, it is recentered to the new range. To do that, `context.temp_override()` is used to pass a timeline region to the `bpy.ops.action.view_all()` factory operator.

Writing the Vert Runner add-on

This add-on animates the selected objects along the vertices of the active object. The vertex coordinates stored in `context.object.data.vertices` are read, while trigonometric functions are used for computing the shortest rotation arc that orients an object toward its next position.

Chapter 8, Animation Modifiers

This chapter covers non-destructive modifiers for animation f-curves and their use in animating procedural effects.

Here's a summary of the topics discussed in the chapter.

Adding f-curve modifiers

F-curve modifiers can be added by selecting a curve in the graph editor and clicking **Add Modifier** in its properties or using the `new()` method from the `modifiers` collection of f-curves.

Writing the Shaker add-on

This add-on uses a **Noise** f-modifier to add a trembling effect on the active object and allows to set the duration and amount of the trembling. *Soft limits* set an initial limitation on the noise strength parameter while still allowing you to type out-of-range values using the keyboard. We add a menu entry for invoking this operator using the right-click menu in the Viewport.

Chapter 9, Animation Drivers

This chapter introduces animation drivers, which are the connections between different properties used to control complex actions. Drivers can incorporate short Python expressions in their logic.

Here's a summary of the topics discussed in the chapter.

Creating and setting drivers

Drivers can be created quickly by selecting **Copy As New Driver** and **Paste Driver** from the right-click menu of Blender properties. Using an object's location as input for its rotation creates a wheel setup since the object rotates when it's moved.

Using Python drivers

Python expression-based drivers can be created quickly by pressing the # key, followed by Python code while editing a Blender property. Oscillatory motions can be created using trigonometric cyclic functions such as `sin`, and the pendulum equation from the physics classroom can be implemented as a driver expression. Object custom properties can be used as parameters in driver expressions.

Writing the Pendulum add-on

This add-on instantly sets up the pendulum expression and parameters. Drivers are added using the `object.driver_add()` method.

Chapter 10, Advanced and Modal Operators

This chapter explains how to write advanced operators by enriching their execution flow and implementing optional methods.

Here's a summary of the topics discussed in the chapter.

Operator execution details

The `invoke()` method of `Operator`, if defined, runs when the operator is launched. Inside `invoke()`, we can switch either to the `execute()` method or to the `modal()` method. The latter listens to user inputs such as key presses or mouse movements.

Writing the PunchClock add-on

This add-on creates time-formatted text in the scene. Its operator sets the initial values of its hour and minute parameters in `invoke()` using Python `datetime` utilities. When adding the operator to a menu, `operator_context` of the layout is set to `"INVOKE_DEFAULT"` so that the execution of `invoke()` is never skipped.

Modal behavior

The operator is added to the modal handlers so that its `modal()` method is run at every update of the UI. Inside the modal, the `"MOUSEMOVE"` events change the displayed hour and minute.

Customizing the undo panel

The undo panel displays the operator properties after the execution is customized by implementing the `draw()` method. With this method, we can design a graphic interface using the same techniques learned in *Chapter 5*.

Part 3: Delivering Output

This section covers the final stages of the 3D pipeline: deformation and rendering.

Chapter 11, Object Modifiers

This chapter covers object modifiers and their use in animation.

Here's a summary of the topics discussed in the chapter.

Adding object modifiers

Modifiers are grouped into four categories: **Modify**, **Generate**, **Deform**, and **Physics**. They are created by clicking the **Add Modifier** button in the **Modifiers** property.

Adding modifiers in Python

The new() method of the object.modifiers collection requires the type modifier as an argument. A list of the possible type keywords can be found by accessing the bpy.types.ObjectModifiers.bl_rna.functions["new"] function and querying its parameters["type"].enum_items.

Writing the Latte Express add-on

This add-on sets up a **Lattice** modifier to deform an object using a three-dimensional grid cage. It finds the center of the model by querying its bounding box and has input parameters for changing the lattice and the object's resolutions.

Using armature deformers

Armatures affect characters using a deformation skeleton. Bones can be created in Python using object.data.edit_bones.new() after switching to **Edit Mode** using bpy.ops.object.mode_set().

Vertex groups are created on the lattice object to bind the lattice vertices to the armature bones. This way, a lattice deformed by an armature can be created via a script.

Creating control shapes

Replacing the default octahedral shape with custom wireframe shapes makes an armature more animator friendly. For that reason, a simple mesh can be created in Python using the mesh.from_pydata method, and assigned to the pose_bone.custom_shape attribute.

Part 3: Delivering Output 321

Chapter 12, Rendering and Shaders

This chapter introduces rendering and materials, the shader editor, and its node tree. Although some steps such as post-processing and video encoding may follow, rendering is commonly regarded as the last stage of a 3D process.

Here's a summary of the topics discussed in the chapter.

How rendering works

A render engine such as Blender's **Eevee** or **Cycles** converts the 3D geometry to finished images using *shaders* to determine how objects look. Blender shaders are networks of operations called nodes, that is, blocks that elaborate and exchange color and geometry information by connecting their input/output sockets.

Writing the Textament add-on

This add-on imports images from disk and creates the **Image Texture** nodes for the current shader. File-import operators derive from two classes, `ImportHelper` and `Operator`, and display the Blender file browser when invoked. The files the user selecteds are accessed as the `directory` and `files` member attributes.

Looking for case-insensitive matches in file names

Uppercase letters and spaces might cause unwanted mismatches, such as the `"base color"` strings not being associated with `"Base Color"`. A function for string manipulation can be written with the usual syntax or defined in one line using a `lambda` expression. Removing all spaces and converting all letters to lowercase becomes the following:

`lambda x : x.lower().replace(" ", "")`

Non-color data in images

Images can contain geometric or masking information. In that case, the `colorspace_setting.name` image attribute must be set to `"Non-Color"`, or Blender will apply color filters that pollute the information.

Connecting images in shaders

Creating a **Texture** node, with `"ShaderNodeTexImage"` as an argument of `node_tree.nodes.new("ShaderNodeTexImage")` allows you to use images in shaders. The connection between a texture node and a shader node input is created using `node_tree.links.new()`.

Normal map textures give the illusion of detail. They must connect to **Normal Map**, which is then connected to the **Normal** input of a shader.

Adding custom buttons to headers

Operators can be added to headers in the same way as they are added to menus: using a function that takes the `self` and `context` arguments, and adds elements to `self.layout`. This function is appended to a *Header Type* in the `register()` function of the add-on.

Arranging nodes in the node editor

Nodes created in Python are positioned at the center of the editor and overlap each other. They can be moved by setting their `location` x and y coordinates. They should be placed on the left-hand side of their output node and sorted vertically according to the order of their output node sockets.

Altering texture colors

The color of a texture can be manipulated by adding a **Mix** node between a texture and its output node. That allows you to change the overall color of an object while retaining the details coming from the image.

Index

Symbols

3D variables
  creating 29, 30
7-Zip 159
  used, for creating .zip file 159
.zip add-ons
  installing 161
.zip file
  creating, with 7-Zip 159
  creating, with Finder on Mac 161
  creating, with Gnome 161
  creating, with Windows File Manager 160

A

Action to Range add-on
  enabling 174, 175
  environment, setting 168
  menu function, writing 171, 172
  operator methods, writing 169
  operators context, fixing 177, 178
  parameters, modifying 175-177
  Python class, finding 173
  registering 172
  register/unregister functions, writing 174
  running 174, 175
  writing 168
Action to Range information
  writing 168, 169
Action to Range operator
  writing 169
active object 42
  modifying 43, 44
active scene 40, 41
add-on preferences
  creating 151, 152
  populating 153
  using 151
  using, in code 154, 155
add-ons 47
  installing 50, 159
  installing, in Blender 48
  object collector, creating 53, 54
  packaging 159
  scripts path 51, 52
  uninstalling 51
add-ons requirements 49
  register() function 49
  script meta info 49
  unregister() function 49

Index

amplitude control
    custom properties, using in drivers 227, 228
    custom property, adding 226
animation curves 179, 180
animation data
    accessing, in Python 181
animation system 163
    current frame and preview range 166, 167
    keyframes 167
    Timeline and Current Frame 164
API documentation 32
arcsine 190
areas 96
armature
    adding, to scene 275, 276
    edit bones, creating 276, 277
    objects, binding to 274, 275
armature bones
    adding 272, 273
armature condition
    adding 275
armature deformers
    using 271
Armature modifier 262
    creating 279
armature objects
    adding, to scene 271, 272
Axis Angle 74

B

Base Color
    mixing 306-308
Bezier curves 180
Bidirectional Scattering Distribution Function (BSFD) 289

Blender
    installing 4
    installing, from Microsoft Store 5, 6
    installing, on Windows 4
    multiple versions, installing on macOS 6, 7
    multiple versions, installing via Windows Installer 4, 5
    portable archive, downloading 6
Blender data
    accessing 33
    elements, removing 40
    iterating, through collections 34
    objects access 33, 34
    objects, creating 37
Blender data, iteration
    avoiding, to reorder via list conversion 36
    dict-like looping 37
    list-like looping 35, 36
Blender modules
    accessing 30
    API documentation 32
    bpy module 30, 31
Blender release
    checking, in interface 10, 11
    checking, in Python scripts 11
Blender Source Bar 57
bones 271
    lattice vertices, assigning to 278
Boolean switches 78
bounding box 265
bpy module 30, 31
button
    adding, for functions 125-127
    displaying 120
    displaying, with operator method 120, 121
    operator properties, displaying 127, 128
    operator properties, setting 124, 125
    operator settings, overriding 123, 124

operator text, setting 121, 122
operator visibility, setting 121, 122
bytecode
  cleaning up 159
bytecode files (.pyc) 59, 60
  .gitignore file, creating 60, 61

C

cached modules
  Developer Extras, using as condition 150
  package modules, reloading 149
  refresh module, implementing 148
  reloading 148
  reloading, via importlib 148
Cast
  used, for modifying object's shape 259
code, improving 59
  bytecode files (.pyc), ignoring 59, 60
  edits, saving automatically 59
  menus, extending 66
  objects collections 65
  operator logic, fixing 62
  re-assignment errors, avoiding 64
  scripts, reloading 64
collections 39
  linking, to scene 39
collection-type items
  finding 259, 260
color feedback
  active object, checking 118
  object selection, checking 118
  providing 117
  red or gray layouts, drawing 118, 119
composite layouts
  dictionaries, populating with 112
  grid_flow layout, using 113

icon keywords, building 113-117
split method, using 111, 112
using 111
context via bl_context
  tabs, grouping in bl_category 102
custom bone shapes
  adding 279
  mesh objects, creating in Python 279-281
  setup, finalizing 281, 282
cyclic motion, driving 216, 217
  amplitude, controlling 226
  pendulum equation, implementing 220, 221
  period, controlling of sin function 219, 220
  rotation point, modifying via
    constraints 217

D

data path 25
defensive programming 144
deformation objects 262
  Lattice modifier, using 262, 263
Developer Extras
  using, as condition 150
display attributes, panel
  context via bl_context, selecting 101, 102
  editor view via bl_space_type, selecting 100
  region via bl_region_type, selecting 101
docstring 27
draw method
  adding 250, 251
driver expressions
  creating, in properties 216
drivers 211
  creating 212-214
Drivers Editor
  wheel, setting up with 214, 215

duplicate transformations, avoiding
 ordering by hierarchy 90, 91
 selected_objects, copying to editable list 90

E

Elevator add-on
 constraints switch, adding 91, 92
 draft, writing 85-87
 duplicate constraints, avoiding 92, 93
 duplicate transformations, avoiding 90
 environment, setting 84
 height, setting in world matrix 89
 input properties, using 87-89
 writing 84
Euler Angles 73
event handlers 238
execute() method
 execution code, writing 56
 execution, planning 55, 56
 implementing 55
 writing 205, 206
external images
 collection, obtaining 143, 144
 icon library, writing 141
 icons, unregistering 143
 packing 140
 pictures, loading from folder 141-143
 relative imports, using 144, 145

F

F-Curve 180
F-Curve modifiers
 adding, in Graph Editor 198-200
 adding, in Python 200
 using 198

Finder
 used, for creating .zip file on Mac 161
F-Modifiers 198
frames per second (FPS) 165
full data path 25

G

get_fcurve method
 keyframes, ensuring 204
 scrolling, through collections 204
 writing 203
getter 45
gimbal lock 72
Git 19
Global Orientation 71
Gnome
 used, for creating .zip file 161
Graph Editor 179
 F-Curve modifiers, adding 198-200

H

Hello World! 9

I

icons
 custom image icons, using 107-109
 viewing, with Icon Viewer add-on 104-106
identity matrix 81
importlib
 cached modules, reloading via 148
import operator
 active node existence, checking 293, 294
 Blender's file browser, using 293
 image files, loading 296
 image texture nodes, creating 297

non-color attributes, obtaining from images 296
texture filenames, matching 294, 295
writing 292
Info Log 12
parameters, modifying 13
Python commands, copying from 12
init file
creating 136, 137
writing 137, 138
integrated development environment (IDE) 17
International System of Units (SI) 220

K

keyframes 164, 167
adding, in Blender 167
adding, in Python 181, 182
Duration and Frame Rate 165, 166
editing 179
objects, animating 167
retrieving, in Python 182-184

L

Last In First Out (LIFO) 172
Latte Express add-on
center of model, finding 265-267
Create Lattice menu item, adding 267
environment, setting 264
information, writing 264
operator, writing 264, 265
using 268
writing 263

Latte Express options
improving 268, 269
lattice resolution, modifying 269, 270
object subdivisions, adding 269
lattice armature
scripting 275
Lattice modifier 262
using 262, 263
lattice vertices
assigning, to bones 278
layouts
columns and rows, arranging 109
composite layouts, using 111
frames, adding with box layouts 110
using, in panels 109
LightTable 18
URL 18
linear algebra 80
Load Textures
Base Color, mixing 306-308
improving 302
shader nodes, arranging 303
Local Orientation 71

M

Mac
.zip file, creating with Finder 161
macOS
Blender, multiple versions installing 6, 7
magic numbers 116
Material Properties
setting 287, 288
Math Vis (Console) add-on
enabling 28

menu function
  writing 171, 172
menus extension
  draw functions 66
  menu entries, adding 66, 67
mesh objects
  creating, in Python 279-281
  subdividing 257-259
Microsoft Store
  Blender, installing from 5, 6
modal behavior
  adding 245
  modal method, writing 247-250
  operator, adding to modal handlers 246, 247
modifiers
  adding, in Python 259
modifiers.new
  using 260, 261
modifiers stack 259
modules
  separating, guidelines 138

N

new() method 37, 38
nodes 289
  connecting 298
  image colors, connecting 298
  normal maps, connecting 298, 299
Node Tree 288-290
normal mapping 298
Notepad++ 17
  URL 17

O

object 34
  binding, to armatures 274, 275
  collections 39
  moving 70
  new() method 37, 38
  transforming 70
  transforming, indirectly 76, 77
object access
  dict-like access 34
  list-like access 34
object collector add-on
  creating 53, 54
  list, refreshing 57
  operator, loading 56
  operators 54
  operator, writing 54, 55
  running 57
  Search Toolbar, running from 57, 58
Object Constraints 198
  adding in Python 77, 78
  attributes, setting 78
  object scale, limiting 79
  using 77
object hierarchies
  using 79, 80
object materials 287
object modifiers 255, 256
  adding 256, 257
Object Properties area
  draw function, executing 103
  icons, displaying 104
  layouts, working with 103
  panel, adding to 102
object rotations
  accessing, in Python 74, 75
  affecting 71, 72

attributes, setting 75, 76
converting, between rotation systems 76
degrees, using 75
issues 72
mode, modifying 73
radians, using 75
object scale
   affecting 71
objects location
   affecting 70
Objects panel
   completing 147
object's shape
   modifying, with Cast 259
offensive programming 144
operator buttons
   adding 158, 159
operator classes
   registering 157
operator flow 237, 238
   execution, steps 238, 239
operator logic
   duplicate collections, avoiding 62
   fixing 62
   object types, querying 63
operator method
   used, for displaying button 120, 121
   writing 169
operator methods, Action to Range add-on
   execute method, writing 170, 171
   requisites, checking in poll() method 170
operator methods, Shaker add-on
   execute method, writing 205, 206
   get_fcurve method, writing 203
   poll method, writing 203
operator methods, Vert Runner add-on
   execute() method, writing 187, 188
   requisites, checking in poll() method 187

operator panel
   draw method, adding 250, 251
   styling 250
operators 30, 54
   adding 155
   execute() method, implementing 55
   loading, in add-on 56
   poll() method, implementing 55
   refreshing, on reload 157, 158
   requirements 54
   writing 54, 55
operators module
   writing 156
operator text
   setting, for button 121, 122
operator visibility
   setting, for button 121, 122

P

package folder
   creating 136, 137
package modules
   reloading 149
panel 96
   adding, to Object Properties area 102
   add-on, drafting 97
   display attributes, setting 99
   environment, setting 97
   repositioning 129, 130
   writing 97
panel add-on
   info dictionary, writing 98
   panel class, drafting 98
   panel registration 99
parent inverse matrix
   used, for creating rest offsets 83, 84

pendulum 216
   reference link 220
pendulum add-on
   class, registering 233, 234
   environment, setting 229
   information, writing 229
   menu, writing 233, 234
   Operator class, writing 230-233
   writing 228
pendulum equation
   Driven Property window,
      displaying 221, 222
   frame per seconds property,
      obtaining 222-224
   implementing 220, 221
   pendulum length, obtaining with
      distance variable 224-226
   variables, adding to drivers 221
Physically-Based Rendering (PBR) 289
Pivot Constraint
   adding 217-219
poll() method
   implementing 55
   writing 203
Pose Mode 271
PunchClock add-on
   default invoke, ensuring in
      pop-up menus 244, 245
   invoke, using to initialize properties 243, 244
   script, creating 240-243
   writing 240
PyCharm 17
   URL 17
Python 3
   adding, in modifiers 259
   animation data, accessing 181
   F-Curve modifiers, adding 200
   keyframes, adding 181, 182
   keyframes, retrieving 182-184
   mesh objects, creating 279-281
Python console 8
   Blender release, checking 10
   functions, invoking 11
   Hello World! 9
   Python release, checking 9
Python features, console's utilities 26
   3D variables, displaying in 3D Viewport 28
   autocompletion 27
   history 27
   multiple input 28
Python features, developer options 24
   data path, copying 25, 26
   Developer Extras 24
   Python tooltips 24, 25
Python Software Foundation 10

Q

Quaternions 73

R

radians 191
refresh module
   implementing 148
regions 96
Render Engine
   setting 286
rigid transformations 70
RNA path 25
rotation pivot
   modifying, via constraints 217

rotations, Vert Runner add-on
executing 194
implementing 191, 192
rotation arcs, representing 190, 191
shortest arc, finding 193, 194

S

script 8
Scripting 8
Scripting workspace
elements 8
Info Log 12
Python console 8
Text Editor 14
scripts path 51, 52
addons folder 52
selected objects
modifying 45, 46
setter 45
shader 288
Shader Editor 289
Node Tree 289, 290
shader nodes
arranging 303
node creation, sorting 304-306
node space, assuming 303
Shading workspace 286, 287
Shaker add-on
Add Object Shake operator class, writing 202
context menus class names, finding 206, 207
environment, setting up 201
info, writing 201
limits and soft limits, adding to properties 202
menu items, adding 206
operator methods, writing 203

registering 207, 208
using 208
writing 201
sine 190
sin function 217
sockets 289
Sphinx 32
structured panel
writing 139, 140
Sublime 18
URL 18
syntax highlighting 14
system path 51

T

Textament add-on
environment, setting up 292
header button, adding 299, 300
import operator, writing 292
information, writing 292
Load Textures, using 300-302
nodes, connecting 298
texture images, using 291
writing 291
Text Editor 14
Python console, copying as script 16
text documents, executing 14, 15
text files, exporting 17
transform matrix 80
matrices, accessing 81
matrices, copying 82
object matrices, storing 82
rest offsets, creating with parent inverse matrix 83, 84
world matrix, using to restore transformations 83

trigonometry 190
tuple assignment 70

U

UI module
  writing 145, 146
user context 40
  active object 42
  active scene 40, 41
  selected objects 44, 45
  View Layers 41
user interface
  adding 145
  importing 146
  Objects panel, completing 147

V

Vectors 70
version control 19
  changes, displaying 20
  repository, initializing 19, 20
  uncommitted changes, reverting 21
Vert Runner add-on
  cyclic animations, creating 189
  environment, setting 185
  menu and register functions, writing 188
  operator methods, writing 187
  rotations, adding 190
  using 195
  Vert Runner information, writing 186
  Vert Runner operator, writing 186
  writing 185

View Layers 41
Visual Studio 18
Visual Studio Code (VS Code) 17, 18
  Blender's text blocks, keeping in sync 19
  scripts folder, loading 18

W

weight painting 274
wheel
  setting up, with Drivers Editor 214, 215
Windows
  Blender, installing 4
Windows File Manager
  used, for creating .zip file 160
Windows Installer
  Blender, multiple versions installing via 4, 5
World Axes 71
world matrix
  used, for restoring transformations 83

‹packt›

www.packtpub.com

Subscribe to our online digital library for full access to over 7,000 books and videos, as well as industry leading tools to help you plan your personal development and advance your career. For more information, please visit our website.

Why subscribe?

- Spend less time learning and more time coding with practical eBooks and Videos from over 4,000 industry professionals
- Improve your learning with Skill Plans built especially for you
- Get a free eBook or video every month
- Fully searchable for easy access to vital information
- Copy and paste, print, and bookmark content

Did you know that Packt offers eBook versions of every book published, with PDF and ePub files available? You can upgrade to the eBook version at `packtpub.com` and as a print book customer, you are entitled to a discount on the eBook copy. Get in touch with us at `customercare@packtpub.com` for more details.

At `www.packtpub.com`, you can also read a collection of free technical articles, sign up for a range of free newsletters, and receive exclusive discounts and offers on Packt books and eBooks.

Other Books You May Enjoy

If you enjoyed this book, you may be interested in these other books by Packt:

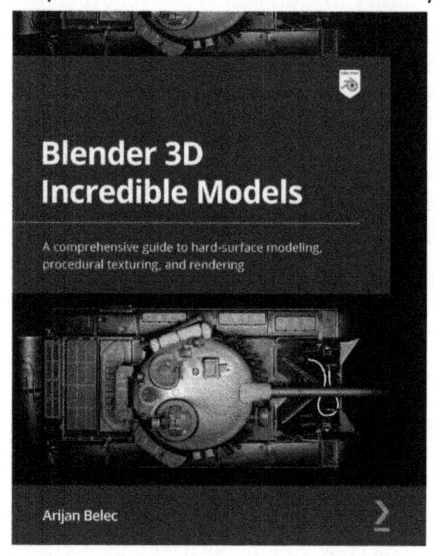

Blender 3D Incredible Models

Arijan Belec

ISBN: 978-1-80181-781-3

- Dive into the fundamental theory behind hard-surface modeling
- Explore Blender's extensive modeling tools and features
- Use references to produce sophisticated and accurate models
- Create models with realistic textures and materials
- Set up lighting and render your scenes with style
- Master the use of polygons to make game-optimized models
- Develop impressive animations by exploring the world of rigging
- Employ texture painting and modifiers to render the tiniest details

Squeaky Clean Topology in Blender

Michael Steppig

ISBN: 978-1-80324-408-2

- Identify the general flow of a model's topology, and what might cause issues
- Understand the topology of a character, and the joints that they make up
- Handle non-quad based topology
- Lay out your meshes for UV seams
- Explore and use hotkeys to get things done faster
- Optimize models for a reduced triangle count

Packt is searching for authors like you

If you're interested in becoming an author for Packt, please visit `authors.packtpub.com` and apply today. We have worked with thousands of developers and tech professionals, just like you, to help them share their insight with the global tech community. You can make a general application, apply for a specific hot topic that we are recruiting an author for, or submit your own idea.

Hi!

I am Paolo Acampora, author of *Python Scripting in Blender*. I really hope you enjoyed reading this book and found it useful for increasing your productivity and efficiency.

It would really help me (and other potential readers!) if you could leave a review on Amazon sharing your thoughts on this book.

Go to the link below or scan the QR code to leave your review:

`https://packt.link/r/1803234229`

Your review will help us to understand what's worked well in this book, and what could be improved upon for future editions, so it really is appreciated.

Best wishes,

Paolo Acampora

Download a free PDF copy of this book

Thanks for purchasing this book!

Do you like to read on the go but are unable to carry your print books everywhere?

Is your eBook purchase not compatible with the device of your choice?

Don't worry, now with every Packt book you get a DRM-free PDF version of that book at no cost.

Read anywhere, any place, on any device. Search, copy, and paste code from your favorite technical books directly into your application.

The perks don't stop there, you can get exclusive access to discounts, newsletters, and great free content in your inbox daily

Follow these simple steps to get the benefits:

1. Scan the QR code or visit the link below

    https://packt.link/free-ebook/9781803234229

2. Submit your proof of purchase
3. That's it! We'll send your free PDF and other benefits to your email directly

Milton Keynes UK
Ingram Content Group UK Ltd.
UKHW051549021224
3319UKWH00040B/853